Africa in Latin America

AFRICA IN LATIN AMERICA

Essays on History, Culture, and Socialization

MANUEL MORENO FRAGINALS, *Editor*
Translated by LEONOR BLUM

Holmes & Meier Publishers, Inc., New York
Unesco, Paris

First published in the United States of America 1984 by
Holmes & Meier Publishers, Inc.
30 Irving Place
New York, N.Y. 10003

Great Britain:
Holmes & Meier Publishers, Ltd.
131 Trafalgar Road
Greenwich, London SE10 9TX

Original Spanish edition:
AFRICA EN AMERICA LATINA © Unesco 1977

This book has been published with the financial assistance of Unesco

Manufactured in the United States of America

Library of Congress Cataloging in Publication Data

Africa en América Latina. English.
    Africa in Latin America.

    Translation of: Africa en América Latina.
    Bibliography: p.
    Includes index.
    1. Blacks—Latin America—Addresses, essays, lectures.
2. Latin America—Civilization—African influences—
Addresses, essays, lectures. I. Moreno Fraginals, Manuel.
F1419.N4A3713   1984   980'.004'96   84-639
ISBN 0-8419-0748-X

Contents

Africa in Latin America

Historical Beginnings:
From Plantation Life
to Class Structure

1
Cultural Contributions
and Deculturation

MANUEL MORENO FRAGINALS

Taking Inventory

The oldest documentation referring to the transportation of Black Africans to America directly from Africa dates back to 1518. The first arrival of individual Blacks in America is even more remote. The last slave cargo of which we have documented proof landed on the Southern coast of Cuba in April, 1873, and was immediately sent to the Juraguá sugar mill near the city of Cienfuegos. There are indications that a few more slave ships came to Cuba after this, but there is no concrete proof of their arrival. Thus, if we establish 1518 and 1873 as limiting dates, we have 355 years of African slave trade. During this time we witness the most massive coercive transport of human beings in history. It is estimated that no fewer than 9.5 million Black Africans arrived in America during those years to labor in six fundamental areas of production: sugar, coffee, tobacco, cotton, rice, and mining.

In the event, the African slave trade reached such vast proportions that thousands of slaves were soon employed outside these productive areas, eventually permeating every corner of all American societies. In the latter part of the nineteenth century we find Blacks born in America (criollos) as well as Africans in the highlands of Mexico and Peru, in New Granada, in Santiago de Chile, and even on the Argentine pampas. Above all, we find them on the Atlantic and Pacific coasts of America. Thousands of pages have been written about these Blacks who were grafted onto predominantly White or Mestizo (a mixture of White and Indian) societies and about their colorful characteristics. Space limitations do not allow us to discuss these geographical regions: this brief analysis will center on Brazil and on the old European colonies in the Caribbean. About 90 percent of the people uprooted from Africa arrived in these areas (or in what is now the southern United States, which is also excluded from this volume).

In attempting to present a global view, fully aware of the dangers involved in generalization, we will concentrate on plantation economies and certain urban centers. The most reliable and best documented estimates show that 65 percent of all Africans brought over were assigned to the production of sugar. Other plantation crops absorbed another 15 percent. As a result of the plantation economy, certain demographic structures appeared in places where the predominance of Africans and their descendants made the conflict between masters and slaves most intense and where we find the most intricate process of transculturation taking place. It is in these areas that a cultural world, so brilliantly termed by Sidney W. Mintz "the Africa of Latin America," was formed and perfected, and is still being created and recreated.

Mechanisms of Deculturation

By deculturation we mean the conscious process by which, for purposes of economic exploitation, the culture of a group of human beings is uprooted to expedite the expropriation of the natural riches of the territory the group inhabits, and/or to utilize the group as a source of cheap, unskilled labor. The process of deculturation is inherent in every form of colonial or neocolonial exploitation. In the case of African slavery in the New World, the destruction of a culture can be seen as an applied technological resource to optimize labor value. Total deculturation, however, is impossible; nor are the exploiters interested in converting the cultural values of the exploited class into a tabula rasa. They only wish to eradicate those elements which create an obstacle to the establishment of the system of exploitation. In fact, it is normal for the dominant class to protect and even to stimulate the development of isolated cultural values of the dominated class, just so long as these values contribute to the reinforcement of the desired structure. African cultural contributions to Latin America and the Caribbean are the result of a cruel class struggle and of a complex transculturation-deculturation process. In such circumstances, the dominant class applies to a maximum its mechanisms of deculturation as hegemonic tools, and the dominated class takes refuge in its culture as a means of identity and survival.

Slavery created a bipolar social structure where class contradictions were expressed in their simplest form: an enormous dispossessed mass, forced to work for its survival, subjected by a small dominant group with all-encompassing powers. Opposite skin colors further differentiated masters and slaves. A typical example of this structure was the plantation system, although the exploitation of Black slaves in the mines was not all that different. Within these socioeconomic organizations, the lifestyle of the slaves was ruled by the pragmatic concept of the economic worth of slave labor. Literature on slaves and Blacks is plagued by lyricisms praising the generosity or demonstrating the cruelty of slaveowners, even pinpointing distinctions between the behavior of Spaniards, Englishmen, Frenchmen, etc. This can be considered literature only in the non-scientific or "Uncle Tom's Cabin" sense of the word. As a matter of fact, whatever the nationality of the master or the ultimate job of the slave, the master was neither interested in torturing nor in pleasing the slave. For the master, the slave was merely one more of the factors of production that brought him wealth. Therefore, the master had no philanthropic or perverse motives. His interests were of a purely economic nature. Since a slave was imported to produce goods for sale on the international market, the resulting profits had to make the total investment in the slave worthwhile. Profitability depended on a series of parameters that varied with the product, with time, place, the availability of productive equipment, and with other factors, some quantifiable, some not. We can thus conclude that the treatment of slaves was strictly a matter of economics.

Setting aside, then, the idyllic interpretations and a few exceptions, we are left with the concrete fact that a mass of Africans were forcibly moved to America and made to work within an organization of prisonlike characteristics for productive purposes. This elementary principle cannot be ignored if one wishes to analyze seriously the cultural contributions of Africans in America. One must keep in mind, moreover, that the majority of these Africans upon arriving in America, did not become integrated into organically created and developed towns. On the contrary, they were taken to uninhabited areas, where homogeneous work groups were formed under the absolute command of certain individuals who forced them to work in the fields or mines. On other occasions they were forcibly incorporated into productive units of this type that were already in operation.

The reliability and productivity of the enterprise to which the African slave was attached was based on its simple organization and jail-like character and on the limiting of communication between its members. In the same manner that a jail is not a society, so plantations and mines do not constitute social organizations, although they may, in the long run, cause a new society to be created. Plantation owners, in fact, had a vested interest in not permitting slaves to interact freely, for with social cohesion might come a sense of solidarity. That is why we can say that deculturation was a technological device applied to the exploitation of slave labor, since a common culture gives a group dignity, cohesion, and a sense of identity.

The Tools of Deculturation

Ethnic Diversity

Large groups of slaves were never made up of Africans of a single ethnic group: that is, of persons of common tribal or cultural origin. In the thousands of documents about African slaves on Brazilian and Caribbean plantations, one can observe a general pattern indicating the care with which slaves from various regions, speaking different languages or dialects, with different religious beliefs, and at times even displaying feelings of hostility towards each other, were deliberately grouped together.

The hatreds among ethnic groups have remote origins which need not be analyzed here; at times they were engendered by the slave traders themselves to bring about the frictions and rivalries necessary for successfully hunting down slaves. Once they were on the plantations, these ethnic rivalries were just as systematically cultivated by the slave owners. Obstacles were thus created to the formation of a class consciousness against common exploitation; in its place the creation of antagonistic groups was encouraged.

In urban centers these ethnic differences were institutionalized. In Cuba, for example, the colonial government that represented the interests of slave owners, sponsored and legalized the formation of *cabildos* (lodge-type mutual-aid associations on a strictly regional or tribal basis, with religious, social, and cultural overtones) where slaves could get together. With the same care displayed by plantation owners, urban authorities encouraged *cabildos* of various ethnic groups to form, making sure that none was sufficiently powerful to overshadow the rest. The urban *cabildos* permitted the survival with a relative high degree of purity, of certain aspects of African culture, including language, which acquired ritual significance. In this respect, the Spanish slave policy differed radically from British colonialism in the Caribbean, which persecuted all African cultural manifestations. As implied above, it would be naïve to see in these different policies of dominance a difference in moral attitude or an expression of respect for African cultures. We are, in fact, faced with two tactics equally disdainful of all that is Black and African, both leading to the same strategy of exploitation of slave labor. Admittedly one tactic had the virtue of preserving the cultural values which the other destroyed.

In plantations and mines, ethnic diversity brought about a fascinating process of interethnic conflict and rapprochement; that is to say, there was a simultaneous process of cultural mixture among people of different African cultures, at the same time as between them and their White masters. All of this occurred within the superimposed framework of deculturation. Later, differences between African- and American-born Blacks, and, because of variations in skin color, between Blacks, mulattoes, quadroons, etc., also developed.

Age and Culture

Until the beginning of the nineteenth century, Africans brought to America were very young, usually between ages fifteen and twenty. After the 1830s, massive imports of children between ages nine and twelve were initiated. Age determined productivity. The mine and plantation system of extensive labor required young, healthy, and strong slaves. In addition, youth ensured the statistical longevity of the slave, which resulted in better training, and of course in greater productivity. A longer life also meant a lower rate of cost amortization and greater profitability.

The age limits of fifteen and twenty were the most logical from an economic viewpoint. Younger slaves would have been assets (in accounting terms) of low productivity, running the same risk of death as more productive slaves. Older slaves would have had great difficulties in adapting to work, a stronger resistance to deculturation, a lower life expectancy and inferior productivity, and would have required a higher rate for amortization of the investment. Only after the 1830s, when the end of slave traffic became certain, were child slaves brought to America as a last recourse for the survival of the plantation system. Other factors contributed to the policy of massive imports of children, but they will not be analyzed here.

The age of Africans, registered at the time of their purchase, was usually estimated by sight, which, of course, is subject to a certain margin of error. But undoubtedly slave traders were experienced at judging age, and probably employed an empirical system of observation that reduced errors to a minimum, especially since their sample was so large. We have documents which provide meticulous descriptions of slave purchases, including physical dimensions, dental conditions, the presence of body hair, etc. Since there were annual inventories of existing slaves on plantations and mines, the calculated age of an incoming African was always registered. The following year, when the new inventory was conducted, notations from the previous year were copied, a year was mechanically added to the age of all surviving slaves, the dead were stricken off the list, and the newborn and new acquisitions were entered. When slaves were transferred from one master to another, the new master often ignored the estimates of his predecessor and fixed the age according to his own estimate.

The survival of thousands of such inventories, which also record sex and other personal items, has permitted the pyramidal graphing of plantation populations. These pyramidal graphs, representing the period of maximum atrocity against slaves, reveal population centers with very few women, even less children (8 to 10 percent between ages 0 and 14) and with a tiny population of elderly people (5 to 7 percent over age 59). These are the demographics of a human nucleus, constituted, ad hoc, for productive purposes, by forced migration. They lack the normal characteristics of pyramidal population graphs, those that occur naturally through vegetative growth. Mortality and migration are the steps of the pyramid without base or top.

While the formation of slave populations of varied ethnic origin was planned to enhance security and further deculturation, the inclusion of mostly young men and children occurred primarily for economic reasons.

Nevertheless, age also turned out to be a deculturation factor. The Africans came from cultures that relied on an oral tradition, where knowledge was the privilege of the elders. In bringing only the young, the least cultured members of a society (cultured with regard to accumulation of knowledge and survival of traditions), were imported. The learned elders seldom came to America; those that did were exceptions. Therefore, incoming slaves, particularly the children, had the least culture to contribute and to transmit. Because of the natural adaptability of youth and adolescence, it was easier to erase in them elements of their own culture and to fix in them the required norms of plantation life. It is fair to say that every African slave by his thirty-eighth birthday had lived longer in America than in Africa.

Sex, Production, and Culture

The standard procedure of the slave trade, until the early nineteenth century, was to import relatively few women. British statistics on slavery (the most complete of their kind) show a 78:22 male-female ratio for slaves brought to America during the eighteenth century. These figures varied over the years, but the proportion of males always remained high until the 1820s. It was only at this time, when the end of the legal slave trade (as opposed to slavery itself) came clearly into view, that more balanced numbers of male and female slaves began to be imported. This tardy development was triggered by the same critical situation that had led to the importation of child slaves: forced by the closing down of their traditional source, slaveowners were building up their breeding stock.

The predominance of male imports, like every other aspect of slavery, was determined by productivity. Women had always been considered, literally, livestock of low productivity. The sole advantage over men was their capacity to increase invested capital by bearing new slaves. This advantage, however, was negated by several factors. First, the very fact of male and female slaves living together threatened the prison-like structure of the plantation or mine, and obliged the masters to allow, if only to a minimal degree, a certain institutionalization of the family or of child bearing. Second, the number of deaths at childbirth was extraordinarily high, which meant a risk in the capital invested in female slaves. Third, Black female slaves always displayed a very low fertility rate, an extremely interesting biological and cultural result to be discussed later. Finally, infant mortality was so high on plantations, that only about 10 percent of the children reached adulthood. During the final stage of slavery, particularly in the nineteenth century, conditions changed.

Under these circumstances, up until about 1815, it was cheaper to purchase an average adult male in the slave market than it would have been to breed and raise to the same age a slave child on the plantation. In the nineteenth century, however, the abolition of the legal trade of Black

Africans and its conversion into contraband, persecuted by Great Britain, drove the price of slaves up yearly. Since the cost of breeding and raising slaves on the plantation rose less rapidly than the market price of a slave, there was a point when the two curves crossed, and projections indicated that it would be less costly to breed than to import. It was this cost relationship, not moral reasons, that led Cuban and Brazilian slave traders (these were the last countries to abolish slavery) to import massive numbers of African women and to alter the prisonlike setup on plantations.

One of the most traumatic experiences of slave life on plantations was the absence of heterosexuality, which led to such behavior as masturbation and sodomy among the slaves placed in constrained quarters with other men only. Unfortunately we lack quantitative studies that would give us an exact idea of the magnitude of the problem. In the Cuban case, we have a list of almost four hundred plantations that reveals the following sex distribution:

African Slave Populations on Cuban Plantations
Distribution in Percentages by Sex

Years	Males	Females
1746–1790	90.38	9.62
1701–1822	85.03	14.97
1840–1849	69.70	30.30
1860–1869	59.80	40.20

Only African slaves are tabulated. Their Creole descendants are omitted. A quick look at these figures indicates that, while legal slave traffic lasted and the cost of a male who could perform according to normal productive standards was relatively low, there was no interest in importing women. This implies that procreation among Creole slaves was minimal. Practically the entire plantation population of both men and women was active; they were all of working age. This explains the fantastic per capita output, as compared to British colonies, where the percentages of women, children, and older people was higher. As we pointed out earlier, as soon as slave traffic became illegal more women were imported, and there was a tendency towards balancing the proportions of the sexes. However, not even in the 1860s, when slave trade was almost extinct, was there ever a perfect balance in the proportion of sexes, nor was there a positive demographic growth rate on the plantations.

The severe disproportion of sexes created an atmosphere of repression and an obsession with sex, which was expressed in many different ways, such as stories, games, songs, dances. In any study of the African cultural heritage regarding sexual relations, one must always keep in mind that even stronger than the cultural tradition was the obsessive world of the plantation. Certain African dances and songs that had no sexual connotation, or that merely sublimated sex, acquired an almost lascivious significance under slavery. It is therefore no coincidence that a large part of the Cuban and Brazilian sex vocabulary originated on the sugar plantations. To summarize: the marked preoccupation with sexual matters to be found among certain sectors of Black American life, far from originating in physiological or cultural causes, is merely a holdover from the inhuman conditions prevailing on the plantation and mines under slavery. In areas where the balance of the sexes was conducive to a more normal life, these behavioral patterns did not occur. However, such balance was the exception. Slavery distorted the slave's sex life, and racists justified these distortions by devising myths about the sadistic sexuality of Blacks, the immorality of Black women, and the libidinous nature of Mulatto females. All this disregarded the fact that in urban areas and in solitary mansions, sex was the only device women could use to improve their economic condition.

In all of the Caribbean, and at a certain time when there was a crisis in the supply of slaves (it is important to recall that this crisis occurred at different times in different colonies) the owners of slaves tried to form compulsory family units according to Western European ethical and cultural norms. These attempts, although encouraged by various religious sects, met with little success. The family, in the White bourgeois conception (here we use the term "White" as a synonym for the European or Creole colonizer), is an institution that thrives only in a favorable setting. Plantations, however, were, culturally, a totally different world. It was not sufficient to give the blessing of the church and to legalize sexual unions that either emerged spontaneously or that were forcefully imposed. Legalization, the ceremony, and the church ritual only created the formal appearance of a family unit. The stabilization and integration of the family core required socioeconomic conditions that were not present on plantations. For example: a family tie could be dissolved by the unilateral and unappealable decision of the master to sell, give up, transfer, or move one or more slaves in a group. Advertisements like "Black woman for sale, with or without her brood" reveal the absolute disdain for motherhood and Black family life held by the dominant, slaveowning class. Such advertisements appeared with frightening frequency in the Cuban and Brazilian press. Furthermore, the European, bourgeois concept of family, with its complex world of interdependent and hierarchical relationships, was incongruous with African cultural norms, and was unviable in a prisonlike setting where individuals lacked the most elementary rights of self-determination, such as ownership of and authority over their own children. A family unit within a plantation was like a naturally rejected foreign body. Since the production and subsistence framework was imposed upon the slaves, they lacked all economic, personal and familial responsibility, as they were not in charge of their own economy and had no control over the hierarchy of blood relationships. They had neither social nor familial responsibilities, inasmuch as all activity was regimented and became a function of production. Free time had been suspended, and after an oppressive and hateful sixteen-hour workday, the few remaining hours could only be used for basic biological survival functions.

These conditions determined the sexual behavior patterns of rural communities descendant from slaves. Instability and fleeting unions based on sexual relations were a plantation routine that was to become the most destructive force within the slave heritage of Antillean society. In many Caribbean islands, and among peasant groups descended from slaves, we still find widespread instances of successive or simultaneous polygamy, whereby men and women frequently change mates and have more than one spouse.

Lacking family, property, and a concept of personal economy, with their worldview reduced from early childhood on to the monotony of the sugar fields and the sugar mill, many African and Creole Black slaves found the abolition of slavery traumatic. Without paternalistic relationships and exploitation, these slaves, particularly the older ones, were left in a state of total helplessness. Incapable of adapting to wage employment, too inept even to comprehend the new economic relationships, lacking in food, clothing, and a roof, all of which had always been provided on the plantation, they sank to the lowest level of social degradation. With sticks and leaves they built their bare homes on roadsides, and there they patiently awaited their slow death. These solitary Blacks with no social or familial ties were a depressing, routine spectacle in the Caribbean after the abolition of slavery.

In brief, in organically originated societies, particularly those formed during the feudal and precapitalist eras, there existed a concrete relationship between production and the institution of the family. However, a plantation, like a jail, is not a society. Seen from any angle, the plantation is an economic enterprise; its population is formed of an aggregate of individuals who are not permitted to interact with each other and whose actions are coercively directed towards one end—production. All the communities to which the Black slaves originally belonged had a series of distinctive institutional relationships. But Blacks segregated from their original communities and enslaved either lost their traditional mores or observed them surreptitiously. Thus the plantation, wherever possible, broke the continuity of African traditions, establishing its foundations upon the destruction of every tie or union, including even that of the family, though families normally develop out of the uncontrollable urge to procreate. The plantation took its toll, leaving the deep sense of instability and discontinuity that had been very useful for maintaining the slaveocracy, but absolutely contradicted what was required of a salaried industrial worker.

An important way in which the socioeconomic structure had an impact on biological urges is revealed by the very low fertility rate of female slaves. Since this fact adversely affected the later plantation economy, it was seriously studied by technical experts of the times. Well-regarded doctors, particularly during the nineteenth century, were urged to find an answer for the apparently unheard-of question of why women with a free sex life, with no concern for virginity, and without the inhibitions of upper class Whites, had a lower fertility rate than the White women. Among doctors of various nationalities who analyzed the problem were the American J. Urdermann, the Frenchmen Bernard de Chateauselins and Henri Dumont, and the Cubans, José R. Montalvo and Luis Montané Dardé. Even though color and class prejudices obscured their scientific reasoning, all the doctors had to recognize that the low fertility of Black women was a consequence of their work routine.

In reaction to her position as a slave, the Black female slave imposed upon herself rigid birth control methods, reviving and generating Malthusian and abortive practices. Contrary to common assumptions, such practices are a cultural phenomenon that occurs at certain critical periods; and they are a part of the cultural practices of so-called "primitive" people. Even today, the pragmatic knowledge of birth control in certain ethnic groups of the Congo astonishes modern gynecologists. Potions prepared with the fruit and leaves of papaya (Carica papaya) were used so frequently in the slave-rich region of western Cuba that the term "papaya" became synonymous with vulva. The persistence of such practices generated innumerable uterine diseases, and inventories of Cuban plantations show that, at times, more than 25 percent of the women had a fallen uterus.

Patterns of Food Culture

Food, dress, and housing are the three needs that make up basic cultural patterns. Africans who were coercively moved to American plantations had dressed and lived in Africa in their own economic and cultural world. Within this cultural and economic environment, each ethnic group had created a system of symbols that constituted the fundamental elements of its culture. To eat, dress, and build or decorate one's home in one way or another was of implicit hierarchical, moral, and religious value. But this cultural world of Africans was crushed by the plantation.

The economic parameters of the plantation determined the slave's nutritional balance. A slave's food intake was determined by his dietary needs (as they were understood at the time, and according to the economic realities of the plantation) and by the market value of various foods, the ease with which they could be transported, and their resistance to lengthy storage periods. The slave, who from the productive point of view was considered a piece of equipment, from the nutritional viewpoint was seen as an ingesting-excreting mechanism that required a daily fuel ration, or source of energy (food), to complete its work and to insure its useful existence for the estimated depreciation period.

A plantation slave had two daily meals, prepared with a generous starch base (rice, corn flour, plantains, etc.) to which was added an ample portion of jerked meat or salted fish. The selection of ingredients varied periodically with market prices and with availability on each plantation. In short, it was food that met dietary, administrative, and even psychological needs, since its abundance even led to a feeling of satiation. The nutrition of slaves was usually maintained within these limits, with numerous variants in form, but not in nutritional value. When they worked on a sugar plantation (as did approximately 65 percent of all imported slaves) slaves usually consumed a large quantity of sugar. They would get the sugar from cane juice while cutting down the cane (this liquid contains about 14 to 16 percent sucrose) or they would drink it directly out of the large open pans used for evaporation. They devoured the pieces of pan sugar that stuck to the containers and coolers; they would abscond with all the sugar they could from the draining room; finally, they would drink large quantities of molasses.

Accounting information from numerous plantations in the Caribbean points to an almost generalized feeding practice over two centuries. The slave was given a daily ration of some 200 grams of jerked meat or salted fish (raw) which contained approximately 70 grams of animal protein, 13 grams of fat, and some 380 calories. The 500 grams of corn flour (or of another starch) added a supplement of 15 grams of vegetable protein, and more than the necessary calories for the daily work routine. This level of nutrition, although deficient, was superior to the normal diet of the African tribes the slaves came from. The population groups of Equatorial Africa had a particularly precarious nutritional level, with little animal protein and an inordinate amount of starch. But the fact that plantation diets were superior to those of Africa does not imply that they were optimal. Plantation life erased all dietary rituals and was characterized by a persistent monotony. Foods were totally lacking in African tastes and flavors. Almost no African culinary art was brought to America. However, in the vicinity of the sugar plantations, people developed a strong taste for sweets, which, in urban areas, engendered a rich variety of sugar-based dishes. This taste for sugar was so extraordinary that the Brazilian sociologist Gilberto Freyre, has mentioned the possibility of writing a "sociology of sweets."

The excessive taste for sugar was paralleled by an equally excessive taste for salt. This was another result of plantation work. Working all day under the hot sun, or in the high temperatures of the boiler room, the

slaves sweated out large amounts of salt, and even required a daily supplement of sodium chloride.

Clothing and Culture

The plantation economy required uniform, low-cost dress for slaves. It is
possible that mass-produced clothing was first made to dress plantation
slaves. It is not known when the dress code typical to all the Caribbean
colonies was first established. However, by the middle of the eighteenth
century, the production of slave apparel had already been standardized so
that each item of clothing had a minimal number of pieces and required
the least amount of sewing. Five commercial sizes were established for
men, and four for women. Boys and girls wore a one-piece shirt with one
lateral seam.

The annual clothing allowance in the eighteenth and nineteenth centuries was as follows: During the months of October and November each
man was given a pair of pants and a shirt (which looked more like a tight,
short tunic), a wool cap, a flannel jacket, and a wool blanket. Women
received a tunic, a kerchief, a cap, a blanket, and a jacket. For the second
semester of the year, men received a pair of pants and a straw hat, while
women were given a dress and a straw hat. Footwear was never handed
out. There was even an eighteenth century French decree forbidding
giving shoes to Blacks because "shoes tortured their feet."

The traditional artisanry of African dress and decoration was lost on
the plantations. Slaves who added some element to their apparel that
differentiated them from others were punished. The only tribal markings
maintained by the Africans were their tattoos and their filed teeth, which
could not be obliterated. Tattoos and tooth filing were forbidden to Black
Creoles; this prohibition, however, was frequently disobeyed.

Housing and Culture

Slaves were housed in huts, built according to a regular pattern that
facilitated surveillance. It was forbidden to place any symbol or distinguishing element either on the façade or in the interior of the hut, since
such symbols could have indicated a special status or might have had
religious significance. In Cuba, where slavery continued after it had been
abolished in the French and British colonies, the owners of the large
plantations of four hundred, five hundred, or more slaves, built rectangu-
lar stone structures, sometimes one hundred or more meters long, with
only one large door in the center of one side of the rectangle, leading to a
large central patio. This was a typical prisonlike structure, with architecture carefully designed to reduce communication between slaves, to make
surveillance easy, and to improve productivity. Housing, like dress, and

nutrition, then, had the objectives of enhancing productivity and of wiping out the African cultural world.

Alienating Work as a Factor in Deculturation

Because plantations were obliged to rely on slave labor, and since slaves were their capital investment, it is logical that production costs were primarily reduced by optimizing labor productivity. From the beginning of the eighteenth century on, we have studies in the Caribbean about the efficiency of workers and their timetables. This data was, in a way, the colonial forerunner of the typical research on division of labor, so fashionable among the encyclopedists.

Present day economists have the erroneous idea that a slaveocracy functioned without technical controls, without the "modern" analytical models on work efficiency. However, by the end of the seventeenth century, the British had already devised control models which followed step by step the production flow on sugar plantations, kept detailed records of the daily activities of slaves, and even permitted the quantification of worker productivity. These models were later improved by the French, and, in the eighteenth century, by Cuban planters. Without exaggeration, it can be affirmed that modern accounting adds very little to the model established by Dutrone de la Couture in 1785, for example. Adam Smith even praised the French for "their good management of their slaves."

If the thesis that industrialization is based on the measurement of work is accurate, we could find in the quantification of slave labor a serious effort towards industrialization without machinery. An analysis of work models reveals that the typical scheme of elementary group work was instituted in sugar plantations. The total volume of production was raised by increasing the number of slaves, equipment and tools. But, since the strength of a group could not grow indefinitely by adding new workers, at a certain point the addition of slaves increased the total volume of production but diminished per capita productivity, since the productivity of each new man was marginal. The large slave concentrations that had emerged from market demand became more ingrown instead of evolving, thus perpetuating the moral and economic degradation of the slave.

Since slave work did not permit specialization, the only possible type of agriculture was extensive "despoliation agriculture," according to Justus von Liebig, which not only progressively lowered agricultural yield, but also, on the long run, impoverished the soil. To stabilize the total production volume it was necessary for the falling curve of agricultural productivity to be compensated by a proportional increase in slave labor. Comparative data on the amount of sugar produced and the size of the slave population in all of the British West Indies, illustrate this process. For example, in Barbados, between 1700 and 1780, slave population doubled, and sugar production went down by approximately 30 percent. In St. Kitts, in 1729, there were 14,663 slaves; towards the end of the century there were 26,000 (77 percent more), but production remained constant. Montserrat also tripled its slave population in fifty years without increasing production. In Antigua, between 1729 and 1780, it was necessary to double the slave force to achieve a production increase of 10 percent.

Extensive labor required not only more men, but a lengthening of the workday. The problem with the longer work day was the same as that of increasing numbers of slaves: production did not grow proportionally because the productivity of each additional hour was only marginal. Thus, being practical, plantation owners sought the optimal limit of productivity as a function of the number of slaves and the duration of their workday. As circumstances became more difficult, the workday was extended to its biological extreme, so that slaves could maximize their output within a previously calculated productive life span.

In Cuba, the extensive work system reached a climax in the 1840s. J. Liggins, an experienced British landowner, visited Cuba and was unable to contain his surprise at the length of the workday. In testimony before a British select committee on slavery in 1853, he repeatedly commented on this: "They worked very slowly and very carelessly, but the advantage of their employment was, it was continuous." James Kennedy, one of the most astute observers in the British diplomatic service, referred to the effects of extensive 18-hour work days: "I have . . . witnessed that. At the end of the crop season . . . [the slaves] look more like idiots than human beings. . . ; they are . . . worn out."

Modern studies on industrial fatigue show that men who have been submitted to extensive tasks over many years are never totally able to regain their energies. Thus, to daily fatigue one must add residual fatigue, accumulated over time, which induces an early reduction of work capacity and premature aging. Residual fatigue could only be eliminated by a proportional amount of rest; but the constant work pace did not permit this, so fatigue set in at the beginning of each workday. After some time this accumulated fatigue became irreversible. The unnatural rhythm must have brought about a deep-seated dissociation between human time and the time required for production, a total lack of synchronization between biological capabilities and the task that had to be performed.

By employing all available biological time for productive labor, social relationships among slaves were suppressed, and slaves only had time to perform their vital bodily functions. In addition to being necessary for increasing productivity, the suppression of the slaves' free time was also intended as a security measure and was part of a deliberate process of deculturation. All slaves were equalized, differences in ability within a group were erased, and communication and interaction among group members were made impossible, since all the slaves were occupied exclusively with one monotonous elementary activity repeated to the limit of physical resistance.

Slaves lost their human significance. They were devoid of personality. Although each had a name for identification purposes, they were all *machine men*, specialized work equipment acquired in the marketplace. They were expected to have a certain productivity and durability, as long as their productive efforts were controlled and they were provided with adequate maintenance. An attempt was made to convert them into mechanisms of maximum efficiency, to make of them a mass with no initiative, but with automatic responses to work stimuli. Siegfried Giedion writes of mechanized barbarism as the most repulsive of all barbarisms: this is what was imposed on Black slaves, both African and Creole, with the difference that the slaves themselves were transformed into machines.

Finally, we must say that, notwithstanding all the efforts made to obliterate ancestral cultural ties and relationships among slaves, despite attempts to create dissension among them, in the long run, there was always a natural feeling of solidarity among the slaves. It is a feeling that emerges in all human beings forced to live together and to share conditions of oppressive exploitation. Since frank and public communication was not possible, horizontal, underground means of communication sprouted. The necessity of transmitting secret messages for the sake of survival created a morale of clandestineness which contributed to the strengthening and syncretization of certain African sects. It is possible, for example, that the key to the social strength of the *abakuá* lay in the necessity to create a gut-system of communication.

Extensive work engendered in slaves a special instinct to survive for the mere sake of survival. This instinct is still operant in certain Caribbean societies in the twentieth century. It is expressed in a Cuban phrase that has its equivalent in Brazilian Portuguese: "The problem here is to keep from dying." This philosophy of simple endurance emerges today as an ancestral, almost atavistic force in human beings who have been exploited and decultured.

The Urban Setting

Plantation colonies producing merchandise for export required large urban concentrations, generally ports, populated by the commercial infrastructure for the sugar, coffee, cacao, and cotton economies. These urban centers also housed the non-absentee or semi-absentee dominant elite, the governing and administrative bodies, the repressive forces, the church, etc. Thus the cities became the heart of the "cultural life," whether scarce or prolific, within the colony.

The infrastructure and productive sector of these cities was always subsidiary to the plantation economy, and required large numbers of free workers and slaves for domestic and nondomestic services. For obvious reasons the urban slave had a better standard of living, and he could communicate more freely with the mass of other slaves and with both the incipient proletariat and urban lumpenproletariat. In the cities, Creole Blacks were more numerous than African slaves, which meant that Blacks born in the colony were selected for infrastructural tasks because they had been subjected since birth to the deculturating process of domestication. Cities also had a more balanced sexual ratio, and, at times, there was even a greater number of females. Undoubtedly it was materially impossible to establish plantation controls on urban slaves; it was therefore essential for the dominant class to establish different systems of subordination and control, which, although sometimes laxer, were not necessarily less efficient. However, as we shall see later, the methods of domination imposed on urban slaves, which endured among the poorest groups of the proletariat after the abolition of slavery, permitted the recreation of symbols and of daily behavioral patterns inherited from Africa.

In our opinion it would be impossible to get to the root of this question by starting off with a fixed anthropological scheme that considers transculturation as a phenomenon of conflict and synthesis between a group of immigrants (coercive or voluntary) inserted into a society with European cultural values. The truth of the matter, at least in what are loosely called "the Black regions of the Caribbean," is totally different. From the very beginning we are dealing with new societies formed of Africans and Europeans who arrived simultaneously: the former as a conquered people in a rapacious, capitalist war, the latter, as a group of exploiters. There was no preexistent European society into which the African imports were inserted. It is therefore methodologically wrong to search for Africanisms and to judge how many of them were accepted into an already established mold. Urban culture in Caribbean societies, just like every other culture, was created, recreated, and updated to conform with group necessities, interactions, and production. To this we can add that it was elaborated, recreated, and updated in conjunction with the contradictions and emergent possibilities of the economic, political, and social situation on the plantations. From their very beginning these were American societies in the process of recreating their Euroafrican components. Within this framework, Black and Mulatto groups made up the poorest, most helpless and most exploited social strata. On the cultural level, they were the objects of prejudice and discrimination, consigned to social pariahdom. They were deliberately isolated or marginalized, with conflicts stirred up among them to make cohesion ever difficult. In this respect, the cultural patterns of these groups, whether handed down, created, or recreated, were closely linked to their specific situation: a situation of neediness, of social marginalization, economic rejections, and cultural nonacceptance. From our point of view, therefore, the current approach to an anthropological study of this sort should lie in the direction of studying the ways in which this culture of exploitation has been created (or recreated) and has endured. And not only the culture of the direct descendants of the old African groups, but also its dynamic spin-offs, which deeply modified the culture patterns of all other exploited groups within the same society, regardless of skin color or "racial" origin.

Once slavery was abolished, the deculturation process continued as a mechanism of subjection in the small Caribbean islands. In Cuba and Brazil it became a divisive factor within the proletariat. An example of the deliberate process of fomenting social schisms, one that involves what has been called "high culture," is given by the following event. During the 1860s, the Anthropological Society was founded in Cuba. It was not an underdeveloped cultural organization that simply imitated its European counterparts. The Cuban Anthropological Society emerged out of the need of the dominant class to face the problems of cultural confrontation on the island. Almost its entire directive body consisted of physicians with the highest qualifications who had studied in Paris. For example, its president, Luis Montané Dardé, besides having been a prominent student in Paris, had been the disciple and later the coworker of Paul Broca (the founder of the *Revue d'Anthropologie*) and of Ernest Theodore Hamy, founder of the Trocadero Anthropological Museum, known today as the Musée de l'Homme. These distinguished scientists discussed, among other things, what was meant by the term "Cuban." Almost unanimously it was decided that a Cuban was a White man born in Cuba. As these meetings were taking place, the Ten Year War had already ended, a war in which many thousands of Blacks and Mulattoes had given their lives in the struggle for Cuban independence. The deputy commander of the Cuban forces had been, precisely, a Mulatto, General Antonio Maceo. This double standard of behavior (at the top and at the bottom of society) shows to what degree cultural differences were more than the theoretical antagonisms between European and African patterns and values: these were no abstract transcultural clashes in empty air, but the highly concrete results of direct class conflict. This led to what some sociologists have called "socialized ambivalence." As Benoist points out, this ambivalence operates both on the broad social level and deep within the individual psyche. Certain cultural values, specific forms of organization and institutionalization, were dynamically preserved (that is, reproduced and regenerated) as a source of orientation, identity, cohesion and dignity for the dominated group. Other standards and values of the so-called "high culture" (those that provided a background of Euroethnocentric dominance) were adopted, reproduced, and recreated as a source of cohesion for the dominant group and as a power mechanism.

In Cuba, where the bloody independence wars were fought by armies that on one side had a large proportion of African descendants (Creoles in the process of becoming Cubanized), national synthesis took place faster than in other countries of the Caribbean. However, U.S. intervention and economic dominance over the island until 1959 revitalized the disaggregating processes of colonial times. The critical decades of the 1920s and 1930s were essential in stirring up the cultural base and in structuring wide unified workers' movements among the physically hungry proletarian groups, which cared nothing for the distinctions, so carefully nurtured by the ruling class, between what was European and what was African. The violent strikes in Jamaica, Barbados, and Guyana and the definitive organization of the Cuban workers' movement took place at this time under the leadership of Mulattoes, to whom "color," whether their own or other people's, was a matter of total indifference. This was also the era of the great dignifying cry for *negritude* which, with time, paradoxically became a submissive, neocolonialist instrument.

To summarize, any analysis of Africans in Latin America taken out of its proper context of class struggle, is merely an empty digression. One cannot forget that the Black African came to America as a production factor, and that his descendants have continued to perform that same function. Sidney W. Mintz, in referring to the theory of marginalization, has shown, with his habitual brilliance, that if Blacks were secularly marginalized with regard to society and culture, they were never marginalized as producers of surplus value. It was upon their shoulders that the large plantation fortunes were created.

The Cuban revolution has performed a social "miracle" by eliminating racial discrimination within a few years. This invalidates the theory of marginalization. The "miracle" was simply the logical byproduct of the definitive rupture of the economic and class structures of capitalism. In a relatively short period, the elements of the dominated culture, jealously conserved and recreated as cohesive modules, have passed into national folklore, or are becoming extinct, now that the reasons for their existence have passed away. For example, music and dances originally linked to African religions have been passing into the national domain without requiring that the public be aware of their symbolic contents. In the same way that outside its original context the *abakuá* ritual loses its transcendental sense, so the dominated culture loses its raison d'être once the class structure breaks down. A book on *Africa in Latin America* must do more than trace the African footsteps, it must analyze how African, European, Asian, and Indoamerican social groups, molded by concrete economic forces, created societies that differed from their components.

2
Flight and Confrontation

German Carrera Damas

The historic perspective that sees a linear development of slavery from the past to the present has painted a picture of slavery in Latin America that omits the most important aspect of this socioeconomic phenomenon. I refer to the fact that, stricktly speaking, Black slavery cannot yet be considered merely as a part of the Latin American past. (In the same vein, one can claim that to this day, or until very recently, Indian slavery has survived in some areas of Latin America, despite its legal abolition four centuries ago.)

The consequences of employing the traditional historic framework in this case are varied and significant.

In the first place, one is forced to think of Black slavery as an historic process that had imprecise origins, that was subsequently controlled through legislation, and that finally culminated in a legislative act: abolition. This perspective confuses the formal existence of slavery with its real existence. In many cases the historic study of the legal boundaries of slavery presupposed that these boundaries in some way reflected reality or even helped to shape it.

In the second place, the above-mentioned evolution of the process is not really taken into account in evaluating and considering Black slavery as an institution. Such evaluations or general considerations that do not consider time spans and occurrences that have been properly described and chronologically determined, lose their concrete significance.

In the third place, the most enduring consequences of the phenomenon of slavery, those that occurred after its legal abolition, have been either totally ignored or reduced to "relics." It may not be exaggerated to see in this approach the effects of the great problem faced by nineteenth-century Latin American liberalism: the persistence of slavery, an institution whose abolition was expressly and definitely called for in all the constitutional texts drafted in expectation of the coming liberal order. Slavery, as a legal institution, should disappear with abolition. The legal act of abolition helped liberalism to clear its conscience, after half a century of incongruent coexistence of liberalism and slavery. For these reasons the economic, social, and political aspects of slavery have been studied in great detail, usually within the judicial framework, while the study of "sequels" or "relics" of slavery is rare or nonexistent. Such a study would undoubtedly have had to come to the uncomfortable conclusion that slavery, far from having been relegated to the Latin American past, is still an integral part of its present.

To summarize, apart from confusing the formal existence of slavery with its real existence, the study of slavery has been reduced to a work relationship that does not deal with the significance of social and racial discrimination against Black slaves, which is of fundamental importance. It does not take into account the fact that, if both aspects have determined slavery, the transformation of the work relationship (often relative), did not necessarily suppress discrimination. This means that it is not possible to explain the new work relationship outside the context of discrimination, for the entire Black sociocultural complex has been, and continues to be, tied to slavery.

Some time ago, I became dissatisfied with this framework and sought a different focus that would be closer to real Latin American social and historical perspectives. This new focus looks at Latin American societies where Black slavery was widespread as societies that are currently undergoing the phase of real abolition of slavery. This present-day abolition is to be understood as a complex and lengthy process through which the socioeconomic institutions and the ideological-political framework are being dissolved.

Thus, Black slavery is not just a part of the past of these societies, but also a current factor, since it is not difficult to see how the present is conditioned and even determined by the tremendous weight of the conventional "past." In other words, slavery did not end with legal abolition, which merely put an arbitrary end to an historic phenomenon, for its existential vigor does not fall within the legislative framework but lies within the socioeconomic structure. More than a century after abolition was legislated, slavery survives as an active component of the sociohistoric picture. Its endurance can be witnessed through social conflicts and tensions that bear a clear relationship to those that existed before abolition.

In colonial societies, where Black slavery reached a significant level, the two most important conflicts revolved around liberation and the struggle for equality, areas in which the incessant confrontation between Creoles, Spaniards, Blacks, and slaves took place.

In the case of the slaves, the struggle for freedom appears to be an individual or collective effort to "escape" slavery without attempting to suppress slavery itself, even though, during the course of the process, certain critical factors evolved, that did, in fact, help in the "suppression" of slavery. Suppression was not a direct result of the struggle for independence. Instead, social tensions were generated that forced the slaveowners to negotiate their way out of the tensions by creating the illusion of the certain or imminent suppression of slavery (such as manumission) or by preserving the essential aspects of the institution and transforming slavery into more or less veiled forms of personal bondage. Abolition became a prerequisite to negotiate the conversion of slavery into forced labor systems (which is what manumission really was) under the guise of peonage, the inseparable companion of Latin American societies.

The intimate ties between the struggle of slaves for freedom and their struggle for equality have attained their full meaning since abolition: there was no automatic correlation between the attainment of freedom (as a consequence of the formal, legal act of abolition) and the attainment of equality. Moreover, the achievement of formal freedom, as it occurred, inspired by liberalism, in the socioeconomic context of implanted Latinamerican societies, was translated into the reinforcement of real inequality and thus, into an absence of freedom.

The intimate relationship between the slave's struggle for his freedom and his egalitarian aspirations, a direct consequence of the dual exploitative and discriminatory nature of slavery, generated an intricate interplay between the individual and collective, active and passive forms of resistance, corresponding to the inherent nature of the deculturation[1] process. This deculturation is fundamental to all Black slavery in Latinamerican societies, since it is a process which attempts to uproot the culture of the exploited to achieve their more effective exploitation.

In the case of the Black slaves in America, the deculturation process inherent, more or less intensely, in every form of colonial or semicolonial exploitation, was applied even more rigorously than in Africa. Slavery not only created the necessary ad hoc conditions, but also served to repress, to a large degree, factors that could operate against deculturation, reducing these to surreptitious practices (even though these practices often filtered into the established coercive norms), leading to a highly traumatic cultural inauthenticity. It was through this inauthenticity that slaves—and thus the Blacks—were forced to abandon their own values and to adopt values whose main effect was to uproot their own. The process of deculturation was imposed upon the following groups:

a. Human beings uprooted from their traditional habitat and grafted, without possibility of return, onto physical surroundings that were in large part totally new to them.
b. Human beings whose social structure was completely demolished from the very beginning (although slavery was not foreign to them), leaving the individuals isolated and deprived of a social position within their group.
c. Human beings belonging to various ethnicities and from various cultures. In the new environment the concentration of individuals of a same tribe was avoided, while preexisting inter-ethnic conflicts were usually maintained and reinforced. New habits were forced upon these groups:

thus the cohesion that brings about culture was dissolved, erasing shared experiences that make possible communication and cooperation.

d. Men brought to America at a very young age. As a rule the ages ranged from 16 to 20 until the 1840s, and from 10 to 15 after that date. (This implies forced massive immigration of children.) Youth made deculturation easier, since the Africans came from cultures based on oral tradition, where knowledge was the sole domain of the older generation, particularly the elders.

e. Groups controlled twenty-four hours a day, whose communications and relations with other groups was forbidden and whose exploitive unit became their universe. The so-called Caroline Black Code, the royal decree regulating the treatment of slaves by their owners and the tasks they had to perform, was issued in Aranjuez on May 31, 1789. One stipulation concerning the types of entertainment permitted to slaves was that "Owners, and in their absence overseers, should see to it that their slaves engage in simple diversions, precluding all contact with slaves of other estates and observing the separation of sexes." The system of extensive labor to which they were subjected sought to have all the slaves' physiologically available time solely devoted to productive work. In addition to its economic value, the suppression of free time also served security purposes. Absorbed continuously with the same elementary activity, repeated to the limits of physical resistance, the differences in ability within a group were eliminated and interaction between group members became impossible.

f. Groups persecuted for their cultural heritage, suppressed as being barbaric, and which was replaced with new cultural forms that were most inauthentic.

g. Groups deprived of alternatives in the way they could satisfy their four basic biological needs: food, sex, dress, and home. These four basic cultural manifestations had to conform to the productive needs of the units of exploitation. Thus, building traditions, dietary and cooking habits, the artisanry of dress and decoration, and the sense of ritual and hierarchy were all disrupted. Sexual behavior patterns were necessarily altered by the unnatural male-to-female ratio of slave groups. At the same time, these groups found themselves forcibly inserted into strange religious and moral frameworks.

h. Men who from their first day in the colony had to adopt the language of the exploiter not only for vertical communication, but also for horizontal communication with slaves from other ethnic groups who spoke different languages.

i. Men who were brutally inserted into a system of production and subordination totally alien to their conception of tribal institutionalization.

j. Men who were forbidden to practice their own religion and upon whom the religion of the exploiter was imposed.

k. Men who were not permitted to have even the most elementary form of identification—not even their own name—since another name was picked for them in their oppressor's language.
l. Men whose possibility of physical survival was reduced to five or ten years of life from the moment they arrived on the plantation (during the days of greatest barbarism); and to ten or fifteen years of life as of 1840 in Cuba and Brazil.

In brief, slavery was what Manuel Moreno Fraginals calls a system of total control over of the physical and cultural personality of the Africans and their descendants that incited an immediate, sustained, and varied resistance.

The ability of the Black slave to cope under these conditions was obviously determined by his instinct for survival. The "physical taking over" that we have talked about, also meant permanently keeping the slave upon that narrow margin between survival and death. Thus, in the worst of cases, the slave could only choose between a survival that annihilated his own identity, and a revolt that would somehow end in death.

The various forms of resistance invite classification. The most common classification uses active or passive resistance as a criterion, while bearing in mind that this differentiation cannot be taken to an extreme. The poles of resistance were established by what may be called the "process of enslavement" on the one hand, and rebellion on the other. Within this spectrum escape and suicide were the most important forms of resistance.

One of the main problems met with in studying the resistance of slaves is that most of the information comes from the enslavers, and, even more significant, from both the judiciary and the police control and repression apparatus instituted by the slaveocrats to preserve and to reproduce the slave system. Thus, any act of resistance acquired a significance that was determined not solely by the act itself or by its particular meaning, but was seen within the framework of control and repression that had been set up to preserve the system.

In contrast to sources on political life in Latin America during that period, supplementary sources on slavery are scarce, and sources generated directly from the slave quarters are practically nonexistent. As a result, we are left with a difficult situation for the historian, who has advanced very little in formulating an appropriate methodology for dealing with these sources. (This is not the case with regard to the economic aspects of slavery, however.)

For example, to underline the importance of this methodological difficulty, we see that, according to "slaveocratic" sources, Black slaves never fought against slavery as a system, since any effort to escape from the system was accompanied, according to confessions frequently obtained through torture, by the purpose of enslaving the White masters, and particularly their women. This was a part of a supposed global scheme to subvert the social order to the point of annihilating all slave-owners and all Whites, to generate a "race war," the idea of which was a constant threat to Creoles from the end of the eighteenth century on.

A very critical source treatment would be required to establish the criteria for classifying the types of resistance employed by Black slaves. At present it is not feasible to put aside the old method based on active and passive resistance.

In response to what we have called the "process of taking over," which was no less than the total domination of the physical and cultural personality of the slave, and which began from the very moment of his capture and removal from his homeland, the predominant form of resistance on the slave's part was purely passive. This passive resistance, as a means of rejecting oppression and channelling the slave's trauma, included simulating obedience while complying only with the minimum of what was ordered, imperfectly and unwillingly, and directing his anger against his tools. The tradition of *ladinismo,* that is, of pretending to perform chores but doing so only partially and inefficiently, has had serious repercussions on today's Black social groups, since it has generated negative work habits. This indirect, passive rebellion, instead of confronting exploitation violently, atomized and neutralized the effects of coercion. However, in the long run, it perpetuated the extensive work system. The violence against the production equipment required that it be designed and built very strong and heavy to reduce the number of breakages. But with this equipment slave labor became slower and less productive, since the slaves now had to work with machetes or hoes that were twice as heavy as those used by free men. There is ample documentation on the low productivity of Black slaves, especially regarding their indolence, their carelessness in the use of tools, their negligent treatment of work animals, their shiftlessness and tendency to pamper themselves. We have, in summary, the slaveowner's view of the slaves' passive forms of resistance, a view that at that time served to promote slavery as a system, and that since abolition, has nourished the stereotypes of racism.

"Active resistance" was displayed through individual or collective forms of rebellion. Although it is hard to measure active resistance in quantitative terms, there is no doubt that it flourished every day on plantations, on estates, and in mines. Even bearing in mind what we already noted, that the descriptions of the slaves' acts of rebellion had as their source the slaveowners' own apparatus for repression, there is no doubt that active resistance became the permanent bugbear of slave society. It was unpredictable and inevitable, and contained great potential for violence that, once unfurled, could multiply a hundredfold the daily accumulation of violence generated through exploitation and discrimination. The words "race war" were a constant threat to slaveowners; they triggered both his violence and his fearful behavior. The racial war in Santo Domingo that occurred as the culmination of the development of slavery at the end of the eighteenth century had such an impact on the Caribbean slave societies that even well into the nineteenth century, the event was used as an argument in the debate on abolition. As for individual acts of rebellion (frequently poorly disguised suicide attempts), their high incidence reflects the violent treatment suffered daily by slaves. Manuel Moreno Fraginals points out that, according to documents of the Permanent Executive Military Commission in the Cuban National Archives, more than one thousand slave owners, overseers, and administrators of sugar plantations were executed by slaves between 1836 and 1870. There is reason to believe that difficulties in communication, the lack of cohesion within slave groups, and the extreme vigilance by the repressive slave system, often prevented group rebellions, but these methods were unable to stop an individual about to commit an act of desperation.

Between the opposite poles of passive and active resistance there were individual and collective ways of escaping slavery through marronage or through suicide.

A maroon was a slave who ran away without having committed any acts of violence against his master or those in charge of him. The Slave Act of 1696 made a distinction between marronage and rebellion. A runaway was a slave who, having lived on the Island of Jamaica for more than three years, fled and hid for less than a year before recapture or surrender. His punishment was a whipping. A slave who had been gone for over a year became a rebel and was punishable by death. A slave who had been on the island for under three years was punished less severely. Captured maroons were sent to "workhouses." Marronage accompanied the development of slavery, from the beginning of the sixteenth century on. In 1523 there were already maroons in the Zapotec region of Mexico, and there is proof of their presence in Santo Domingo in 1545, in Darien in 1548, in Castilla de Oro in 1575, and in Panama and Uruguay in 1574. At the beginning of the eighteenth century there were some twenty thousand maroons in Venezuela.[2] Repression of maroons was accomplished not only by punishing their flight, but also by finding the most efficient methods of preventing their escape. It therefore was considered necessary to take specific measures, including special laws and traditional forms of harsh punishment, even though the futility of these measures was frequently noted.

In Cuba, as in the rest of America, marronage is as old as slavery. However, the institutionalization of counter-measures (forced return to the place of work, punishment, and imprisonment) only began in 1796. In that year the King approved the "new regulations and rewards applicable to the capture of runaway slaves." Written by Francisco de Arango y

Parreño, the law summarized and adapted all the old and diffuse legislation on fugitive slaves to conditions on Cuban plantations. The law, in
effect until 1870, institutionalized the system of slave-hunters (the *ranche-
adores*) prisons ("depositories") and applicable forms of punishment. A
"correction house" was even established to punish maroon slaves and
others who were considered by their masters to be in need of punishment.

Suicide was the most expeditious way for slaves to escape, either
through an act of self-destruction or by rebelling under conditions that
guaranteed death. Chroniclers of the early colonial period document how
the enslaved Indians deliberately sought their own death, individually or
collectively, and would thereby frustrate the expectations of slave traders
or masters. Suicide was also a frequent practice among Black slaves, a
desperate response to their excessive workload, to hunger, or to punishment. Suicide was so prevalent on Cuban sugar plantations that an inves-
tigation was started in 1840, compiled in a voluminous file now kept at the
National Cuban Archive, entitled "Causes that influence the frequency of
suicide of our slaves and measures that must be adopted to avoid them."
The Bishop of the Cathedral, the prosecutor of the "Audiencia Pretorial"
and a commission of the most prominent rural slaveowners named by the
Royal Development Board, all testified at the hearings. It was agreed that
the problem was "appalling," since two to three suicides were occurring
each year on all large plantations (those with 250 or more slaves), that the
suicide rate was higher among men than among women, who "rarely
commit suicide," and that, as the Bishop stated, "It is not the ill-treatment
of the slaves that produces frequent suicides, but their lack of religious
instruction." According to incomplete urban statistics, which, of course,
did not include the large number of suicides occuring on plantations, 83
percent of Havana's suicides during the 1840s were those of Black
slaves.[3]

The various forms of resistance to slavery created a climate of severe
social tension by the end of the eighteenth century. This resulted in a
hardening of the position of slaveowners, shown by their attempts to
make the means of controlling slaves more efficient. To summarize, one
cannot say that slave resistance considerably weakened the slave system.
However, the flareup of political events in North America and Europe at
that time makes it difficult to evaluate to what extent the slave system was
weakened, if it was, particularly because the slave question became a part
of the general crisis within colonial society.

The growth of slavery during the seventeenth century created, among
other things, severe and ever-growing inequalities between the "White"
and the "non-White" population of Latin America, affecting particularly
the Blacks and the Mulattoes, given the decreasing importance of the
Indian population. Tensions arose that kept slaveowners constantly on
guard, once they realized the various difficulties involved in maintaining

tranquility and control over their slaves. Through the above-mentioned Black Caroline Code, the King claimed to have consistently established, observed, and followed a system that would make slaves useful, and that "set the rules for owners to provide their slaves with whatever education, treatment, and occupation was required, according to the rules and principles dictated by religion, humanity, and the good of the state, compatible with slavery and with public peace." Three factors directed at overcoming the slaves' struggle for freedom were thereby established: the normative, regulatory influence of the state; religious indoctrination; and the repressive vigilance of slaveowners.

Moreover, according to historic documents from the end of the eighteenth century, the effect of the regulatory and control factors that guaranteed the stability and the proper functioning of the slave system were nullified by the repercussions of the "occurrences in Santo Domingo and Guarico." The social climate of the time, admirably portrayed by Alejo Carpentier in his novel *Century of Lights,* reflects the interaction between the crisis-generating factors within the slave system and the new currents and ideas emerging from the crisis of the old French regime. The stimulus received from these new currents by the struggle of Black slaves for their freedom and equality contributed to the development of a social situation in Latin America in which the attitude towards slavery rapidly became the key to evaluating the scope of ideologies and movements. It is impressive to note that, at a very early stage, a group was formed that proposed the liberal answer to the slave question. Their three main principles were: the preservation of the economic structure; harmonization of the liberal principles of property, liberty, equality, and fraternity; and a guarantee of White hegemony.

It might be worthwhile to look at the Venezuelan case in more detail, because it illustrates the process so well, and because circumstances in Venezuela so accurately reflect the general history. Events that took place in Venezuela in 1797 were shaped by men whose connection with the French revolutionary thought of 1793 has been proven, and whose position on slavery was clearly defined in the constitutions or ordinances written by Juan Bautista Picornell, instigator of the so-called "Picornell, Gual, and España" conspiracy. In fact, the first two principles were clearly spelled out in articles 32, 34, 36, and 37 of the ordinances, as follows.

32. Inhabitants of all provinces and districts are hereby declared equal, and it is urged that total harmony should reign between Whites, Indians, and Blacks, and that they all view each other as brothers in Christ, equal before God, seeking advantage only through merit and virtue, which are the only two real distinctions among men that will from now on be recognized among individuals of our Republic.

34. Slavery is of course abolished because it denies humanity: therefore, all slaveowners are expected to present to the governing junta of their towns a list of their slaves, which will include their name, mother country, age, sex, job, costs, years of service, and a note on their conduct and their illnesses, if any, so that, in their presence the General Junta can determine and order the just payment out of the public coffers to their respective owners. All slaves shall remain in the service of their masters until the General Junta decides otherwise.

36. All new citizens must swear their loyalty to their country, which they will serve as members of the militia until freedom of the country has been attained, as long as circumstances so require. To prevent the neglect of agriculture, plantation workers, slaves and servants living in the interior of the country shall remain with their old masters, and shall receive fair wages for reasonable work. To avoid all excesses and damages by one side or the other, no servant or new citizen may leave his master without a valid reason, approved by a member of the governing junta who will be named as judge.

37. Once the Nation has attained independence, the new citizens will be discharged and will be offered all help deemed necessary.

The reaction of Venezuelan Creoles to the "Picornell, Gual, and España" movement was to close ranks in defense of the colonial order and its slave structure. This reaction was dictated, with regard to slavery, by the necessity to exert effective controls, not only over slavery, but over the entire non-White population. The conspirators of 1797 seemed quite aware of this crucial question, which is why they included in article 7 of their ordinances that the governing junta of each city or village should be formed by ". . . Only those local estate-owners, who had already shown beforehand unequivocal proof of their constant patriotism, of their love for the poor, and of their knowledge about government."[4]

The importance of maintaining effective controls over society not only served to sustain the right of property and the economic structure, but also increased as a consequence of the "racial war" that broke out in Santo Domingo. This war determined the immediate objectives of regulating the growth of the Black population and of perfecting the means of control and repression. The first objective was accomplished through the decree of August 14, 1810, drawn up by the Supreme Junta of Venezuela which stated, "The introduction of Blacks into these provinces is forbidden." The second objective was accomplished by creating a national guard with the specific mission of repressing slaves.

Thus, the crisis in the slaveocracies of Latin America resulted from the coincidence of the slavery crisis with the societal crisis in Europe and was characterized by the following events: in the first place, the dominant Creole classes became aware that in establishing new countries they had to offer an answer to the slave question. In the second place, from the very beginning of the crisis, a basic norm was established regarding slave expectations that, with certain variants, was reproduced throughout Latin America.

In the third place, the methods used by slaves in their resistance to slavery were changed, quantitatively and qualitatively, when they were called upon to participate in the struggle for independence (which they associated with their aspirations of freedom and equality). This call to action from without, unrelated to the slaves' aims, in the end had the effect of changing into a struggle against slavery what had previously been basically the individual slave's fight for his freedom.

It was during the wars of independence that the slaveowners, the Creoles and the Spaniards, first experimented with a new attitude towards slavery. I will venture to explain some of the stages and ideas developed during this period.

It is interesting to note that at the beginning of the period, which varied in duration in each area, rebels and loyalists both made efforts to win the slaves over to their cause by urging them to participate in the struggle. This encouragement to fight (often consisting of pure and simple recruitment) did not necessarily include an offer of freedom, as it did in the case of the slave rebellions against the first Venezuelan Republic (1811–1812) promoted by the clergy.

It was during the second phase of this period that participation of slaves became a prerequisite for freedom, as can be observed in Bolivar's decrees of 1816 (as in the ordinances of 1797). However, some of the revolutionary heroes were genuinely in favor of abolition. The constant debate between those who in some way encouraged the participation of slaves in the wars and those who, aware of the system's requirements, were in favor of keeping the slaves on the sidelines of the struggle as a means of avoiding the proliferation of the non-White population, accompanied the various phases of the independence period.

In the absence of any systematic study of the participation of Black slaves in the wars of independence, it has been difficult to establish the connection between the resistance to slavery and the new political situation. However, it is clear that by the end of the wars, the liberal republic had developed the following attitudes towards the slave question: *(a)* slavery as an institution was condemned through legislation and according to ideological principles, even though its real extinction was subordinated to economic, financial, and political considerations; *(b)* slavery as a system was structurally affected by prohibition of the slave trade, reinforced by the new world order that had been initiated and promoted by Great Britain; and *(c)* slavery as a socioeconomic structural order was generally preserved through legislative provisions, administrative proceedings, and the tolerance of some illegal practices.

To summarize, a situation was created based on two powerful concerns of the new dominant class: In the first place, the effective control of societies disrupted by the war was resumed, which implied the reestablishment of slavery. This is why we can speak in terms of the recurrence of slavery after independence. In the second place, the White sector of the population was invigorated by realigning previously incompatible groups and by encouraging large waves of White immigrants to enter the countries, while prohibiting Black immigration (the prohibition of the slave trade soon developed into the pure and simple prohibition of Black immigration).

The establishment of republican regimes became a severe threat to the Creoles, since the rupture with the colonial order was brought about by lengthy wars that were cruel and filled with profound social repercussions. The recurrence of slavery, the growing non-White population, the demographic and social weakening of the Creoles, all played a crucial role in the rapid process of disenchantment that followed initial illusions that the coming of a new social order would replace with positive values the somber traits of the old colonial order.

The Creole, oppressor and exploiter of Indians and Blacks, imposed upon the colonial order a new social order in which he became a member of the dominant class. As the heir to the destiny of the "implanted" Latin American society, he faced the challenge of turning into reality the national ideal, so laboriously formulated during the war. It is impossible, in this short essay, to mention even briefly the problems of establishing the new republic. Let it suffice to point out that it soon became obvious to the dominated classes that, with regard to slavery, the new order was a reflection of the old, though without the presence of royal representatives.

It became quite clear that, as far as slaves were concerned, the reestablishment of the economies destroyed by the war was to be achieved by a more rational and careful exploitation of their work, by prolonging and reinforcing the slave system (in spite of the existence of a system of manumission which was as grudging in theory as it was disregarded in practice) by controlling the situation through police force and judicial repression, conditions that echoed those at the end of the eighteenth century. Thus, conditions were created that encouraged the same forms of resistance to slavery as those practiced under the Spanish colonial order, such as unwillingness to work, marronage, and rebellion.

It is worth mentioning that for the republican period, the problems regarding historic sources are identical to those of the colonial period. The persistence of maroon settlements and the frequency of notices in the republican press offering rewards for fugitive slaves point to the conflict between reality and ideology in the doctrine of militant liberalism.

The difficulties encountered by Creoles as they established the republic soon led to a desperate search for explanations, which attempted to uncover the root of their failures and to present curative proposals. The extensive list of remedies served basically to absolve the ruling class of all responsibility and placed the blame for all failings squarely upon the shoulders of all Indians, wherever there were Indians, and upon Blacks, wherever these accounted for a large part of the population.

It thus became possible to strengthen even further the social and ethnic discriminatory web that had entangled both slave and Black almost since the discovery of America. The Black was no longer merely a hindrance: he was now the real obstacle to the development of society and the achievement of the republican order. Not slavery: the Black. In such an ideological climate, it is understandable that the legal abolition of slavery became basically a political and an administrative problem. The fundamental problem was no longer the incorporation of a contingent of slaves into a free society, but rather the existence and growth of a large sector of non-Whites inexorably marching towards control of the society. Abolition, once the right of property was guaranteed, resolved a number of problems, not only economic but also social: it dissipated tension, conflict, and even the potential of insurgency, which could have become particularly dangerous given the ethnic composition of the population; it homogenized the dominated class under conditions that made control easier; and it opened an escape valve for egalitarian pressures. It revealed, in sum, that, as slaves, Blacks had the ability to exert pressure disproportionate to their numbers, whereas, atomized by a "free" society, they became pariahs, overwhelmed by the weight of deculturation and servitude. It would be hard to find a more important political step than abolition taken by the Creoles once they became aware of the threat represented by the non-White population, and once they were convinced of the futility of their efforts at demographic and social reinforcement through massive immigration of Whites. Their wisdom was revealed by their eagerness to abolish slavery, and thus take away the detonator that could blow up the volatile social situation.

The negative portrayal of Blacks as the explanation for the chaotic situation in some of the Latinamerican republics in the nineteenth century was reinforced in the years following abolition. The racist simplicism that Blacks were not the prime cause of all delays because they were slaves, but because they were Blacks, gained popularity. The unrelenting and insidious debate on the abilities of Blacks, a debate in which racism used every possible argument and the social context was deliberately ignored, placed Blacks in a very difficult position. They were operating in a discriminatory social order and had to carry with them the burden of slavery as a social and a cultural reality.

During this new phase of slavery, flight and confrontation were no longer viewed as resistance to slavery. Among freed Blacks one can find similar reactions to a society marred by racial prejudice and by the marginalization of Black people.

Rebellion as a way of escaping slavery merged into civil war before and after abolition in those Latin American societies that had broken their colonial ties at the beginning of the nineteenth century. One example was the rebellion of free Blacks at Aponte, that took place in Cuba in 1811.

Flight and marronage also had their counterparts among the free groups before and after the abolition of slavery. Perhaps one could also include in this analysis Black attempts to return to Africa, as well as the isolation of many units of the Black population. However this should not be the definitive explanation for such phenomena.

In societies where Blacks were few or very dispersed, abolition was the final blow to resistance to deculturation, even though this might seem to contradict the deculturing nature of slavery. In fact, the last possibilities of resistance vanished as soon as direct coercion ceased, as soon as Blacks were faced with the problems of becoming incorporated into a discriminatory society without even the support of a viable cultural identity. The large Black populations of Cuba and Brazil had a totally different experience, since it was possible for them to preserve and to cultivate a part of their cultural identity.

Thus a situation developed which I will refer to as "cultural marronage," by which I mean a flight from all that was Black. This occurred when socioeconomic progress, in a medium where all that is African was rejected through prejudice, could only be achieved by denying one's Black African past. Cuba offers some incredible examples of cultural marronage. The most important Black cultural society was called the "Athens Club," and the most important Black recreation society was called "The Young Waltzers" (later the spelling was changed to the Spanish *vals*). It is also significant that a group of Black university intellectuals in 1902 asked for and obtained from the government the prohibition of other *comparsas* and other forms of Black dance and music.

However, the mimicking of "White" values to escape slavery, which affected both freed slaves and old slaves once abolition had occurred, when seen in a sociocultural context, does not really become an alternative to the reestablishment of "Black" values. Structural conditions determined both alternatives and usually they would evolve into a cultural confinement for the Black man, a cultural confinement that only differed from that of other exploited sectors within society because it carried with it the additional burden of discrimination that was part of the legacy of slavery. In summary, a situation developed in which Blacks were simply denied access to the higher cultural levels and to the social participation that would have permitted them to act efficiently whether mimicking "White" values or revaluing "Black" values.

Therefore, one must study this problem in the context of social structures and of possibilities for vertical mobility. Such possibilities must be understood not as exceptions that existed even in times of the most rigid slavery, but as institutionalized and regular guidelines. One should not lose sight of the fact that even though the slaveowners wanted to maintain a system of exploitation, they were no less interested in preserving White hegemony. For this reason it was essential that Black freedom, no matter how obtained, should not bring with it more than a rhetorical equality, never a real one. The health of the system and of the entire society hinged upon this. Thus, abolition never contemplated the fact that the old slave could have any other destiny than that of swelling the ranks of the peons, both ignorant and poor. That was the reason for rigorous social stratification, and social and racial discrimination.

The "re-evaluation of Black values," seen neither as a position of retreat nor as a historically reactionary evocation of nostalgia, must occur intrasocially, or else it becomes a sort of autosegregation. This presupposes the development of a set of social, economic, and cultural attitudes that could not appear within the framework of social structures that would have to be shaken to their roots in order for such a revaluation to occur. Therefore in republican societies that developed as a result of the crisis in the structure of the colonial societies of Latin America, pro-African or anti-African, pro-Black or anti-Black positions have all been the result of a class struggle in which class was determined by skin color. But when the class structure is annihilated, such ideology also dies, although not immediately, since mental attitudes often survive the structural reasons that accounted for their existence.

To summarize, the absolute destruction of slavery in Latin America does not seem possible within a framework of a society divided into classes, such as the capitalist society, not only since its "unequalizing" effect counters the egalitarian aspiration of the former slaves, but also because capitalism reinforces the inequitable principles of a slaveocracy. So long as this situation remains unchanged, the resistance to slavery initiated by Black slaves and continued by freed Blacks before and after abolition, can enrich itself with new forms of struggles or witness the transformation of a few nuances, yet under such circumstances the struggle against slavery and its lasting effects will never cease.

NOTES

1. This section is based principally and extensively, on concepts first put forth by Manuel Moreno Fraginals.

2. Miguel Acosta Saignes, *Vida de los Esclavos Negros en Venezuela* (Caracas: 1967), pp. 249–250.

3. Information made available by Manuel Moreno Fraginals.

4. Casto Fulgencio López, *Juan Picornell y la Conspiración de Gual y España* (Madrid: 1955).

3

Social Organization and Alienation

Octavio Ianni

Race and Culture

In Latin America and in the Caribbean, the Africans became Blacks and Mulattoes. During the course of centuries, and under the most varied social conditions, the Africans' many personifications or social figurations came to include the following: slave, newly arrived African, Creole, Ladino, free born, freedman, Mulatto or Black. Confronted with Whites, Indians, Mestizos, European immigrants, Asian immigrants, and other social groups, Africans were gradually transformed into Blacks and Mulattoes. And it is Blacks and the Mulattoes who appear on the White social horizon, and on their own social horizon, in the twentieth century. They appear in work relationships, in politics, in religion, in play, in sex and in other relationships as social types that differ from Whites in their physical, phenotypical, psychological, and cultural attributes.[1] With regard to social relations Whites and Blacks themselves end up thinking and acting as though Blacks had a different culture—another way of evaluating relationships among people, with nature, and with the supernatural. In general, theirs is a subordinate race. Blacks are not like Whites: they are different and strange. In almost all countries, Blacks appear as the second or third race after Whites and Indians.

This is the psychological significance of the Black race. The racial differences, socially reworked, engendered, or codified, are constantly being recreated and reproduced, preserving, altering, reducing, or even accentuating the physical, phenotypical, psychological, or cultural traits that distinguish Whites from Blacks. The biological, cultural, national, linguistic, religious, and other distinctions and differences are constantly being recreated and reproduced in the relationships between persons, families, groups, and social classes. Within the various strata of social organization, in work relations, in religious practices, in the relationship between the sexes, in the family, in regard to artistic production and free time, or in other situations, the races are constantly being recreated and reproduced as socially different and unequal. In every country the social criteria employed to classify people, groups, or classes can vary. But in each case, for the White, the Indian, the Mestizo, the Italian, the German, the Japanese, the English, the French, and others, Blacks belong to a different race, to a universe of values and sociocultural norms that can be somewhat or very different from that of Whites.

More specifically, the criteria that define social races differ from one region to the other in the Americas. In one region the important criterion is *ancestry,* in another *sociocultural* criteria prevail, and in the third, *physical appearance* is the fundamental base for the classification of social races. As a result, a different number of social races and a different structural ordering of racial relations emerges in each one of these regions. The different ways in which each region conceives of the social races reflect the relations between people of various biological and cultural origins within a large society.[2]

It is in these terms that Blacks emerge on the horizon of scientific analysis. They appear to Whites, and even to themselves, as social types whose sociability and culture present traits that differentiate them from Whites. Some of their activities, as well as the values that organize these activities, seem to differentiate and to discriminate against Blacks to the point of transforming them into a problem or a challenge to Whites and to themselves. The White attempts to find in the Black the motive for the social distance, the prejudice and the tensions that appear in the relationships between the two. The Black, on the other hand, tries to enter and to move within the network of social relations where he appears different, alienated, and discriminated against by the White. The identity of the White contains a kind of reflection of the identity he gives to the Black. And the latter, to achieve an identity, must accept passively or critically the identity given to him by the White. This is the core of the tense social universe within which the Black appears as a problem not only to the White but also to himself and to the social researcher.

This search for the social and cultural particularity of Blacks is present in a large body of the research and interpretations of anthropologists, sociologists, historians, and other social researchers who have worked with the problem of social relations between Whites and Blacks in Latin America and the Caribbean. Fernando Ortiz, Gilberto Freyre, Melville J. Herskovits, E. Franklin Frazier, Frank Tannenbaum, Marvin Harris, H. Hoetink, Eugene D. Genovese, J. Halcro Ferguson, Sidney W. Mintz, David Brion Davis, Magnus Mörner, Verena Martinez Alier, Florestan Fernandes and Roger Bastide are some of the social scientists interested in researching and explaining the historic and cultural contents of the relations between Blacks and Whites in Latin American and Caribbean countries. It is the problems discussed above that appear on the cultural scale devised by Herskovits, first published in 1945.[3] His system categorizes information based on the presence of African cultural elements in various American and Caribbean countries. This chart permits us to see how the cultural elements are distributed among various types of activity into which Black and White relationships are organized, such as technology, economic life, social organization, institutions, religion, magic, art, folklore, music, and language. Although Herskovits tried to

TABLE 1

Intensity Scale of Africanisms in the New World
(In each group only the greatest degree of preservation is shown)

	Technology	Economy	Social organization	Independent Institutions	Religion	Magic	Art	Folklore	Music	Language
Guyana (Bush)*	b	b	a	a	a	a	b	a	a	b
Guyana (Paramaribo)	c	c	b	c	a	a	b	a	a	c
Haiti (peasant)	c	b	b	c	b	a	e	a	a	c
Haiti (urban)	e	d	c	d	b	b	d	a	a	c
Brazil (Bahia-Recife)	d	d	b	d	a	a	e	a	a	a
Brazil (Porto Alegre)	e	e	c	e	a	a	b	a	a	c
Brazil (Maranhão, rural)	c	c	b	e	c	b	e	b	a	b
Brazil (Maranhão, urban)	e	d	c	e	e	b	e	d	a	b
Cuba	e	d	c	b	a	a	e	b	a	a
Jamaica (maroons)	c	c	b	b	b	a	e	a	a	c
Jamaica (Morant Bay)	e	c	b	b	b	a	e	a	a	a
Jamaica (general)	e	c	d	d	b	b	e	a	b	c
Honduras (Black Caribs)**	c	c	b	b	b	a	e	b	a	e
Trinidad (Port of Spain)	e	d	c	b	a	a	c	b	a	e
Trinidad (Toco)	e	d	c	c	c	b	e	b	b	d
Mexico (Guerrero)	d	e	b	b	c	b	e	b	?	e
Colombia (Choco)	d	d	c	c	c	b	e	b	c	e
Virgin Islands	e	d	c	d	e	b	e	b	a	e
United States (Gullah Islands)	c	c	c	d	c	b	e	a	b	d
United States (Rural South)	d	e	c	d	c	b	e	b	b	b
United States (Urban North)	e	e	c	d	c	b	e	d	b	e

(a) Very African; (b) quite African; (c) somewhat African; (d) slightly African; (e) traces or absence of African customs; (?) no information available.

*Refers to Negroid villages formed by descendants of former maroons.
**The influence of Carib Indians is strong in this culture.

40

show how African culture persisted in the American and Caribbean countries, we can also view the table of cultural Africanisms as a table of cultural losses, or as a scale of recreated cultural forms (see Table 1).

Another significance of the data presented by Herskovits could be to show how researchers attempt to explain, through cultural Africanisms, the metamorphosis of Africans into Blacks and Mulattoes. Understanding how Africans changed into Blacks and Mulattoes is certainly a crucial question, as is the reason why White, Black, and Mulatto relationships became marked and tainted by racial differences rather than extinguishing or diluting such differences. To explain this metamorphosis, anthropologists, sociologists and historians turn to the relationship between race and culture.

Let us therefore examine how the relationship between African culture and the Black condition are usually treated. To understand the social condition of Blacks in Latin America and the Caribbean we can begin by looking at what appears to be the peculiarity of their culture. There are at least three different interpretations of the cultural contribution of African people and their descendants to Latin American and Caribbean societies. Let us describe them briefly:

The first interpretation establishes that African culture, as such, is present in all slave societies. This culture exists, of course, in varying degrees, in different social activities and organizations such as religion, folklore, music, language, the family, cooking, etc. It also emerges in different intensities according to country, region, and locality, but it is always present, and can be recognized as being originally African, distinct from European, Asian, or Indian cultures. This means that some aspects of the social and cultural life of Black populations in Latin America and the Caribbean, as well as certain aspects of the relationship between Whites and Blacks, are influenced by African cultural elements. These elements are preserved by the descendants of Africans as cultural survivals that are transmitted to individuals, families, groups, and communities.

As for the second interpretation, it maintains that the culture brought by the Africans was more or less destroyed and reworked through slavery. With regard to the social and technological organization of production relations, slavery brought its own culture that had little or nothing to do with European, African, Indian, or Asian cultural elements. The centuries of slave work broke all the preexisting cultural contributions and produced a peculiar, vigorous culture that took root and expanded within the society, among individuals, families, groups, and social classes. Therefore, what appeared later, in the nineteenth and twentieth centuries, as Black culture was only a culture produced by slave society. Within the former slave societies, typical slave cultural elements persisted well into the twentieth century. These were the elements that appeared in religious practices, magic, music, family organization, cuisine, and other aspects of

Black social activity in Latin America and in the Caribbean. Few African elements were preserved; those that did survive would have been reworked by relationships and structures deriving from slavery.

A third interpretation maintains that both the African and slave cultures were destroyed and superseded by the capitalist relationships and structures that became predominant in Latin American and Caribbean societies in the twentieth century. Of course one can still identify African and slave cultural elements in the life patterns of Blacks and Whites in the twentieth century; such elements can be detected in religion, music, folklore, family organization, cooking, language, and other aspects of social life. However, the dominant trait is capitalist culture—a heterogeneous culture, unequal as well as contradictory, whose relationships and structures only make sense in terms of the capitalist mode of production.

These three interpretations are not necessarily mutually exclusive. One can be a part of another. In a certain way the first and second can be encompassed within the third. The fact that capitalist relationships and structures create their own cultural elements, be they material, organizational, or spiritual, does not prevent the coexistence of certain African and slave-related cultural elements. Capitalist relationships and structures have the ability to create and to recreate the new as well as the old. The heterogeneity, inequality, and cultural contradictions (in both material and spiritual terms) must be a part of the heterogeneity, inequality, and contradiction typical of capitalist relationships and structures.

The common denominator of each of these interpretations of the cultural contribution of Africans to Latin American and Caribbean societies, is the uniqueness of the Black. On what terms and for what reasons does the Black appear to the White and to himself as a unique social type, a different race with a different way of thinking, feeling and acting?

To become Blacks in twentieth-century Latin America and the Caribbean, Africans were not only first slaves, but they were also transformed into laborers. Furthermore, in the twentieth century Blacks were transformed, or transformed themselves, into industrial workers, agricultural workers, day laborers, specialists, functionaries, employees, merchants, politicians, intellectuals, or other social types. And it is under those circumstances that they do not reproduce themselves as Africans or as slaves in the twentieth century. What remains of the African or of the slave in their culture or in their Weltanschauung, can hardly be explained as the survivals, the mixture of cultures, or the syncretisms that hide the ex-African or the ex-slave. What remains of the African or the slave in the culture and the worldview of Blacks in Latin America and the Caribbean is that which is continuously recreated and reproduced. But this constant recreation and reproduction is not decided or acted upon by Blacks themselves, but by the conditions and the relationships of interdependence, alienation, and antagonism determined by capitalism.

This is true to the point that what seems to be African or Black culture in Latin America and the Caribbean really consists of components intrinsic to the present-day, living culture of these countries. In *santería,* in *voodoo,* in *candomblé,* in *umbanda,* and in other expressions of the religious culture of Blacks and Mulattoes, we find not only elements of spiritism and Catholicism, but we also find White, Indian, Mestizo, German, Italian, and Polish elements. Black religions, just like magic, music, folklore, and other expressions of Black and Mulatto life, are more or less absorbed or reworked by the existing cultural systems in those countries. It is not by chance, exoticism, or cultural survival that certain "African," "slave," or "Black" cultural elements emerge and reemerge, are created and reproduced in the big cities and in the large industrial centers of each country. In Latin America and in the Caribbean, the Black cultures— working class, middle class, or other—are popular dimensions of the political and economic relationships that guarantee the reproduction of society with its harmony, inequality, and contradictions.

Social Reproduction of the Races

In the twentieth century Blacks and Mulattoes are continually recreated and socially reproduced by the same social relationships that recreate and reproduce members of the other "races," such as Whites, Indians, Mestizos, Japanese, Chinese, Spanish, Portuguese, Jews, Italians, Germans, British, French, Dutch, Northamericans, and others. In each of the national societies that form Latin America and the Caribbean, some, and at times all, of these groups are socially recreated and reproduced by the social relationships that organize and move each society. In work, political, religious, sexual, recreational, and other relationships, they reproduce socially. Therefore anthropologists, sociologists, linguists, and other social researchers find different signs of "European," "African," "Asian," and "Indian" cultural elements in the social organization in economic, religious, and other activities.[4]

It must be understood that the continuous reproduction of racial categories also implies the recreation and reproduction of African and slave cultures. On plantations, in haciendas, sugar mills, factories, and offices, at home, in schools, barracks, churches, temples, etc., the African and slave cultural elements appear, sometimes clearly, at other times blurred. However, in every case, the elements appear and reappear only because they are recreated and reproduced socially by the various races in their activities and in their political, economic, and cultural relationships. Generally, it is the course of concrete social relations in the material and spiritual spheres (hacienda, factory, school, church, etc.) that determines the invention and reinvention, or the recreation and reproduction, of the cultural values, behavior standards, ideas, ideals, thought patterns, racial characteristics, phenotypical traits, and cultural traits that determine whether the Black, the Mulatto, the White, the Indian, the Mestizo, and others will be taken practically and ideologically as different and unequal racial categories.

Reviewing the entire picture and focusing on some characteristics of the relationships between African, slave, and Black cultural and social organization in Latin America and the Caribbean, Roger Bastide gives us the following summary:

> In the first place, Black society has never been a separate society. Black society and slavery . . . have destroyed the African models, and the Black man has reacted by restructuring his community. He was no longer a man surrounded by nature, but formed new institutions; he gave himself a new life style and he created for himself his own organization, apart from the Whites. . . .
>
> In the second place, we have learned to distinguish, depending on the region, two types of communities: those in which African models persist, of course under pressure of the environment, and which certainly are forced to change in order to adapt themselves and to be accepted; we will call these "African communities." And those, in which, to the contrary, the pressures of the environment have been stronger than the pieces of collective memory, who were employed as servants for centuries, but where racial segregation has not permitted that the descendants of slaves accept the cultural models of their masters; in these cases the Black man has had to invent new life styles within the society, in response to his isolation, to his work patterns, and to his new necessities; we shall call these "Black communities." Black, because the White man is excluded from them, but not African, because these communities have lost the memory of their former mother country.
>
> These two types of communities are no more than ideal abstractions. In fact, we are faced with a continuity between the two types. Thus, one sector of a society can remain purely African, such as religion, while another responds to the new environment, such as the family or economic structure. Naturally, the Black maroon communities are closest to the first type, those formed by new arrivals from Africa. The communities formed following the abolition of servile labor, such as the Creoles who lived in isolation in the countryside, are closest to the second type. Within the Black villages of the Caribbean and South America we find an intermediate type, because "nations" could easily be formed during the slave era, without White control, in order to secretly hold on to traditions. However, among themselves, these Blacks were forced to comply to the State's matrimonial, economic and political laws, and thus to adapt to the model imposed upon them in exile.[5]

The social recreation and reproduction of Blacks and Mulattoes, among other racial categories, occurs only within political and economic relationships that establish the basis for the continuing recreation and reproduction of the society's relationships and structures. In this perspective the great complexity of racial composition that organizes and moves the relationships between Blacks, Mulattoes, and Whites, begins to become clearer. At first the racial map of Latin America and the Caribbean seems quite complex, heterogeneous, and even contradictory. But, when seen in the context of politicoeconomic conditions in which social relations and structures are reproduced, this map acquires more precise contours and movements. In an article on Caribbean societies, Sidney W. Mintz describes in a fairly clear manner some of the aspects of the relationship between race and social organization. The relationships between the structural differentiation process and the recreation, reordering, and reproduction processes of relationships and categories become obvious:

> Caribbean "racial" composition is highly diverse. First, the phenotypic variety of Caribbean peoples is unusual, due both to the circumstances of immigration, and to the lengthy colonial careers of their component societies. Second, the codes of social relationships typifying these societies take account of phenotypic variety, but each society employs its code in its own distinctive fashion. Hence, while "race" is important throughout, its significance and its particular uses in social assortment vary from one Caribbean society to another. If one conjures up a "racial map" of the region, employing the criteria common to white middle-class North Americans, one finds societies such as Haiti or Jamaica, in which nearly everyone appears to be of African or largely African origin, and others such as Puerto Rico, Cuba, Saba, or the Cayman Islands, where this is much less the case. But since perceptions of physical type are culturally conventionalized, such a map does violence to the realities of Caribbean social life. A more effective map would depict *perceived* "race," for those persons who fall within all of the *locally defined* categories between black and white. While a number of writers have contributed significantly to our understanding of what this map might be like, it remains largely imaginary, and its complexity is difficult to grasp. Yet a third such imaginary map could deal with ethnic divisions— with those population segments falling outside any black-white scale—for which perceived cultural differences (including stereotypes), rather than perceived physical differences, appear to constitute the primary basis of social assortment or allocation.
>
> But "maps" of these societies in terms of "race," perceived race, and ethnicity evade what many theorists would regard as a much more obvious and fundamental basis of assortment: the class structure. Caribbean societies are, of course, stratified and class-differentiated entities. Color and ethnicity are not neatly correlated with class membership, even if it was once generally true—and, to a very large extent, still is—that lightness or whiteness and upper status tend to accompany each other, much as do darkness and lower status. What is more, the introduction of large populations that are not perceived to be aligned along any single gradient from blackness to whiteness, such as the Indians in Trinidad or the Chinese in Cuba, has made much more complicated any analysis of the relationship among economic status, physical type, and ethnic identity.

While many features of the traditional stratification systems of the region are still operative, changes in class structure have proceeded along different lines, such as the decline of local planter classes, the emergence of corporate, foreign plantation systems, the growth of tertiary, service-rendering sectors, the development of externally oriented consumer economies, the emigration of large populations, etc. These changes have affected the distribution of persons of particular physical or ethnic identities within local social systems, and the linkage between these identities and class membership has accordingly become more nuanced. Changes in political arrangements have also altered the traditional picture. To note but two very different cases, in recent decades in both Cuba and Haiti a clear upward movement in position or in life-chances for substantial numbers of darker persons has marked political change; many would argue for parallel phenomena in other parts of the region as well. In these ways, the sociological complexity of these societies may be seen to have increased significantly, in accord with political, economic, and demographic processes that extend themselves over time.[6]

The same basic differentiation process of the social structure has also occurred in the Latinamerican societies outside the Caribbean. In the twentieth century, the social division of labor and the expansion of productive forces brought about, in some cases, the massive immigration of Europeans and Asians into the area. It is obvious that this immigration modified the characteristics of the White population of Spanish, Portuguese, English, French, and other origins. This means that the immigration altered the entire demographic, racial, social, and cultural context within which the Blacks and Mulattoes operated.

Nowadays there are further expansions of urbanization and of productive forces in the industrial sector. Along with agriculture, mining, and other activities, the service, transportation and commercial sectors have become more dynamic. In some cases, industrialization as a basic process decisively influences and even determines social relations.[7] Urbanization and industrialization occur simultaneously with migration from rural areas and small towns to larger urban centers. Sometimes these large urban centers are also important industrial centers. From an historical-structural perspective, the social division of work, the expansion of productive forces, urbanization, industrialization, and the growth of the commercial, transportation, and service sectors modify the structure of social and racial relations quite profoundly. The African and slave cultures "get lost" in the capitalist culture. That is, in a society based on salaried work, on production and earning requirements, and the supremacy of capitalist monopoly, the values and cultural norms inherited from Africa and from slavery lose their original meanings and acquire others. As the twentieth century progressed, we find that the capitalist organization of production relationships became dominant. Gradually, all aspects of social life became determined, or recreated and reproduced, according to the requirements of the politicoeconomic relationships of capitalism. In this context, what appears to be the survival of an African or slave cultural trait can only be understood as a cultural element inserted into current capitalist relationships. What seems to predate capitalism only preserves this appearance. Just as the social relationships or the politicoeconomic structures are recreated and reproduced according to the conditions and necessities of the forces that are dominant in society, the same applies to the cultural elements.

Thus, in the social formation of capitalist societies, social organization continuously redistributes and reclassifies persons, families, and groups by sex, age, educational level, religion, ethnicity, race, and social class, in addition to fundamental or secondary attributes. Therefore, in the twentieth century people are also classified as White, Black, Mulatto, Indian, Mestizo, Italian, German, Japanese, and so forth. In the social reproduction of life, in factories, haciendas, schools, churches, barracks, and other areas of society, both the material and the spiritual are reproduced. In recreating and reproducing social relationships, society is constantly reproducing the White and the Black—and other races—according to the attributes and to the images that each and all have of themselves, and that some have with regard to others.

Awareness of Alienation

Among Blacks and Mulattoes of Latin America and the Caribbean an awareness of alienation is most frequently perceived in the realm of religious values and practices. Under slavery, as well as in the class societies of the twentieth century, Black religion seems to be the sociocultural sphere in which the understanding, be it naive or critical, of the alienated lifestyle of Blacks and Mulattoes is most evident.

In this perspective, the two forms of religion presented by Roger Bastide can be considered as two types of organization of Black awareness. Bastide classified the stabilized religions as those "in preserve" and "live" religions. Both are religions lived by Blacks, Mulattoes, and also some Whites. However, whereas one group is relatively stable, the other changes. Bastide places the Afro-Brazilian religions in the first group and Haitian *voodoo* in the second group.

> *Religions "in preserve"*: . . . Against the unrelenting corrosion by society, Black culture resists by congealing, becoming immobile, for fear that any change could indicate its end. Thus a phenomenon, if we can thus call it, of cultural mineralization, occurs; or, if one prefers a comparison with what an individual experiences when he feels his integrity endangered by the environment, a defense mechanism. Religion is what is lived but what is not

living, in the sense that it does not develop, that it does not change with time, that it is fixed in accordance with what has been taught by the ancestors. . . . In fact, Brazil has never been isolated from Africa, and after a relative period of isolation, communications are currently being resumed. Thus the Afro-Brazilian sects remain in contact with their mother religions. *"Live" Religions:* This is not the case with other Afro-American religions, particularly with regard to Haitian voodoo. . . . The result has been the lack of centralization of one religion, which, having been cut off from its African links, burst into multiple sects, that, having departed from one nucleus, each developed in their own manner. . . .

In fact, voodoo has become, as we have already said, the sword to fight against European culture, an expression of the organization, the necessities and the aspirations of the national peasant society, that will change, as a consequence, as the agrarian structures change.

The religions that stabilized or were "preserved" and the "live" religions can thus be taken as two different types of organization of the social conscience of the Black and Mulatto populations. It so happens that in religion, the critical awareness always appears in its "innocent" form, stylized, sublimated, and inverted. In Black religion Blacks also seek refuge, preserve themselves, and become organized to confront the Whites, the power of the state, and other expressions of alienated social relations. In Brazil, the Afro-Brazilian centers or cult sites, must register with the police, which is not the case with other churches and sects.

Most researchers recognize that there are African cultural traits in the Black religions of Latin America and the Caribbean. Together with music, folklore, and magic, religion is the part of social life in which many originally African cultural traits remain. Even when Black religion in a given country is strongly impregnated with elements of spiritism or Catholicism, researchers tend to believe that beneath the appearances of syncretism there exists a basically African religion. Some authors suggest that the borrowing of non-African cultural elements, such as Catholicism, spiritism, and Indian religions, does not alter the African spirit of Black religion. Even in cases where the experience of slavery was quite deep and lengthy, religion (together with folklore, music, and magic) is considered a social trait in which African cultural elements prevail or persist. Herskovits explains that music, folklore, magic, and religion retained more of their African nature than economy, technology, and art, because, during slavery, the masters were far more interested in controlling the economic and technological aspects of the life of their slaves. What was expressed in legends or in songs was of little importance to the masters, who therefore mounted few obstacles to its preservation. There were some external controls on religion; magic, since it was mostly secret, was not directed by the masters. Herskovits accounts for the failure of African art to survive in places other than Guyana, and to a lesser degree Brazil, by proposing that the life of slaves was so strictly organized for productive purposes that there was little time for artistic expression.[9]

In view of all this, Bastide suggests that the Black religions are not African, but largely syncretic. He believes that the slave trade and slavery vastly destroyed African culture. Bastide describes the varying degrees of syncretism as follows: Ethnically, syncretism is far more pronounced in the case of the Dahomans than the Yorubas, and it is less pronounced in the Bantu who were the most vulnerable to external influences. Ecologically, syncretism is stronger in rural areas than in towns, where freed slaves could form their "nations." Institutionally, syncretism is more active in "live" than in "preserved" religions. Sociologically, syncretism varies depending on the morphology, the institutional level, and the level of occurrence of collective awareness. And Bastide concludes:

> It is necessary to take into account the nature of the occurrences that are being studied. The rule for religion lies in the establishment of correspondences; the rule for magic lies in accumulation.
>
> Syncretism through the correspondence of gods and saints is a fundamental process and therefore the most researched. It is explained, historically, through the necessity of slaves, during colonial times, to hide their pagan ceremonies from the eyes of the whites; thus they danced before a Catholic altar, and the masters, in view of such an extravagant act, did not imagine that the Black dances were directed to the African divinities, rather than the paintings and statues of saints. . . .[10]

During the course of centuries of slavery, relationships of political domination and economic appropriation permitted the master class to destroy and to recreate or restructure the cultural elements of the slave class. Observe that slavery was the form taken by the acculturation of Africans, and that this acculturation was enforced, submitted to, and organized according to the interests and the predominance of a caste of Whites. Thus, even for Bastide, what was once African became Black through slavery. Through this process, Black religion became a more or less autonomous, totally syncretic form. With this interpretative perspective, Bastide unravels the mixtures and correspondences between Black and White, or Catholic and Afroamerican divinities. This data is represented in table 2.[11]

It has already been suggested that Black religion is a religion of the defeated; of the defeated who maintain in their religious practice a fundamental element of resistance to the domination of the conqueror. A religion of the defeated, a subculture, or a counterculture, these are the hypotheses or interpretations that emerge from some of the analyses. For beneath the Africanisms, or under the mixtures and correspondences of religious syncretism, there was presumed to be a subculture or a counterculture of a socially subordinate nature.

TABLE 2
The Correspondence of Gods and Saints

Saints	Brazil (Yoruba)	Cuba (Yoruba)	Trinidad (Yoruba) (Fon)	Haiti (Fon)
Jesus Christ	Obatalá	Obatalá		Aizan
Our Lady of the Rosary	Yemayá			
Our Lady of the Candles	Ochún (Bahía)			
Our Lady of the Immaculate Conception	Ochún (Porto Alegre)			
Our Lady of Pleasures	Ochún (Recife)			
Our Lady of Regla		Yemayá		
Our Lady of Charity		Ochún		
Mater Dolorosa				Ezili
Saint Anne	Anamburucú		(Ochún) (Agbe)	
Saint Barbara	Yansan	Changó		
Saint Catherine	Oba		(Oia) (Avlekete)	
Saint Benedict			(Obatalá)	
Saint Patrick				Damballa (Oueddo)
Saint Anthony	Ogún		(Da Zodji)	Legba
Saint George	Ochosi (Bahía) Ogún (Rio)	Ochosi	(Shakpanan) (Obo Zuin)	
Saint Jerome	Changó			
Saint Hubert transformed into Saint Albert		Ochosi		
Saint Michael			(Ogún)	
St. Sebastian	Omolú			
St. Francis	Iroco	Orumila	(Osaín) (Abodogji)	
St. Lazarus	Abaluayé (the oldest Omolú)	Babaluayé		
St. John the Baptist	Changó		(Changó) (Sobo)	
St. Peter	Echún (Porto Alegre)	Ogún		Legba
Souls in Purgatory		Eleguá		
The Devil	Echún (Bahía, Recife, Rio)			
St. Cosmo and St. Damian	The Ibeji	Los Jimaguas (The Twins)		The Marassa

It has frequently been noted that, when an invading people imposes its religion upon the defeated, a disequilibrium of values occurs, following the transition of the more or less egalitarian society into one that is more or less stratified. The religion of the conqueror becomes the only valid public religion for the masses, while the religion of the defeated . . . degenerates into magic or is transformed into a clandestine religion based on initiation rites and secrecy. . . . This secrecy, however, bothers the Whites, who believe that, within the places of worship of closed sects frightening forces are being manipulated, and since they don't always have a clean conscience regarding their relations with Blacks, they fear that these forces could be used against them. This thought does not lack substance, as slaves, in effect, used Ochún, Ogún and the herbs of Osaín to fight against the economic and racial oppression of the dominant class.[12]

This interpretation is quite attractive and presents some convincing elements. It shows that Latin American and Caribbean Blacks of the twentieth century hold on to, or recreate cultural elements that originated in Africa to defend themselves and to oppose the domination of Whites. In this sense, the Black religion, be it syncretic or not, is a type of spiritual catacomb in which the Black seeks refuge, hides, resists, or expresses some struggle against the supremacy of the White.

But the interpretation of Black religion as a type of counterculture does not clarify two basic questions. In the first place, it is based on the Black-White opposition, considered, basically, as racial. There is no doubt that the relationships of interdependence and alienation between Whites and Blacks generate an antagonism that is unbearable for Blacks. To the ideology of White supremacy (in countries where Whites dominate the political and economic power structures), Blacks tend to present an opposing counterideology. In the Black *Weltanschauung,* with regard to racial categories based on social relations of production that also include Whites, it is obvious that religion could have the nature of a counterculture or could inscribe itself within the framework of a counterideology. For this purpose—and in the second place—it would be necessary for the contents of the Black religion to be the expression of the interdependence and alienating relations that mark the Black-White relationship. However, it has still not been proven that the content of Black religion is really a counterculture or a counter-ideology.

As long as these two questions are not answered, the critical nature of Black religion remains to be demonstrated. Notice that I do not deny that Black religion in the Caribbean and in Latin America has a critical nature or will eventually develop this nature. Likewise, it can be said that there is a critical component to Black religion. Brazilian *candomblé,* Haitian *voodoo,* and Cuban *santería* all contain social elements that express worldviews that are not shared by Whites (other than those who participate in negrism). There are many indications that Africanism and syncretism hide some resistance to the worldview expressed by the racial ideology of the White, or to aspects of the dominant culture.

What I am suggesting is that the Africanisms that persist in Black religion, or in the syncretic forms assumed by this religion, do not in themselves make it a resistance front in defense of the Black and in opposition to the White. It is evident that the existing relationships of interdependence and alienation between Black and White generate antagonisms. What is not clear is that those antagonisms express and exhaust the position of Blacks versus Whites. The Blacks I refer to in Latin America and in the Caribbean are also industrial workers, agricultural laborers, functionaries, employees, soldiers, students, merchants, intellectuals, petit bourgeois, etc., and so are the Whites. It is therefore crucial to clarify how *race* and *class* reciprocally contain each other; or, when and how the policy of racial antagonism implies or is manifested in the policy of class antagonism.

Political Awareness

The metamorphosis of the slave into a Black or a Mulatto was also the metamorphosis of one form of alienation into another. Through slavery, slaves were alienated from their work product and from themselves. And it is because of this condition that they reworked or recreated elements of their African culture, combined with the culture of their own slave condition. In this context, religion, magic, music, folklore, and language became expressions of an effort to guarantee a restricted sociocultural universe in which the slaves sought refuge, expressed themselves, asserted themselves, and resisted the slave culture. The master class permitted them this refuge. It even took this sociocultural universe as proof that the slave class was in fact a different race. Nonetheless, the relationships, values, and structures expressed through religion, magic, music, folklore, and language turned into the sociocultural universe in which slaves found refuge and upon which they focused their rebelliousness, their protest, and their denial of the slave condition. Blacks and Mulattoes are here defined by their condition as slaves, while in the class society, the Black is a free worker. Despite the adverse conditions in which Blacks were placed within the work force, where they were obligated to compete with Whites, Indians, Mestizos or others, in the class society Blacks could negotiate their labor value. As people they were formally free. They were citizens, although second-class or dependent ones. But they were alienated from the product of their labor (when they were wage earners) and in their condition as citizens. They were Blacks or Mulattoes in addition to being wage earners. In addition to being industrial or agricultural workers, functionaries or employees, they were Blacks or Mulattoes. As a result of this condition, they reworked and recreated the cultural elements of their social and racial condition. As Blacks, Mulattoes, or wage earners, they recreated and reworked the cultural elements of their class condition and of their slave past. The collective and historical experience of having been a slave for two, three, or four centuries, was recreated and reworked, together with the current experience of being Black, Mulatto, or a member of the working class (urban or rural), of the middle class, of the petit bourgeoisie or of another social category.

Therefore, in the twentieth century class system, the types of awareness of alienation are more differentiated. It is true that religion, magic, music, folklore, and language continue to be aspects of an important sociocultural universe. But the sociocultural and political meanings of this universe are given by the interdependent, alienated, and antagonistic relationships of the social classes. The racial and class conditions are intertwined.

The politicoeconomic content of the social condition of Blacks, meanwhile, only developed in an irregular and at the same time contradictory manner. The doubly inferior condition of the majority of the Black and Mulatto population in almost all the countries of Latin America and the Caribbean made the transition from an "ingenuous" (or alienated) awareness of alienation to an adequate, politically organized, and critical conscience, quite difficult. Blacks and Mulattoes were frequently doubly alienated, because they were alienated as members of a different, inferior *race* vis-à-vis the Whites, and as members of an equally subordinate social class, of which the majority could be White. There are times when this situation became even more complicated, since a Black majority could be subordinated to White and Mulatto groups.

Under these circumstances, as in the case with other races and subordinate classes, consciousness of alienation did not immediately present itself as a political consciousness in the case of the Blacks and Mulattoes. In every subordinate social category, political awareness develops mixed with religion, morals, play, and other activities. The political values of the dominant classes or races invade and permeate the consciousness of the subordinates, mixing and confusing their understanding of their own lifestyle.

The double alienation of the Black in almost all the Latin American and Caribbean countries has created various responses. In addition to religion and art in general, and to political organizations (associations, syndicates, parties), the Black is now organizing his awareness and political practices. In Brazil, for example, in the 1930s, he organized the Brazilian Black Front, suppressed by the Getulio Vargas dictatorship in 1937. Between the abolition of slavery and the creation of a more explicit political movement, several significant expressions of political awareness took place.

> The formation of Black clubs and organizations began in 1915, and was intensified around 1918–1924. The organizations that emerged did not, however, pursue "racial regimentation," their purposes were purely "cultural

and welfare oriented." They evolved naturally, after 1927, under the pressure of the economic and social position of the Black man in São Paulo. . . . Other organizations, born from the incipient collective assertiveness of Blacks, have more defined and combative purposes. The "Brazilian Black Front," for example, was formed in 1931, to "congregate, educate, and orient" the Blacks of the State of São Paulo. A parallel evolution took place in the city's Black press. The first Black newspapers published between 1915 and 1922, started off as literary, but later turned into "educational or protest vehicles," on account of the social problems afflicting the colored people. . . .[13]

At the same time, Brazilian Blacks organized conferences, debates and discussions to reestablish, develop, or deepen the understanding of their problems with regard to the Whites and to themselves. They also organized artistic movements such as plays and dances to recreate and to develop their creativity and to stamp them with the individuality and originality of their lifestyle, feelings, thoughts, and doings. In more recent years, between 1945 and 1975, the Brazilian Black has voted in political elections for Black candidates. Blacks in Brazil do not have a party, since this was forbidden by the 1969 Constitution, but Black groups in various states (the country's administrative units) have elected councilmen and state and federal deputies. There is a definite politicization of Black groups, both within the proletariat and among those who have entered or are entering the middle classes. As a group, from an historic perspective, the Brazilian Black is evolving from a condition of anonymity that has existed since the abolition of slavery, to a class situation. Following abolition in 1888, in many parts of the country Blacks became unemployed, almost forming a lumpenproletariat, because of the adverse conditions they had to confront competing with Whites, immigrant, Italians, Germans, and other Brazilian racial groups. During that period, Blacks were probably the main element in the reserve army of labor. Later, they gradually became absorbed in wage occupations that multiplied and became more differentiated with urbanization and industrialization. Thus, gradually, they turned into workingclass Blacks, both in industry and in agriculture. Notice that being *Black* and being *workers* have been the two constants in the lives of the majority of Blacks and Mulattoes.

It is obvious that the changes in social consciousness are not homogeneous, nor are they the same in different Latinamerican and Caribbean countries. In each country the capitalist social formation assumes a particular shape. In addition the social structures of each society differ; they reflect the degree of urbanization, industrialization, agricultural development, demographic makeup, and distribution of the races within each social class. As a whole, however, there is evidence of a progressive transition from a *religious awareness* of the Black condition to a *political awareness*. Observe that the transition from the religious awareness to the political awareness does not mean the substitution of one for the other. They are not exclusive or unique. There are, for example, artistic forms that can express one type of awareness or another of the alienated condition felt by the Black. Poetry, theater, music, painting, and movies can express religious or political kinds of awareness as well as other ways of understanding, accepting, or rejecting the condition of being a subordinate race.[14] There are a variety of forms of awareness the Black man has expressed and developed. The tendency, however, is for the political consciousness to assert itself, or to begin to assert itself over the others.

This politicization process progresses at a variable pace in the different countries of Latin America and the Caribbean. In Mexico, Colombia, Venezuela, Peru and some other Latinamerican countries, Black groups are forced to subordinate their religious, artistic, and political activities to the structures that were created and directed by Whites, or by Indians or Mestizos. In Brazil, the same type of subordination exists, but with some idiosyncracies. In some regions of the country, as for example in the cities of Salvador, Rio de Janeiro, São Paulo, and Porto Alegre, religious, artistic and political activities seem to develop more and more. There are also indications that Blacks and Mulattoes see themselves each time more clearly as social categories with political potential. Racial alienation produces political developments, in spite of the vigorously promoted myth of racial democracy that confuses Whites, Blacks, and Mulattoes. Obviously, the situation differs in some Caribbean societies where the Black and Mulatto population is a majority or forms part of the government. In these cases, the Black and Mulatto political movements acquire some or a great deal of autonomy compared to religion and to other forms of social awareness. They assert themselves and reject White political proposals. But they assume political power without altering the class structure into which Blacks and Mulattos are divided. In these cases, the Blacks and the Mulattoes are the ones to confront directly and explicitly the double alienation in which they have lived historically: they find themselves structured into social class hierarchies, without having overcome the racial subdivisions of Black and Mulattoes—or poor and rich Blacks and Mulattoes—the product of past and recent relationships with Whites, be they colonizers or not. In this case, the racial condition can become subordinate to the class phenomenon, either gradually or rapidly, depending on the context of interpendence, alienation, and antagonism of relationships generated by the reproduction of political and economic structures.

It so happens that Blacks resist the real conditions of their lifestyle as well as the racial ideology of Whites. A Black worker, for example, does not have the same rights as the White worker in the same condition. To be equal to the White worker, the Black worker must be better than the

White one. In the occupational structure and in the wage scale, Blacks are in a worse situation. In addition, they suffer prejudice, discrimination, and also segregation. In other words, Blacks see themselves in a subordinate position, both in practice and in ideology. White racial ideology rejects or confuses them; it does not consider them equal. Paternalism, ambiguity, the myth of racial democracy, and other expressions of White dominance confuse or irritate Blacks. It is with regard to this practical or ideological situation that Blacks become aware of their double alienation: as members of a *race* and as members of a *class*. In this sense, in order to reduce or to eliminate their alienating conditions and their doubly subordinate condition, Blacks must build a double political awareness: they must see themselves and have Whites see them as members of another *race* and as members of another *class*. As members of a race, they are alone, and they must fight this condition. As class members they mix with elements of other races, and they must struggle against this condition. In this context, race and class are in constant interplay, making the Black political awareness and practice more and more complex.

NOTES

Except in cases where the country and the period are specified, the discussion covered in this essay includes all countries of Latin America and the Carribbean with African slaves and descendants. At no point does the discussion focus on the racial situation in socialist Cuba.

1. From this point on, the term "Black" will often include both Blacks and Mulattoes. Sometimes, depending on the context, I will differentiate one from the other.

2. Charles Wagley, *The Latin American Tradition* (New York: Columbia University Press, 1968), p. 156. Quote from chapter 5, "The Concept of Social Race in the Americas," pp. 155–174.

3. Melville J. Herskovits, *The New World Negro* (Minerva Press: 1969), p. 53. The table on Africanisms is in the chapter entitled "Problem, Method and Theory in Afroamerican Studies," pp. 43–61.

4. Ibid.; Melville J. Herskovits, *The Myth of the Negro Past* (Boston: Beacon Press, 1958); Roger Bastide, *Les Amériques Noires* (Paris: Payot, 1967); Magnus Mörner, ed., *Race and Class in Latin America* (New York: Columbia University Press, 1970).

5. Bastide, *Les Amériques Noires,* pp. 49–50.

6. Sidney W. Mintz, "The Caribbean Region," *Daedalus* (Cambridge, Mass.: Harvard University (Spring 1974) pp. 45–71; citation from p. 52.

7. Ibid., p. 53.

8. Bastide, *Les Amériques Noires,* pp. 133–137 and 201–202.

9. Herskovits, *The New World Negro,* p. 55.

10. Bastide, *Les Amériques Noires,* pp. 158–159 and 160–196.

11. Ibid.

12. Roger Bastide, *Les Religions Africaines au Brasil* (Paris: Presses Universitaires de France, 1960), pp. 548–549.

13. Florestan Fernandes, "A luta contra o preconceito da cor," in Roger Bastide and Florestan Fernandes, *Brancos e negros em São Paulo,* 2nd ed. (São Paulo: Companhia Editora Nacional, 1959), pp. 269–318 and 281–283. Also see *A integração do negro na sociedade de classes,* 2 vols. (São Paulo: Dominus Publishers, 1965).

14. Jean Franco, *The Modern Culture of Latin America* (Penguin: 1970), esp. pp. 131–140; Cesar Fernandez Moreno, ed., *America Latina en su Literatura* (Mexico: Siglo XXI, 1972), esp. pp. 62–69.

Cultural Forms:
Religion, Literature, and Music

4

Religion and Black Culture*

JUANA ELBEIN DOS SANTOS
DEOSCOREDES M. DOS SANTOS

I

There is nothing more evasive or more delicate than the historic changes of perception and interpretation of transplanted Black African* religions and their complex process of continuity and discontinuity in the New World. A sensible and incisive chronological reading of the titles that categorize the literature would give us the material for an instructive history of racial prejudice, or better yet, of interethnic and intercultural relations, in Latin America, including the volatile Caribbean region. These relationships were shaped by the strong cultural ethnocentrism of the elites that held the official institutional power, and by the international interests and conditions that accompanied the development of slavery, which was a product of European mercantilism. To view the development of these relationships in terms of the world economy provides a fascinating backdrop that permits a coherent understanding of the role of religion.

The subject of African religion in the Americas—its origins, its areas of influence, its dogma, doctrine, liturgy, priesthood, mutilations, persecutions, transformation, values, diversity of styles, and latent epistemological unity, although apparently well studied, is actually in urgent need of reinterpretation. Such a revision should encompass an almost total reformulation of terminology and concepts; it must offer a broad enough perspective to permit—in addition to an in-depth study of the religious structure, its philosophical, mystical, and symbolic contents, and the variety of ways in which they are expressed—an interpretation of its historic and contemporary meaning. The last is the fundamental element that permitted the dramatic struggle for psychic integrity and made possible the preservation of a specific latent ethos that survived all pressures from the elite who held political and institutional power.

Beginning with studies on witchcraft, magic, superstition, fetishism, animism, and syncretism, and extending to the most sophisticated classification of Afro-American cults, the old system of analysis implicitly

---

*The term *Black* is used here to refer both to Africans and to their descendants in America. It encompasses diverse models and cultural and genetic traits, both those that were inherited and those that are new, reworked within their social and historic contacts and contexts in the New World.

61

denies the classification of religion to the mystical system left by Africans, and reworked by their descendants. This denial not only pushes aside the transcendental values of the culture brought by the slaves (thus justifying the lucrative arrogance of repression, be it forced or indirect) but it fundamentally diverts and submerges the underlying unity, the transnational character of African religions. Above all it covers up the fact that religion, as a transmitter of institutional continuity, permitted the formation of groups and communities that became the centers of organized cultural resistance. More than any other aspect of culture, religion, and its related activities, contained the elements that permit us to restructure the "communality" within the Caribbean that Sidney W. Mintz refers to, and the so-called "cultural focus" that Edward Brathwaite mentions in referring to Black religions.

Just as Grecoroman civilization expanded through changing forms of Christianity, the Black African civilization expanded and spread in the diaspora by means of various changes and reformulations of traditional Black religions. We will attempt to examine to what degree this adaptability both created new forms of religion as dynamic replies to new social and historical contexts, and also permitted the latent transmission and homogenization of the essential elements of its original source.

The emergence and development of these variables, which at once hid and expressed a strong resistance to adaptation, and the fact that they could not be absorbed by the church of the dominant class, clearly shows an institutional incompatibility between religions. Black American religion, as an elaboration of its African models, became a religious superstructure that gave meaning to and permitted the physical and spiritual survival of important sectors of the Black population in the Americas. It also served as an antithetic response to the paternalism imposed by the Christian church, which was one of the official ethnocentric systems.

In the old analyses, variables were studied separately within the geographic boundaries of national societies whose linguistic differences sometimes hid similar phenomena; material was collected and described without any deep interpretive analysis of the symbolic structural system, or, what is worse, with foreign interpretations or fantasies. All this prevented, with rare exception, a view of religious expressions as fragments of a whole.

There is no doubt that Black American religion, just like Christianity, is the result of a long process of selection, association, synthesis, and reinterpretation of archaic elements, as well as an absorption and elaboration of new ones, with variations based on the cultural baggage of each local ethnic group and on socioeconomic interrelationships, all nonetheless conforming to and tracing out a basic, central system.

From this point of view, syncretism is understood to be a variable within the overall system. It is a significant affirmation of continuity and expansion, a process in search of an original medium to survive in, integrated into the religious superstructure which we have agreed to call Black American religion, and always interpreted in terms of its African roots.

A global view would permit us to have a coherent understanding of the various models and situations that are the fragments of a Neoafrican continuity, of that mystical and symbolic system—so different from, and yet dialectically a part of Latin America—that places a portion of this continent within the orbit of a transatlantic community that still lacks a self-awareness.

Nevertheless, at this stage of research, it remains difficult to introduce this new perspective on Black American religion. We are still in dire need of in-depth and updated studies of each region, and of a rigorous critical revision of the vast existent bibliography, which could in itself provide us with enough material for an entire volume. In addition, the rich oral documentation has barely been researched and worked with, even though among groups that use a ritualistic language it is particularly expressive, and could therefore be an invaluable source of information coming straight from the communities. Documents written by public officials have not all been found and systematically analyzed, nor has the field been subject to analytical studies that use contemporary methodology. There has, in fact, been no valid interchange among the specialists on each region, nor any field work or technical, international, interdisciplinary work.

We need studies on basic subjects and comparative essays including not only the various Latin American regions, but also Africa. Such comparative studies would point out the specificity of the models and of their components and would permit us to analyze analogies that would, in turn, reveal continuities and discontinuities, selective transmissions, innovations, and the interplay between the African and the American heritage. They would enable us to sketch out a global scheme, a vast scaffolding into which we could fit all known variables with their characteristic and distinctive traits, and which would be broad enough to encompass those vast and important areas that are still unknown, but that will be the focus of future research.

In a prior essay[1] we insisted on two essential points. First, we showed the importance of comparative studies that would consider migrations, influences, and cultural continuities; but we insisted that these generalizations would only be scientifically valid if they were based on systemically developed research, and if the existing material were subjected to critical revision. Second, we argued that the important and defining themes should include studies of the religious system, thereby filling our lacunae of knowledge in that area. Basic concepts of the religions, such as the nature of the Supreme Being or universal originator of matter, the other world, spiritual elements that form a part of a person, the deep significance of sacrifice, the dynamic principles and initiation rites, oral traditions, and rhythm, would all have to be studied. Rare are the studies that do exist on these matters; most of them are not published and therefore do not receive adequate distribution.

Roger Bastide was well aware of these lacks and difficulties. After almost thirty years of dedication to Black American studies, with an emphasis on Afro-Brazilian studies (under the current classification system), Bastide emphatically maintained that: "There was an extremely rich and subtle philosophy behind this religion." He also had the intellectual honesty in one of his last articles to recognize that "Although I entered *candomblés* as a member, not merely as an observer, the rules of maturation of secrets prevailing in religions requiring initiation would consider me profane, and would barely permit me to acquire a Black vision of the world. Only a cult priest of very high status could write the type of text that I was hoping to write."

He proceeds to mention the types of studies he is referring to, and continues: "Unfortunately, at this time, such texts that reveal the wealth of esoteric Afro-Brazilian thought, can only be found in the form of manuscripts, since the authors have been unable to interest Brazilian editors who seem to feel that the intellectual security of White society would be threatened if *candomblé* were accepted as a philosophy, rather than as folklore or an artistic spectacle; a philosophy that I will refer to as 'negritude,' by which I mean real negritude, not the negritude that is merely a political ideology."

This text immediately confronts us with various very important problems, such as the contents of a religion requiring initiation and cultural controls on the one hand, and the intellectual control of a dominant elite on the other. However, for the time being we only wish to highlight the concept of negritude, of "real negritude," not negritude as a political ideology, that Bastide portrays as an "existential affirmation." In this sense, negritude would be an expression of African latency, that ethos, that "communality," that in some more or less obvious ways unites the various expressions of Black American religion. From this perspective, and were it not for the association of negritude with the well-known position of a group of Black intellectuals, the most appropriate title for this chapter would have been "Religion and Negritude."

One thing is clear: as we have insisted from the beginning, religion was and is the most powerful transmitter of the essential values of Afro-American negritude. These values never remained frozen; quite to the contrary, they managed to survive with vigor in a medium with powerful repressive pressures, precisely because of their extraordinary plasticity and vitality, because of this dialectic process of resistance-accommodation that generated the diversity that is referred to by some specialists as a lack of continuity within continuity.

It would be absolutely inaccurate to interpret fidelity to African roots as a copy, as something immutable and frozen, particularly with reference to the cults that most clearly reveal their African origins or "Africanism," since they are still in the process of restructuring their original elements and their inherited systems. To talk about a freezing of values would reveal on the one hand, a lack of knowledge of the dynamism within the African-inherited system and its ability to renew its structure and to incorporate change, both in continuity and in stability; on the other hand, one would be guilty of unconscious ethnocentrism if one registered as changes only those that reveal any visible elements of Western origin.

Changes are less well perceived by social scientists in the "traditional" cults because social scientists, generally members of the White world, do not know enough about the original systems to appreciate the changes that occurred in the new medium over successive periods. In addition, these researchers have an external, indirect knowledge that does not permit them to perceive the changes that do occur, since the new traits are so profoundly assimilated.

Thus, those new elements that are "Africanized" are not perceived or accepted as changes. They are attributed a static quality that has nothing to do with the functional reality of these cults. This dangerous conclusion has led to the unfortunate naming of those cults that have a strong basic unity as "canned religions."

The preservation of their basic structure has permitted these cults to adapt without becoming "Whitened" by interpreting the new elements in terms of a philosophy in which the values of the past are renewed as a source of continuity and stability, and as a nexus with history and belonging. This renewal within stability, this peculiar mobility, became the best transmitter of negritude, which, according to Bastide is the existential affirmation, fundamental for the continuity of the Black ethos. Paradoxically, Bastide looked at the negritude of the cults that have a strong basic African unity, and considers them congealed. We disagree. It was through these cults that the most creative phenomena of Afroamerican negritude were produced and extended.

There are numerous examples. To summarize one, in order to achieve institutional and patrimonial continuity, Ashé Opó Afonjá, one of the most representative communities of Nagô descent in Brazil, created, as a part of its basic structure, a civil society within the framework of the national society, whose governing body consisted of the prominent members of its religious hierarchy. This civil society gave the community an official acknowledgement and legally regulated its relationship with the rest of the world.*

*It is interesting to point out that this same community, which is considered one of the most "traditional and pure," is now in the process of reaching an agreement with the educational authorities of Salvador to establish an experimental community school of a multicultural nature.

Thus, we can say that, with regard to the degree of retention and elaboration of the basic African elements, a greater or lesser ability to rework foreign elements into the structure of their African roots would give us the degree of negritude of the variables.

To offer an extreme example, we can look at the jazz phenomenon. It is obvious that Black urban music in the United States, as in the case of the Brazilian, shows its deep negritude despite all the foreign elements that it has incorporated and reworked, beginning with the musical instruments. Virgil Thompson classifies jazz as "the tacit reference," to the expression of all that is Black. And he adds: "Classical European composition, Anglo Saxon folklore, the meter of an Hispanic dance, hymns, drums, the German Lied, ragtime, Italian opera, all are food for the insatiable Black appetite, *provisions to be chewed,* as though within all Black North Americans, when it comes to sound, there exists an old African enzyme that can digest voraciously whatever it finds in its path" (our italics).

This ability to "digest or to Africanize" contributions, as opposed to "adding and summing them" while leaving their various components visible, would give us sufficient material for a primary classification of the various expressions of Black American religion into *homogeneous* and *heterogeneous* variables. We would include among the homogeneous variables, all the religious expressions of the Gêgê Nagô complex in Brazil, *lucumí* and *ñáñigo* in Cuba, *rada* in Haiti, *shangó* in Trinidad and Grenada; and among the heterogeneous ones, the various cults of Bantu influence from the Congo and Angola, with ramifications in all of Latin America and the Caribbean; the *petro* complex in Haiti; the various forms of *umbanda, caboclo,* and *payelanza* in Brazil, *maria lionza* in Venezuela; the *myal, cunfa,* and *poco* forms with their variations in Central America and the Caribbean (particularly in Jamaica and the Antilles); the various forms that center on baptism and that are influenced by other Protestant sects in the Antilles (shakers, shouters, *convince,* etc.); as well as the cults practiced in Suriname, where the Ashanti elements are added to Fon, Hueda, Yoruba, and Christian elements.

This organization of Black American religion into homogeneous and heterogeneous variables is simply heuristic and should not be too rigid. Into *rada* in Haiti, considered a homogenous variable of basic Fon structure, were absorbed elements of *aizan, nagô, guedeví, hueda,* and Catholicism.

On the other hand, a heterogeneous variable like the *caboclo*** cult covers the immemorial necessity and strong African traits of worshiping the ancestral owners of the earth, but with pseudo-Indian symbolic elements, such as feathered headdresses and bows and arrows, that have little resemblances to the real ones. In the *caboclo* rites, the Brazilian Indian pantheons that sometimes appear in *payelanza* are not venerated;

instead they worship the individual and collective spirits of various tribes, particularly those of the original owners of the lands onto which the Blacks were settled. The cult really involves the worship of native forerunners in typical Bantu African style; and in many cases, either on successive or alternating days, the *prêtos velhos* (old Blacks), the spirits of the ancient slaves, the first ancestors of the Blacks in America, are added to the worship list of Indian spirits.

The *caboclo* cult contains in its heart some of the essential characteristics of the African system: its sense of continuity, its ties with the past, its stability, expressed in a stable relationship between humanity and nature, between humanity and the earth, which is the symbol of eternal rebirth. This type of continuity could not be found by African descendants in White culture, since the Whites were foreigners and conquerors; it could only be found in Indian culture, among the natural ancestors of the land. Thus, one can examine a heterogeneous variable that shows a foreign element as its manifest cult object, but that has internalized basic African contents.

It is important to point out that the *prêto velho*, the African ancestor, and the *caboclo*,* the Indian ancestor, are not at all similar, even though they belong to the same category. There is evidence of an addition, a pluralism, not a fusion of values; each one has its own characteristics that don't mix; there is a formal, spatial, and temporal separation. Whereas the supernatural entities show up simultaneously in homogeneous cults, they only appear separately in heterogeneous cults, thus pointing to the diversity of their origins.

This also occurs, to a certain extent, in the *umbanda* cults, where added elements appear next to a few syncretic mechanisms, such as the *pontos riscados,* the cabalistic drawings that were sketched by the *prêtos velhos.* The *orishás,* (Nagô supreme beings) are saved, while St. Ciprian, St. Michael and the *falanges,* spirits originating in the Congo and in Angola, are worshiped simultaneously. On the altars one can find images of Christ, St. Joseph, St. George, next to sirens, water goddesses, *caboclos, prêtos velhos,* seals of Solomon, stones, and sea shells. The earth is saved by pouring libations of water and rum and making the sign of the cross. The supernatural beings appear in successive groups in the *giras* but never mix; one moves *(vira)* from one *gira* to another, which sometimes occur on separate days.

The homogeneous variables can follow two processes if they are unable to maintain a balanced dynamic between their basic structure and new contributions: they can either lock themselves defensively into their African roots and thereby really freeze, become reduced, or disappear;

Caboclo: name given in Brazil to the Indian-White Mestizo, and by extension to the Mulatto of a coppery-red skin color.

or, they can add, without "digesting" them, new elements, thereby pluralizing and transforming themselves into heterogeneous variables.

The heterogeneous variables have the potential of integrating their original elements, becoming homogeneous, and thus creating a new model or Black American religious system. So far there is no example of such an occurrence. To this date, the homogeneous variables continue to be those that center on African elaborations, and the heterogeneous ones remain pluralistic.

Still, the heterogeneous variables run the risk of changing, or of serving as alienating pseudo identifications with the very negritude they would like to unify. It is on this level that one should understand the fierce struggle between the so-called *umbanda* of the *morro* and the *umbanda* of the "asphalt" and the two federations that represent them.

The *morro* contains the largest portion of the colored population and it also absorbs and miscegenates the poorest White groups. *Morro* groups living in *favelas* continue to reinterpret, within their own heterogeneous elements, the fundamental structure of *nagô,* which permits them to elaborate a specific or particular cultural continuity that expresses their negritude or their "existential affirmation."

The groups of the "asphalt" adopted the standards of the White culture, at least as far as the class-culture structure permitted them to. They structured their cults according to the image that the White man has of the Black, adding magic and exotic stereotypes, thus transforming a seeming identification process into a process of alienation.

Obviously, specialized literature has contributed a great deal to the prolonged survival of such stereotypes, not to mention the negative role of the press. Concepts used to describe Black religion that were employed fifty or seventy years back are repeated to this day.

Fetishism, and above all, animism, continue to be discussed in recent specialized publications. But we shall return to these concepts.

Before beginning an analysis of the formal content and structure of Black American religion, we need to establish a structure that will frame its totality. We should also include among the variables a series of occurrences that, although on the one hand have served to atomize Black religion into innumerable groupings of traits and styles, on the other, have irradiated a Black ethos outside the institutionalized groups.

We refer here to numerous persons, who, regardless of whether initiated into organized cults or simply autoinitiated, "savage" participants, practice individual or family cults, or go to the homes of others to conduct ceremonies and rites. Some of these are transmitters of homogeneous variables who often combine their individual practices with those they share with their groups. Such is the case with many priests who have been initiated into the knowledge or oracles or the handling of herbs. Others form personal cults, consisting of various combinations, additions, and recreations of heterogeneous elements. This is quite common in remote places, far from urban centers. Finally, there are others who present more extreme innovations and therefore find it difficult to attach themselves to preexisting groups. As time goes by, if these innovations are in tune with the real adjustment needs of a community, small groups will form around these individuals for an unspecified duration of time. This seems to have occurred on several occasions in the Caribbean. One example is *petro* in Haiti, originally started by the Creole Don Pedro. This group developed very stable heterogeneous variables, in contrast to Bedwardism* and others that disappeared with the death of their founders.

Just as we noted the presence of Christian elements in the Black American variables, we cannot neglect the influence of Black norms on the Christian cults that eventually permeated the entire society. This influence is apparent, not in the liturgy or the dogma of the Christian church, but in the selection of certain elements and concepts as opposed to others, particularly among the ecumenical any syncretic elements of Christianity, all of which are quite obvious in Latin American Catholocism. In areas where descendants of Africans constitute 30 to 70 percent, or even 90 percent of the population, one should not be surprised that Black forms and habits spill over their own boundaries to affect all the religions and lay manifestations of the national society.

The covert processes that Africans employed to adapt their own religions to the conversion process required by their masters are well known. By worshiping their own supernatural beings while associating them with specific saints and Catholic festivities, they tried to deceive their masters. It is difficult to determine to what degree this was possible. A lengthy array of delicate mechanisms, either fictitious or real, has created a wide fringe of uncertainties and mutual influences. Various authors have spent time constructing graphs to establish the various associations between African and Christian supernatural beings; we will not go over them again.

One must realize, however, that these associations are not sufficient, in their present state of processing, to characterize a new religious system. Syncretisms, as mechanisms of interethnic and intercultural contact, were, and still are, undoubtedly real. But, with regard to Christian influence they were not reworked homogeneously to create a new and unique institution capable of syncretizing into a dogma and a liturgy the contributions of various incompatible institutions. On the other hand, due to their compatibility, syncretisms deriving from various African ethnic sources occurred naturally; they constituted the basic unit of the homogenous and the transmitter of negritude in the heterogeneous variables.

*A religious, initiation-based movement, founded in the middle of the nineteenth century by a Black Jamaican, which disappeared with the death of its founder.

Although we are once again tempted to talk about a sum of characteristics, Afro-Christian syncretism in Latin America is more evident on the individual level. It is a well-known fact that almost all, if not all, the Blacks of Latin America are Christian, usually Catholic. At least they have been baptized and go to church more or less frequently.

Despite the fact that there are no statistics on this phenomenon, it is possible to determine empirically that a high percentage of the Mestizo population goes to or belongs to some group or community that practices a variant of a Black American religion. If the parallel practice of two religions creates syncretic mechanisms, these are not translated into the institutionalized organization of either religion; each maintains its own basic structures, clearly separate, except for some complex traits, that, in one sense or another, surpass the cultural class-group limits without altering them.

Still no new religion exists; no new whole different from the original religions has developed; there is a change or addition of beliefs, each with its own values and structures, practiced separately in their appropriate places. Two liturgies are practiced: the Christian or official one in the church; alongside it the Black or unofficial one, practiced either in temples, homes, or places that have been duly consecrated.

If we insist on these concepts it is in part because we believe them to be highly relevant when examining the meaning of the various categories of syncretism and association resulting from the dialectic of adaptation; but above all, because they are in their diversity a part of the underlying unity of Black "communality." Let us try to examine, from the perspective of religion, what this negritude consists in, what transforms the various fragments into the variables of a basic system. It is a system that is reformulating Africa in Latin America, giving it, together with "indigenismo" a singularity or a specificity uniting it both culturally and spiritually, with a greater or lesser degree of awareness and official acceptance, to Black Africa.

II

We will not spend time here discussing the historical development of Black American religion, nor on detailed descriptions of its variables. For this we refer the reader to the existing bibliography, even though in-depth studies are needed. It is our ambitious purpose to integrate all the variables and contradictions into a dynamic graph of structural elements, and to try to highlight and to examine their abstract and concrete relationships within the continuity of the religious system as a whole, as well as its manifestation through its variables.

African culture constitutes a dynamic interrelationship of variables, with religion as its fundamental expression. In the rich culture of the various kingdoms of Occidental and Equatorial Africa that are the source of almost all Africans in America, religion impregnated and marked all activities, pervading and regulating even the profane.

In the diaspora, religion was the most important factor that permitted the *institutionalized regrouping* of Africans and their descendants. This is very important. Religion became a cohesive element that permitted the formation of groups and associations whose system of beliefs, a result of ethnic heredity and sociohistorical adaptations, prescribed particular interrelationships, norms, actions, and values that transformed the groups into real communities with their own characteristics. During the diaspora, the geographic space represented by native Africa and its contents were transferred into houses, temples, or rooms, where the power of ancestors and supernatural beings that guaranteed not only a continuity to existence but a lifestyle, were "planted," next to the symbolic elements.

Terreiro, tenda, casa, cabildo, hounfort, sect, center—whatever the name of the group—these are communities that, through their religious practices, maintained a cohesive, collective consciousness of belonging. They also contained the material and spiritual belongings, the structural elements and their variables. An analysis of these contents gives us information, not only on the religion, but also on the essential aspects of the African system they are a part of.

It was through the continuous practice of religion that Blacks maintained a profound sense of community. In Latin America a cultural complex was implanted and reformulated whose prime form of expression was religion, and it was this religion that served to preserve and to renew certain specific parts of the original system.

Throughout the entire process of slavery, and even during later interethnic conflicts, religion and the communities observing the religion became the bulwark of the Black psyche and of its cultural dignity and integrity, since, for a long time, they were the only source of inviolable, spiritual freedom.

Since religion became the only cultural element of cohesion within these communities, it has been common to see the communities themselves as mere religious groups. This error overlooks the significance of the communities as the institutionalized instruments of continuity and reelaboration of a basic cultural system that insisted tenaciously and dynamically on participating with its own values, in a variety of ways, in the national social structure.

These communities appeared both in rural areas and in urban centers, on estates, in small landholdings, and in homes, even concentrated in a single room. They all present certain common traits:

A portion of the members live in the place of worship or in its vicinity, sometimes forming a neighborhood or a village. Other members live at various distances, but come regularly to spend longer or shorter periods at the place of worship, where they often have a room or some type of lodging. The link between the community members is unrelated to their place of residence; the limits of the groups do not coincide with the physical limits of the place of worship. The community tends to spill over its material boundaries, which serve as the point of concentration and irradiation from where it disperses to permeate the rest of society. The members of the community circulate, move, work, have ties with society as a whole, and constitute a fluctuating community that concentrates and expresses its own structure in the consecrated places.

Furthermore, these communities form an extraordinary system of alliances. This system varies, depending on whether the community practices homogeneous or heterogeneous variables, from the simple and generic "fraternity" to the more complex hierarchical organization that establishes communal relationships, recreating ties of lineage and of the extended family as they existed in Africa. Blood relationships are replaced with community membership that is judged by age, obligations, and initiatory lineage.

No matter who the supernatural being to whom a female priest is consecrated may be, she is part of a whole, a "blood" member tied through initiation rites to the gods that are worshiped as well as to the initiated, to the authorities, and particularly to the forefathers and ancestors of the community. She is the repository of a force of which she is the receiver, and, as times goes by, the transmitter. This force or supernatural power, transmitted during the initiation of the oldest or newest members, is kept and accumulated through the practice of the ritual, which continuously revitalizes the community.

This brings us back to two interrelated subjects: the uniqueness of the religious system, and the intrinsic elements that result from its structure, dogma, and liturgy and permit it to maintain its own continuity and that of the communities and groups of which it is the center.

At the beginning we talked about the necessity of a total reinterpretative examination. We expressed the need to adjust analytical and interpretative instruments to arrive at an internal perspective on Black American religions. We could have attempted a methodological revision at that time. However, we prefer to introduce it now that we have achieved a certain distance from academic orthodoxy and can penetrate the intricacies of the Black system.

We have elsewhere referred to the problems researchers meet when they bring their academic baggage and their personal history with them, leading them to use as references the class and culture they belong to. We also underlined and analyzed the pros and cons of the *actor* or *observer* position, adopted according to whether one did or did not belong to the cultural community being studied. We pointed out that the *observing* scientist, no matter how careful he is, cannot easily shed his own history and the frame of reference of his own historic process, and that the *actor,* a member of the group, would fail to perceive the abstract and structural realities of the system that he is living in. We thus pointed out two viewpoints that, although difficult, are not impossible to complement.

Black religion constitutes an *initiatory experience,* "during the course of which, knowledge is obtained through a lived experience on a bipersonal or a group level, through *gradual development,* through *transmission* and *absorption* of power and the symbolic and complex knowledge at all levels of the person who represents the vivid incorporation of all the collective and individual elements of the system; therefore it would seem that the perspective we conventionally called the 'insider's perspective,' becomes inevitable."

It is true that the absorption of a series of collective and individual values and the act of reliving them through a group interaction, are not sufficient to analyze and interpret them. It is necessary to place them in perspective and to consciously restructure the elements and their particular relationships, thus revealing their symbolism.

We even insist that: "to be initiated," to learn the elements and values of a cult as an "insider," through interrelationships within the heart of a group, and at the same time to be able to abstract from this empirical reality the mechanism of the whole and its dynamic significance, its symbolic relationships, while at the same time consciously abstracting "like an outsider," is an ambitious aspiration and a fairly unlikely combination. Perhaps it is unlikely; but since we are dealing with a system of initiation, it is not only desirable, but it seems to us inevitable. With regard to Black American religion, seeing and building "from the inside to the outside" leads us to focus on three aspects: the factual, critical revision, and interpretation.

By "factual aspect" we mean a dynamic description of the homogeneous and heterogeneous variables of a religion; an exact and detailed description of the ritual, from its most complex ceremonies and the composition and morphology of the group, its hierarchy, places, and objects, and deities, down to the smallest gesture within the ritual. Included, of course, is research into the oral traditions, the importance of which we will discuss later.

We have already insisted several times on a critical revision, and this aspect is very important when the cultural realities of the communities are looked at "from the inside." We are concerned with demystifying imported or superimposed ideologies, discarding ethnocentric European ideas, so that we can see and place specific group values in their true light. Such ethnocentric distortion has been one of the most severe barriers to the comprehension of Black American values.

In this revision we will include, not only a critical rereading of a specialized bibliography that will place Black American values back into their historic perspective, but also a deep conceptual examination of the terminology that denatures and corrupts the perception of a religious system.

Although we do not hope by this synthesis to revise terminology, we would like to call attention to some words and their associations.

Fetishism was, and continues to be, the most prevalent classification of African religions transferred to Latin America. As is well known, the word comes from the Portuguese *feticio,* a thing that has been accomplished, or prepared, and was first applied by the Portuguese sailors to objects and ritual images which began to be called *fetiches*. Thus, the Portuguese attributed object worship to Africans, without perceiving that the material objects were not the subjects of worhsip, that they were instead, symbolic representations that had been duly consecrated, and were a part of a complex system of very abstract and mystical relations. We are not dealing with divinity-objects, omnipotent fetishes that control their worshipers, but emblems consecrated through special ceremonies that are accepted as symbols of beings and spiritual forces. "The initiate does not bow before a stone, wood, clay, or porcelain, but before a sacred abstraction, in the same manner that a Catholic does not adore the material images of saints and crucifixes, but the mystical spirit they symbolize." The sacred objects are not autonomous, they form a part of a whole and acquire its significance by participating in a liturgical system into which all manifestations of the sacred are organized.

We would also recommend a revision of translated terms that prevent a proper understanding of the structure of the system. Thus, *masked* or *mask* is applied to the spirit of an ancestor whose materialized representation is invoked in ancestral worship. The very word *mask,* continuously used in the language of ethnology and in the prestigious art books, comes from an erroneous translation that alters the cultural significance of the objects it attempts to define, and has nothing to do with the terms applied to those objects in their original communities.

The talk of critical revision must be undertaken by the researchers as they come across descriptions and concepts in specialized literature that relate to their field experience, as they analyze the ritualistic texts and the concepts used by the hierarchy of participants in a religion. Thus, for example, restricted access to some ceremonies, particularly those related to offerings, has often been attributed to the barbaric nature of these practices, to fear of the law or to a desire to discourage scientific curiosity. In fact, only certain types of individuals are not permitted to be present. We pointed out earlier that the initiation development was progressive, and that it depended on the acquisition of certain attributes and powers. Therefore, access to certain rituals and ceremonies is determined by the degree of initiation of an individual, his or her physical and spiritual ability to participate in mystical experiences during the course of which powers that are difficult to manage and that have a deep meaning are released and invoked. The precaution of keeping these ceremonies private stems from the nature of the religious structure and has nothing to do with immorality, barbarism, or other projections of the values of another cultural system.

Revision also leads us to a problem that has been difficult to solve: how to find in the national language words that are equivalent to the cultural concepts used in the communities. There are no possible translations for *orishá, vodun, ashé,* etc., concepts than can be analyzed but not translated. This forces the specialist to overburden his work with unknown words, or to repeated explanations when terms such as *vodun* are redefined to correct their inappropriate former ethnocentric usage.

Our third concern is that of interpretation. The perspective of "from the inside to the outside" is developed with greater depth at this level. Here we must analyze the nature and significance of factual material, discover underlying symbols, and reconstruct the significance of the signs as a function of their internal interrelationships and their interplay with the outside world. The symbolic interpretation is the least studied aspect of Black religion even though it permits us to see the ritualistic sequences and to give them a logical structure. Religion, its morphology, its practices and all its contents are expressed through symbols or through complex symbolic structures. Reciprocally, we can say that, by unveiling the correspondence of symbols and interpreting them, we will be able to explain the contents of the ritual and its variables.

These three aspects of religion—the factual, critical revision, and interpretation—are all interrelated and become the interchangeable instruments of a technique that must be adjusted to the slow but progressive field work related to the study of "initiation."

III

We will attempt to examine some essential aspects of Black American religion and the elements through which it expresses itself; in other words, we will look at the underlying relationship between the various visible contents, a relationship that determines the level of "communality," Africanism, or negritude.

The main defining aspect of the religion we are concerned with is the fact that it is an initiatory system. It is acquired, transmitted, and developed in a specific manner. The initiated partake of an experience, during the course of which, either through a direct or a gradual interrelationship, they receive, absorb, and develop a mystical and symbolic power permitting them to become integrated with, and to identify with, the elements of a dynamic system that they help to mobilize. We have already referred to this fulfillment process to which we attributed the development of the most precious content of the communities, responsible for the very existence of the religions through the mystical alliance, the "consanguineous" current, between the past, the present, and the future.

This power, known as *ashé*, a Nagô word, or *sé*, a Fon word, is the beginning that makes all vital processes possible. It is passed through material and symbolic means and it is cumulative. It is a force that can only be acquired through introjection or through other forms of contact. It cannot be transmitted through objects or human beings.

According to Mopoil, it refers to "the invisible force, the magical-sacred force within every divinity, every animate being, of everything." But this force does not appear spontaneously and must be transmitted. An object, a being, or a sacred place can only become sacred by acquiring *ashé*. The community with all of its material contents and initiates must receive *ashé*, must accumulate it, maintain it and develop it.

The quality of the power varies with the combination of elements it contains and directs; each combination is the transmitter of a power that permits the occurrence of certain happenings. *Ashé*, like all forms of power, can diminish, expand, or become stronger. These changes are determined by activities and rituals.

> Conduct is determined by the scrupulous observation of duties and obliga-
> tions, guided by doctrine and liturgical practice, that the holder of *ashé*
> observes himself, in his attitude towards the group he belongs to, and to-
> wards the community. The more active and ancient the group, the more
> elevated its degree of initiation, and the more powerful will be the commu-
> nity's *ashé*. Knowledge and the development of initiation are a function of
> the absorption and elaboration of *ashé*, and are transmitted through specific
> combinations that contain material and symbolic representations, that are
> individualized and thereby permit a specific meaning. Each combination is
> unique and is determined by its function and its ritual. Ritual permits the
> accumulation and revitalization of individual and collective *ashé*, and there-
> fore, the continuity and vitality of the community itself.

A proper understanding of this power that permits the existence and the transformation of a group is imperative to grasp the profound significance of sacrifice and offerings as particular and symbolic ways of conveying *ashé*.

Ashé is not learned, it is received, becomes enriched through the ritual and the mystical experience; it is shared and distributed. *Ashé* is received from the hands and the spirit of those who are more advanced, it is conveyed from person to person through a live and dynamic relationship. It is received through body and psyche and touches the deepest levels, it can be conveyed through symbolic elements, through blood, fruits, ritual-istic herbs, words, mystical pacts, and relationships that are established with the ancestors, with nature, and with the group as a whole.

The higher the hierarchical status, the more advanced is the mystical development, permitting a greater accumulation of *ashé* and of initiatory knowledge. The degree of initiation is determined by the years gone by since initiation, not by the chronological age of the participant. Performance of the ritual will permit further development of a participant's *ashé* and will decide his place within the community. The community is socially structured according to the higher or lower levels of *ashé* of its participants. *Ashé* is transmitted during the various degrees of initiation and is reinforced during transition rites from one level to another and by confirmation rites in which individuals are designated to hold certain positions within the hierarchy.

The heads of the communities are also their priests or priestesses. Upon being invested, they become the maximum bearers of *ashé* within the community, receiving and inheriting all the material and spiritual powers of the community since its creation. They are responsible not only for the care of the temple, its altars, ornaments and all other sacred objects, but they are also in charge of preserving, developing, and strengthening Ashé, thus keeping alive the community. Whatever the religious variable may be, be it homogeneous or heterogeneous, the head of the group, be it *iyalashé, hugan, hunon mokongo, tata, graman,* etc., will be the depository of maximum mystical and initiatory powers and liturgical knowledge. The cult priest distributes or "plants" power by initiating novices and infusing them with the power of which he is the depository.

It is this process that permits the internalization and mobilization of symbolic and spiritual elements, both individual and collective, that transform the human being into a real live altar in which the presence of the supernatural beings can be invoked. These supernatural forces or beings, *models and symbolic regulating principles of cosmic, social, and individual phenomena,* are incorporated, known and lived, through the experience of "possession."

Possession accounts for another unique characteristic of Black religion that classifies the different groups into one basic system of variables. Possession institutionalizes a complex system of identification and recreation mechanisms; it updates and elaborates, either individually or collectively, the cultural values of Latin-American negritude in the most faithful African manner.

The dynamics of possession keep alive the cult of supernatural entities. The beings are manifested through the body of the priestesses or the initiated—talking, dancing, blessing, advising, using emblems and parameters, communicating their origins, history, and significance. It is not a matter of *recalling* the past, of myths or prototypes, of forces and cosmic elements. It is a matter of *reliving* through a dynamic experience a communication and identification with supernatural beings that transmits an order, a moral discipline, and cultural forms and values that go beyond the liturgical plane and the individual experience, to become a part of the life of the community.

During the experience of possession, the entire religious system, its theogony and mythology, are relived. Each participant is the protagonist of a ritualistic activity, in which Black historic, psychological, ethnic, and cosmic life is renewed. The dynamics of possession psychologically re-create here and now the existence of a system of knowledge that is drama-tized through a personal experience. This system can only be understood as it is lived through the ritualistic experiences, the analogies, the myths, and the reenacted legends; knowledge only becomes significant when it is *actively* incorporated.

We are thus pointing to one of the most, if not the most, important aspect of the system, which in certain ways is causally linked to factors we have pointed out before. Two persons, at least, are indispensable for transmission through initiation. Knowledge passes directly from one be-ing to another. No reading, explanations, or logical thought is required on a conscious or intellectual level; the transfer of the complex code of symbols is achieved through the real presence of people and their dy-namic interrelationship. Material symbols and gestures; words that are uttered, pronounced, and infused with life; modulations, emotions, and the personal history of the one who utters them: all are a part of the process of transmission. The word becomes so strong because it is im-pregnated with power, with *ashé;* it goes beyond its rational, semantic content to become the instrument for the conductor of *ashé. Oral transmission* is a technique used within the dynamic system and is also basic to the initiation system, present in all variables of Black American religion.

The dynamic structure of religion employs a type of communication that must be constantly self-fulfilling. To utter a word or a formula in a certain way, or in a certain context, becomes a unique circumstance. Each word is born, accomplishes its function, and then disappears. Each repetition has a unique result. Oral expression signifies interrelationships and interactions on two levels; the social and the individual. In the social context, the word is conveyed from one person to another, it is uttered to be heard and is communicated from mouth to ear. It is the transmission of the experience of one being to another and from one generation to another and conveys the concentrated *ashé* of the ancestors to present-day gener-ations. On the individual level, the utterance of the word is the culmina-tion of a communication process or an internal polarization. The sound always presupposes the presence of something that is expressed and that tries to reach its speaker.

Within the Black system, sound is invested with power and is a transmitter of action. The dynamic interaction of active sounds appears with all its symbolic content in formulas and ritualistic invocations as well as in the sounds emitted by the instruments used in the ritual. Of course the instruments are prepared, consecrated, and receive the appropriate *ashé* to accomplish their functions, and they can only be used by certain members of the group. The combination of sounds produced by these instruments, playing alone or with others, accompanied by the clapping of hands, the spoken or sung word, are formidable in summoning the supernatural entities, in transmitting action, and in promoting communication between the present and the past, between this world and the parallel supernatural world.

Sound is a synthesis; it is born from the interaction of two types of generative elements, and itself becomes a third element; it is a dynamic structure, resulting in a third element and originating movement. In the entire system the number three and its various combinations is always associated with movement.

The word as an invocation relies on the dynamic power of sound. The ritual texts and songs are invested with this power. Whether they are recited or sung, whether they are or are not accompanied by instruments, they mobilize ritualistic activity. All oral communication is a part of the dynamic transmission system, where transmission is accomplished at a level of *concrete interpersonal relations*.

It is important to notice the peculiar rhythmic structure of the ritualistic language. A special symbiosis is established between the dynamic oral expression and its rhythmic structure. We would like to speak about rhythm as an aspect that is unique to Black religion in every variable. But we cannot spend too much time here discussing the significance of rhythm as a social expression in which cosmic movement and harmony are relived.

Even though oral transmission is so important in this system of an essentially participatory individual, namely the Black, it is necessary to place it within a global perspective, as one of the elements of the complex dynamic structure wherein the basic principle is the interpersonal relationship.

Knowledge is not stored and frozen into writings and archives, it is permanently relived. The archives are alive, they are chains whose links are the wisest individuals of each generation.

The study of written texts can help catalogue aspects of religion and give them a more or less rational explanation, but only the development of initiation through the liturgy will permit the communication of integral knowledge. The upper hierarchy of the cults generally opposes giving information outside of the ritualistic context and refrains from writing theological treatises. This is not only because they wish to keep secrets or to maintain their position, or to selfishly hold onto knowledge. It is because written transmission goes against the very essence of real mystical knowledge, which can only be acquired through interpersonal relationships. It is possible that this essential aspect has contributed to the absence of written notations in Black African languages. The introduction of a written form of communication creates problems that shock and weaken the very foundations of the dynamic relationships of the system.

Africans believe that existence occurs simultanously on two levels: in the world or physical universe inhabited by human beings, and in another world—abstract, infinite, and unlimited—inhabited by supernatural beings, including divine beings, ancestors, and spiritual doubles of all that concretely inhabits our universe. The *alem* is not particularly associated with any part of the real world. It is an abstract concept, a world parallel to the real world that coexists with it, with all of its contents. Everything that exists in the real world has its counterpart or its spiritual double; the opposite is also true, all that exists in the supernatural world has its counterpart, its material or corporal representation in the real world. This concept, which is the result of the dynamic interrelationship of the parts that constitute the system, represents another essential African concept that has been transmitted through Black American religions, namely the two levels of existence: the real and the spiritual, or abstract, which are parallel and inseparable. Thre is no dichotomy between them, their own survival depends upon their dynamic interrelationship. This is expressed in myths and representations, as well as in the ritualistic and communal happening itself; it is seen quite clearly in the homogeneous variables and somewhat more indirectly and in a more fragmented manner in the heterogeneous variables. The presence of supernatural and abstract beings in the body of the priestess, through a complex initatory and liturgical process ritualizes the existence of both worlds and makes it symbolically irrefutable.

We cannot spend too much time on explanations of the concept of material correspondence to every spiritual element. This concept is inherent in the system and expresses itself in the selection of specific material elements that contribute to the formalization of an emblem; it manifests itself through those who hold and link ashé, the power of fulfillment, to the point that each natural being is conceived a a concrete and individualized piece of being as well as an abstract, spiritual, generating-mass principle.

There is a constant relationship, an incessant current of transfer of spiritual and material elements between the two worlds. This current carries the essential burden of the supernatural power, the power of fulfillment that mobilizes the entire system and that is orchestrated through birth, death, real and ritualistic rebirth—in other words, through the constant transfer and redistribution of *ashé,* symbolized and regulated by the ritual.

The initiating momentum is provided by the essence of existence and the knowledge of past generations, to which is added that of present generations, thus insuring the dynamic continuity of the community by regulating the symbolic interrelations between the two parallel worlds. It is not natural for Eshú, the supernatural being of the Nagô pantheon symbolizing the dynamic principle of *ashé,* to have been transposed from its ethnic origins, and to have become one of the most extensively worshiped beings in both the homogeneous and the heterogeneous variables. Also known as Elegbara, Elegba, or Legba, the conveyor of the power of fulfillment, it regulates communications between the multiple components of the system. It is therefore the principle of individualized life that promotes and develops individual destiny and that of the community as a whole.

Having worshiped for so long a being like Eshú, which represents the principle of expansion and of offspring, transporting and regulating offerings, returning and redistributing element-symbols loaded with significance and power, the Nagô have internalized a principle that elaborates the harmonic relationship, the cohesion and continuity of the system and the group. Eshú, whose latent significance is expressed by a variety of symbols, paraphernalia, iconography, and rites is the most complete and complex representation of the dynamic structure of Black American religion.

The Supreme Being, be it, according to its ethnic origin, Olorún, Mawú, Naná, Nyane, Zambí, etc., emanates and returns the power of fulfillment, a power that contains existence, direction, and objectives. But it is a power that is "replenished" through its own dynamic of existing on two levels, the natural and the supernatural. As we have already pointed out, the supernatural world exists only as long as the real world exists, and vice versa. The Supreme Deity, the origin of origins, the spiritual and material promoter at both levels of existence, is constantly delegated and restored through the configuration of symbolic beings, *orishá, vodun, loa, inquisi, winti,* etc., that are representations and patterns of cosmic, social, and individual elements, renewing themselves at different levels of power through individualized elements or generalized ones that are linked to the ritual. The Supreme Being is the recipient and distributor of this power that regulates and mobilizes all existence. He is called in communities that center on the rites of Nagô, Alaabé l'aashé, the one who is and has the purpose and power of fulfillment. Because of its specificity, we insist on the concept of Supreme Being, who encompasses all "space," the contents of the natural and the supernatural world, transmitting and receiving in the permanent, dynamic circle the powers that form and activate the universe and its existence.

We do not wish to expand upon the idea of a Supreme Being, a difficult task that must still be accomplished, despite the existence of a few published studies. In this synthesis we have limited ourselves to an examination of a little-known aspect and one that is unique to this religious system. It is easy to figure out that the real concept of a Supreme Being is inscribed in and participates in the dynamic structure that interrelates and characterizes all the components of the system.

We also wish to point briefly to another aspect of this interrelationship, expressed in the importance of ancestor worship. Often organized into secret societies but sometimes a part of the normal liturgy of the communities, usually known by the variables that are worshiped (*egungun, guede, esa, yorka, gabida, prêto velho,* etc.), ancestor worship internalizes the concept of belonging to a social structure. The forefathers become identification models and guardians of morality and discipline within the community. By insuring individual and collective immortality, they institutionalize the continuity between life and death, between past and present, and embody the survival of the community itself.

Social consensus, collective acceptance through initiation and ritual, permit the introjection, transference, representation, materialization, and activation of a complex, basic system that expresses the underlying cultural identity, the "communality" or negritude, with all its varieties, to be found in Black American religion.

This structure is prolonged and accomplished through a series of material objects and activities. We are referring to the very rich patrimony of ritualistic objects, such as dress, metal, pottery, stone, sculptures, objects made of leather or rafia, music with its complex rhythmic structures superimposed on texts and chants that complement one another. They all constitute a powerful means of communication that, through representations and esthetic explorations, formally and conceptually express and relive the principles, the values, and the particular cosmic vision of the Black religious and cultural system.

This has not been an attempt to exhaust the subject, particularly because we are dealing with variables in transformation. Nor do we wish to minimize the differences between variables. It was our intention to introduce a perspective that, through a collection of the existing information, would permit us a global, coherent, and articulate vision of a group of phenomena whose most essential elements delineate a significant path that expresses and constitutes, as few others do, the irrefutable continuity of Africa in Latin America. Although it is not a passive continuum, it justifies its own structural heritage by being versatile, resistant, and vital, giving place to a dialectic process that makes the culture of Blacks in Latin America unique, and possibly heading towards a new humanism based on the existential multidimensionality of the human being.

NOTE

1. Deoscóredes M. Dos Santos, *Axé Opô Afonja* (Río de Janeiro: Instituto Brasiliero de Estudos Afro-Asiáticos), 1963.

5

African Influence on Language
in the Caribbean

RICHARD ALLSOPP

In the Hispanic and Portuguese-speaking countries of Latin America, serious scholarly attention has for many years been given to African linguistic survivals in the New World forms of Spanish and Portuguese spoken in these countries. As long ago—for the business of linguistics—as 1924, Fernando Ortiz's famous *Glossary of Afronegrism* presented a vocabulary of some twelve hundred African terms in Cuban Spanish. The author's care in explaining his dissatisfaction with the label *Africanismos* (and preference for *Afronegrismos*) established a respect for the identity of this corpus of African contribution to his country's language that both made the work uniquely ahead of its time and indicated the approach which others elsewhere have followed.

> The words studied in this book comprise our *Africanisms;* not only those that we could call *Afrocubanisms,* but also some that could be presented as *Afrohispanicisms.*
> These voices comprise our *Africanisms;* nevertheless, we have not wanted to call them that, because this nomenclature, which suggests geography, does not give the idea exactly. These words come from Africa; but not from the Arab peoples, not from the Turks of Egypt, not from the Boers of the Transvaal, etc.; concretely, they come from "the Blacks of Africa." Therefore, we have preferred to coin the word *Negroafricanism,* or *Afronegrism,* which we consider of good alloy. [Introduction, p. xiv]

Thus it is the linguistic contribution from Black Africa that, says Ortiz, must undoubtedly be acknowledged.

In Brazil, where distinguished anthropologists and historians have for decades recognized the Black contribution to that vast country's culture, particular writers have focused attention on the linguistic contribution as well. Professor João Ribiero devoted part 3 of *O Elemento Negro* to "A Influencia do Elemento Negro na Linguagem" (pp. 78–143, with an appendix, pp. 157–186); and other writers have also dealt with the matter in detail, one of the most fulsome treatments being Nelson de Senna's *Africans in Brazil.* The bulk of this latter work (the last nine chapters, pp. 69–274) is given to detailed lists and related studies, in keeping with the author's claim that "Consequently, scholars have an extremely wide field

83

of literary, philological, and scientific activity in that badly explored and inexhaustible search for the Afronegrisms that enrich the vocabulary of the Portuguese language as spoken in Brazil" (p. 21).

In Puerto Rico, Nazario's *El Elemento Afronegroide en el Español de Puerto Rico* was a further massive contribution (453 pages) to the inventory of African *aportaciones* to transatlantic Spanish; and although he saw the words of African root as being "de menor importancia . . . en el conjunto del vocabulario hispanopuertorriqueño" (p. 202) he notes the greater vitality of these words in the areas of greater concentration of Black people. It is also interesting to note that his grouping of the *léxico afronegroide* according to subject matter reveals that the survivals related to the cultural life of the Negro (though he calls it *Vida espiritual*— ceremonies, superstitions, music, and dancing) are the most significant in number.

In addition to these general studies, which stand like monuments in the sparsely built domain of studies of African linguistic diaspora, there stand to the further credit of Hispanoamerican scholarship one or two works in Brazil and Cuba concentrating on the survival of a particular African language. Such a work as Lydia Cabrera's *Anagó: Lucumí Vocabulary*— setting out as it does, in over three hundred packed pags, a listing of seventy-five hundred words of Yoruba spoken in Cuba—is conclusive evidence, in this writer's view, that the African linguistic presence in the New World is of such obtrusive importance that neglect of it can no longer be excused even on the traditional emotional grounds.

In areas of Dutch control on the South American mainland circumstances forced acknowledgment and study of the African linguistic influence, especially in Suriname. In that country, a firmly established Negerengelsch, confronting official Dutch, necessitated attention, and the establishment of a Taalbureau and a Bureau Volkslectuur in Paramaribo brought scholarship to bear on this distinctly Afro-influenced language whose rise in national status and lingual credit is indicated by the replacement of the pejorative name *Taki-taki* with the respectful *Sranan Tongo*. Moreover, the distinguished work, first of the anthropologists M. J. and F. S. Herskovits[1] of Northwestern University, and then of the linguist Jan Voorhoeve of the University of Leiden, have brought to international attention the fact that the most solidly preserved African linguistic survivals in the New World are to be found in Suriname, and independently of the Sranan Tongo language. Saramaccan, the collective name given to the "Bush dialects" spoken along the Suriname and Saramacca rivers, is actually a tone language—

a kě = he wants (mid-tone on *a*)

á kě = he does not want (high-tone *a*)[2]

—with a significant number of other African features, phonemic, lexical, and sentence-pattern. Djuka[3] is a third distinct language of Suriname showing distinctive African features, though not as many as Saramaccan. Again in Curaçao, Papiamento, having by sociohistorical accident become the common tongue, has stimulated controversy because of its Creole status. But thereby it has also commanded serious attention, and in 1951 Navarro Tomás argued in a brief but resounding article, that that language had its origin in the Portuguese pidgin of the West African coast in the slave era. True, Navarro Tomás, like so many others after him, typically stressed the Portuguese element and dynamics of this pidgin, but even so, the African influence, if grudged at that time, was indisputable.

The record of study of African linguistic survivals in the Anglophone and Francophone Caribbean is far less substantial than that with which the Hispanic, Portuguese, and Dutch scholars can be credited. The reason lies in the social history of these places: in contrast to the Hispanic and Portuguese New World societies, the English and French colonial societies were sharply anti-integrative—so were the Dutch, but then Sranan and Papiamento profited from special circumstances[4]—and in those colonies the association of Creole speech with Black people and with the lowest social stratum meant that it was sharply despised by the whole society, including the Creole speakers themselves. This is still the case today, and since the Creole tongues—which may be regarded as dialects in the Anglophone, but properly as languages in the Francophone places—are the repository of all the surviving Africanisms; the study of Africanism has had to await the change in attitudes brought about by the recent, almost sudden scholarly "discovery" of the linguistic importance of the Creoles. And still, the preference of modern linguistics for heuristic rather than historical investigations—synchronic vs. diachronic studies—has meant that the African linguistic influence, for example in West Atlantic Black English, denied until L. D. Turner's famous work *Africanism in the Gullah Dialect,*[5] is still a greatly underdeveloped area in the domain of language study in the Anglophone and Francophone New World. Indeed such a reputable American scholar as Professor Robert Hall, Jr. still maintains in principle that any African influence is superficial, failing to reach the grammatical dynamics of the Creoles:

> The surface characteristics of the various pidgins and creoles may often be quite far from those of English, French, or the other Indo-European languages; but, on a deeper level of grammar, all varieties of Pidgin English and creoles that have grown out of them have an underlying identity of structure with English, and similarly for the French-based, Spanish-based, and Portuguese-based pidgins and creoles. No matter how much they may have changed and have been brusquely restructured near the surface, they still maintain a basically Indo-European pattern. This observation, incidentally,

forces itself on the observer even against his will: three times I have begun work on a pidgin or creole language (Neo-Melanesian, Stranan, and Haitian Creole) with the determination to find in it a non-Indo-European structure, and each time the language itself has compelled recognition of its basically English or French pattern, as the case might be.[6]

It is worth quoting this opinion, presented in 1966, if only to contrast it sharply with the older one of the Brazilian Professor João Ribiero (1939?) which the facts of this paper seem better able to support:

That which we call the "black element" designates all the sorts of alterations produced in the Brazilian language through the influences of the African languages spoken by the slaves introduced into Brazil.

These alterations are not as superficial as some scholars claim; on the contrary, they are rather profound, not only in respect to vocabulary, but also in regard to the grammatical system of the language.[7]

It would therefore seem opportune to engage the rest of the present article in giving special attention to the African influence to be found in the Anglophone and Francophone areas of the Caribbean.

II

The "alterations produced . . . through the influence of the African languages spoken by the slaves introduced" into the New World were indeed "rather profound" for two important reasons. The first is that these "alterations" go back to the *origins* of the development of the New World Creoles in the fifteenth and sixteenth centuries on the West and Central African coasts. The second is that Creolisms, often unsuspected, continue to characterize the idiom and the general dynamics of the language that is being standardized today, especially in the Anglophone territories, bringing with them the same African linguistic conditioning that have made them Creolisms.

Let us look first at the important matter of origins. Although the progeniture of the New World Creoles remains a matter of controversy, no credible theorists today deny a notable degree of West African input; but the widely accredited basic theory is that a willfully simplified Portuguese—a sailors' pidgin—was the communication vehicle to which various African adjuncts were admitted or clung; that when the French, English, and Dutch (in that order) followed the Portuguese into coastal trade, they used the same Portuguese vehicular structure only "relexifying" it— i.e., replacing the Portuguese lexicon wholesale with their own,[8] so that whichever European culture the slaves fell under determined the "Euro"- variety of pidgin they learned, but the species was congenitally Portuguese, which would explain the striking similarity of their deformities in Indo-European terms.

The first aspect of this theory to be questioned is that, if the linguistic thrust in the creation and maintenance of this new "talk" was both basically and persistently European, why is it that the result was structurally so often far from any of the European progenitors? Compare commonplace expressions like

Papiamento: nan ta bai

Spanish: ellos van
Portuguese: eles vão

Antillean French Creole: yo ka alé

French: ils vont

Jamaican Creole: im a go

English: she is going

and one is immediately struck not only by the irreconcilable differences of structure horizontally but, at the same time, by the remarkable similarities of structure vertically. In other words the Creoles (on the left) clearly have something structurally in common, and clearly also whatever is responsible for the obvious genetic linkage in the Creoles, it is *not* Portuguese—nor any other of the European languages in the picture. The only reasonable conclusion is that that "something" is African, an African structural base! Admittedly the example is a small one, and since it contributes to the rather crucial contention that the progenitor "pidgin" of the Caribbean—and New World—Creoles *was more African than it was anything else,* it is pertinent, especially in the context of this paper, to show why this is probably a more reasonable hypothesis than the generally accepted one of essentially Portuguese production of the initial "pidgin."

In the circumstances of the slave trade, certain postulates in regard to language would seem indisputable:

a. In the contact situation the West African was the *host* culture and the European the *visitant.* The host culture—and its basic cultural uniformity has been cogently brought to attention by Mervyn Alleyne[9]—would be in a stronger position to influence, characterize, indeed stabilize the means of communication than the visitant culture, simply because it had a fairly stable and (at contact points) specially motivated resident majority using the new *interlingua,* while the visitant culture was a minority partner which was both irregular and unstable, migratory and changing in personnel from one ship's crew to the next, and periodically also changing in nationality.

b. The interlingua or "new code" would be pressed into service by the hosts to discover the newcomer's intentions, decide on and establish the nature of relationship with them, test their trustworthiness and (very importantly) circumscribe the limits of their intrusion. The visitors however would need the new code for self-protection, for situation control, and to pursue their intended (commercial) objectives. Self-interest and self-protection would motivate both sides, with the minority visitors—especially in the early stages which are notably important, after all, in the formation of a pidgin—feeling their way vitally into the hosts' understanding, and the hosts critically assessing meaning and testing the worthiness of entertaining an intrusion. In such circumstances the "prestige" of the visitor's language and its "dominance" in the production of the new code are assumptions which, though common among all writers on the subject,[10] seem rather questionable, if they are tenable at all. On the contrary it seems quite possible that a situation in which a belief in mutual integrity would have been to the advantage of the minority visitors should have reflected mutuality in the "code" it produced.

c. A pidgin is product and instrument of an exclusively oral situation; and a pidgin situation is also obviously dominated by performance, in the linguistic sense of this term. In the African or host culture language is also exclusively oral, every "speech event" being characterized by an *actuality* and certain "performance factors"[11] that are, in contrast, not notable in European languages. It would therefore seem reasonable to conclude that the coincidence of these important African language characteristics with certain important characteristics of a pidgin situation should be to the advantage of the African "side" in a process of pidginization with a European "side."

In the face of such arguments it is difficult to see how the pidgin or protopidgin which is postulated as the progenitor of our Caribbean Creoles can be called "Portuguese pidgin" or "pidgin Portuguese" or a "Portuguese pidgin [from] medieval Sabir":[12] and the fact seems to be overlooked that this "Portuguese pidgin" is largely postulated and no one has ever found a working sample of it yet—in the ship's logs, diaries, or travel accounts of the period. The proposition rests largely on a few words—far too few: Professor F. G. Cassidy makes the case for six in Jamaican Creole—*savvy, pickaninny, dobl, candle, paen, sampata*—and the argument of a Portuguese progeniture as against other later European possibilities for the last four of these is not conclusive, as Cassidy himself indicates.[13] Moreover, one of the supposedly Portuguese words that evidently continues to excite much interest in the genesis theory is the Portuguese feminine prepositional particle *na,* serving as a regular prepositional particle in different Creoles, which Douglas Taylor (1960: 157) has shown to be used in Sranan and Phillipine Creoles in a way quite "common" in Ibo, but quite "foreign to English, Spanish, and Portuguese." Again, as Ian Hancock[14] points out, "the grammatical structure shared by these English-derived Atlantic Creoles is no closer to Portuguese than it is to any other European language," and, except for Saramaccan, have a negligible percentage of their vocabularies traceable to Portuguese.

Altogether then, the case for Portuguese influence is patently thin and indeed no case has ever been made for a Portuguese grammatical sub-stratum coming through the "Portuguese pidgin" to the resultant Creoles. On the other hand, that there is a case against an African substratum to our Creole structure has been agreed on by scholars of such widely differing views as Hall (1966:58, 86) and DeCamp, the latter concluding that "there could not have been any significant systematic African 'substratum.' "[15] A basic problem, therefore, is: exactly what framework then was "relexified?" The answer, if the theory is accepted, must be an *Afroportuguese contact vernacular* and this, following the indications in this paper, and against opinions such as DeCamp's, was likely to be "significantly" African. The distinguished sociolinguist William Labov has remarked that "the penetration of one language by another, in lexicon and grammatical subsystems, is . . . much deeper than most linguists would have been willing to believe possible;"[16] but when this interesting statement is applied to the Afro-Portuguese case it seems that "interpenetration" would more properly describe what took place, and *inter*penetration is, of course, not relexification. Indeed Weinreich, some time ago now, (1958:379), seems still to have said the most apt word on the matter among the scholarly voices: "In the formation of the Creoles, *an unknown African substratum, mutual interinfluence,* and the 'minimization' (or 'optimization') of grammar which seems to be universally attendant upon improvised communication conditions, all played a role [emphasis mine]." In addition, Taylor (1963:813) at the end of a long article on the origin of West Indian Creoles concluded that "if there was continuity in the use of a grammatical system, everything points to Africa as the place of that system's origin—probably not in any one African language, but more likely in some Afro-Portuguese pidgin."

There is, therefore, both evidence and scholarly support for an Afro-Portuguese contact vernacular with a strong African substratum as the basic language of the Portuguese fifteenth and sixteenth century trading on the West African Coast. Indeed the strong African character of the vernacular may be the reason why no written samples of it appear in ship's logs, diaries, etc., as has been pointed out. One can well imagine Portuguese reluctance or inability to write down rather un-Portuguese vocables. Nevertheless the Portuguese had long enough to learn, to "institutionalize," this vernacular—a century of uninterrupted contact from 1441, before the French intruded, as Cassidy (1964: 269) has noted. In fact this is *too* long a time, as pidginization theory goes,[17] for the term "pidgin" to be still applicable to the "talk," and "vernacular"—an established, home-grown, utility "talk"—is a more apt label. This, then, would have been the established *auxiliary vernacular* that the Portuguese would have taken with them in their later trading expansion around the world. And this, too, would have been the basic auxiliary language that the African hosts would have kept going as new waves of Europeans—French, English and Dutch in that order—began from about 1550 to establish business contact with them: *it is this auxiliary language that would have been "relexified."*

The next problem is who did the relexifying—who made the postulated "lexical shifts" replacing vocabulary from one source language by "widespread borrowings" from a new source language (Stewart: 1962). J. Voorhoeve[18] points out that the supposed relexification which produced the prototype of the French Creoles clearly did not pass through a French pidgin stage—and everyone must agree, since French Creoles are a very far cry from what *Frenchmen* would have done to their language to "simplify" it. Indeed the French Creoles and French are and evidently have always been mutually incomprehensible! But the theory actually requires that the French, English, and Dutch "used the Portuguese pidgin as the basis and model for pidgins of their own."[19] This means that the Frenchmen would have learned an ongoing Portuguese pidgin as a second language (!) and thoroughly enough to produce a third language (why ??) very much like the second and very unlike their first in character except for mass change in lexicon, and that Englishmen simultaneously, and Dutchmen later, would have done the same. Such developments seem most unlikely. If, on the other hand, one were to see the African *hosts* as *agents* of the change, relexifying their own century-old auxiliary language to accommodate new European trading nations, with each set of European nationals readily cooperating in the development of a trade language specially for their advantage, at least illogicalities disappear. The only difficulty with this approach is the question of whether there were sufficient and significant enough similarities in the multifarious West African (and later also Central African!) languages to justify postulating "an unknown African substratum." The argument for a "basic cultural uniformity of West Africa" with an "African-derived deep-structure" in language has already been referred to above (and see note 9). The matter must, however, be taken further than that, and it can be. The now widely accepted work of Greenberg (1966) based on the twin principles of "mass-comparison" of "linguistic evidence only" groups the great bulk of the languages in some three million square miles of Subsaharan Africa as genetically related within a vast Niger-Congo family; and Armstrong ended his great essay (1964: 23) emphasizing "the immense antiquity of West African languages" and their "fundamental and elaborate unity" (which he backed up with thirty-eight pages of illustrative lexical appendix).

III

Such highly respected scholarly opinion is not the only basis on which the thesis of uniformity of structure of a multilingual West African product rests. The evidence of certain features of language in the Caribbean is that there are common structures peculiar to them which can only be accounted for by a conceptual uniformity intrinsic to their African progeniture. The examples that follow now add to the minimal sample offered above at the beginning of section 2.

Perhaps the simplest feature to bring to attention first is that of *word formation* in the languages that have surfaced in the Caribbean. The surface word for Standard English (SE) "tears" in many Caribbean Creoles is a lexicosemantic structure made up of "eye" + "water." For example:

Guyana Creole *Jamaica Creole*	eye-water
Sranan Tongo (Suriname)	watr'ai
Patois Guyanais (Fr. Guyana)	dileau-ouèye (de l'eau + oeil)

And the parallel lexicosemantic structure may be found in many African languages. For example:

Mandingo (Gambia)	na-giyo eye-water	
Mende (Sierra Leone)	ngayei	< ngamei + njei face (eyes) water
Twi (Ghana)	ani - suo eye water	
Fante (Ghana)	nyinsuwa	< enyiwa + nsu eye water
Yoruba (W. Nigeria)	omi - oju water eye	
Igbo (E. Nigeria)	anya - miri - akka eye water flowing	
Efik (E. Nigeria)	mmong - eyet water of the eye	
Luo (Uganda)	pi - wang water eye	

Lingala	mayi-ya-miso
(Zaire)	water of eyes
Ci-Nyanja	misozi<liso (pl. "maso") + manzi
(Zambia-Malawi)	eye water

The number and wide scatter of these African examples—from Gambia to Zambia—demonstrating a sameness in word formation that is reflected both in the Anglophone and Francophone Caribbean Creoles indicates *(a)* that the parallel emergence was possible through slaves' *calquing* from their different native tongues into the same European language whether on the West African coast or in the New World; and *(b)* that this parallelism was due to the characteristic similarity of African patterns.

Such deep-structure similarity—especially if it spread beyond word-structure level—would contribute to an easy *business* communication among Africans themselves—a multilingual facility making possible an auxiliary vernacular. One can see this "vernacular," with the universal working principles of pidginization (see Weinreich's remark above) as an added factor, being transferred to a business contact situation—whether as trader or slave—with Europeans, the latter's needs helping further to unify the African product. In this light the African linguistic base of the New World products would be seen as substantial, integrative, and primary rather than parasitic.

Indeed the evidence may be strengthened from an examination of the idiomatic structures and the kind of conceptualization that came through to the Creoles, where such structures both show a uniformity and indicate African progeniture. Space must limit us to two categories of examples here, the one of idiom and the other proverbs.

The first is a classic Creole structure which has been called *"predicate-clefting"* or better *"front-shifting"* or *"front-focusing."* It is an aspectual feature involving reduplication of the verb nucleus to emphasize the actuality of a piece of information. An example from *Haitian Creole* that Albert Valdman calls "a special case of embedding"[20] is:

(1) sé   manjé   l   ap   manjé

    is   eat   he -ing eat
    (= He's really eating)

Similar examples may be cited from other French Creoles, for example Taylor's Caribbean examples (1951: 50) which he calls "a special kind of inversion." The structure is "special" to Europeans, but it may be found in all the Anglophone Creoles and post-Creoles except present Barbadian. So, for example, in *Guyanese Creole:*

(2) a   fraikn   dem   bin   fraikn
    it's   frighten them   (past)   frighten
    (= They were very much frighened)

and Bailey's (1966:86) *Jamaican* example:

(3) a   tiif   Jan   tiif   di   manggo
    it's   steal   John   steal the mango
    (= John did, in fact, steal the mango)

and Hendrik Focke (1855, Intro.: X) notices the structure with examples, in Suriname's *Neger-Engelsch:*

(4) Da   skrífi   mi   de   skrífi
    it's   write   I   -ing   write
    (= I am actually writing)

Again *Papiamento* has this structure to express emphasis (Goilo, 1962: 89):

(5) Ta   ke   mi ke   bo   bai
    Is   want   I want you   go
    (= I do want you to go)

This very particular type of reduplicative structure is as notably foreign to Portuguese and European languages as it is notably present in African languages. The following examples,[21] taken from languages of places as widely separated as Senegal, Nigeria, and Zambia—and from language families as distinct as West Atlantic, Kwa, and Bantu—suggest that we have here a *generic* African idiom:

(6) *Wolof:*   Tayal   la   tayal   rek
    (Gambia)   Laziness it is laziness only
               (= He is/they are just lazy!)

(7) *Mende:*   ngufei mia   i wufei nga   la i lowu
    (Sierra Leone) nga
               shame (emph.) he be ashamed (past) (emph.) he
               hide (past)
               (= It was really from shame that he hid)

(8) *Twi*   wawu   no,   na owu   ara   na   wawu
    (Ghana)   He died he, that he die even   that   he died
               (= Having died, he was dead) (Christaller:147)

(9) *Nupe:*   li lo   nan wo lo nan, U gala ewun   be
    (Nigeria)   O
               The go(ing) that you go that it which fight bring
               (terminal emph.)
               (= The going that you went there caused trouble)

(10) *Yoruba:*   Pipa   ni   nwon pa a
     (Nigeria)   Killing it is they kill him
                        (= They actually killed him) (Rowlands, 1969:210)
(11) *Kikongo:*   Kanuini   ko, yela ketua   yela
     (Zaire)   Not he drink not,   sick he is   sick
                        (= He is not drunk, he is actually sick)
(12) *Ki-Yaka:*   Ayandi ! Ubela   ka   bela
     (Zaire)   It is so! Sick   he   sick
                        (= He is actually sick, not pretending)
(13) *Ci-Nyanja:*   Kupita angapite, koma   atate ače
                        azakalipa
     (Zambia-Malawi)   To go he can go but   father his   he will be
                        angry
                        (= He may certainly go but his father will be angry)

We may turn now to the field of proverbs, which, though widely scouted by folklorists and anthropologists, seems to have remained virtually untouched by linguists. Yet the proverb is the *esin òrò* ("horse word") or vehicle of thought to the African, as one Yoruba proverb puts it, and is intrinsic to serious dialogue right across Africa. It would be preposterous to suppose that the conceptual structure of African proverbs can have been lusitanized by Portuguese trade-contact, and furthermore it would be hardly possible to imagine their translation on any scale into a Portuguese coastal pidgin. Yet it seems an increasing matter of fact that a body of evidently *generic* African proverbs arrived in the New World *calqued* in the Creoles of whatever "base," evidently from some common *conceptual African frame.* The evidence is best illustrated by one of the many examples in such a work as David-Jardel's *Créole Proverbs of Martinique,* a rich collection of proverbs in which those of the Francophone Caribbean are mingled with those of West and Central Africa. Thus (pp. 53–54 of that work):

(14) *Dominica:* Faute manman ou ka tété magranne
(15) *Haiti:* Lors ou pas gan manman ou tété grande
(16) *Louisiana:* Quand na pas manman, tété grand-maman

with which are paralleled also.

(17) *Mali:*   Faute d'avoir tété sa mère a tété sa
                 grand-mère *(Fulani)*
(18)   A défaut du sein de sa mère, on tète celui
                 de sa grand-mère *(Bambara)*
(19)   Celui qui n'a pas de mère prend le sein de
                 sa grand-mère *(Malinke)*
(20) *Senegal:* A défaut de ta mère, tu tètes ta
                 grand-mére *(Wolof, Serer-Non)*

(21) *Guinea:* Celui qui n'a pas de mère prend le sein
de sa grand-mère *(Mandinka, Dyula, Fulani)*
(22) *Chad:* Si tu ne peux téter ta mère, il te reste
les tétons de ta grand-mère *(Mbai)*
(23) *Congo:* L'enfant privé de sa mère suce les seins
de sa grand-mère *(Kongo)*

And to David-Jardel's impressive collection may be added another Caribbean relative:

(24) *Guyana:* Picknie can't get mamme, he suck granny

The parallel occurrence of such particular conceptualization—the kind of data selected as carrier—of what is a commonplace of human thought—that "one must make the best of what there is if better cannot be found"—and the persistence of this occurrence through *calques* into new language bases make it difficult to avoid the conclusion that there is an African way of putting things that may be as deep and pervasive for Africa as Whorf's Standard Average European (SAE) for Europe.[22] In other words a kind of Standard Average African or SAA. Indeed the evidence almost tempts the suggestion that linguistically SAA may have a deeper common conceptual base than SAE; but whether that be so or no the evidence for a kind of SAA would explain an African facility for acquiring other, *not necessarily neighbouring,* African languages—his noted *Afromultilingualism*—by a process of *calquing.* However upon his contact with non-African languages—those of Europe—the principle of *calquing* would influence only the *intellectual* base of the necessary new code, the vocabulary being built upon universal principles of pidginization.

Now the role of *calquing* in pidgin-Creole evolution has been variously noted by writers on the subject, but not emphasized: Taylor[23] bases an important paper on the "striking structural similarities between members of lexically differently based groups which cannot be attributed to the 'source language'." Hancock[24] concedes "extensive calquing and Africanization of the Creoles," but does not allow that this process had already begun in Africa. Hoenigswald[25] in some revealing paragraphs suggests, in general terms, that "conditions of 'intimate' contact. . . . between grossly different languages may lead to excessive borrowing of loan words and creating of calques and loan-translations (process 1) with effects that would resemble rapid 'learning' uncorrected by any ironing-out of flaws (process 2)." The argument of the present paper is that African *calquing* is central to the origin of New World and probably other Creoles, that the Africans, first in Africa and later in the New World, interpreted or *calqued* ther native structural patterns *in* Portuguese or French or English or Dutch—this accounting for the indisputable structural similarities between Papiamento and English-based and French-based Creoles. This contention accordingly supports the thesis of Mono-genesis of the Creoles, identifying the latter more precisely, however, as what may be called an *Afrogenesis* of Creoles of whatever base.

IV

We remarked earlier that "Creolisms"—those features of New World IndoEuropean languages that bear the historical coloring of Africa—continue to characterize these languages today. Attention may be drawn first to a suprasegmental or "prosodic" conditioning that is especially noticeable, at least in the English of the Creole-based speaker, which distinguishes it in a systematic way from homeland or "British" English. This feature has been observed both at sentence and at word level and there can be little doubt that it is, once again, generically African.

At sentence level, Cassidy (1961: Chapter 3) has demonstrated very effectively that the *intonation* of Jamaican speech bears an accidental resemblance to Welsh or Irish English, which is nonfundamental, but that "the only possible alternative source for the characteristic Jamaican into-nation is the African languages that the slaves spoke when they came" (p. 31) the Africans "carrying over into English some of the accidentation of pitch to which they were accustomed" in such languages, as he shows, as Twi. This systemic intonation, though strongest at folk level, is still very noticeable at the standard level of Jamaican English; and the same remark applies to the Englishes of other Caribbean territories, which, though they have distinctive intonational features to Caribbean ears, are all different from British or North American varieties.

At word level another feature that may be observed, the *semantic pitch differentiation of homonyms and homographs,* seems to be clearly a resi-due of phonemic pitch from the tone languages of Africa, as it is not a feature of original English.[26] Since the words involved are not African, but English, the feature—so subtle that it has long lain undetected by scholars for what it is—involves a carryover onto English homonyms of the Afri-can capacity to signal difference in meaning by change of pitch only, without interfering with the words' stress pattern. Obviously the feature is more easily demonstrated on words of more than one syllable, but Prof. J. Berry, the distinguished Africanist scholar at Northwestern University, has identified the feature on monosyllables working with Jamaican infor-mants distinguishing *tonemically,* for example, the minimal pairs

bank (of a river)	glass (a tumbler)	pen (for writing)
bank (for money)	glass (a window pane)	pen (for cows)

The following examples of disyllabic pairs are, however, taken from the present writer's own experience as a native speaker of Guyanese

English. (The stress is indicated in capitals, and the pitch by the customary use of numbers, 1, 2, 3, etc., representing relative levels from low upwards.) Most of the examples apply also to present Barbadian English and some (plus others not given here) also to St. Vincent, St. Kitts, Antigua, Grenada, and Dominica, as checked by the writer with informants from those places.

Item		*Pitch Patterns*
	/12/	/2'1/
ARCHer		
BUTCHer		
COOPer	Family	Ordinary words
FRIday	Names	(S.E. usage)
MAson		
PORter		Ordinary words
TAYlor	Family names	(S.E. usage)
WELcome		(tailor)
etc.		
UGly		ordinary adjectives
WICKed	Nicknames	(S.E. usage)
STUpid		
BROther	Members of	
FAther	religious	Blood
SISter	organization	relatives
MOther		
ANSwer	arithmetical result in classwork	reply to a question
WORKer	Seamstress	Workman
FIGure	Shape of female	(a) number
etc.	body	(b) guess
	LESSon	LESSen
	FLOWer	FLOur
	etc.	

The feature means, of course, that sentences like

(25) He is a *butcher*
(26) She is a *mother*

will each have very different meanings in these societies depending on the pitch pattern used on *butcher, mother*. Though the feature is most commonly noticeable in disyllabic words, it is not limited to these, and trisyllabic and quadrisyllabic examples can also be found—e.g.,

BEAUtiful /1'1 2/ nickname	/2'2 1/ S. E. adjective
COMmon ENtrance /1'12'2/ a School examination	/2'21'1/ regular public gateway

However, these prosodic subtleties are by no means the only Creol-isms that mark the cultivated language of the Anglophone Caribbean areas. Less subtle but nearly as pervasive African influence can be identified at the *morphosyntactic* and *idiomatic* levels. The chief mor-phological feature attributable to the African linguistic heritage is the use of the uninflected English verb more in lexical than syntactic function, the nature rather than the time of an action (see note 11) being commonly signaled in the speech and writing of persons at many socioeducational levels:

(27) I hear so yesterday.
(28) He say he is going.
    etc.

The idiomatic cases are often readily spotted by English-speaking for-eigners to the region and a few examples will suffice as illustration at this stage.

to be able with someone	(= to manage or cope with someone easily)
to be hard-eared	(= to be obstinate)
to be big-eyed	(= to be covetous or gluttonous)
to be two-mouthed	(= to be deceitful)
their eyes made four	(= their eyes met)
to have a basket to carry water	(= to have a nearly impossible task)
to want to die laughing	(= to be extremely amused)
to have to call somebody uncle	(= to be the person's nephew or niece)
"I'm there!"	(in reply to the greeting "How are you?")
	(2nd person plural pronoun)

each of which may be shown to be an exact or near calque, often from more than one African language.

Purely lexical remainders from African languages have been left for last since these, the most obvious *apports* identifiable today have been the subject of more common attention and therefore require simpler comment in the present paper. Moreover, the appearance of the brilliant historical

Dictionary of Jamaican English (1967) has minimized the necessity today of listing surviving African words still to be found at folk level in the Caribbean. A count of the words in that dictionary whose etymology has been either clearly identified as African or indicated as likely to be has produced 473 cases out of an estimated 15,000 entries, or just about 3 percent. The low proportion is significant but, in the historical, social and educational circumstances, does not need to be explained. The same percentage probably applies roughly to other Caribbean territories here and there, with significant exceptions—again for historical reasons—such as Barbados, where traces have been more massively eroded. It is the near absence of this evidence of African survivals in the New World that has led superficial investigations into serious misjudgments and misled educators in the Anglophone territories into thinking that the English superstructure had totally suppressed the African linguistic presence, so that the learning of English needed only the educational routines designed in England. But the truth, far from this, is that the lexical is about the least of the African influences, which, as we have seen, are, in the wise words of João Ribiero "rather profound."

NOTES

1. See M. J. and F. S. Herskovits, *Rebel Destiny—Among the Bush Negroes of Dutch Guiana* (New York, 1934), which discloses the depth of African culture preserved by the people living on the banks of the Saramacca River; and *Suriname Folklore* (New York, 1936), in which there is also a section of "Linguistic Notes" (pp. 117–135).

2. J. Voorhoeve, "A Project for the Study of Creole Language History in Suriname," in *Creole Language Studies II,* ed. R. B. Le Page (Macmillian, 1961) p. 105. See also the same author's "Le Tom et la grammaire dans le Saramaccan" *Word* 17 (1961).

3. Dyuka is the collective name of the Bush dialects spoken along the Mavowijne River of Suriname. See Voorhoeve, "Creole Language History," pp. 100ff.

4. Prof. Sidney W. Mintz's paper "The Socio-Historical Background to Pidginization & Creolization," in Dell Hymes, ed., *Pidginization and Creolization of Languages,* pp. 481–96, is an excellent account of the contrasting situations in these colonial societies.

5. L. D. Turner's (1949) massive evidence of Africanisms in the Gullah Dialect of the South Carolina-Georgia coast defeated such rash assertions as Prof. Krapp's (quoted by him p. 6) that "it is reasonably safe to say that not a single detail of Negro pronunciation or Negro syntax can be proved to have any other than an English origin"; but some scholars still wish to defend some of this ground.

6. Robert R. Hall, Jr. (1966:58). He however admits (p. 86) that "extensive carryovers of patterns from the substratum (native) languages" will have been

added to the "simplified versions of the fundamentally European linguistic structures" which the Creoles are.

7. João Ribiero, *O Elemento Negro,* p. 83.

8. The term *relexification"* must be credited to W. A. Stewart (1962), though others have contributed to the theory. The dominant role of a Portuguese pidgin, as an inevitable lingua franca is the nucleus of this theory.

9. See Dr. Alleyne's telling article "Acculturation and the Cultural Matrix of Creolization," in Hymes, pp. 169–86, and esp. pp. 175–6, where he argues that the relative basic homogeneity of the cultural area of West Africa would have had "correlates" in the linguistic deep-structure.

10. Even those who are openly suspicious of the "Portuguese pidgin" hypothesis seem ready to concede, like Dr. Alleyne (ibid., p. 175) that "the African community saw it in their interests to learn the languages of the European."

11. It is a well-known and widely encountered feature of the West African languages (see, for example, Turner, 1949:225–27) that the nature of a "happening" (called *aspect* by the grammarians) in more important than the time of the "happening," because the time (i.e., "tense") in such cases is already determined by "present" contextual reference and "present" situational factors so that the verb, doing what is properly a lexical job of signaling "nature" rather than "time," often needs no morphological or "tense" change at all, or only a change in syllabic pitch. Also, the only vocabulary there is is actually functional, there being no provision for "lexical sedimentation," which writing permits (Alexandre, 1972:32). It is to such characteristics that I refer in the term *actuality.* Related to this are the "performance" factors of pitch-differentiation (in "tone" languages, which are very common in West Africa) and the immediacy of the operation which a speech event is, in contrast to a written "event"—that is, there is no provision in oral cultures for the maturation of a speech event that writing permits; and it is a fair question whether *performance*—in the linguistic sense, as distinct from the speaker's ultimate grammatical *competence*—is differently, more deeply, developed in oral than in scribal cultures. Another point is that multilingualism—another set of calls on a speaker's "performance"—is an old habit of West African cultures (Alexandre, 1972: 16–17) in contrast with monolinguistic European cultures.

12. These are the terms which Hymes, De Camp, and Whinnom among others use in their papers in Hymes, pp. 4, 23, 107.

13. In his article "Tracing the Pidgin Element in Jamaican Creole," in Hymes, pp. 203–221.

14. Ian Hancock, "Provisional Comparison of the English-derived Atlantic Creoles," in Hymes, pp. 287–291.

15. In his introductory article in Hymes, p. 20.

16. "The Notion of System in Creole Languages" in Hymes pp. 447–472.

17. Hall's view (1966:116) that "half a century is, if anything a long time in the time-perspective of pidgin languages" is not contested in principle by other scholars.

18. In a note in Hymes, p. 189.

19. Cassidy, in Hymes, p. 203.

20. Prof. Albert Valdman of Indiana University, in a note describing "The Language Situation in Haiti" in Hymes, p. 61.

21. I am indebted to the following very gracious informants, native speakers of the languages, for the data given, though any faults in the presentation must be attributed to me:

Mbye Cham	- Wolof
Momo Bangura	- Mende
Jonathan Ndagi	- Nupe
Ungina Ndoma	- Kikongo
Yamvu Makasu A M'Toba	- Ki-Yaka
Obi Mazombwe	- Ci-Nyanja

For a typographical facility I have used the ẹ, °, ⁿ, to represent the phonemes / / / / / / where they occur. Tone has not been marked.

22. "It also became evident that . . . the grammar of European tongues bore a relation to our 'Western' or 'European' culture. And it appeared that the interrelation brought in those large subsummations of experience by language, such as our own terms 'time,' 'space,' 'substance,' and 'matter.' Since, with respect to the traits compared, there is little difference between English, French, German, or other European languages with the possible (but doubtful) exception of Balto-Slavic and non-Indo-European, I have lumped these languages into one group called SAE or 'Standard Average European.'"—B.L. Whorf (ed. Carroll, 1956: 138).

23. In Hymes, p. 293.

24. Ibid., p. 289.

25. Ibid., p. 478.

26. Phonemic pitch (which is typically African) must not, of course, be confused with phonemic stress (which is typically English). A full treatment of pitch-differentiation of homonyms, especially in Guyanese English, is given in my (forthcoming) "Some Suprasegmental Features of Caribbean English and their Relevance in the Classroom." Some of the examples that follow are taken from that paper.

BIBLIOGRAPHY

Alexandre, P. *Languages and Language in Black Africa,* trans. F. A. Leary. (Chicago: Northwestern U. Press), 1972.

Armstrong, R. *The Study of West African Languages,* (Ibadan U. Press) 1964.

Bailey, B. L. *Jamaican Creole Syntax,* Cambridge, 1966.

Cabrera, L. *Anago: Vocabulario Lucumi.* (Havana), 1957.

Cassidy, F. G. *Jamaica Talk* (London: Macmillan), 1961.

———. "Toward the Recovery of Early English-African Pidgin," *Symposium on Multilingualism* (Brazzaville, 1962) (CSA/CCTA Publ. No. 87), London: Commission de Cooperation Technique en Afrique, 1964.

——— and Le Page, R. *Dictionary of Jamaican English* (Cambridge), 1967.

Christaller, J. G. *A Grammar of the Asante and Fante Language called Twi.* Basel: Gregg Reprint, 1964, 1875.

David, B. and Jardel, J. P. *Les Proverbes Créole de la Martinique.* C.E.R.A.G., 1969.

Focke, H. *Neger-Engelsch Woordenbock,* Leiden, 1855.

Goilo, E. *Papiamentu Textbook,* (Aruba, N.A.: de Wit), 1962.

Greenberg, J. *The Languages of Africa,* Mouton: IJAL Monograph 25, 1966.

Hall, R. A., Jr. *Pidgin and Creole Languages,* Cornell, 1966.

Hymes, Dell, (ed.) *Pidginization and Creolization of Languages,* Cambridge, 1971.

Navarro R. Tomas, T. "Observaciones sobre el Papiamento," *Nueva revista de filologia hispanica* 7 (1951), (pp. 183–89).

Nazario, M. A. *El Elemento Afronegroide en el Espanol de Puerto Rico.* San Juan, 1961.

Oritz, F. *Glosario de Afronegrismos.* Havana, 1924.

Ribiero, J. *O Elemento Negro: Historia—Folklore—Linguistica.* Rio de Janeiro, 1939.

Rowlands, E. *Teach Yourself Yoruba,* English U. Press, 1969.

de Senna, N. *Africanos No Brasil.* Bello Horizonte, 1938.

Steward W. A. "Creole Languages in the Caribbean," in *Study of the Role of Second Languages,* ed. F. A. Rice. Washington: C.A.L., 1962.

Taylor, D. "Structural Outline of Caribbean Creole," *Word* 7 (1951): 43–59.

———. "Language Shift of Changing Relationship," LJAL 26(2) (1960): 155–61.

———. "The Origin of West Indian Creole Languages: Evidence from Grammatical Categories," *American Anthropologist,* 65(4) (1963): 800–814.

Turner, L. D. *Africanisms in the Gullah Dialect.* U. Chicago Press, (1963), 1949.

Weinreich, U. "On the Compatibility of Genetic Relationship and Convergent Development," *Word* 14 (1958).

6

The African Presence
in Caribbean Literature[1]

Edward kamau Brathwaite

in december to about april every year, a drought visits the islands. the green canefields take on the golden deciduous crispness of scorched parchment. the blue sky burns muted. the dry air rivets the star nights with metallic cold. it is our tropical winter. this dryness, unexplained, is put down to 'lack of rain.'

but living in st lucia at this time, i watched this drought drift in towards the island, moving in across the ocean from the east, obscuring martinique, obscuring sails beating towards castries and i suddenly realized that what i was witnessing—that milky haze, that sense of dryness—was something i had seen and felt before in ghana. it was the seasonal dust-cloud, drifting out of the great ocean of sahara—the harmattan. by an obscure miracle of connection, this arab's nomad wind, cracker of fante wood a thousand miles away, did not die on the sea-shore of west africa, its continental limit; it drifted on, reaching the new world archipelago to create our drought, imposing an african season on the caribbean sea. and it was on these winds too, and in this season, that the slave ships came from guinea, bearing my ancestors to this other land. . . .[2]

Even before the first slaves came—bringing, perhaps, Precolumbian explorers[3]—there was the wind: an implacable climatic, indeed, geological connection. Along its routes and during its seasonal blowing, fifteen to fifty million Africans were imported into the New World,[4] coming to constitute a majority of people in the Caribbean, and significant numbers in the New World.

Transference and Adaptation

Now there is a persistent, established theory which contends that the Middle Passage destroyed the culture of these people, that it was such a catastrophic, definitive experience that none of those transported during the period from 1540 to 1840 escaped trauma.[5] But modern research is pointing to a denial of this,[6] showing that African culture not only crossed the Atlantic, it crossed, survived, and creatively adapted itself to its new environment. Caribbean culture was therefore not "pure" African, but an adaptation carried out mainly in terms of African tradition. This we can

This essay is dedicated to John La Rose.

determine by looking at what anthropologists have called its culture-focus. This concept posits that each culture has a distinguishing style or characteristic; it may be sun-centered or acephalous, ceremonial or casual, materialistic or contemplative. And everyone agrees that the focus of African culture in the Caribbean was religious.

The anti-African argument claims, however, that it was *only* religion that the slaves brought with them, and a religion already tending more to fetish and superstitition than to theology and ethics, and therefore weak and unviable. They claim (and their twists of evidence would fill a whole paper in itself) that the slave had no philosophy, no military organization, no social life, no family structure, no arts, no sense of personal or civic responsibility.[7]

I fundamentally disagree with this view which I consider based (and biased) on (1) mistaken notions of culture, culture change, and culture transference; (2) untenable, sometimes ignorant, concepts of African culture; (3) a lack of intimacy with traditional African culture (most of those who have written on Africa have been European scholars, with both intellectual and interpersonal problems relating to Africa); and (4) an almost total ignorance of Afro-American folk culture.[8] Until sensitive *African* scholars begin to contribute to the study of New World and Caribbean folk cultures, the presence of African elements within this subculture is bound, for fairly obvious reasons, to remain obscure. How can we explain the success of the Haitian Revolution, for instance, unless we consider it a triumph of Afro-Caribbean folk arts and culture over European mercantilism? Toussaint was a slave (a coachman) and an herbalist, not an academy-drilled, socially motivated vaulter like Napoleon.

Religious Focus

The story really begins in the area of religious culture-focus already mentioned. A study of African culture[9] reveals almost without question that it is based upon religion—that, in fact, it is within the religious network that the entire culture resides. Furthermore, this entire culture is an organic whole. In traditional Africa, there is no specialization of disciplines, no dissociation of sensibilities. In other words, starting from this particular religious focus, there is no separation between religion and philosophy, religion and society, religion and art. Religion is the form of kernel or core of the culture. It is therefore not surprising that anthropologists tell us that African culture survived in the Caribbean through religion. What we should alert ourselves to is the possibility, whenever "religion" is mentioned, that a whole cultural complex is also present. Of course we have to take into account the depredations and fragmentations imposed upon African culture by the slave trade and plantation systems; but this should not alter our perception of the whole.

Emancipation

This African culture, focused upon a religious core which survived and flourished under slavery, came under very severe attack at emancipation. Under slavery, it had been possible for plantation slaves—those not immediately or always under the surveillance of the master—to continue practicing their religion and therefore their culture, or at least those elements of it that had survived under the conditions—elements signaled by things like drum, dance, *obeah*,* song, tale, and herb. At emancipation, however, all this came under attack from a number of quarters.

In the first place, the missionaries were naturally against African or African-oriented religious practices among their ex-African adherents. Hence the banning of the drum (voice of god or worship: *nyame*—one of three Akan names for the Supreme Being); the gradual replacement of African foods and foodstyles *(nyam†/yam)* by European or Creole substitutes, and the Christianization of names (*nommo*—Bantu for the Word) and ideas *(nam)*. It was possible after emancipation to do this more and more effectively because there was no longer the legal restriction on missionary activity that had existed under slavery. Slowly the ex-slaves began to lose or disown the most crucial elements of their culture in the very area where it was most important and venerable. They began, in other words, to go to churches and chapels rather than to beat their drums.

Second, the process of education began—first clerical, then secular,

---

*The African religious complex, despite its homogeneity, has certain interrelated divisions or specializations: (1) "worship"—an essentially Eurochristian word that doesn't really describe the African situation, in which the congregation is not a passive one entering into a monolithic relationship with a superior god, but an active community which celebrates in song and dance the incarnation of powers/spirits *(orishá loa)* into one or several of themselves. This is therefore a social (interpersonal and communal), artistic (formal/improvisatory choreography of movement/sound) and eschatological (possession) experience, which erodes the conventional definition/description of "worship"; (2) *rites de passage;* (3) divination; (4) healing; and (5) protection. *Obeah* (the word is used in Africa and the Caribbean) is an aspect of the last two of these subdivisions, though it has come to be regarded in the New World and in colonial Africa as sorcery and "black magic." One probable tributary to this view was the notion that a great deal of "prescientific" African medicine was (and is) at best psychological, at norm mumbo-jumbo/magical in nature. It was not recognized, in other words, that this "magic" was (is) based on a scientific knowledge and use of herbs, drugs, foods and symbolic/associational procedures (pejoratively termed *fetishistic*), as well as on a homoeopathic understanding of the material and divine nature of Man *(nam)* and the ways in which this could be affected. The principle of *obeah* is, therefore, like medical principles everywhere, the process of healing/protection through seeking out the source or explanation of the cause (*obi*/evil) of the disease or fear. This was debased by slave master/missionary/prospero into an assumption, inherited by most of us, that *obeah* deals *in* evil. In this way, not only has African science been discredited, but Afrocaribbean religion has been negatively fragmented and almost (with exceptions in Haiti and Brazil) publicly destroyed. To properly understand *obeah*, therefore, we shall have to restore it to its proper place in the Afroamerican communion complex: *kumina-custom-myal-obeah-fetish.*

†West African (Mende, Ashanti, etc.) and Afrocaribbean for "food," or "to eat."

but always colonial. Depending on who owned the territory, the ex-slaves were to be molded into the British or the French or the Spanish system. They began to learn to read and write so that they were diverted from the oral tradition of their inheritance; they became literate in a language which was foreign to them, "liberated" into a culture which was not theirs. They began, in other words, to read about Versailles and cake and Lord Nelson and Robin Hood and all those frescoes which, some time ago, the Mighty Sparrow‡ de-celebrated in his calypso, "Dan Is the Man in the Van." At the same time, there was no countervailing influence to help them learn about their own tradition. This of course did not "have to" happen. It is conceivable that this education could have been truly bicultural, so that, who knows, we might have struggled through Asante Twi and the Zulu epics as well as French, Latin, and Anglo-Saxon. However, under the dictates of mercantilism, education had a more monolithic and materialistic aim: control of the ex-slaves for the profit of their labor.

Third, since the object of the plantocracy was to retain its wall of social and political authority in the Caribbean, it supported these two "missionary" drives with social legislation designed to prevent the former slaves from achieving very much in the community. Their voting rights were restricted, their socioeconomic mobility curtailed, and their way of life brought under subtle but savage attack. *Shango, cumfa, kaiso,* tea-meeting, *susu, jamette*-carnivals§—all had to go.

The situation has been very slow to change. The law banning *cumfa* in Suriname was only rescinded in 1971,[10] and it is not unlikely that, technically at least, laws against *shango, bongo, poco,*[11] and *obeah* are still in force in the region. Recently, for instance, Dr. Eric Williams, Prime Minister of Trinidad and Tobago and author of the radical antimercantilist dissertation, *Capitalism and Slavery,*[12] remarked with sardonic disap-

---

‡The name used by Slinger Francisco, the most talented and popular calypsonion of recent times. Sparrow has dominated the calypso art form since the 1950s.

§*Shango:* an Afrocaribbean form of worship, centered mainly on Shango, the Yoruba god of thunder and creativity, and most closely associated with the island of Trinidad.

Cumfa: one of the possession dance/ceremonies of the New World found under this name mainly in the Guianas. In Jamaica, it is known as *kumina.*

Kaiso: an early form/word for calypso.

Tea-meeting: a speech contest and exhibition, at which syntactical logic is increasingly abandoned or transcended. A kind of possession by the Word.

Susu: Yoruba/Caribbean word for cooperative group.

Jamette-carnival: Jamet, supposedly French Creole for *diametre* (literally, "the other half"), was a term applied in Trinidad to the underworld of prostitutes, rudies, and, by extension, the black poor. The *jamette*-carnivals were obscured by the establishment on grounds of "obscenity" (first routes, then hours of performance were restricted, until these "ole mas" bands could appear only in the foreday morning—*jou'vert*—of the first day), and thus became a *maroon* feature of the culture—a dark area of celebration where the folk expressed themselves without much reference to middle-class inhibitions and styles. *Mokojumbies, jonkonnus, calindas* (stick-fight dancers) and nation-bands (Shango, Congo, etc.) were other features of this carnival.

proval that he didn't think it would be long before the *obeah* man would be rehabilitated in the Caribbean.[13] Such is the success of the Europhone establishment at devaluing African culture in the New World. Not surprisingly then, the teaching of African history at the University of the West Indies has been, to say the least, spasmodic. The subject's most distinguished native scholar, Walter Rodney, was cashiered from Jamaica in 1968[14] and there has been no continuity of instruction since then. African *culture* is not "taught" or even thought of at all, a fact reflected in the dearth of books, records, films, and lectures on these matters available to the public. Moreover, when an individual or group protests about this or tries to *do* something about it, a multiracial howl goes up. The protesters are accused of overemphasis on Africa (!) and asked to remember that they are Dominicans, Bahamians, or what have you, with their own distinctive (!) and locally rooted (?) cultures. In August, 1973, for instance, a Bajan cultural group, Yoruba House, commemorated Emancipation/Freedom Day by issuing a number of awards in the arts—the first such recorded in Barbados or indeed in the Anglophone Caribbean. These were not awarded on the basis of annual competition/performances but in consideration of contributions to the discovery, recognition, and status of the African presence in the community. On this, the island's (then) only newspaper felt it necessary to editorialize:

> Our heritage is the result of exposure to many cultures, with some having a greater influence than others. It is because of this greater influence which has been mainly of British origin in Barbados, that much of our African heritage has become submerged or even diluted to the extent that it can no longer be identified as such. . . .[15]

With Africa, then, diluted, even submerged, and certainly safely out of the way, the article goes on to salvage from the cultural wreck the multiracial (Creole) notion of "Caribbean": "not totally European, nor is it pure African." it also referred to extremists who "become fanatical in their thinking about things African" (one wonders where or when!), warns against "emotionalism" sweeping into the discussion, and finally concedes that Yoruba could play "a big part in bringing into proper perspective what we owe to the African side of our heritage." My contention is that the creation of this "proper perspective" requires more than lip service from the establishment. It requires information, and an educational program based on a revolutionized value system.

Religious Continuity

On the eve of the Morant Bay Rebellion, thirty years after emancipation, there was a "strange" movement in Jamaica which, significantly, took the form of a religious revival. Social and political unrest centered in the

Baptist churches, which the slaves had always preferred, mainly because of the "African" nature of their adult baptism and the comparative freedom of their communal worship.[16] Especially militant were the Black or Native Baptist churches, started at the time of the American Revolution when loyalist colonists fled from what was to become the United States with faithful slaves or ex-slaves, some of whom (George Leile, Moses Baker) were helped or encouraged by their masters to spread the gospel of Christ on the island.[17] As a result, certain churches shifted away from a Euro-American kind of organization into congregations that were not only run by Blacks, but included African religious elements into their services. In 1865, on the verge of the Rebellion (in fact a symptom and symbol of it), there was a sudden proliferation of these churches.

This was followed by an even more "startling" phenomenon—the public reappearance of *myalism,** which had no connection whatever with Christianity. *Myal*[18] is a fragmented form of African religion expressing, through dreams, visions, prophesying, and possession dances *(kumina†),* what the establishment called "hysteria" and later *pocomania:* "a little madness."[19] Thousands of black Jamaicans became involved in this revival which ranged from "left wing" Christian (Baptist) to Afro-Jamaican radical or anarchic *(myal).* The Rebellion itself was a militant political movement closely related to these. The leaders, Mulatto George William Gordon and Black Paul Bogle, pastors of Baptist and Black Baptist churches respectively, worked in close alliance. Bogle (like Toussaint, and Sam Sharpe later) probably carried the *myal* title of "Daddy" *(Dada)* as well, although more research will have to be done to confirm this. At present we know next to nothing about him,[20] but there is evidence[21] that some of his followers took oaths and drank rum and gunpowder, leading some contemporary observers to speak of "the supernatural workings of Satanic temptation."[22] There was also an emphasis on color ("We must cleave unto the black")—all of which suggests that a radical Afro-*myal* movement underlay the more liberal/reformist Creole concern with justice and land.[23] Elements similar to this were present in the ferment surrounding Cuffee in Guyana (1763), Dessalines in Haiti (1799 to 1800), Bussa in Barbados (1816) and Nat Turner in the United States (1831), so that we witness again and again a chain reaction moving the ex-African's core of religion into ever-widening areas. It is this potential for explosion and ramification that has made blackness such a radical if subterranean feature of plantation political culture; for the African "phenomenon," continuously present, like a bomb, in the New World since the abduction of the first slaves—a phenomenon subsisting in bases

---

**Myal:* divination aspect of Afrocaribbean religion. The term is most commonly associated with Jamaica.

†*Kumina:* Afrojamaican possession/dance ceremony, similar to *cufa* in the Guianas.

deep within the Zion/Ethiopian churches of the United States[24] and in the *hounforts*‡ of the Caribbean and South America—triggers itself into visibility at each moment of crisis in the hemisphere: 1790 in Haiti, 1860 in Jamaica, 1930 in the West Indies, and 1960 in the New World generally.

II

I cannot maintain that African continuities are as easily traced in our literature as in the social/ideological world I have so far described. This does not mean there is no African presence in Caribbean/New World writing. It simply means that because of its almost inevitable involvement with the establishment through education, communication and sales processing (mercantilism), much of what we have come to accept as "literature" is work which ignores, or is ignorant of, its African connection and aesthetic.

Until, therefore, our definition of "culture" is reexamined in terms of its totality, not simply its Europeanity, we will fail to discover a literature of negritude and with it, a literature of local authenticity.[25] Likewise, the African presence in Caribbean literature cannot be fully or easily perceived until we redefine the term "literature" to include the nonscribal material of the folk/oral tradition, which, on examination, turns out to have a much longer history than our scribal tradition, to have been more relevant to the majority of our people, and to have had unquestionably wider provenance. In other words, while a significant corpus of "prose" and "poetry" has been created—and read—by a few pesons in the major Antilles; folk song, folk tale, proverb, and chant are found *everywhere* without fear or favor and are enjoyed by all. It is from "the guitars of the people," as Nicolás Guillén recently put it, that the "*son* went to the salons of the aristocracy,"[26] With this re/vision in mind, we see an African literature in the Caribbean beginning to reveal itself.

Slavery

On the eve of emancipation, at a *crise de conscience,* when the European planters in the West Indies were becoming aware of the *plural society*[27] developing around them and conscious of the need, if they were to retain their hegemony, to destroy, subvert, psychologically control the Black majority, a few books began to appear which described slaves in terms of their own culture.[28]

The most outstanding example in English is a novel, anonymously written called *Hamel the Obeah Man* (1827), which for the first time

‡Name given in Haiti to the compound (courtyard and buildings) where *vodun* services are conducted.

describes a slave, Hamel, as a complex human being. In order to do this, the author had to give him a cultural context, and, significantly, he chose a cultural context based on his *obeah—obeah* seen not as a debasement but as a form of African religion of which he was a priest. Hamel was placed in ideological opposition to a white missionary. The plot of the book is, in fact, designed as a struggle between the white missionary and the African priest. Out of a personal sense of loyalty, Hamel uses his *obeah* to support righteous planter against subversive missionary. Nevertheless, Hame's intransigent opposition to the institution of slavery is clearly established. It is suggested that, had he, rather than the missionary, fomented the slave revolt which climaxes the novel, it would have been practically uncontrollable. The book, in other words, is an antimissionary tract. But it is also a remarkable act of fiction (for its genre) in that Hamel is seen "whole," with real doubts and passions, and so provides some insight into the West Indian slave experience.[29]

After emancipation, due to the sociocultural disengagement between Black and White, there were no further works by White/Creole writers, even approaching the standard of *Hamel.* Since 1900 there has been a certain reappearance of the White writer: H. G. DeLisser (Jamaica), Alfred Mendes and Ian McDonald (Trinidad), J. B. Emtage and Geoffrey Drayton (Barbados), Phyllis Shand Allfrey and Jean Rhys (Dominica), and Christopher Nicole (Guyana), to name perhaps the most important.[30] But with the exception of DeLisser in *Jane's Career,* none of these writers has (yet) become centrally concerned with Caribbean Africans (or Indians); most of them (again with the exception of *Jane's Career*) seem romantic, while a few are the opposite—callous (Mendes in *Pitch Lake*) or just plain boorish (Emtage)—and betray what Kenneth Ramchand, using a phrase of Fanon's, has called "terrified consciousness."[31]

Indigenism/Negrismo

The above, however, is not intended in any way to exclude White West Indian writers from our literary canon. In fact, in another study,[32] I have attempted to show how the work of Roger Mais, a "White" Jamaican, could in many ways act as a model for our developing critical aesthetics. But the majority of White West Indian writers, it seems to me, are not yet prepared to allow their art to erode the boundaries set up around their minds by the physical/metaphysical plantation, and so do not yet recognize that their world has become marginal to the majority sense of local reality; or rather, that the plantation has transformed itself into other, new mercantilist forms, in which they are enslaved as surely as the descendants of their former bondsmen. It is only when this comes to them as crisis, it seems to me, that the White West Indian writers will find their voice.

The postemancipation period, therefore, has been one of literary hiatus. Caribbean (written) literature, as truly native enterprise and expression, does not begin, in fact, until, in response to the American occupation of the Greater Antilles,[33] certain artists in Cuba and Puerto Rico began to develop distinctive literary, and creative forms that have come to be called indigenism and *negrismo*. This is interesting because the populations of these two territories are predominantly ex-Spanish, rather than ex-African. Unlike those in the rest of the Caribbean, the majority in Cuba and Puerto Rico is "White" rather than "Black" Creole. Nevertheless, the literary expression which came out of these White Creoles (and Mulattoes) was Black-based; they recognized that the only form of expression which could be used as a protest, or an authentic *alter/native,* to American cultural imperialism, was ex-African. This is at least part of what the Cuban thinker Juan Marinello had in mind in the 1930s when he said that due to the extinction of the Amerindians and the fact that they had left "no architecture or literature," the Negro had assumed a "specific significance." "Here the Negro is marrow and root, the breath of the people, a music heard, [an] irrepressible impulse. He may, in these times of change, be the touchstone of our poetry.[34]

Crisis/Response

The best way to understand this in its fullest literary sense—one, that is, which includes the oral tradition—is to see it and the other expressions of the African presence which followed as responses to White cultural imperalism. During slavery, White cultural imposition was responded to with worksong, gospel, blues, the spiritual, *mento* (a secular Jamaican folk song form), *shanto* (the word in Guyana for *mento*), *shango* hymn, a folk tale. The postemancipation crisis saw a certain erosion of folk tales, especially in the more urbanized areas, but it saw the entrenchment of the literature of the *hounfort*. Urban immigration, from the end of the nineteenth century, saw the formation of Black ghettos and the emergence of a new urban folk art—the dozens, urban blues, new urban shouter churches, the Harlem Renaissance, Garveyite creative work,* Rastafari,† the Nation of Islam, and Carnival.

The crisis of American imperialism brought us Price-Mars and Hippo-

*Marcus Garvey was one of the first Black leaders to begin the resuscitation of self-help folk entertainment, especially in the urban ghettos.

†The Rastafari are a dynamic and distinctive ("dreadlocked") group in Jamaica, who consider themselves Africans, recognize the Emperor Haile Selassie as the Living God, and declare it their certain destiny to return to Africa (I-tiopia). As such—a kind of modern maroon group—they refuse to acknowledge the materialistic governments of Babylon. Rastafari art (including song, dance, drum, music, poetry, painting, carving, craftwork, and above all word/symbols) is revitalizing Jamaican folk culture, and their philosophy and lifestyle are already beginning to reach Black communities elsewhere.

lyte and Jacques Roumain in Haiti, José Martí and *negrismo* in the Spanish Antilles and, in a way, the international emergence of the calypso in Trinidad.[35] The crisis of European imperialism, as reflected in World War II, produced the *negritude* of the French-speaking expatriate colonials as well as a more locally based *tigritude*[36] literature in the Black colonies of Africa and the Caribbean. The recent crisis of neocolonialism and indigenous disillusionment has seen the Black Power movement and its various ramifications, the explosion of urban folk in Jamaica and the United States, the reemergence of "native" churches, a certain revitalization of calypso, and a generally increased awareness of the authenticity of folk forms. And as the Carifesta Revolution (1972) in Guyana clearly demonstrated, these Caribbean folk forms continue to be uniquely, vitally, and creatively African in form, rhythm, and soul.[37]

III

There are four kinds of written African literature in the Caribbean. The first is *rhetorical*. The writer uses Africa as mask, signal, or *nomen*. He doesn't know very much about Africa necessarily, although he reflects a deep desire to make connection. But he is only saying the word "Africa" or invoking a dream of the Congo, Senegal, Niger, the Zulu, Nile, or Zambesi. He is not necessarily celebrating or activating the African presence. There are also elements of this romantic rhetoric within the other three categories. The second is what I call *the literature of African survival*, a literature which deals quite consciously with African survivals in Caribbean society, but without necessarily making any attempt to interpret or reconnect them with the great tradition of Africa. Third, there is what I call *the literature of African expression*, which has its root in the folk, and which attempts to adapt or transform folk material into literary experiment. Finally, there is *the literature of reconnection*, written by Caribbean (and New World) writers who have lived in Africa and are attempting to relate that experience to the New World, or who are consciously reaching out to rebridge the gap with the spiritual heartland.

Rhetorical Africa

> Tambour
> quand tu résonne,
> mon âme hurle vers l'Afrique.
> Tantôt,
> je rêve d'une brousse immense
> baignée de lune,
> où s'echevellent de suantes nudités.
> Tantôt
> à une case immonde
> où je savoure du sang dans des crânes humains.

Drum
when you make sound
my soul curls back to Africa.
Sometimes
I dream of a great moonlit forest
alive with leaping nudes.
Sometimes
there is a simple hut
where I drink blood out of human skulls.[38]

Carl Brouard

There are many such poems in this category, among them work by Daniel Thaly of Dominica/Haiti, Pales Matos of Puerto Rico, Claude McKay and George Campbell of Jamaica, and E. M. Roach of Tobago. Perhaps the most famous, a romantic/rhetorical poem as distinct from but still connected to the primitive/rhetorical tradition of Brouard and Pales Matos, is the Black American Countee Cullen's "Heritage":

What is Africa to me:
Copper sun or scarlet sea,
Jungle star or jungle track,
Strong bronzed men, or regal black
Women from whose loins I sprang
When the birds of Eden sang. . . .[39]

In the Anglophone Caribbean, this is echoed in poems like Philip Sherlock's "Jamaican Fisherman":

Across the sand I saw a black man stride
To fetch his fishing gear and broken things,
And silently that splendid body cried
Its proud descent from ancient chiefs and kings. . . .[40]

It is this kind of concern, persistent from the earliest days of Black New World expression, which finally feeds into and influences the literature of rehabilitation and reconnection:

C'est le lent chemin de Guinée
La mort t'y conduire. . . .[41]

Jacques Roumain

In general, however, rhetorical literature is static, wishful and willful in nature. Although it betrays a significant instinct for Africa, the instinct is based on ignorance and often, in the case of Brouard and his generation and class, on received European notions of "darkest Africa." Louise Bennett was quite right in humorously rejecting that kind of reconnection:

Back to Africa Miss Matty?
Yuh noh know wha yuh dah-say?
Yuh haffe come from some weh fus,
Before yuh go back deh?[42]

From this attraction/ignorance too, springs the sense, as in Leon Laleau[43] and Derek Walcott,[44] that the two cultures present a dichotomy and that one must choose between them. Dantès Bellegarde, a leader in the early 1940s of one of Haiti's anti-Africanist groups, held that "We belong to Africa by our blood, and to France by our spirit and by a significant proportion of our blood."[45] In Andrew Salkey's novel, *A Quality of Violence,* the debate is expressed as follows:

> We not frighten by white fowl talk or Africa or slave power! We don't belong to them things. . . . We is people who live on the land in St Thomas, not Africa. . . . We is no slave people, and there is no Africa in we blood the way you would-a like we to believe. . . .
>
> But you wrong, Miss Mellie. Me and you and the rest-a-people in St Thomas all belong to the days that pass by when slavery was with the land. Everybody is part of slavery days, is a part of the climate-a-Africa and the feelings in the heart is Africa feelings that beating there, far down. . . .[46]

In contrast, we have the *acceptance* of this dual cultural inheritance by a poet like the Cuban Mulatto Nicolás Guillén.

> We have been together from long ago
> young and old,
> blacks and whites, all mixed,
> one commanding and the other commanded,
> all mixed;
> San Berenito and another commanded,
> all mixed . . .
> Santa Maria and another commanded,
> all mixed
> all mixed

But always there is the refrain with its positive recognition of Africa:

> I am yoruba, I am lucumi,
> mandingo, congo, carabali. . . .[47]

The Literature of African Survival

The literature of African survival inheres most surely and securely in the folk tradition—in folk tale, folksong, proverb, and much of the litany of the *hounfort*. Here, for example, is a *marassa* (spirit twins) lament from a *vodun** ceremony:

Vodun is the largest and most public African-derived (Dahomey: *vodu*) religious form in the Caribbean, centered in Haiti. See also *shango* (in Trinidad), *poco* (in Jamaica), *santería* (in Cuba) and the *candomblé* or *macumba* (in Brazil). Often, in this text, the term *vodun* is used to apply to Afro-New World religions generally. In the culture of Dahomey, from which Haitian *vodun* is derived, twins are held in special reverence. In *vodun*, they are apotheosized as *marassa* (spirit twins).

Marassa élo, I have no mother here who can speak for me
Marassa élo
I have left my mother in Africa
Marassa élo
I have left my family in Africa
I have no family to speak for me
I have no relations to speak for me
Marassa élo[48]

The connection between this and African elegies is obvious; as is the connection with African lamentations in "New ships," "Tano," and "Wake" from my own *Masks* and *Islands*.[49] There is also, in the *hounfort*, the use of language based upon what are often only fragmented phonetics of an ancestral African tongue, as in this *shango* hymn to Ajaja:

Ay ree ah jaja
Ay ree leh
Ah jaja wo goon
Ajaja way geh

which has been interpreted to mean

We are searching for you
Wherever you are
Show yourself
We want to see you
We are searching for you
Come let us speak to you
We call you, we speak to you
Wherever you are[50]

Similarly from Jamaican *kumina* comes this poem in which *so-so* means water, and *kuwidi* means "call *(ku)* the dead *(widi)*."

Tange lange Jeni di gal eva
Wang lang mama o
Di le kuwidi pange le
So-so lange widi gal
So-so lange mama o

Dance tall Jenny gal
Walk tall mama o
The dead come to greet you
Water long like the dead, gal
Water long, mama o[51]

In "William Saves His Sweetheart," the folk imagination is again concerned with water,[52] but this time its expression is entirely in intransigent non-English or, as I prefer to call it, *nation-language*, since Africans in the New World always referred to themselves as belonging to certain *nations* (Congo, Kromantee, etc.)[53] Here there are no African word-fragments or phrases as in the *hounfort,* but the tonal shape of the language, its rhythm changes, structure, contours of thought and image, eruption into song/dance/movement, make it clearly recognizable as African speech-form:

an a so dem doo. dem kal de gal, an she kom. an im seh, yu nyaam mi peas tiday? him seh, nuo ma, me no heat non. Him seh, aa'right, kom, we go doun-a golli-ya. we wi' faen out. him tiek di gal an im go doun-a di golli, an when going doun too di golli, im go op pan im laim tree, an im pick trii laim. im guo in-a fowl ness, im tiek trii eggs . . . an im staat, an haal im suod . . . an im go goun-a di golli. im pu-doun di gal in-a di lebble drai golli, an seh, *see ya! tan op deh.* mi de-go tell yu now, ef yo heat mipeas, yu de-go drounded, bot if yu nou heat ih, nottn wuon doo yu. so swie, yu bitch! swier! seh yu no heat ih, while yo nuo yu heat ih. an she lik doun wan-a di laim a-doti so, wam! an di drai golli pomp op wata, kova di gal instep. de gal sah, *mai! puo mi wan!* a-whe me deh go-do tiday? him seh, *swie! swie!* yu bitch! an im lik doun wan nedda laim so, *wam,* an di wata mount di gal to im knee. di gal seh

laad ooi! mi wilyam ooi!

ih im sweethaat im de-kal

mi wilyam ooi!
puo mi wan ooi! peas ooi!
oo, mi dearess wilyam oo
rin doun peas oi ai! a rin doun!
oo, rin doun[54]

There is also considerable metaphysical life and symbolic association contained and hidden away in some of the folksongs and poems that have been preserved, often accidentally. Take this French Creole song, for instance, "Three Leaves, Three Roots," about change and timelessness:

Trois fé trois ci-tron oh!
Trois fé trois ra-cine oh!

Moin dit, rwo, youn jour ou wa be-soin moin!
Trois fé trois ra-cine oh!

Moin dit oui, youn jour ou wa be-soin moin!
Gain'-yain bas-sin moin

trois ra-cine tom-bé la-dans
Quand ou wa 'bli-é

fau' ra-mas-sé chon-gé[55]

Similarly, there is a fragment of a charm, collected by the Jamaican historian, H. P. Jacobs, which reads:

Bear up, mi good tree, bear up!
Mi father alays cut a tree,
The green tree falls and the dry tree stands!
Shemo-limmo! mi toto! beng! beng![56]

The paradox *dry tree stands* and *green tree falls* is yet another illustration of the levels of expression possible within the folk tradition. This fragment is especially interesting because the folk/metaphysical mind can be seen working in concert with African symbolism. For *Shemo-limmo,* which is the secret name of a bull in certain Afrojamaican folk stories,[57] is also connected to *lemolemo,* the Yoruba for "locomotive"; and the locomotive has become one of the guises[58] of Shango, god of thunder and creativity, in the New World.[59]

There is very little in the written "educated" tradition which offers anything approaching these insights into our collective psyche. Seldom do our writers reach beyond descriptive rhetoric when they treat "*hounfort-happenings.*"

Most of the people on the veranda and some of those who squatted on the stones in the front yard formed a group round the three women and waited for Mother Johnson to make a statement. She asked for her bandana which she wrapped round her right forearm. She knotted it. Everybody watched her as she tucked in the loose ends and patted the bulky parts of the folds into shape.

She said: "I hope everybody see how I just tie up the bandana?" There was a chorus of muttered affirmatives. "Well," she continued, "I telling you, now, that that is the same way that somebody tie up poor, innocent Doris brain. That somebody is well beknown to all of us in St Thomas. That somebody is a selfish, class-warring, sort of house-enemy. Is a person who looking to destroy Miss T happiness and peace-a-mind." She paused for breath. She again patted the bandana, and pointing to it, she continued: "As the dead body of my husband, Dada Johnson, who everybody here did well know and like as a great prophet/'mongst us . . . I telling you, once and for all, that Miss T gal pickney, Doris, is under a spell that she can't budge from, without plenty working of the good Lawd work on her, to bring her round again."

The gathering muttered: "Oh! Jehovah! Yes, Lawd!"

Mother Johnson cleared a space on the veranda steps, and sat down.[60]

The descriptive/dramatic power of this passage is typical of the excellence of *A Quality of Violence,* but as Salkey approaches the central and most sacred experiences of the *tonelle,** his knowledge and involvement falter, to be replaced by passages that ring more of melodramatic brass than responsive silver:

Dada Johnson held a cutlass high above his head, sliced the air in wide circular movements and threw it in front of the deputy. It landed blade first. The deputy dropped the white rooster, grabbed the cutlass and also made

*The *tonelle* is the inner area of the *hounfort.* On the floor or ground are to be found the *vèvè* (symbols) of the gods to be welcomed, and at the center of the tonelle the *poteau-mitan:* stick, whip, or ladder of god.

slicing movements in the air. The chanting sisters started to gyrate once more, pummelling their stomachs with clenched fists. . . .[61]

No matter how apparently violent (and not all possessions are violent), there is nothing in the choreography of Afro-Caribbean folk religion that is uncontrolled: flung *hounsis** are softly caught; no one, except them, ever touches another, despite the complex movements and the limited space; and there is never a pulled muscle or a cricked neck.

Salkey's verbs—"grabbed," "gyrate," "pummel"—are all suddenly wrong. Or, to put it another way, the description of possession demands of the writer a choice of words, of traditions. Salkey, in the heart of the *tonelle,* opts for the Eurorational/descriptive and therefore fails to celebrate *with* his worshipers, which in turn leads to the alienation of "In one action, they gathered up their calico gowns, stooped lower to the body of the deputy and *urinated on him.*"[62] But such is the thirst of Salkey's literary ear that fragments of litany, of powerful enigmatic metaphor soon appear and give his work a new dimension in passages like the following (which gains in power when we know that in *vodun,* and Afro-Creole religion generally, the crippled [lame] god of the crossroads, Legba, is the first to be praised in the *hounfort*):

> The chanting sisters had stopped chanting but were still standing in front of Dada Johnson who was saying a silent prayer. The deputy had crawled under the meeting-table. Suddenly, the chanting sisters sprang back and cried out: "And Jonathan, Saul's son, had a son that was lame of his feet!" There was about five seconds' silence and the deputy crawled from under the meeting-table. He stood erect and raised his right hand towards the chanting sisters who screamed: "Him have the sacrifice in him hand! *See God dey!*" The deputy sprang around and faced Dada Johnson who bowed and snatched the white rooster out of his right hand. Dada Johnson said: *"Cock blood pour down like rain water! Cooking fowl is cloud! Cloud burst open and blood bring rain!"*[63]

The surreal images here (italicized) could hardly have been conceived outside the *hounfort.* And yet Salkey, like so many others caught up in the tradition of the Master, remains ambivalent in his attitude to the African presence in the Caribbean.[64] Vera Bell, in "Ancestor on the Auction Block"[65] betrays an even more direct uncertainty of response:

> Ancestor on the auction block
> Across the years your eyes seek mine
> Compelling me to look.
> I see your shackled feet

---

*The *hounsi* are servitors, usually female, of the *vodun* complex. The religious leader (invariably male) of the *hounfort* is the *houngan,* his chief female assistant, the *mambo.*

Your *primitive* black face
I see your humiliation
And turn away
Ashamed.

Across the years your eyes seek mine
Compelling me to look
Is this *mean creature* that I see
Myself?

Philip Sherlock in "Pocomania"[66] betrays this psychic dichotomy in a crucial choice of work—namely, the use of *grunt,* instead of *trump,* to describe the deep rhythmic intake/expulsion of breath which precedes possession:

Black of night and white of gown,
White of altar, black of trees,
Swing de circle wide again,
Fall an' cry, me sister, now.
Let de spirit come again,
Fling away de flesh an' bone
Let de spirit have a home.

Grunting low and in the dark,
White of gown and circling dance.
Gone today and all control,
Here the dead are in control,
Power of the past returns,
Africa among the trees,
Asia with her mysteries. . . .

Earlier in the poem, the loss of "control" under these Afro-Asian mysteries (why "Asia" isn't clear) is even more pejoratively stated:

Black Long Mountain looking down
Sees the shepherd and his flock
Dance and sing and falls away
All the civilised today. . . .

No wonder Fola, the young Black educated sister in George Lamming's *Season of Adventure,* was afraid to enter the *hounfort*[67] But what is really surprising, given the Caribbean psychocultural inheritance, is not really the fear/avoidance response with regard to the African presence in the New World, but the persistent attempts, at all levels, to deal with it. No writer in the plantation New World can, in fact, ignore "Africa" for long, though it is interesting to note that outside of literary *negrismo* circles, there has been more active and public interest in this area of our culture from historians, sociologists, and social anthropologists than from writers and artists generally.

Maroons*

One area of African survival is that of physical and psychological marronage. From the moment of arrival in the New World, the people of Africa
were concerned with response: suicide, accommodation, escape, rebellion. Escape/rebellion often led to the setting up of African communities
outside of and often in opposition to, the great Euro-Creole plantations.
In Suriname, for instance, the Njukka, Saramaccar and other groups,
usually blanketed under the term "Bush Negroes," established indepen-
dencies along the rivers and waterways of the forested Guyanese hinter-
land from the middle of the seventeenth century. In Jamaica, Maroons
quickly established themselves in five independent towns in the inaccessible Blue Mountains and Cockpit country, fighting the British almost to a
standstill in two highly organized guerrilla wars during the eighteenth
century. There are militant Black Caribs (Afro-Amerindians) in the Wind-
ward Islands, particularly St. Vincent, and significant Afro-Maroon
groups in most of the other slave islands, especially Saint Domingue
(Haiti). The most spectacular maroon community, however, was that
established at Palmares, in Brazil, in 1631, which was able to maintain its
independence (with ambassadors, traders, etc.) for over seventy years.[68]
And yet there are only two novels in English, known to me, which attempt to come to terms with even one aspect of this experience; and I
suspect that the story is very much the same in the rest of the region.
This, again, is a tribute to European brainwash. Many Caribbean writers
don't even *know* that these communities existed and that some still exist;[69]
and the few who *do* are too cut off to conjure line or metaphor from this
matrix. Of the two Anglophones who have attempted imaginative fiction
in this field, one, Namba Roy, was himself a (Jamaican) Maroon. Unfortunately, he did not attempt, in the only novel he ever wrote,[70] more than a
romantic tale of "brave warriors" and internecine conflict. Wilson Harris,
on the other hand, uses in *The Secret Ladder* the presence of an ancient
Black chieftain of the swamps to initiate a whole series of perceptions into
the question of marronage, ancestry and filiation.

> I feel I have stumbled here in the Canje [writes Fenwick, the persona
> through whom we perceive the interests of "progress" in this novel] on an
> abortive movement, the emotional and political germ of which has been
> used in two centuries of history. . . . What will you say when I tell you I
> have come across the Grand Old Man of our history. . . ?[71]

But Harris' vision is too ecumenical for it to allow him to accept too easily
this celebratory gift of an ancestor.

---

*Maroons is a term springing from historical marronage to connote areas of African
cultural survival, or isolated resuscitation, resistant to the blandishments of the plantation.

To *misconceive* the African [Fenwick's letter continued] . . . is to misunderstand and exploit him mercilessly and oneself as well. For *there,* in this creature Poseidon, the black man with the European name, drawn out of the depths of time, is the emotional dynamic of liberation that happened a century and a quarter ago. . . . Something went tragically wrong then. Something was misunderstood and frustrated, God alone knows why and how. . . . Maybe it was all too emotional, too blinding, this freedom that has turned cruel, abortive, evasive, woolly, and wild everywhere almost. . . .[72]

It is a salutary caveat, although Harris is himself guilty of misconceiving the African—certainly the Maroon. For the cruel abortion of freedom he speaks about, the over-"emotional" negritude, was and is not only a function of maroonage, it was and is even more certainly the consequence of opposition to the plantation. How else can we interpret the fate and history of Haiti, the greatest and most successful Maroon polity of them all? But Harris, ambivalent like most of us, finds "West Indian [protest] politics and intellectualism" sterile,[73] so that, as with the cultural pessimists we referred to earlier, he concludes that the African slave, originator and conditional body of Caribbean militance, must/could have come here equipped with very little—with very little to offer:

One must remember that *breath* is all the black man may have possessed at a certain stage in the Americas. He had lost his tribal tongue, he had lost everything except an abrupt area of space and lung: he possessed nothing but the calamitous air of broken ties in the New World.[74]

And yet, whereas with Naipaul,[75] Patterson,[76] even Derek Walcott,[77] this nothing yields nothing, with Harris this ruin/vestige, shred of breath, vital possession of the dispossessed, becomes the survival rhythm from which transformation may proceed.

The Literature of African Expression

Limbo [is] a dance in which the participants have to move, with their bodies thrown backwards and without any aid whatsoever, under a stick which is lowered at every successfully completed passage under it, until the stick is practically touching the ground. It is said to have originated—a necessary therapy after the experience of the cramped conditions between the slave decks of the Middle Passage. Now very popular as a performing act in Caribbean night clubs.[78]

> And the limbo stick is the silence in front of me
> *limbo*
>
> *limbo*
> *limbo like me . . .*

> long dark night is the silence in front of me
> *limbo*
> *limbo like me*
>
> stick hit sound
> and the ship like it ready
>
> stick hit sound
> and the ship like it ready
>
> *limbo*
> *limbo like me. . . .*[79]

Limbo then reflects a certain kind of gateway or threshold to a new world and the dislocation of a chain of miles. It is—in some ways—the archetypal sea-change stemming from Old Worlds and it is legitimate, I feel, to pun on *limbo* as a kind of shared phantom *limb* which has become a subconscious variable in West Indian theatre. The emergence of formal West Indian theatre was preceded, I suggest, by that phantom limb which manifested itself on Boxing Day, when the ban on the "rowdy" bands . . . was lifted for the festive season. . . . I recall performances I witnessed as a boy in Georgetown . . . in the early 1930s. Some of the performers danced on high stilts like elongated limbs while others performed spreadeagled on the ground. In this way *limbo* spider and stilted pole of the gods were related to the drums like grassroots and branches of lightning to the sound of thunder.[80]

The power and progress of image in these quotations illustrate what I mean by transformation. In terms of literary craftsmanship, they represent a shift from rhetoric to involvement. The beginning of this is evident, for example, in the poem "Pocomania," by Philip Sherlock, which we have already considered. Note its new rhythmic emphasis:

> *Black* the stars, *hide* the sky,
> *Lift* you' shoulder, *blot* the moon

and the appearance of dialect:

> Swing de circle wide again,
> Fall an' cry, me sister, now

The most significant factor in this process, however, is its connection with the *hounfort:* the heart and signal of the African experience in the Caribbean/New World. We have already witnessed the operation of this in Salkey's *A Quality of Violence,* and in the *limbo* quotations, above. But the Caribbean writer who has been able to move fearlessly/innocently into this enigmatic alternative world and has therefore been able to contribute most to the literature of African expression is George Lamming. In *Season of Adventure* we watch a young girl dance toward the gods at a *vodun* ceremony. As she dances, we become involved, until we find that Lamming's language has become an image of the child's possession:

> The child was wide awake. . . . The dance was an instinct which her feet had learnt. . . . The women's chant was broken by applause. The child heard the voices competing in her praise. She became hysterical; wild, light as air and other than human, like the night clouding her eyes. Her voice had cried out: "Hair, hair! Give all, all, all, hair." And she clapped until there was no feeling in her hands.
> And the voices came nearer than her skin: "Dance, Liza, dance! Dance! Dance! Liza, Liza, Liza, dance! Dance, Liza, dance."[81]

The only time Lamming falters in this astonishing participation in Afro-Caribbean worship is with the word/perception *hysterical*. It is similar (and present for similar reasons) to the false notes already noted in Salkey, Bell, Brouard, and Sherlock. But the faltering is only momentary. As Liza/Lamming dances to incarnation, Caribbean literature, through this encounter with the *loa,* begins its transformation into a new species of original art:[82]

> Fire of the spirits in her eyes, and no longer a child as she watched the shadows strangled by her wish for hair blazing from the summit of the bamboo pole! She trampled upon the circle of maize, exploding shapes like toys under her feet, dancing the dust away. For the gods were descending to the call of voices: "Come! Come! in O! In O spirit of water come! Come!"
> Now: gently, stage after gentle stage and feather-wise as if now orphaned of all sound, the voices were dying, second by full measure of second: then died on the gentlest of all sounds, "come, come, in O spirit of water come, come, come. . . ."[83]

Nommo

The process of transformation which Lamming so remarkably undertakes here—the art of the *hounfort* into the art of the novel—has its roots in a certain kind of concern for and attitude to the *word,* the atomic core of language. This is something that is very much present in all folk cultures, all preliterate, preindustrial societies. Within such cultures, language was and is a creative act in itself. Think of our love for the politician or the word of the preacher. Indeed, it is one of the problems of our political life how to separate the word and the meaning of the word.

The word (*nommo* or name) is held to contain secret power. Monk Lewis, who was a novelist himself, visited Jamaica (where he had some estates) in 1815–1816 and described this kind of attitude among his slaves:

> The other day. . . a woman, who had a child sick in the hospital, begged me to change its name for any other which might please me best: she cared

not what; but she was sure that it would never do well so long as it should be called Lucia.[84]

People feel a name is so important that a change in his name could transform a person's life. In traditional society, in fact, people often try to hide their names. That is why a Nigerian, for example, has so many names. Not only is it difficult to remember them, it is difficult to know which is the name that the man regards or identifies as his. If you call the wrong name you can't damage him.[85] Rumpelstiltskin in the German fable and Shemo-limmo in the Jamaican tale above are other examples of this. In H. G. DeLisser's *Jane's Career,* there is an interesting variation in which an earthquake, a natural divine phenomenon, becomes an aspect of *nommo:*

> . . . many persons talked of the recent [1907] earthquake as *something that could hear what was said about it,* and take action accordingly. To Sampson and many others like him, the earthquake was a living, terrible force. . . . [86]

Aimé Césaire takes this a stage further with:

> I would recover the secret of epic speech and towering conflagrations. I would say storm. I would say river. I would say tornado. I would say leaf. I want to pronounce tree. I want to be soaked by all the falling rains, dampened with all the dews. I would roll like frenzied blood in the slow current of the eye of the word's mad horses' newly born formations of the fire. . . . [87]

This is a kind of conjuration/divination, or rather, it comes from the same magical/miracle tradition as the conjure-man. Vibrations awake at the center of words. From the pools of their *nommo,* onomatopoeia and sound-symbols are born: *banggarang, boolooloops* and *boonoonoonoos* (Jamaica); *barrabbattabbattabba* and *bruggalungdung* (Barbados); *umklaklabulu* ("thunderclap": Zulu); *dabo-dabo* ("duck"), *munumm* ("darkness": Twi); *pampam, primprim, prampalam* (Bajan/Twi sounds of contact/movement); *patoo* ("owl": Asante/Jamaican); *felele* ("to blow in the wind, to flutter": Yoruba). In Black America it lives in the preacher/signifying tradition and the dozens, and surfaces scribally in areas of Ralph Ellison's *Invisible Man* and James Baldwin's *Go Tell It on the Mountain.* It is apparent in Ishmael Reed's *Yellow Back Radio Broke-down:*

> A terrible cuss of a thousand shivs he was who wasted whole herds, made the fruit black and wormy, dried up the water holes and caused people's eyes to grow from tiny black dots into slap-jacks wherever his feet fell. . . . [88]

and in Imamu Baraka's (LeRoi Jones') "Black Art":

Poems are bullshit unless they are
teeth or trees or lemons piled
on a step. Or black ladies dying
of men leaving nickel hearts
beating them down. Fuck poems
and they are useful, wd they shoot
come at you, love what you are,
breathe like wrestlers, or shudder
strangely after pissing. We want live
words of the hip world live flesh &
coursing blood. Hearts Brains
Souls splintering fire. We want poems
like fists beating niggers out of Jocks
or dagger poems in the slimy bellies
of the owner-jews.......................................
.... we want "poems that kill."
Assassin poems, Poems that shoot
guns ....[89]

Similarly, the Surinamese word see-er or seer Robert Ravales (Dobru)
tells us

> write no words
> write grenades
> to eradicate poverty
> write no sentences
> write guns
> to stop injustice[90]

This concept and use of word is found throughout the entire Black/
African world. It is present in modern as well as traditional African literature.[91] In the Americas, it reveals itself in our love of courtroom scenes
(both factual and fictional), the rhetoric of yard quarrels,[92] "word-
throwings,"[93] tea-meetings, and preacher/political orations.[94] The whole
living tradition of the calypso[95] is based on it. But it goes deeper than this,
as the metaphysical and symbolic qualities of some of the Afro-Carribean
fragments we have already discussed, indicates. Language, as we saw in
the discussion of names, may be conceived as having the power to affect
life. And again it is Lamming who exposes us to an interior view of the
process:

The words seemed to come like the echo of other voices from outside: "is
so, same so. . . ." Syllables changed their phrasing; words showed a length
that had suffered by the roughness of an accent uttered in haste. Surfacing
slowly . . . [they] seemed uncertain of their alliance. At every stage of
awareness she could feel the change, until the rules of college speech gave
way completely to the private dialect of her own tongue at home: "is same
ever since and it been the same, same so ever since. . . ."[96]

This way of using the word depends very much upon an understanding of the folk tradition out of which it comes. This folk tradition has received (not surprisingly) very little attention from scholars. There has been work by Nina Rodrigues, Renato Mendoza, Arthur Ramos, and Donald Pierson in Brazil; Fernando Ortiz in Cuba; for Jamaica there has been Martha Beckwith and more recently Ivy Baxter; for Trinidad, Errol Hill and J. D. Elder. For the Caribbean generally, there has been the work of the Herskovitses and Roger Bastide.[97] But even where these studies are comprehensive, they seldom attempt to describe the sociology of nation-language. Few of them, certainly, attempt a critical/aesthetic appraisal of the word, as found in its Creole context, or as illuminated in the work/thought of say, Kagame, Ogotemmêli, St. John of the Gospel, Father Placied Tempels, or Jahnheinz Jahn, within the African "Great Tradition."[98]

Techniques

In addition to sound-symbols, nation-language sets up certain tunes, tones and rhythms which are characteristic of the folk tradition, and are often essential features of its expression. The overall space/patterns of this language, we might say, are controlled by a *groundation** tendency, in which image/spirit is electrically conducted to earth like lightning or the *loa* (the gods, spirits, powers, or divine horsemen of *vodun*):

> Mr. Frank
> my gentleman, de Lord know
> is you dat did show de way
> nourish we spirit
> when we did nothin, nothin.
> Like a fowlcock
> early pon a morning
> *jooking in de straw*
> *scratchin de rockstone*
> *nastyin up 'e beak*
> *in de muddy gutter water. . . .*[99]

Notice how, since what we *see* is in fact the speaking (seeking) voice, pause and cadence become important:

> 'e eye ball sharpen
> to catch de teeny weeny bit . . .
> before it loss away
> okra sauce slippin through de gullet

Groundation or *groundings* (verb: *to grounds*) is a term for a rap session. But since the word/idea (contributed by Rastafari) comes from the experience of religious possession, its ripples of meaning reach further than the idea of simple, secular "grounding."

> hot, quick gone 'long for ever/ /
>
> An' is you dat did dey . . .[100]

Bongo Jerry's sound-system poetry is instinctively quicker—urban ghetto—but the cadence/pauses are still there, as in "Learning Rhymes":

> I want to know the truth.
> But they tell me to wait.
> Wait till when?
> Till I'm seventy.
> Or eighty and eight.
> I can/not/wait . . .
> To them truth is when you don't tell lie or when you face
>   don't show it
> Hoping that they could hide the truth and I would never
>   know it./ /
> Dem cold.[101]

His poem, "Mabrak," is in itself, a brilliant example of groundation:

> Mabrak:
>   NEWSFLASH!
> "Babylon plans crash"
> Thunder interrupt their programme to
> announce:
>
> BLACK ELECTRIC STORM
>   IS HERE
> How long you feel "fair is fine
> (WHITE)" would last?
>
> Hog long calm in darkness
>   when out of BLACK
> come forth LIGHT?
>
> [the dry tree stands and the green tree falls]
>
> Every knee
>   must bow
> Every tongue
>   confess
> Every language
>   express
>   W
>   O
>   R
>   D
>   W
>   O
>   R
>   K
>   S[102]

Again, in the ballad tradition of Sparrow's "Dan is the Man in the Van" and "Parables," or a Jamaican ska like "Salaman A Grundy," Jerry trans/ fuses weather forecasts, ("fair to fine"), Christian liturgy ("Every knee/ must bow"), and children's game songs ("ringing rings of roses") and whatever other significant demotic of the moment he can find; (Babel-land/Babylon into his African vision:

> SILENCE BABEL TONGUES; recall and
> recollect BLACK SPEECH.
> Cramp all double meaning
>   an' all that hiding language bar,
> for that crossword speaking
>   when expressing feeling
> is just English language contribution to increase confusion in
>   Babel-land tower—
> delusion, name changing, word rearranging
>   ringing rings of roses, pocket full of poses:
> "SAR" instead of "RAS"[103]

Improvisation

Some time ago, I wrote an exploration into West Indian literature in which I tried to use jazz[104] as an aesthetic criterion for understanding what certain of our writers were trying to do. My assumption was that all African-influenced artists, whatever their individual styles, participated in certain modes of expression, and that understanding the patterns of one could lead to an understanding of how the work of all relates together in a mutual continuum.[105] I also found in that study that just as a cardinal element in jazz was improvisation (rhythmic and thematic), so were similar features clear in Black/African literature. Bongo Jerry's "Mabrak," above, is one example of this. Nicolás Guillén's well-known "Sensemayá" is another:

> ¡Mayombe-bombe-mayombe!
> ¡Mayombe-bombe-mayombe!
> ¡Mayombe-bombe-mayombe!
>
> La culebra tien los ojos de vidrio
> La culebra viene y se en reda en un palo
> Con sus ojos de vidrio, en un palo
> Con sus ojos de vidrio. . . .
>
> The snake has eyes of glass
> The snake appears and winds itself round the post
> With eyes of glass round the post
> With eyes of glass. . . .[106]

The same strong rhythmic pulse, leading to variation, is present in Césaire:

> Au bout du petit matin
> un grand galop de pollen
> un grand galop d'un petit train de petites filles
> un grand galop de colibris
> un grand galop de dagues pour défoncer la poitrine de la
> terre[107]

and throughout the word play in Leon Damas' *Pigments*

> Sans nom
> sans lune
> sans lune
> sans nom
> nuits sans lune
> sans nom sans nom
> ou le degout s'andre en moi. . . .[108]

and in Jamal Ali:

> Rocket up to the moon
> Living up to the moon
> Cost of living up to the moon
> Death toll sky high, twisting, up to the moon[109]

and in my own "Negus" which begins as a raindrip or drum beat and develops into cross rhythms:

> It
> it
> it
> it is not
>
> it
> it
> it
> it is not
>
> it is not
> it is not
> it is not enough
> it is not enough to be free
> of the red white and blue
> of the drag, of the dragon
>
> it is not
> it is not
> it is not enough

it is not enough to be free
of the whips, principalities and powers
where is your kingdom of the Word?

It is not enough
to tinkle to work on a bicycle bell
when hell
crackles and burns in the fourteen-inch screen of the Jap
of the Jap of the Japanese-constructed
United-Fruit-Company-imported
hard sell, tell tale tele-
vision set, rhinocerously knobbed, cancerously tubed. . . .[110]

Call/Response

But rhythm is not the only feature of improvisation in the literature of the
African presence. It can also involve chantwell and chorus, as in spiritual,
secular soul-litany, gospel, and above all, worksong:

> Cayman ah pull man,
>> *timbakay,*
> Cayman ah pull man
>> *timbakoo,*
> Cayman ah pull man,
>> *timbakay,*
> Cayman ah pull man
>> *timbakoo.*
>>> "Timber Man" (Traditional Guyana)

and in *calinda* calypso:

Sparrow: Well they playin bad,
  They have me feeling sad;
  Well they playin beast,
  Why they run for police?
  Ten criminals attack me outside of Miramar

Chorus: *Ten to one is murder!*

Sparrow: About ten in de night on de 5th of November

Chorus: *Ten to one is murder!*

Sparrow: Way down Henry Street by H. E. M. Walker

Chorus: *Ten to one is murder!*

Sparrow: Well the leader of the gang was hot like a pepper

Chorus: *Ten to one is murder!*

Sparrow: And every man in de gang had a white handled razor

Chorus: *Ten to one is murder!*

Sparrow: They say I push de girl from Grenada

Chorus: *Ten to one is murder!*[111]

It will be found in sermons like this Spiritual Baptist's from Silver Sands, Barbados:

I can say what troubles . . .
      have we seen . . .   *oh yea*

an' what conflicts . . .
      have we passed. . . .   *oh yeas*

There were many walls with*out* . . .
      and fears within . . .   *oh yeaa*

but God has *preserved* us by His power Divine   *oh yes*

the sun shone on our path sometimes   *oh oh!*

sometimes it was very rainy   *oh yes*

But there is no captain . . .   [humming begins]

      if he only rows . . .
         near the shore   *uh!*

      and still waters   *uh!*

. . . .
we've got our glory . . .   *hello!*

      we've got our shame . . .   *oh yes!*

some have said this . . .

      and some have said that . . .

but *regardless* to what happened . . .
      we are *still* moving on!   *ah yes!*[112]

A folk-poet like the Barbadian Bruce St. John captures all this, and, significantly, the very essence of the Bajan psyche with:

Stokeley like he mad   *Da is true*
He outah touch wid de West Indies   *Da is true*
He ain't even discreet!   *Da is true*
He can't be pon we side   *Da is true*
He mussy working fuh de whites!   *Da is true*
Dem thrives pon we division   *Da is true*

<table>
<tr><td>So they wouldn't let 'e talk!</td><td>*Da is true*</td></tr>
<tr><td>Suppose he right though?</td><td>*Wuh da?*</td></tr>
<tr><td>Suppose he right though?</td><td>*Da is true*</td></tr>
<tr><td></td><td>*Da is true*[113]</td></tr>
</table>

Transformation

Improvisation can also invade and erode the shape/sense of the word as in my "Mother Poem":

> Muh
> muh
> mud
> me mudda
>
> coo
> like she coo
> like she cook
> an she cumya to me pun de grounn
>
> like she lik mih
>
> like she lik me wid grease like she grease mih
> she cum to me years like de yess of a leaf
> an she issper
> she cum to me years an she purr like a puss an she essper
>
> she lisper to me dat me name what me name
> dat me name is me main an it am is me own an lion eye mane. . . .[114]

It is evident also in the "surrealism" of Césaire's:

> that two plus two makes five
> that the forest meows
> that the tree gets the chestnut out of the fire
> that the sky strokes its beard
> etcetera etcetera[115]

and in the passage in George Lamming's *The Pleasures of Exile* where a plough/slave is transformed into a plough/sword, omen of revolt:

Imagine a plough in the field. Ordinary as ever, prongs and spine un-changed, is simply there, stuck to its post beside the cane shoot. Then some hand, identical with the routine of its work, reaches to lift this familiar instrument. But the plough escapes contact. It refuses to surrender its pre-sent position. There is a change in the relation between this plough and one free hand. The crops wait and wonder what will happen next. More hands arrive to confirm the extraordinary conduct of this plough; but no one can explain the terror of those hands as they withdraw from the plough. Some new sights as well as sense of language is required to bear witness to the miracle. . . . For as those hands in unison move forward, the plough achieves a somersault which reverses its traditional posture. Its head goes into the ground, and the prongs, throat-near stand erect in the air, ten points of steel announcing danger.[116]

The Literature of Reconnection

The literature of reconnection has become an active and fairly widespread concern, particularly in the Black United States, since the Black Power Revolution of the mid-1960s. Writers and jazz musicians began leaving their slave names and taking on African *nommos* and poets like Don Lee, Marvin X, and Alicia Johnson, developed a certain concern with Africa, at least as a source of inspiration/validation. Among the younger Anglophone Caribbeans, Elizabeth Clarke's poem "Mudda Africa" and Tito Jemmott's "A Tale" are indicative of this new orientation.[117] But the solid work was really done before this phase, by poets like Melvin Tolson (1898–1966)[118] and Robert Hayden[119] in North America; and by Guillén, Roumain, Césaire, and Damas in the Caribbean. My own trilogy[120] is another effort in this direction.

But the example I should like to close with is Paule Marshall's novel *The Chosen Place, The Timeless People*.[121] I have developed my comments on this remarkable piece of work in the *Journal of Black Studies*.[122] The following excerpts illustrate quite unequivocally what I mean by the "literature of reconnection": a recognition of the African presence in our society not as a static quality, but as root—living, creative, and still part of the main. Take, for instance, this passage describing the famous Bathsheba coast. The people of Barbados know this coastline—wild, Atlantic, and rocky. But how many, looking down on that surf, those reefs, from Horse Hill and Hackleton, realized that there was nothing but ocean and blue between themselves and the coast of Africa—that Barbados, the most easterly of the West Indies, is in fact *the nearest to Africa*. Certainly no major Barbados writer known to me had ever made the point. Marshall, whose parents are Bajan and whose childhood was divided between Barbados and Brooklyn, saw the connection immediately:

It was the Atlantic this side of the island, a wild-eyed, marauding sea the color of slate, deep, full of dangerous currents, lined with row upon row of barrier reefs, and with a sound like that of the combined voices of the drowned raised in a loud unceasing lament—all those, the nine million and more it is said, who in their enforced exile, their Diaspora, had gone down between this point and the homeland lying out of sight to the east. This sea mourned them. Aggrieved, outraged, unappeased, it hurled itself upon each of the reefs in turn and then upon the shingle beach, sending up the spume in an angry froth which the wind took and drove in like smoke over the land.[123]

And from nature to the people who inhabit and inherit the landscape, Paule Marshall uses the word, her words, not to say "it is so," but to say, as the conjuror says, *this is how it could/should be*. So her Bajans become more than Bajans: they develop historical depth and cultural possibility—Fergusson, the cane factory mechanic, for instance:

> [A vociferous] strikingly tall, lean old man, whose gangling frame appeared strung together by the veins and sinews, standing out in sharp relief beneath his dark skin. . . . His face, his neck, his clean-shaven skull, had the elongated intentionally distorted look to them of a Benin mask, or a sculpted thirteenth century Ife head. With his long, stretched limbs he could have been a Haitian Houngan man.[124]

It is Fergusson who, like an Ashanti *okyeame,* kept the memory of the ancestral dead alive with his interminable rehearsal of the tale of Cuffee Ned, the slave rebel. Cuffee Ned becomes the ancestor of the whole village, and it is his memory and the whole African tradition which depends on it, that keeps these people inviolate under the pressures of commercialization and progress.

Then there was the Ashanti chief himself, Delbert, the shopkeeper and truck owner:

> He was lying propped up on a makeshift bed amid the clutter behind the counter, a broken white leg in a cast laid up stiffly in the bed. He was huge, with massive limbs. . . . He was the chief presiding over the nightly palavering in the men's house. The bed made of packing cases was the royal palanquin. The colorful Harry Truman shirt he had on was his robe of office; the battered Panama hat . . . his chieftain's umbrella, and the bottle of white rum he held within the great curve of his hand, the palm wine with which he kept the palaver and made libation to the ancestral gods.[125]

It is rhetorical, even romantic. But Paule Marshall's *intention* is crucial, and in it she unquestionably succeeds: to transform the Afro-Bajan out of his drab, materialistic setting with meaningful correlates of custom from across the water in ancestral Africa.

Finally, at the end of the book, there is a carnival. It is not a particularly typical Bajan happening, but Paule Marshall does not intend it to be. She links the Afro-Caribbean experience of Bajan (Chalky Mount) Maroons with Trinidad carnival and Montserrat masquerades.[126] Every year the people of Bournehills put on the same mas'—the same pageant—*The Legend of Cuffee Ned*. They will not change a single iota of their metaphor. There is of course an outcry against this from other parts of the island: "Oh you poor people from the slave days, every year you doing the same thing." But Bournehills is making a point: until there is a change in the system, we will always be slaves, and until there is change, we must continue to celebrate our one, if brief, moment of rebel victory:

> *They had worked together!*—and as if, in their eyes, this had been the greatest achievement, the thing of which they were proudest, the voices rose to a stunning crescendo that visibly jarred the blue dome of the sky. Under Cuffee, they sang, a man had not lived for himself alone, but for his neighbour also. "If we had lived selfish, we couldn't have lived at all." They half-spoke, half-sung the words. They had trusted one another, and set aside their differences and stood as one against their enemies. *They had been a People!* Their heads thrown back and the welded voices reaching high above New Bristol's red-faded tin roofs, they informed the sun and afternoon sky of what they, Bournehills People, had once been capable of.
>
> Then abruptly, the voices dropped. . . . They sung then in tones drained of their former jubilance of the defeat that had eventually followed . . . in voices that would never cease to mourn . . . for this too, as painful as it was, was part of the story.[127]

NOTES

1. This is an edited transcript of a talk given at the Center for Multi-Racial Studies, Cave Hill, Barbados, in February, 1970; revised and extended in October and December, 1973.

2. Edward Brathwaite, *Rights of Passage,* Argo DA 101 (1968), sleevenote.

3. The most detailed examination of this possibility is the almost ignored Leo Wiener, *Africa and the Discovery of America,* 3 vols (Philadelphia: Innes and Sons, 1922). More recently, there has been Harold G. Lawrence, "African Explorers of the New World." *The Crisis* (June–July 1962). For a useful bibliographical essay, see Floyd W. Hayes III, "The African Presence in America," *Black World,* 22, No. 9 (July 1973), pp. 4–22.

4. The latest estimates/discussion are in Philip D. Curtin, *The Atlantic Slave Trade: A Census* (Madison, Wis.: University of Wisconsin Press, 1969); Walter Rodney, *How Europe Underdeveloped Africa* (London and Dar-es-Salaam: Bogle-L'Ouverture, 1972), pp. 103–112.

5. See, for example, the work of E. Franklin Frazier in the United States, Orlando Patterson in the Anglophone Caribbean. M. G. Smith's "The African Heritage in the Caribbean," *Caribbean Studies: A Symposium,* ed. Vera Rubin (Seattle: University of Washington Press, 1960), pp. 34–46, is perhaps typical.

6. See, for example, M. J. Herskovits, *The Myth of the Negro Past* (New York: Harper and Brothers, 1941) and the work of the Herskovitses generally. Then there are the works of W. R. Bascom, George E. Simpson, Alan Lomax (in cantometrics), R. F. Thompson ("African Influence on the Art of the United States"), Pierre Verger, Janheinz Jahn, and Maureen Warner (on the Yorubas in Trinidad) to name a few, and my own *The Folk Culture of the Slaves in Jamaica* (London and Port-of-Spain: New Beacon Books, 1970). A summary of work and ideas in the field appears in my Introduction to M. J. Herskovits' *Life in a Haitian*

Valley [1937] (New York: Doubleday, 1971), revised in African Studies Association of the West Indies *Bulletin* No. 5 (Mona: 1972). A detailed consideration of the entire question is the subject of my *Africa in the Caribbean* (forthcoming).

7. See, for example, Orlando Patterson, *The Sociology of Slavery* (London: Macgibbon and Kee, 1967).

8. For more on this, see my review of Patterson's *Sociology* which appeared in *Race,* 9, No. 3 (1968). My own position is set out in *The Development of Creole Society in Jamaica* (Oxford: The Clarendon Press, 1971).

9. Studies of African culture are now so easily available and in such quantity that a listing here would be pointless. I would like to draw attention to the following, however: M. J. Herskovits on Dahomey; R. S. Rattray on the Ashanti; M. J. Field on the Ga; Afolabi Ojo on the Yoruba; John Mbiti, J. B. Danquah, Marcel Griaule on African religion and philosophy; and the collection edited by S. and P. Ottenberg, *Cultures and Societies of Africa* (New York: Random House, 1960).

The question of the unity of African culture, or at least of those areas of Africa involved with or contingent upon the slave trade, is obviously one of the critical assumptions of this paper, permitting me to speak of "Africa" instead of, say, Senegal, the Gold Coast, Dahomey. For discussions on this point, see, among others, Cheikh Anta Diop, *L'Unité Culturelle de L'Afrique Noire* (Paris: Présence Africaine, 1959); Melville J. Herskovits, *The Myth of the Negro Past,* esp. Ch. 3; and Alan Lomax, "Africanisms in New World Negro Music," *Research and Resources of Haiti* (New York: Research Institute for the Study of Man, 1969).

10. "Appreciation for Cumfa," *Evening Post* (Guyana), August 29, 1972.

11. See George E. Simpson (for Trinidad) in *Religious Cults of the Caribbean* (Rio Piedras, Puerto Rico: Institute of Caribbean Studies, University of Puerto Rico, 1970), pp. 82–85. Until the advent of "Papa Doc" Duvalier, *vodun* in Haiti also found itself under pretty regular attack from church and state, starting with the Liberator himself, Toussaint L'Ouverture. See Simpson, pp. 254–256. The news that Guyana was to abolish its *obeah* laws came in November of 1973. The reverberations from church, press and other states (fear, ridicule, caution: when Prime Minister Forbes Burnham of Guyana visited Jamaica soon afterwards, he was met by at least one anti-*obeah* demonstration) indicate the revolutionary depth of the announcement.

12. Eric Williams, *Capitalism and Slavery* (Chapel Hill: University of North Carolina Press, 1944).

13. Eric Williams, *Some Historical Reflections on the Church in the Caribbean* (Port-of-Spain: Public Relations Division, Office of the Prime Minister, 1973), p. 11.

14. During this "October Crisis," the entire Jamaican mass-media apparatus came out against Rodney, Black Power, and "Cave Mona" (a punning editorial pejorative for the University of the West Indies at Mona), and clearly had little time for analysis or facts. The best and perhaps the only "Diary of Events" was therefore the students' publication, *Scope*—in the excitement, undated, but with a picture of Dr. Rodney on the cover. Rodney's own comment is in *The Groundings with My Brothers* (London: Bogle-L'Ouverture, 1969), pp. 59–67. It is interesting to note that the nonestablishment newspapers that appeared as a result of this crisis carried African *(Abeng, Moko)* or Amerindian *(Tapia)* names.

15. "Yoruba and Our African Heritage," *Advocate-News* (Barbados), August 20, 1973. In addition to Yoruba House in Barbados, mention might be made here of Maureen Warner-Lewis' Omo Ajini (Children of Africa) at Mona. Mrs. Lewis

has been teaching her group Yoruba songs she recorded in Trinidad during her research into the Yoruba presence there, and restoring them to life (movement and setting), using Yoruba dances she learned while living in Nigeria. But it must be borne in mind that before Yoruba and Omo Ajini, there were several folk/ survival groups, most of them ignored by the establishment.

16. Philip D. Curtin, *Two Jamaicas* (Cambridge, Mass.: Harvard University Press, 1955), esp. pp. 158–177.

17. W. H. Siebert, *The Legacy of the American Revolution* (Columbus: Ohio State University Bulletin, April 1913); Curtin, *Two Jamaicas,* pp. 32 ff.; Brathwaite, *Creole Society,* pp. 253–255 and *passim.*

18. For discussion, see Martha Beckwith, *Black Roadways* (Chapel Hill: University of North Carolina Press, 1929); Curtin, *Two Jamaicas;* and the F. G. Cassidy/R. B. Le Page, *Dictionary of Jamaican English* (Cambridge: Cambridge University Press, 1967), pp. 313–314.

19. For this and Afro-Aamaican religion generally, see J. C. Moore, "The Religion of Jamaican Negroes . . . ," Ph.D. thesis, Northwestern University (1953); Edward Seaga, "Cults in Jamaica," *Jamaica Journal,* 3, No. 2 (June 1969), pp. 3–13; and Simpson, *Religious Cults.*

20. See, for instance, Sylvia Wynter's *Jamaica's National Heroes* (Kingston: Jamaica National Trust Commission, 1971).

21. *Facts and Documents Relating to the Alleged Rebellion in Jamaica* (Anonymous) (London: 1866), pp. 12, 13, 38, 57.

22. Curtin, *Two Jamaicas,* p. 174.

23. Noelle Chutkan, "The Administration of Justice . . . as a Contributing Factor [in] the Morant Bay Riot of 1865," unpublished History Seminar paper, University of the West Indies, Mona, 1969.

24. The names of the churches are significant: First *African* Baptist Church (Savannah), *African* Baptist Church (Lexington), *Abyssinia* Baptist Church (New York), Free *African* Meeting House (Boston), etc. For full list, see St. Clair Drake, *The Redemption of Africa and Black Religion* (Chicago and Atlanta: Third World Press and Institute of the Black World, 1970), p. 26. Closely connected with these were the "Back to Africa" movements—militant under slave rebels; religious/secular with people like Paul Cuffee, Martin Delany in the U.S., Albert Thorne in Barbados, and George Alexander McGuire in Antigua, through Bishop Henry Macneil Turner, Alfred Sam, Edward Blyden, DuBois, to Marcus Garvey with the *grito:* "Africa for the Africans at home and abroad." For a discussion of these see, among others, Edwin S. Redkey, *Black Exodus* (New Haven, Conn.: Yale University Press, 1969); Vincent Bakpetu Thompson, *Africa and Unity: The Evolution of Pan Africanism* (London and Harlow: Longmans Green, 1969); and St. Clair Drake, op. cit. The Garvey bibliography, needless to say, is an industry in itself. In addition, there was the presence and influence of literate (slave) Africans like Phyllis Wheatley, Ottobah Cugoano, and Ignatius Sancho, some of whom, like Mahammedu Sisei, Mohammed Bath, Olaudah Equiano, actually returned to Africa. See Paul Edwards' "Introduction" (p. lx) to *Equiano's Travels* (London and Ibadan: Heinemann Educational Books, 1967); Janheinz Jahn, *A History of Neo-African Literature* (1966), trans. Oliver Coburn and Ursula Lehrburger (London: Faber & Faber, 1968), p. 40. Sisei and Mohammed Bath are treated in unpublished papers by Carl Campbell, Dept. of History, University of the West Indies, Mona, 1972–1973.

25. For a development of this point, see my "Foreword" in *Savacou* 3/4 (December 1970/March 1971).

26. Nicolás Guillén, "Interview with Keith Ellis," *Jamaica Journal,* 7, Nos. 1 & 2 (March/June 1973), p. 78.

27. The concept derives from M. G. Smith's classic, *The Plural Society in the British West Indies* (Berkeley: University of California Press, 1965).

28. See, for instance, Abbé Raynal, *Histoire philosophique et politique des établissements et du commerce des européens dans les deux Indes* (1770); and Thomas Southey, *Chronological History of the West Indies* (1827). These works are examined in Elsa Goveia's *A Study on the Historiography of the British West Indies to the End of the Nineteenth Century* (Mexico: Instituto Panamericano de Geografia y Historia, 1956). On the other hand, works like the anonymous *Jonathan Corncob* (1787), J. B. Moreton, *Manners and Customs* (1790); and Edward Long, *History of Jamaica* (1774), no matter what their other qualities, were little more than travesties of Black reality. See my "Creative Literature of the British West Indies During the Period of Slavery," *Savacou,* 1 (June 1970), pp. 46–73.

29. This novel, probably written by an Englishman with some knowledge of the West Indies, is discussed in detail in my "Creative Literature." The most imaginative insight into slavery from the Anglophone Caribbean is perhaps James Carnegie's unpublished novella, *Wages Paid,* a long extract of which appeared in *Savacou* 3/4 (December 1970–March 1971), as "Circle."

30. DeLisser published ten novels in the period 1913–1958, including *Jane's Career* (Kingston: The Gleaner Co., 1913; London: Methuen & Co., 1914) and the well-known, *The White Witch of Rosehall* (London: Ernest Benn, 1929). Jean Rhys, who left the Caribbean c. 1912, when she was sixteen, and has never returned, has written at least six novels, only one of which deals with the Caribbean: *Wide Sargasso Sea* (London: André Deutsch, 1966). Nicole, who also makes his home outside the Caribbean, has written many novels, including a whole series of detective tales under a pseudonym. Among his books dealing with his native land are *Off-White* (London: Jarrolds, 1959) and *White Boy* (London: Hutchinson, 1966). The contribution of the other writers listed in the text is as follows: Mendes, *Pitch Lake* (1934), *Black Fauns* (1935); McDonald, *The Humming-Bird Tree* (1969); Emtage, *Brown Sugar* (1966); Drayton, *Christopher* (1959), *Zohara* (1961); Allfrey, *The Orchid House* (1953). I have not included the work of Roger Mais here, because his novels deal almost exclusively with the Black proletariat and peasantry. See note 32.

31. Kenneth Ramchand, *The West Indian Novel and Its Background* (London: Faber & Faber, 1970), pp. 223–236.

32. "Jazz and the West Indian Novel," *Bim,* 44–45 (1967–1968).

33. Cuba and Puerto Rico were occupied by U.S. forces in 1898 as a consequence of the Spanish-American War. The Dominican Republic and Haiti were occupied during the First World War.

34. Juan Marinello, "Sobre una inquietud cubana," *Revista de Avance* (February 1930); and *Poética, ensayos en entusiasmo* (Madrid: 1933), p. 142, quoted and translated by G. R. Coulthard in his *Race and Colour in Caribbean Literature* (London: Oxford University Press, 1962), p. 29. Coulthard's book is an invaluable and still, after more than ten years, unique source of information about literature in the French and Spanish Caribbean.

35. The first big "hit" was a song, delivered by a White American group, the Andrews Sisters, called fittingly, "Rum and Coca-Cola."

36. "A tiger is not conscious of his stripes, he pounces." A statement, attributed to the Nigerian writer, Wole Soyinka, and indicative of a general Anglophone

reluctance to accept the theoretical apparatus of negritude. The term also suggests something of the postcolonial difference between French and English-speaking African writers: the former tended to be expatriate, the later lived and worked, on the whole, in their own countries.

37. See my series of articles on Carifesta in the *Sunday Advocate News* (Barbados) (October–December 1972).

38. Carl Brouard (Haiti), "La trouée," *La Revue indigène* (October 1927), my translation.

39. Countee Cullen, "Heritage," *Color* (New York: Harper & Bros., 1925).

40. Philip Sherlock, "Jamaican Fisherman," *Ten Poems* (Georgetown, Guyana: Miniature Poets Series, edited and published by A. J. Seymour and *Kykoveral,* 1953).

41. Jacques Roumain, "Guinée," *La Revue indigène* (September 1927).

42. Louise Bennett, *Jamaica Labrish* (Kingston, Jamaica: Sangster's Book Stores, 1966), p. 214.

43.

> And this despair, equal to no other
> for taming, with words from France,
> this heart which comes to me from Senegal

Laleau, "Trahison," *Musique negre* (Port-au-Prince: Imprimerie de l'Etat, 1931) trans. Coulthard, op. cit., p. 43.

44. Derek Walcott's preface to *Dream on Monkey Mountain and Other Plays* (New York: Farrar, Straus & Giroux, 1970) and his play *Dream on Monkey Mountain* are explicit explorations of this theme and "problem," memorably crystallized in his poem, "A Far Cry from Africa," *In a Green Night* (London: Jonathan Cape, 1962), p. 18.

> I who am poisoned with the blood of both,
> Where shall I turn, divided to the vein?
> I who have cursed
> the drunken officer of British rule, how choose
> Between this African and the English tongue I love?

45. Dantès Bellegarde, *Haiti et ses problèmes* (Montreal: 1941), pp. 16–17, quoted in Coulthard, op. cit., pp. 73–74.

46. Andrew Salkey, *A Quality of Violence* (London: New Authors Ltd., 1959), p. 151.

47. Nicolás Guillén, "Son Numero 6," from *El son entero* (Buenos Aires: Editorial Pleamar, 1947), trans. George Irish in *Savacou* 3/4 (1970/1971), p. 112.

48. In Alfred Métraux, *Le vaudou haitien* (Paris: Gallimard, 1958), trans. Hugo Charteris as *Voodoo in Haiti* (New York: Schocken Books, 1972), pp. 152–153.

49. Edward Brathwaite, *Masks* (London: Oxford University Press, 1968), pp. 38–39, 68–69; *Islands* (London: Oxford University Press, 1969), pp. 51–53.

50. George Simpson, *The Shango Cult in Trinidad* (Rio Piedras, Puerto Rico: Institute of Caribbean Studies, University of Puerto Rico, 1965), p. 45; reprinted in his *Religious Cults of the Caribbean,* p. 40.

51. Moore, op. cit., pp. 174–175, reprinted in Brathwaite, *Creole Society,* pp. 224–225, 329–331.

52. In Cuba and Brazil, Yemajaa, the Yoruba goddess of the sea, dominates ceremony and dance. In Haiti, important customs surround Agwe, the saltwater

power, whose boat is annually sent drifting back to "Ibo." In folktales, *fair-maids* and *water-mammas* play important roles. In songs originating from the *hounfort,* we are always crossing the river, and the importance of the Baptists has already been mentioned.

53. See "Jazz and the West Indian Novel," *Bim,* 45 (1967), p. 41.

54. Adapted from R. B. Le Page and David De Camp, *Jamaican Creole* (London: Macmillan, 1960).

55. In Harold Courlander, *The Drum and the Hoe* (Berkeley and Los Angeles: University of California Press, 1960), p. 248.

56. "The Little Boy Who Avenged His Mother," in H. P. Jacobs, "An Early Dialect Verse," *Jamaican Historical Review,* 1, No. 3 (December 1948), pp. 279–281.

57. See Walter Jekyll, *Jamaican Song and Story* (1907; New York: Dover Publications, 1966).

58. For an account of some of these, see Tony Harrison, "Shango the Shaky Fairy," *London Magazine,* New Series, 10, No. 1 (April 1970), pp. 5–27.

59. The "rock-and-roll" base of Black American music is another aspect of Shango, as is "boogie-woogie" (piano imitation of the train), and the innumerable spirituals and gospel songs that not only *sing* about trains, but become possessed by them. Listen, for example, to use recent examples, to Aretha Franklin's "Pullin' " *(Spirit in the Dark:* Atlantic SD 8265) or the Staple Singers' "I'll Take You There."

60. Salkey, *A Quality of Violence,* p. 109.

61. Ibid., p. 61.

62. Ibid., p. 66.

63. Ibid., pp. 60–61.

64. This applies not only to writers, but to Caribbean critics as well. See my commentary on this in "Caribbean Critics," *New World Quarterly,* 5, Nos. 1–2 (1969), pp. 5–15; *Critical Quarterly,* 11, No. 3 (Autumn 1969), pp. 268–276. Salkey and Sherlock particularly, however, have developed significantly during the Black Consciousness period of the 1960s. Salkey's collection of stories, *Anancy's Score* (London: Bogle-L'Ouverture Publications, 1973) is an especially fine example of the new writing.

65. Vera Bell, "Ancestor on the Auction Block," *The Independence Anthology of Jamaican Literature,* ed. A. L. Hendriks and Cedric Lindo (Kingston, Jamaica: The Arts Celebration Committee of the Ministry of Development and Welfare, 1962), p. 85. For a detailed analysis of this poem, see George Lamming, "Caribbean Literature: The Black Rock of Africa," *African Forum,* 1, No. 4 (Spring 1966), pp. 32–52.

66. Philip Sherlock, "Pocomania," *Caribbean Quarterly* (Federation Anthology of Poetry), 5, No. 3 (1958), pp. 192–193.

67. George Lamming, *Season of Adventure* (London: Michael Joseph, 1960), pp. 44–50.

68. For details of the various Maroon groups see, among others, Philip J. C. Dark, *Bush Negro Art* (London: Alec Tiranti Ltd., 1954); Jean Huraul, *Africains de Guyane* (Le Havre and Paris: Editions Mouton, 1970); R. C. Dallas, *The History of the Maroons [of Jamaica],* 2 vols., (London 1803); Sir William Young, *An Account of the Black Charaibs in the Island of St. Vincent* (London, 1795); Douglas C. Taylor, *The Black Carib of British Honduras* (New York: Wenner-Gren Foundation for Anthropological Research, 1951); Edison Carneiro, *Guerras do los Palmares* (Mexico: Fondo de Cultura Económica, 1946).

69. The Maroons of Jamaica, the Black Caribs of Honduras, and the Suriname groups.

70. Namba Roy, *Black Albino* (London: New Literature Press, 1961).

71. Wilson Harris, *The Secret Ladder* (London: Faber and Faber, 1963), p. 23.

72. Ibid., p. 39.

73. Wilson Harris, *History, Fable and Myth in the Caribbean and Guianas* (Georgetown, Guyana: National History and Arts Council, Ministry of Information and Culture, 1970), p. 29.

74. Ibid., p. 28.

75. "History is built around achievement and creation; and nothing was created in the West Indies," V. S. Naipaul, *The Middle Passage* (London: André Deutsch, 1962), p. 29.

76. "This was a society . . . in which all forms of refinements, of art, of folkways were either absent or in a state of total disintegration," Orlando Patterson, *The Sociology of Slavery,* p. 9.

77.

> those who remain fascinated,
> in attitudes of prayer,
> by the festering roses made from their fathers' manacles,
> or upraise their silver chalices flecked with vomit . . .
> crying, at least here
> something happened—
> they will absolve us, perhaps, if we begin again,
> from what we have always known, nothing . . .
> while the silver-hammered charge of the marsh light
> brings towards us, again and again, in beaten scrolls,
> nothing, then nothing,
> and then nothing.

From *Another Life* by Derek Walcott (New York: Farrar, Straus & Giroux, 1973), p. 144–145.

78. Brathwaite, *Islands,* pp. ix–x.

79. Ibid., p. 37.

80. Harris, *History, Fable,* pp. 9–10.

81. Lamming, *Season of Adventure,* p. 29.

82. The only other Caribbean writer who has been able to enter the *hounfort* in this way, it seems to me, is Alejo Carpentier in *El reino de este mundo* (Mexico: EDIAPSA, 1949). But Wilson Harris, in a remarkable passage in a public lecture, demonstrates that he too (as one would expect) is fully aware of the implosive links between *vodun* and the folk literature of the New World:

> All conventional memory is erased and yet in this trance of overlapping spheres of reflection a primordial or deeper function of memory begins to exercise itself. . . .
>
> That such a drama has indeed a close bearing on the language of fiction, on the language of art, seems to me incontestable. The community the writer shares with the primordial dancer is, as it were, the complementary halves of a broken stage. . . .

"The Writer and Society," *Tradition, the Writer and Society* (London and Port-of-Spain: New Beacon Books, 1967), pp. 51–52.

83. Lamming, *Season of Adventure,* pp. 29–30.

84. M. G. Lewis, *Journal of a West Indian Proprietor* (1834; London: G. Routledge & Sons, 1929), p. 290.

85. For more on this, see Placide Tempels, *Bantu Philosophy* (1946), trans. Colin King from the 1952 French edition (Paris: Présence Africaine, 1959), pp. 69–74.

86. DeLisser, *Jane's Career,* p. 120.

87. Aimé Césaire, *Cahier d'un retour au pays natal* (1939; Paris: Présence Africaine, 1956), p. 40, my translation.

88. Ishmael Reed, *Yellow Back Radio Broke-down* (1969; New York: Bantam Books, 1972), p. 9.

89. LeRoi Jones, *Black Magic Poetry* (Indianapolis and New York: The Bobbs-Merrill Co., 1969), p. 116; which should be *heard* on *Sonny's Time Now Now* (Jihad 663), with Sonny Murray (drums), Albert Ayler (tenor sax), Don Cherry (trumpet), and Henry Grimes (bass).

90. R. Dobru, *Flowers Must Not Grow Today* (Paramaribo, Suriname: Afi-Kofi, 1973).

91. The presence and use of *nommo* is too pervasive and evident in modern African literature for us to do more than refer, among many others, to Gabriel Okara's *The Voice,* Wole Soyinka's *The Road;* the plays by Robert Serumaga *(Renga Moi)* and Duro Ladipo (for example, *Oba koso*), based closely on traditional ceremony; Camara Laye's *L'enfant noir,* the novels of Amos Tutuola and the long poems of Okot p'Bitek. For traditional African literature and thought, see, among others, William Bascom, *Ifa Divination* (Bloomington: Indiana University Press, 1969); Ruth Finnegan, *Oral Literature in Africa* (Oxford: The Clarendon Press, 1970); S. A. Babalola, *The Content and Form of Yoruba Ijala* (Oxford: The Clarendon Press, 1966); J. H. Nketia, *Funeral Dirges of the Akan People* (Achitoma, 1955); Marcel Griaule, *Dieu d'eau: entretiens avec Ogotem-meli* (Paris: Editions du Chêne, 1948); Tempels, *Bantu Philosophy;* and Chinua Achebe "Foreword" to *A Selection of African Prose,* ed. W. H. Whiteley (Oxford: The Clarendon Press, 1964), pp. vii–x.

92. See *Minty Alley* [1936] (London and Port-of-Spain: New Beacon Books Ltd., 1971), pp. 21 and 23.

93. See DeLisser, *Jane's Career* (reprint London: Heinemann Educational Books, 1972), p. 79.

94. Listen, for example, to *Message to the Grass Roots from Malcolm X* (Afro Records, AA 1264); *Martin Luther King* (Mercury 20119). Writing *about* oratory has not been particularly successful (c.f. Marcus H. Boulware, *The Oratory of Negro Leaders* (Westport, Conn.: Negro Universities Press, 1969). Although Roger Abrahams' work on this aspect of Afro/New World folk art should be specially mentioned: "The Shaping of Folklore Traditions in the British West Indies," and "Traditions of Eloquence in Afro-American Committees," *Journal of Inter-American Studies and World Affairs,* 9, pp. 456–480 and 12, pp. 505–527.

95. In this paper I have concentrated on the religious aspects of Caribbean folk culture. There is, however, an important secular development, magnificently expressed in the carnival and calypso of Trinidad especially. This secular aspect of our culture is as comprehensive (life-centered) as the religious art-styles being discussed. See Errol Hill, *The Trinidad Carnival* (Austin: University of Texas Press, 1972).

96. Lamming, *Season of Adventure,* p. 91.

97. From the work of the writers cited in this paragraph (themselves a selec-

tion), the following may be noted: Nina Rodrigues, *Os Africanos no Brasil* (1905; São Paulo: Cia Editora Nacional, 1932); Renato Mendoza, *A influenca Africana portugesa do Brasil* (Rio de Janeiro: 1934); Fernando Ortiz, *Hampa Afrocubana: Los Negros Brujos* (Madrid: Editorial-America, 1906); Arthur Ramos, *O Negro Brasileiro* (Rio de Janeiro: Civilizacão Brasileira, 1934); Donald Pierson, *Negroes in Brazil* (Chicago: University of Chicago Press, 1942); Ivy Baxter, *The Arts of an Island* (Metuchen, N.J.: The Scarecrow Press, 1970); Errol Hill, *The Trinidad Carnival;* J. D. Elder, *Evolution of the Traditional Calypso of Trinidad and Tobago. . . .* (Ann Arbor, Mich.: University Microfilms, 1966, 1970); Roger Bastide, *Les Amériques noires* (Paris: Payot, 1967).

98. See Alexis Kagame, *La philosophie bantu-rwandaise de l'être* (Brussels: 1956); Griaule, *Dieu d'eau;* Tempels, *Bantoe-Filosofie;* Jahn, *Muntu* (1958), trans. Marjorie Grene (London: Faber and Faber, 1961) and *A History of Neo-African Literature.* In the New World, studies of the African word in Creole speech include Lorenzo Turner, *Africanisms in the Gullah Dialect of the Southern United States* (Chicago: University of Chicago Press, 1949); J. J. Thomas, *The Theory and Practice of Creole Grammar* [in Trinidad] (Port-of-Spain, 1869); F. G. Cassidy and R. B. Le Page, *Dictionary of Jamaican English;* F. G. Cassidy, *Jamaica Talk* (London: Macmillan, 1961); Mary Jo Willeford, "Africanism in the Bajan Dialect," *Bim,* 46 (1968), pp. 90–97, and Fernando Ortiz, *Glosario de Afro-negrismos* (Havana: 1923). But the really illuminating studies, often providing a meaningful context for understanding the presence of the Word, are (among others), Mervyn Alleyne, "The Linguistic Continuity of Africa in the Caribbean," *Black Academy Review,* 1, No. 4 (Winter 1970), pp. 3–16; LeRoi Jones, *Blues People* (New York: Grove Press, 1972); Sylvia Wynter, "Jonkonnu in Jamaica," *Jamaica Journal,* 4, No. 2 (June 1970), pp. 34–48; and Jean Price-Mars, *Ainsi parla l'oncle* (Port-au-Prince: Imprimerie de Compiégne, 1928).

99. Monica Skeete, "To Frank Collymore on His Eightieth Birthday," *Savacou* 7/8 (January/June 1973), p. 122.

100. Ibid.; my notation.

101. Bongo Jerry, "The Youth," *Savacou* 3/4 (December 1970/March 1971), p. 13. My notation.

102. Bongo Jerry, "Mabrak," *Savacou* 3/4, pp. 13–14.

103. Ibid., p. 15.

104. Edward Brathwaite, "Jazz and the West Indian Novel."

105. I have developed my ideas on this still further in my "Introduction" to Roger Mais, *Brother Man* (1954; London: Heinemann Educational Books, forthcoming in 1974).

106. Nicolás Guillén, "Sensemayá" from *West Indies Ltd* (1934), in *El son entero,* pp. 60–61.

107. Césaire, *Cahier* (1956 ed.), p. 50.

108. Leon Damas, "Il est des nuits," *Pigments* (Paris: Guy Lévis Mano, 1937), p. 24.

109. Jamil Ali, "Dimensions of Confusion," *Savacou* 9/10 (forthcoming in 1974).

110. Brathwaite, *Islands,* pp. 65–66.

111. The Mighty Sparrow, "Ten to One is Murder," transcribed in his *One Hundred and Twenty Calypsoes to Remember* (Port-of-Spain: National Recording Co., 1963), p. 37. Errol Hill in *The Trinidad Carnival,* p. 70, comments on the *calinda*-style performance as follows: "The form seems simple enough on paper, but it is highly effective and dramatic in performance. The rapid alternation from

solo voice to chorus creates a feeling of tension. Sometimes the leader will anticipate the end of the chorus line and come in over it; at another time he will appear to drop behind the regular meter in starting his verse, then suddenly spring forward on a syncopated beat. He improvises not only with his lyric but also with the melody; he ornaments his short passage[s] in subtle ways, but is always constrained to return to the original tune by the insistent power of the chorus. It is as though leader and chorus complement and contradict each other simultaneously."

> Sparrow: Well I start to sweat,
> An I soakin wet,
> Mamma, so much threat,
> That's a night I can never forget
> Ten o' dem against me with fifty spectator
>
> Chorus: *Ten to one is murder!*

112. Pastor Williams and Spiritual Baptist Congregation, Silver Sands, Barbados. Transcription of cassette tape recording: October 15, 1972. We could also refer to the second preacher in the Jamaican film, *The Harder They Come,* and recordings such as the Reverend Kelsey (Brunswick OE 9256) for the United States. Examples could also be cited for Haiti, Brazil, Africa.

113. Bruce St. John, "West Indian Litany," *Savacou* 3/4 (December 1970/ March 1971), p. 82.

114. Unpublished manuscript.

115. Césaire, *Cahier* (Paris: Présence Africaine, 1971 ed.), p. 72.

116. Lamming, *The Pleasures of Exile* (London: Michael Joseph, 1960), p. 121.

117. See Elizabeth Clarke, "Mudda Africa," *New Writing in the Caribbean,* ed. A. J. Seymour (Georgetown: National History and Arts Council of Guyana, 1972), p. 60–62; Tito Jemmott, "A Tale," *Savacou* 3/4, pp. 60–64.

118. Melvin Tolson, *Libretto for the Republic of Liberia* (New York: Twayne Publishers, 1953).

119. Robert Hayden, "Middle Passage," *A Ballad of Remembrance* (London: Paul Breman, 1962), pp. 60–66.

120. Brathwaite, *Rights of Passage* (1967), *Masks* (1968), *Islands* (1969), published under single cover as *The Arrivants* (London: Oxford University Press, 1973).

121. Paule Marshall, *The Chosen Place, the Timeless People* (New York: Harcourt, Brace and World, 1969).

122. Brathwaite, "West Indian History and Society in the Art of Paule Marshall's Novel," *Journal of Black Studies,* 1, No. 2 (December 1970), pp. 225–238.

123. Paule Marshall, *Chosen Place,* p. 106.

124. Ibid., p. 121.

125. Ibid., p. 123.

126. For the close connection between the Montserrat masquerade bands and their counterparts in West Africa, see the articles by Simon Ottenberg, Phillips Stevens, Jr. and John C. Messenger in *African Arts,* 6, No. 4 (Summer 1973), pp. 32–35, 40–43, 54–57.

127. Marshall, *Chosen Place,* p. 287.

7

African Influence in Latin America: Oral and Written Literature

Samuel Feijoo

Oral Literature

To understand, even superficially, the Black influence, its efficient development as it permeated the complexities of Latin American culture, it is necessary to know which were the dominant folk cultures brought to America by the African groups, how they merged and mixed their folklore, and how this mixture was later inserted into the general cultural environment.

The following pages only attempt to analyze briefly one aspect of the problem: the African influence on oral and written Latin American literature. Oral literature is a difficult subject to deal with because it is so complex and because we still do not have sufficient live, accurate, and clean texts on national variations and influences to permit us to make deep and accurate judgments. Nevertheless, through existent research it is possible to assert that the imprints of African oral literature are deep and quite obvious in some countries, and that they are weaker in the countries that have a lighter African demographic density.

What is known, for example, about the fate of African oral folk culture in Mexico, its absorption and its transformation into the general Mexican culture? There may still be folk tales, Mexican ones narrated by Whites or Mestizos, as is the case, for example, of the amusing adventures of the ingenious "Little Black Poet." However, this poem or Black myth has barely influenced Mexican literature, and has practically disappeared from it.

And the Black in Peru? Has the influence of the strong Black or Negroid folk forms been analyzed in the general Peruvian literature or in oral folk literature? What about Ecuador? In Colombia, where linguistic research has been seriously conducted, cultural anthropology is becoming more significant and folk researchers are conducting important studies in Black areas, such as the Alto and Bajo Chocó, on the idiosyncratic cultures, their variants, transculturation, etc.

In Argentina, where Black slaves lived primarily in Buenos Aires, they had only a very scant influence on general Argentine folk poetry, stories, refrains, and myths. There are caricatures of the newly imported slave in the songs of the ancient carnival groups, made up of Whites, who imitated the songs of the *candombé*. These were Americanized songs that mockingly used the neo-Spanish language of the Africans:

> Candombe, candombe,
> Candombe, candombe,
> Candombe, candombe,
> Candombe, candombe,
> Buriay curumbamba
> María Curumbé.
> Hé, e,
> Hé, e, he Maruay Curumbé.

It is clear that the Black context in this way left its impression on satirical popular speech: but here imitation implied nonrecognition. Later on the Black became a subject of Argentine literature, like the Black poet in the national poem "Martin Fierro," who expresses himself like an Argentine without maintaining any ties with the culture of his ancestors. This Black improvisor is a symbol, he is a model of the Black born in America; he and his American descendants are just like the gauchos. They are completely Americanized.

The depth to which the oral elements of Black literature have influenced Venezuelan folklore is still unknown because of lack of research. In Brazil the Black has left a deep musical and religious imprint. Many important anthropological studies have been conducted by Nina Rodrigues, Arthur Ramos, Mario de Andrade and others; yet, we lack specialized texts on the literary heritage of the Black in Brazil. Nevertheless, in the studies of Rodrigues, Ramos, and Andrade we find much oral African or Neoafrican poetry in religious songs that have been collected. Some examples follow. Ramos describes a ritual ceremony that contains Black Brazilian songs:

> The high priest begins the service by invoking the protecting saint. The mediums are arranged in two lines, the women to the left, the men to the right. The *filhas de santo* are dressed in a white cotton skirt and robe, the men wear pants and shirts made of canvas of the same color. The *umbanda*, standing before the altar, stretches his arms forward and utters an unintelligible prayer. Immediately he turns towards the audience and shouts: "Ogún!" He appears in *candombé*, "pulls out" the songs and begins to sing:

Saint George is in our circle	Está na ronda San Jorge
Because of his bravery	Pela sua alta vanentía
Let us salute Ogún	Vamos saudar Ogún
Ogún!	Ogún!

The rhythm is marked through the clapping hands, percussion instruments such as drums, tambourines, timbrels. The *candombé* continues, accompanied by the chorus:

Saravad Ogún	Saravad Ogún
Ogún, my father,	Ogún, meu pae
Oh George, oh George	O Jorge, ó Jorge
Come from Luanda	Vem da Loanda
Have mercy on your children	Tem copaixdo de seus filhos
He overcame the demand	Venceu a demanda
Ogún is	Ogún-é
Ogún is macumba!	Ogún macumba-é!

Enter the chorus:

Save Angola!	Salva Angola!
Save the Congo!	Salva Congo!
Save the Congo!	Salva Congo!
Because Umbanda has arrived.	Que Umbanda chegou.

Nina Rodrigues collected stories from Black descendants of Dahomans in Bahia. In one of them, which narrates the adventures of a turtle, there is an African style song that is very rhythmic and very closely related to African stories and to the African stories of the Antilles:

Otavo otavo longozoe
ilá pono éfan
i ve pondereman
hoto ro men i cos
assenta ni ananá
ne so aroro ale nuxá
avun-cé, mababú,
avun-cé, nogo-e-zin
avun-cé, mababú,
avun-cé, nogo-zo
avun-cé, mababú
avun-cé, nogo-abo,
avun-cé, mababún,
avun-cé, aue-na
a son coticoló ke
babúm.

Another Congolese song was discovered by Mario de Andrade in a Catholic ceremony in Rio Grande do Norte; it has a fetishist background:

Solo: Já mutum, já mutum, já mutum, gangulé!
Chorus: Eh, alelé, já mutum, gangulé!
The little Blacks are dancing for the White man to see!
Eh, alélé, já mutum, gangulé!
Blessed be he for whom we had the feast!
Eh, adélé, já mutum, gangulé!

Another is a Black Brazilian song to Obá, goddess of the Obá River in Africa. This nostalgic song maintains its vigorous African rhythm, its power, and its language in the New World:

> Xangó olé bondilé ó-la-lá
> Con gon gon gondilá.
> Xangó olé, gondilé, olé-olé
> Con gon gon gondilé.
> Con gon gon gondilé
> Iemanjá otó bajoré
> O yá otó bajoré
> O remanjá otó bajoré
> O ya otó bajoré o.

Blacks have also left their imprint on oral Latin-American folklore, through what we could call the discriminatory folklore which makes fun of the Black. This style already had its precedents in the "Black Wedding" by the poet Quevedo, who wrote during the Golden Century of Spanish literature. All this must be counted in the general context of Black influence in Latin America.

Americanization and the Colonial Context

The refrains, stories, myths, fables, and poetry of oral African and neo-African literature reappear and expand throughout America, not to evoke a feeling of nostalgia for Africa in the descendants of Africans, but to become a more American element. Thus the Black or Mulatto uses immemorial sources and adds to them American variants, characters, vegetation, voices, and idiosyncracies. The Blacks born in America, the Mestizos, have become a part of the general American style. Present-day Blacks and Mulattoes, like Cubans, Haitians, and Brazilians, are living parts of their respective homelands, and are linked to these homelands like all other inhabitants: they are Blacks and Mulattoes who share a general culture. However, in some countries, the United States for one, they still suffer from tremendous racial, social, and economic discrimination. Discrimination is less pronounced elsewhere, and is nonexistent in Cuba, where it was decisively eliminated with the triumph of the revolution. Therefore a nostalgia for Africa appears only very rarely in the writings of Blacks in the Americas, and Mulattoes. It is no longer an important psychological factor in Creole Blacks or their descendants; nor is it even a distant folk theme: it no longer exists, it has disappeared. Blacks have become citizens, an original, cultural, telluric force, a creative part of each new nation where they live, maintaining their own music, song, and dance in the face of poor living conditions, racial discrimination, and the lack of education that corresponds to their low social status.

This is why Blacks and Mulattoes who learned how to read and write during the course of the nineteenth century did not write about their ancestors or the folk literature of their forebears. They wrote instead in the style of the dominant Spanish or Portuguese cultures, the contemporary style, with its colonial or nationalistic roots deriving from independence from Spain or Portugal. A Black singing in the Pampas sang like a *gaucho;* and the Cuban poet Plácido, writing in a country colonized by Spain, wrote like a White poet, penning odes, the "Moorish romances" that were in fashion, poems, and talented Spanish epigrams. The same was true of the literate Black Cuban slave poet Juan Francisco Manzano; he wrote sensitive, talented verses, in the style of contemporary White poets, that fit into the dominant Spanish literary context.

However, Manzano left the world, in his autobiography, composed on request, the most heartrending antislavery document ever written, portraying the inhumanity and the horrors of the slave system. It is the most tragic autobiography, an incomparable human document, the most unique accusation against slavery and the slave trade.

There are numerous examples of the writings of assimilated, literate Blacks that we will not reproduce here, since they fall into a research, rather than an analytical context. However, it would be helpful to provide an example of how White folklore penetrated the Black communities and was generally accepted by them: we refer to the inflammatory, *"porfía"* poetry of Colombian Blacks in Chocó, collected by Rogerio Velazquez during a recent trip to the fabulous Colombian Black region. These aggressive couplets are part of the tradition of "troubadour" contests, between improvisatory poets that is strong in certain Latin-American countries like Cuba, Argentina, Venezuela, the Dominican Republic, Puerto Rico, and Colombia. The form is Spanish, a combination of couplets and rhyme. The images and stylistics are Colombian, accentuated here by the African mode, its idiosyncratic expressions and concepts. Here are some brief examples of a folk art of Americanized Blacks:

Yo soy el José Tomás
de los ojos colorados,
hasta los diablos me huyen
porque en el infierno he estado.

I am Joseph Thomas
Of the red eyes
even the devils flee from me
because I have been in hell.

Quien vaya a cantar conmigo
que examine su memoria,
porque yo aprendí a cantar
con angeles de la gloria.

Whosoever will sing with me
should examine his memory
because I learned to sing
with the angels of glory.

El que va a cantar conmigo
beba primero la tonga,
me llamo José María,
hijo de la negra conga.

Whoever sings with me
let him first drink a round
My name is José María
and I am the son of a Black Congolese.

These are songs of Black American singers who suffered because their Black skin set them apart, who were immersed in a Mestizo culture, often in the process of becoming Mulattoes, but who were always discriminated against. This discrimination gave cultivated Black and Mulatto writers a social, political, and cultural conscience, always expressed in sharpness, satire, active protest, and a secret knowledge of the injustice committed against a very important racial element that was crucial to the formation of their country. It is always expressed in literature or in American song: "There is as much difference between a Black Antillean and a citizen of Dakar, as between a Brazilian and a person from Madrid."

Oral Neo-African Literature in the Antilles

In the Spanish Antilles, Cuba, the Dominican Republic, and Puerto Rico, Spanish style was always the aesthetic standard of "high" culture. This was so even at a time when a nationalist conscience began to emerge, when the desire for independence strengthened, even, in the Dominican Republic, which had a very active Black folk culture due to its proximity to Haiti. In Cuba the situation was different. By the time political pseudoindependence was achieved in 1902, following the interventionist war of the United States against Spain, the French aesthetic standards of the "modernist" movement had already begun to dominate cultured poetry.

In the Spanish Caribbean, as in other Latin-American areas, there is an extensive folk literature based on Black themes. This literature does not reflect an African or a Black influence, instead it reflects the inheritance of slavery. Its favorite subject is ridicule of the Black, which indicates the prejudice that originated with slavery. Two couplets from Puerto Rico show this shameful attitude (there are similar examples in the Dominican Republic, Colombia, Venezuela, etc.):

El negro no tiene sesos,	The Black man has no brains,
ni huesos, ni coyunturas,	no bones and no joints,
y para mayor vergüenza	and what is even more shameful,
tiene la cabeza dura.	he has a hard head.

El negro y el sinvergüenza	The Black man and the scoundrel
nacieron de una barriga;	were born from one belly;
el negro nació debajo	the Black man was born at the bottom
con el sinvergüenza arriba.	with the scoundrel on top of him.

Naturally these couplets often brought a defensive reply from the Black. The following replies were found in Puerto Rico:

El que me dijere negro	Whoever calls me Black
es ponerme una corona	Is crowning me
porque de negro se visten	because the three divine persons
las tres divinas personas.	are all dressed in black

Hay muchos negros aquí;	There are many Blacks here;
al decirlo no me escondo;	while saying so I do not hide;
el que no tiene de congo	whoever is not part Congo
tiene de carabalí.	is part Carabalí.

Such folk expressions generally lack literary merit, but they are important sociological documents. Puerto Rican folk culture is full of praise for the female Mulatto, and so is the folklore of the rest of Latin America. Although these folk songs seem complimentary, they are really reflections of racial prejudice:

Una mulata que tenga	A Mulatto woman who has
su nariz muy perfilada	a very fine nose
y su frente desarrollada	and a developed forehead
¿quien no suspira por ella?	Who will not sigh for her?
Y si es simpatica y bella	And if she is charming and beautiful
pues vale mas que una blanca.	she is worth more than a White woman.

Cuba

Cuba and Brazil have examples not only of oral literature, but also of written Black, Mulatto, and White literature influenced by general Black culture or by the subject of African slaves and their descendants in Latin America. In Cuba and in Brazil there exist very accomplished, beautiful, and universally resonant music and dance with African references. In Cuba the first antislavery novels were written by Whites. They described the physical environment of the Africans and their descendants, in the countryside and in the cities, mentioning the horrors to which the Blacks were subjected. Examples include *Francisco* by Anselmo Suarez y Romero, and *Cecilia Valdés,* by Cirilo Villaverde. Cuba offers ample examples of the bold appearance of African culture on the island, its peculiar, already Creole characteristics, displayed in folk and cultured poetry. Cuba was the center of the development of a "Black Poetry" movement that made its way into universal anthologies. Therefore, we will briefly discuss Cuba in our description of the general awareness of Blacks, their culture and their vivid contributions to America.

Following the genocide of the Cuban Indians there remained of their culture, regardless of its status or conditions, only some beautiful words, some lovely names, usually of places, and some of the obscure myths of their cosmogony. Thus, when the African slaves arrived, their culture only had to confront that of the White masters and the new culture of the first White Creoles that was beginning to emerge in America in adaptation to a novel and different medium conducive to new styles.

With the years, after the African cultures had mingled on the island, the slaves and their Creole children still refused to assimilate the dominant culture of the White without distorting it. How could the slaves survive in such a different, hostile, condescending, and cruel atmosphere without secretly clinging to their folk culture? The first Africans and their children were all a part of such a folk culture. The mass of slaves resisted, for the sake of survival, all the foreign influences of their masters, searching their inner being, their knowledge, and their beliefs in order to reject this alien culture. The vitality of the African slave sought refuge in religion and in folk culture, legitimately resisting the power of the White exploiter. Dances, songs, myths, voices, liturgies, foods, and medicines were the more appreciated and the more unifying because they marked the slaves' determination, from the very beginning, to resist the oppressive culture into which they had been so violently inserted, to save the rich inheritance of their own culture, even using it to transform and to add gaiety to the culture of their oppressors.

By the third or fourth Black generation in Cuba, according to Cuban scholar Julio Le Riverend, "The Black man rapidly lost the elements of his culture, because his servile condition, besides mixing [different cultures] together, imposed upon him a government, authorities, laws, and constraints which made the survival of his own [cultural] creations impossible. In some cases, however, he preserved with extreme faithfulness, essential traits like religion and magic, music, folk tales, and the language that survived slavery. It must be kept in mind that many of the Black groups that came to America were by no means the barbarians described by apologists for slavery and therefore, many of them not only preserved elements of their own culture, but were even able to transmit them to other Black slaves of different origins with whom they cohabited. They even passed them on to some Whites."

The slave folk culture expanded, but was always looked at with suspicion and contempt by the governing class and the high and small bourgeoisie that was emerging in these countries. But people in general enjoyed the Black music, dances, fables, sayings, and sense of humor, all of which gave them real pleasure. One must not forget that there was a time, in the fourth quarter of the nineteenth century, when the Black Cuban population was the largest in the country. During that time Blacks and Mulattoes preserved their folk culture, by then already in its mixed form or somewhat changed, but still alive, beautiful, and attractive, and despite its transculturation, no less powerful.

In the African-influenced oral literature one observes religious myths and the glorification of the heroic feats of the gods. There are also animal stories with monkeys and elephants, and once in a while a European bear makes an appearance. There are stories filled with rhythmic songs and swift adventures, sometimes followed by moral teachings, other times told for the sake of pure enjoyment, containing a happy sense of humor and excellent narrative skills. Such is the nature of the tightly knit, attractive, simple fables set in the Antilles.

The pithy power of African slave literature was passed on to their children. A number of refrains responding to the new condition of the Black in America were generated. Some of these have been collected, and it may be helpful to get to know them briefly. The following sayings were taken from a collection put together by the researcher Lydia Cabrera in the 1950s:

> Head cannot go through ear.
> The turtle tried to fly and broke its shell.
> The same stick that will kill a White dog will also kill a Black dog.
> A Black woman for a Black man, a White woman for a White man, yet both
>   of them are mothers.
> All hearts are red.
> If the ox is not born, the Black man must pull the cart.
> Happiness has a skinny body.
> The pan is used to having its bottom burned by the flame.
> The mother of misfortune is poverty.
> They can't stand a poor man with a large basket.
> A gentleman may eat gold, but he shits filth.
> Guilt always hangs over the Black.
> On White man's fishing trip the Black man carries the nets.
> Necessity is the father of the Mulatto.
> From the bishop to the governor all equally bad.
> In a chicken court, a cockroach has no vote.
> A cockroach won't greet Mr. Rooster.
> Give your clothes to a tiger, and he will break your neck.
> The head gets its advice from the ear.
> The peacock believes he is king: he better not look down at his legs.
> Some day the spider may have to pay rent.

Rafael Roche compiled refrains in Náñigo, revealing the persistence of African language, by then part of the jargon, and its noticeable influence on Cuban folk vocabulary:

> Malarica bira guañañongo ecombre.
> (Whitey, if you don't know, just keep out of it.)
> Acua embore boroquí mangue.
> (The goat is castrated just once).
> Aseré abasillaberomo ita maribá endié ecruloró.
> (When the sun rises, it rises for everyone.)
> Chequedenque longosiremó.
> (He who doesn't have a heart won't go to war.)
> Efique, efique butón, efique, efique quenamiró aguana toitó.
> (I am poor, but with my family I am rich.)

White Influence of Blacks in Nineteenth-Century Cuba

Despite the constant suspicion on Black culture, some colored men excelled in nineteenth-century Cuban literature. They were either truly Black, sons of slaves, like Juan Francisco Manzano or Ambrosio Echemendia, both of whom were slaves themselves until manumitted by compassionate White literary figures who pitied them for their living conditions; or they were Mulattoes like Gabriel de la Concepión Valdés (Plácido), the son of a Spanish woman and a Mulatto. But these descendants of Africans, we repeat, were dominated, in their style and their subject matter, by Spanish usages; they were writers who had been inserted into the Spanish-dominated Antillean literature.

The following are brief examples of the neoclassical style of Plácido, who wrote poems, romances, and epigrams with Cuban themes. Colonial censorship did not allow for sharpness and strength of style, even though Plácido was able to ridicule the censorship with great ability, as we will show later on.

These are fragments of fashionable neoclassicism; they show Hispanicized Cuban peasants using *rebecs* that had never been used before by Cubans:

Del céfiro halagados mis oídos resonaba el rabel de los pastores,	In my ears flattered by zephyr the rebec of the shepherds resounded
que al alba festejaban divertidos cantando por las selvas sus amores.	they were merrily feasting at dawn singing their loves in the forests.

This is a strictly European Arcadia, since in Cuba shepherds did not exist. The verses are purified through the neoclassical style of colonized Mulattoes. What other types of poetry did the despotic colonial government of Cuba permit?

Desde el manso Almendar la bella ninfa	From the gentle Almendar the beautiful nymph
Tu oriente ensalza entre tu clara linfa	praises the source of your clear waters
De límpido cristal.	of transparent crystal.
Su manto de zafir, su faz riente,	Her sapphire mantle, her smiling face,
De oro sus rizos, de jazmín su frente,	Her golden hair and jasmine forehead,
Su carro de coral.	Her coral cart.
Su nevado cendal ciñen claveles,	A snowy scarf encircled by carnations
Orna su sien de auríferos laureles	decorates her temples with golden laurels
Con ademán gentil	with gesture soft

Y en tu natal las almas enajena

Pulsando así con dedos de azucena
Su plectro de marfil.

And at your source enraptures the
  spirits
plucking with lily-white fingers
Its ivory plectrum.

El Sueño (The Dream)

Plácido was shot during the terrible slave slaughter called the "Conspiracy of the Ladder," in which Blacks and Mulattoes were tortured with a cruelty rarely seen in America. It is quite possible that some of his poems brought about his death—possibly the antislavery poems, since this sensitive Mulatto knew discrimination at close hand and used symbolic means to attack slavery in Cuba:

Gran confusión se notaba
en los siervos de una finca,
y ningún de su choza
solo en la noche salía.
Súpolo el dueño, juntolos,

y preguntó qué tenían.
Ellos dijeron que un bulto
en la oscuridad se vía
que era como un tigre grande.
El amo dijo: magnífico
anima mea!... ¡la cruz!...
Más una negra ladina
contestó: señor, no es eso;
ese tigre es sin mentira
el alma del mayoral
que se murió el otro día.

There was great confusion
among the estate slaves
and no one from his shack
would leave alone at night.
The master knew of this and
  gathered them together
and asked them what was wrong.
They said there was a shape
they had seen in the dark
that was much like a large tiger.
The master said: Bless
my soul!.... the cross!
But a Black woman slave
answered: Sir, it is not that,
this tiger is without a doubt
the soul of the overseer
who died the other day.

La figura de un alma (The figure of a spirit)

The fame of Plácido was immense; he was the natural pride of dark-skinned and Black people. His is the most important expression of Mulatto poetry of the nineteenth century in Latin America. He even ridiculed the racial boundaries set up by "pure" White men:

Siempre exclama Don Longino:
soy de sangre noble y pura
....
y con su rostro cetrino
que africana estirpe indica
alucinado publica
ser de excelsa parentela.
Que se lo cuente a su abuela

Don Longino always exclaims:
I am of noble and pure blood.
....
And with his sallow face
showing his African extraction,
deluded, he proclaims
his noble parentage.
Let him tell that to his grandmother.

Que se lo cuente a su abuela (Let him tell that to his grandmother)

He does even more. He suggests a liberation struggle, the war against the racist oppressor. To do this he employs the simple fable, "The Man and the Canary." A man asks a canary:

Animada miniatura	Animated miniature
¿por qué con tu suavidad	why don't you, with your gentle-ness
no entonas, y con dulzura,	sweetly sing,
los trinos de libertad	the trills of liberty
que aprendiste en la espesura?	that you learned in the thickets?
Cuanto quieren enseñarte	Whatever they wish to teach you
humilde, lo aprendes todo,	humbly, you learn it all,
y puedes tanto olvidarte	Do you forget yourself
de tí que no buscas modo	to the point that you don't ever search
ninguno de libertarte?	for a way to seek freedom?

And the canary responds:

Lo que se me enseña canto,	I sing what I am taught
porque con mis trinos bellos,	because with my beautiful trills,
aunque vierta oculto llanto,	even though I secretly cry
hago lo que mandan ellos	I do what they want me to do
para no padecer tanto.	so that I need not suffer too much.
Sé que no puedo quebrar	I know that I can't break
estas varillas de alambre:	these metal bars:
me dan vida por cantar,	they let me live so I may sing
y si persisto en callar	and, if I persist in keeping quiet,
me harán perecer de hambre.	they will starve me to death.
Que le adulo en la apariencia	My master thinks I adore
piensa me dueño, y se hiochiza;	his presence and he is bewitched;
mas, mirándolo en conciencia,	but, looking at things honestly,
yo engaño al que me esclaviza	I trick the one who enslaves me
por conservar mi existencia.	to preserve my own existence.
. . . .	. . . .
Vivir, y hallar la ocasión	To live and to search for the right moment
de libertarse, es cordura.	To become free, is to be sane.

The ex-slave, Juan Francisco Manzano, who wrote "Anacreónticas" and "Odes" composed the famous sonnet in which one can feel the pain suffered by the ex-slave expressed in the purified classical European form, its rhythm and its restrictions. It is entitled "Thirty years":

Cuando miro el espacio que he cor-rido	When I consider the distance that I have run
desde la cuna hasta el presente día,	From my cradle to the present day,

tiemblo, y saludo la fortuna mía más de terror que de atención movido.	I tremble, and greet my fortune moved more by terror than by attention.
Sorpréndeme la lucha que he podido sostener contra suerta tan impía, si tal llamarse puede la porfía de mi infelice ser, al mal nacido.	I am surprised by the struggle that I have sustained against bad luck, if I can thus call this stubborn fight for my unhappy existence, since I was born to this ill fate.
Treinta años ha que conocí la tierra; treinta años ha que en gemidor estado triste infortunio por doquier me asalta.	For thirty years I have known this earth thirty years have gone by while in my moaning state, sad misfortune assaults me from all sides.
Mas nada para mi es la cruda guerra que en vano suspirar he soportado si la calculo Oh Dios! con la que falta.	But nothing to me is this crude war that with vain sighs I have borne if I match it, Oh God, with what is yet to come.

The rhythm of the African musical dances and its voices, the revolutionary awareness of the discriminated-against Black Cuban, reappears many decades later, in the 1930s in "Black Poetry."

Black Influence on Cuban Writers of the Nineteenth Century

In response to its ugly manifestations, an antislavery sentiment began to emerge among Cubans, which found expression in their literature. This literature continued to employ the Spanish literary forms until the end of the century, at which time slavery was abolished. As was mentioned earlier, this awareness gave birth to some fine antislavery novels, such as *Cecilia Valdés* by the anticolonialist patriot Cirilo Villaverde, and *Francisco* by the delicate, nature-loving Anselmo Suárez y Romero.

These works were instrumental in the development of a general consciousness of the abuses of Spanish colonialism and of the vile nature of the slave trade. *Cecilia Valdés* was Cuba's *Uncle Tom's Cabin*. The Cuban novel was neither romantic nor "sweet," instead it was sober, realistic, and powerful.

The subject of slavery was not a common one in colonial Cuban poetry, since the topic was considered dangerous and was usually censored. We do, however, have a Cuban ballad by José Fornaris, a "White" poet, famous for originating the anticolonial Siboney Movement of Cuban poetry, which lead to his exile from Cuba. "The Sad Flute" is about a sad African slave who sits up all night to guard his master's estate. To keep himself awake he plays a "rustic" flute:

Esa tosca flauta anuncia	This rustic flute announces
al mayoral de la estancia	to the overseer of the estate
que está velando el esclavo	that the slave is alertly watching the
y alerto los camps guarda.	fields.
Bien sabe que si se duerme	For he knows that if he falls asleep
el mayoral se levanta	the overseer will get up
y con el látigo horrible	and with a horrible whip
lo azota y lo despedaza!	he will beat him and tear him to
	pieces.

The flute resounds with the "deep lament of the Ethiopian race." Tired, the slave is overcome by sleep, and in his dreams he returns to his country, which the poet describes as Arcadian:

Soñó ver, lleno de gozo,	He dreamed that he saw, with great
	pleasure
las costas de Senegambia,	the shores of Senegambia,
y al son de los atabales	and to the beat of drums
volvió a divisar sus playas.	he once again saw its beaches.
Soñó que a su pobre madre	He dreamed that to his poor mother
un beso en la frente daba,	he gave a kiss on the forehead
y que risueño corría	and that with a smile he was run-
	ning
ya en la fiesta, ya en la caza,	at festivals or in the hunt,
o por la orilla del Níger	along the shores of the Niger
en alegre caravana . . .	in a happy caravan.

As soon as the overseer no longer hears the flute, he gets out of bed and runs to whip the slave. The overseer's daughter intervenes and asks for mercy for the slave. The overseer gives in to her demands. The daughter kneels before a crucifix and exclaims:

Dios de los orbes, Dios mío!	God of this earth, Oh my god!
Apiádate de esta raza:	Have mercy on this race:
extiende tu mano, borra	extend your hand and erase
el sello vil que la marca,	the vile seal that marks them
y hazla sentar al banquete	and let them sit at the banquet
de la gran familia humana!	of the great human family!

It was not this type of poem that redeemed Cuban slaves. However, when Carlos Manuel de Céspedes rebelled against Spanish colonial power in 1868, he took his slaves with him and granted them their freedom. The Blacks were great fighters during the Cuban insurrection, and prominent leaders like Maceo, the Moncadas, the Crombrets, all had Black blood.

During the nineteenth century there was a significant Black influence on the popular theater, known as the *"bufo"*. The *"negritos,"* a product of the Spanish *sainete,* or one-act farce, were Cubanized, and became important characters in the most outrageous comedies, filled with Cuban slang and Black slave language. These *"negritos"* were Whites with blackened faces, like the Northamerican minstrels. They were always happy, full of snappy expressions, and they brought to the stage popular dances, mixed with Black rhythms and songs. *Rumbas* and *guarachas* were danced and sung, but they never expressed the misfortunes of the Black social condition. What mattered was the acceptance of mixtures of Mulatto-influenced rhythms, dances, and songs with *guarachas* and "White" literary styles. Some, like "María Belén" were quite ironic:

La negra María Belén	The Black woman María Belén
dice que fue seductora	said she was seductive
y sin rival bailadora	and an unrivaled dancer
de danzas y de minué.	of dances and the minuet.
Refrain:	
Y hoy vive desesperada	And today she lives in desperation
porque ya no vale nada.	because she is no longer worth anything.
Al ponerse ella una bata	And, when she put on a robe
y un pañolito en la sien,	and a kerchief over her forehead,
era la negra más sata	she was the most flirtatious Black woman
la negra María Belén.	the Black woman, María Belén.

There were others that were satires, like "Rice and Beans":

Un blanco con una negra	A White man married a Black woman
se casaron hace un mes:	a month ago:
el marido tiene suegra	the husband has a mother-in-law
y creo que bruja es.	and I think that she is a witch.
Refrain:	
Tiene tres bemoles	They have great difficulties
pareja tal	this couple,
Que arroz con frijoles	that everyone calls
se suele llamar.	rice and beans.
Como los dos se casaron	How the two got married
yo no puedo comprender . . .	I cannot understand
Sin duda que se avidriaron	They must have become empty-headed
para tal barbarie hacer.	to do something so outrageous.

Other *guarachas* praised the Mulatto female:

Yo soy la reina de las mujeres	I am the queen of women
en esta tierra de promisión;	in this promised land;
yo soy de azúcar, yo soy de fuego,	I am made of sugar and fire,
yo soy la llave del corazón.	I am the key to the heart.
Refrain:	
No sé lo que tengo aquí,	I don't know what I have here

ni lo que me da;
ay, ay, ay!
No tiene cura mi enfermedad.

nor what afflicts me
ay, ay, ay!
there is no cure for my malady.

Yo soy la causa de que los hombres
a las blanquitas no den amor,
porque se mueren por mis pedazos

y los derrito con mi calor.

I am the reason why men
don't love their little White women,
because they die for certain parts of
me
and I melt them with my warmth.

Es mas dulce que el azúcar
cuando quiere una mulata,
entre todas las mujeres
sin duda es la flor y nata.

It is sweeter than sugar
the love of a Mulatto girl
among all women
she is undoubtedly the flower and
the cream.

Then, we also have the Black man Valentín, a showoff and a ruffian, later to be used by the "Black Poetry" movement in a different manner:

Aquí ha llegado Candela,
negrito de rompe y raja,
que con el cuchillo vuela
y corta con la navaja.

Candela has arrived
a little black rough and tumble boy
he is swift with his knife
and he cuts with his razor.

Candela no se rebaja
a ningún negro valiente;
en sacando la navaja
no hay nadie que se presente.

Candela will not lower himself
to any brave Black man
when he pulls out his knife
there is no one who will challenge
him.

All this sensational tough talk, all this Creole jargon and rhymed couplets, is accompanied by negroid rhythms which did not match the Spanish style. To bring together Spanish style and Black rhythm was the fecund success of later "Black Poetry."

The Black Poetry Movement in the Twentieth Century

Poetry with Black and Mulatto sounds, rhythms, and themes became prominent in Cuba in the 1930s, as did its natural forerunners both folk and cultured. This is not the place to dwell on this poetry, since whole books have been written on its merits and on its great poets. We will give a short summary of this movement, which gave the world a genuine Latin-American expression based on the rhythms of Cuban Mulatto dances, which passed into the rhythm of verses, creating something totally new.

Forerunners

Religious songs and the "Songs of the Cabildos" were the origins of this movement. Voices and rhythms linked to percussion instruments opened the path towards a new poetic language based on original forms. Lydia

Cabrera, in her book *The Forest,* gathers sung prayers of Black *mayom-beros* in which magic and religion are linked. The following are some examples of this rhythmic style:

Casimba yeré	Casimba yeré
Casimbangó	Casimbangó
Yo salí de mi casa	I left my house,
Casimbangó	Casimbangó
yo salí de mi tierra,	I left my land
Casimbango	Casimbangó
yo vengo a bucá . . .	I come to look . . .
Dame sombra Ceibita,	Give me shade little Ceiba tree,
Ceiba da yo sombra.	Ceiba give (I) shade.
Dame sombra palo Cuaba	Give me shade Cuaba tree
Dame sombra palo Yaba	Give me shade Yaba tree
Dame sombra palo Caja	Give me shade Caja tree
Dame sombra palo Tengue	Give me shade Tengue tree
Dame sombra palo Grayúa	Give me shade Grayúa tree
Dame sombra palo Wakibango	Give me shade Wakibango tree
Dame sombra palo Caballero	Give me shade Caballero tree
Yo vine a bucá . . .	I came to look for . . .

There are verbal rhythms like those in the "Song to Lower a Palm Bag By":

> Patti patti patti
> npémba simbico!
> Patti patti patti
> npémba simbico!
>
> . . . .
> Ya e yá patimpolo
> yá yá yá patimpolo
> Que yamos a ver
> Goya ya que patimpolo
> Pa tolo mundo, simbico.
> Yá yá yá, María Nganga
> Lo simbico, que patimpolo
> Mambé mambé dió!

Refrains and vocal rhythms follow the rhythm of the Black Cuban song. There are numerous prayers and magic songs, such as the "Songs of the Cabildo," which have the rhythm of a new poetry:

> Engó teramene!
> Jabre cutu güiri mambo.
> Engó teramene!
> Jabre cutu güiri mambo.
> Engó teramene!
> Jabre cutu güiri dinga.
> Engó teramene!

To these we might add the carnival songs and the "Songs to Kill Snakes," where the rhythm is dominant and the voices are a simple pretext for the dance rhythm:

Mamita mamita!	Mammy, mammy
Yen, yen, yen.	Yen, yen, yen,
Culebra me pica!	A snake is biting me!
Yen, yen, yen.	Yen, yen, yen.
Culebra me come!	A snake is eating me!
Yen, yen, yen.	Yen, yen, yen.
Me pica, me traga!	It is biting, it is swallowing me!
Yen, yen, yen.	Yen, yen, yen.
. . . .	. . . .
Culebra se muere	The snake is dying
Sángala muleque!	Sángala muleque!
Culebra se muere!	The snake is dying
Sángala muleque!	Sángala muleque!
La culebra se murió!	The snake is dead!
Calabasó-só-só!	Calabasó-só-só!
Yo mimito mató!	I myself killed it!
Calabasó-só-só!	Calabasó-só-só!

All these songs and rhythms became more common during the nineteenth century. In the twentieth century, the cultured Cuban poets found a splendid national treasure of sung and danced folklore, to which they gave a unique and original dimension.

Black Poetry

"Black Poetry" began in Cuba with Black and Mulatto folk elements; later it became fashionable, and finally it turned into a powerful literary movement that traveled to the other Antilles and to Latin America in general. In Europe there had already been studies on African myths, fables, and statuary. When Lydia Cabrera edited her *Black Cuban Stories* there had still been no systematic production of "Black Poetry" in Cuba despite repeated admonitions, such as those of Domingo del Monte in the nineteenth century: "The Blacks on the island of Cuba are the source of our poetry, and there are no two ways about it. But not just the Blacks, but the Blacks with the Whites, all mixed together, it is they who will shape the tableau, the scenes. . . ."

In 1928, the magazine *Atuei* published José Z. Tallet's "Rumba" signaling the dawn of "Black Poetry." The poem is based on the rhythm of the *rumba* and describes the dance spectacle. Black dancers, described by a blond White author, gripped by the rhythm of the dance. The following are fragments:

Zumba, mamá, la rumba y tambó!	Zumba, mamá, rumba, and drum!
Mabimba, mabomba, mabomba, y bombó!	Mabimba, mabomba, mabomba, and bombó!
Zumba, mamá, la rumba y tambó!	Zumba, mamá, la rumba and drum!
Mabimba, mabomba, mabomba, y bombó!	Mabimba, mabomba, mabomba, and bombó!
Como baila la rumba la negra To-masa!	How Black Tomasa dances the rumba!
Como baila la rumba José Encarnación!	How José Encarnación dances it too!
Ella mueve una nalga, ella mueve la otra,	She moves one buttock, she moves the other,
el se estira, se encoge, dispara la grupa,	He stretches, he shrinks, he shoots out his rump,
el vientre dispara, se agacha, camina,	He shoots out his belly, he bends down, walks
sobre el uno y el otro talón.	on one heel and then the other.
Chaqui, chaqui, chaqui, charaqui!	Chaqui, chaqui, chaqui, charaqui!
Chaqui, chaqui, chaqui, charaqui!	Chaqui, chaqui, chaqui, charaqui!

Based on refrains and onomatopoetics, the poem continues. It is included in the repertoire of many famous Cuban actors, as well as foreign ones. It has even made it to Hollywood.

Another White poet who started out by writing in the same vein was Ramón Guirao, a student of Black poetry and author of *Orbita de la Poesía Afrocubana,* whose first poem was "Rumba Dancer," very stylized, but always revolving around the spectacle of the dance. A fragment follows:

Bailadora de guaguancó,	Guaguancó dancer
piel negra	of black skin
tersura de bongó.	as taut as a bongo.
Agita la maraca de su risa	She shakes the rattle of her laughter
con los dedos de leche	with the fingers of her milky
de sus dientes.	white teeth.
Pañuelo rojo	Red kerchief
-seda-,	-silk-,
bata blanca	white robe
-almidón-,	-starch-
recorrer el trayecto	to walk the path
de una cuerda	of a rope
en un ritmo afrocubano	in an Afro-Cuban rhythm
de	of
guitarra	guitars,
clave	claves
y cajón.	and cajón drums.

The theme of *comparsos,* or carnival street dancers, with their imaginatively dressed musicians and dancers, tempted poets like Pichardo Moya, a White man, Emilio Ballagas, another White man, and Marcelino Arozarena, a Mulatto, to name a few of the most important ones. The poems were based on the dance spectacle, creating a genre of poetry that had never been heard before in the Spanish language:

Bailan las negras rumberas	The Black *rumba* dancers are dancing
con candela en las caderas	with a fire on their hips
abren sus anchas narices,	they open their wide nostrils
ventanas de par en par,	like windows
a un panorama sensual . . .	to a sensuous panorama
La conga ronca se va	The conga dancer goes away hoarse
al compás del atabal.	to the rhythm of the drum.

In 1930 Alejo Carpentier also published a Black poem, entitled "Liturgia," in the *Revista de Avance:*

La Potencia rompió	The Power has started out
¡yamba ó!	yamba ó!
Retumban las tumbas	The drums rumble
en casa de Acué.	in the house of Acué
. . . .	. . . .
A é, aé,	A é, aé,
cencerro de latón,	Brass bells
de paja la barba,	beard of straw
de santo el bastón.	staff of a saint
¡Tiembla congo! ¡Dale candela!	Tremble Black man! Set him on fire!
¡Chivo lo rompe! ¡Chivo lo pagó!	Goat breaks drum! Goat paid for it!
Endoco endiminoco,	Endoco endiminoco,
efimere bongó,	efimere bongó.
Enkiko baragofia,	Enkiko baragofia
¡yamba ó!	yamba ó!

Nicolás Guillén

But the greatest of all was the real master of the movement, Nicolás Guillén, a Mulatto born in 1902. By first dwelling on the spectacle, he attained its innermost parts faithfully depicting the Black, the Mulatto, and even the White, in poetry of broad themes based on the rhythm of the *son,* one of the strongest, most incisive forms of Cuban music. To accomplish his powerful poetic work, Guillén immersed himself into the most authentic *son* music of his country, which he converted into Black poetry. Though he also used classical forms, the basic element that can be heard in his work is the primary beat of the *son*. His general form of expression had already been shared by the Spanish classicists, such as Góngora, Quevedo, and Lope de Vega, who, during Spain's Golden Century, wrote poems with words and rhythms of Black dances. Guillén employs the purest and most appropriate Spanish language, yet his style is Cuban and American.

Guillén collected Black themes and talked about the Black, the Mulatto, and the Cuban people in his initial *Motivos del Son (Motifs for the "Son")*. Here he refers to their flat noses, coppery, woolly hair, and thick lips. At first his work was considered derisive and disrespectful by "whitened" Cuban Blacks.

The rhythms of the *son* were faithfully caught, for the first time, in a joyful language:

> Sóngoro Cosongo
> songo bé;
> sóngoro cosongo
> de mamey;
> sóngoro, la negra
> baila bien;
> sóngoro de uno,
> sóngoro de tré.
> aé,
> Bengan a bé;
> aé
> bamo pa bé;
> bengan sóngoro cosongo,
> sóngoro cosongo de mamey.
>
> (Si tú supiera . . .)
> (If you only knew . . .)

Guillén is a poet who emerged out of Cuba's folk song and dance. Guillén, born from a *son,* grew into its perfect exponent. He created a special literature that was at once national and folkloric. It grew with its creator, just as the anonymous music of the island emerged from the virtuosity of the Cuban people and achieved its perfect artistic form. In publishing his *Motivos del Son* a rite was established in Cuban and universal poetry that became known as "Black Poetry." With more than an intuitive knowledge of folklore, Nicolás Guillén carried folklore within him, and took it to its musical apex in the words he so naturally conquered; and, because he conquered them so well, he was able to use them to conquer his people, since the *son* was their root, the taste and essence of their creation. The *son* was a part of the people without the elaborate form of expression that marks the cultured writings. It was a part of the floating folklore that fills everything with a vivacious air and is always in search of the natural artist who will conquer it. Nicolás Guillén took the *son* that he was so intimately acquainted with, which he had chosen because it was good and beautiful, and developed it into a style that became the center of his life and work.

The masterful command Nicolás Guillén had of Cuban folklore, and of its purity, is essential to the universality and originality of his poetry. Guillén's poetry is not just Mulatto poetry. It is the total understanding of the musical rhythm of his country translated into verse form, expressed in the melodic Cuban rhythm, the popular and the universal Cuban verbal rhythm. The run-of-the-mill, fashionable poet hit upon the rhythm and the accent of the Mulatto Cuban style and of Black literature, but never progressed beyond it. Guillén entered the territory of *son* and made his way triumphantly, because he penetrated it with his Creole and his personal joy and thus conquered it.

What was written during or after the fashion of the *son* (what is known as "Black Poetry" because it uses the form of Black or Mulatto Cuban poetry) was beautiful and was literature, but it was only words. The *negrismo* of Ballagas, Carpentier, and even Tallet won the heart with its poetry) since it was the life, the essence, and the style of the people. But by incorporating himself into this major national style, Guillén did away with the literary fashion, the artistic findings. Out went the fashionable Black French prose. This is what Guillén had to say about the Black:

> We bring our features to the definitive profile of America.
>
> "The Arrival"

He describes the laughter, the speech, and the rhythms of Blacks:

Yambambó, yambambé!	Yambambó, yambambé!
Repica el congo solongo,	The solongo congo drum reverberates
repica el negro bien negro;	the Black, the real Black reverberates
congo solongo del songo	congo solongo of the songo
baila yambó sobre un pie.	dance yambó on one foot.
Mamatomba,	Mamatomba,
serembe curserembá.	serembe curserembá.
El negro canta y se ajuma,	The Black man sings and gets drunk
el negro se ajuma y canta,	The Black man gets drunk and sings
el negro canta y se va.	The Black man sings and goes.
Acuememe serembó,	Acuememe serembó,
aé;	aé
Yambó,	Yambó,
aé.	aé.

"Yambambó"

In the "Ballad of the Two Grandfathers," Guillén points out his Mulatto blood, referring to his White grandfather and his Black grandfather. He forces them to embrace for the sake of Cuba. That is why he satirizes the false White, thoughtless and corrupt politician, and the false Black. About the White he says:

Me río de tí porque hablas de aristocracias puras
de ingenios florecientes y de arcas llenas

I laugh at you because you talk about pure aristocracies
Of flowering sugar mills and of filled coffers.

"West Indies Ltd."

Of the "assimilated" Black he says:

Me río de tí, negro imitamicos,

que abres los ojos ante el auto de los ricos,
y que te avergüenzas de mirarte el pellejo oscuro
cuando tienes el puño tan duro!

I laugh at you, monkey-aping Black,
You open your eyes to stare at the car of the rich
and you are ashamed of looking at your Black skin
even though you have such a hard fist!

"West Indies Ltd."

This is how "Black Poetry" acquired, in Guillén, a social conscience and a rebellious character. The following is his description of the Antilles:

El hambre va por los portales
llenos de caras amarillas
y de cuerpos fantasmales;
y estacionándose en las sillas
de los parques municipales . . .
. . . .
Hambre de las Antillas
dolor de las ingenuas Indias Occidentales

Hunger enters the portals
that are full of yellow faces
and of ghostlike bodies
and perching on chairs
of municipal parks
. . . .
Hunger of the Antilles
pain of the ingenuous West Indies

"West Indies Ltd."

Para encontrar la butuba
hay que trabajar caliente;
para encontrar la butuba
hay que trabajar caliente;
mejor que doblar el lomo
tiene que doblar la frente.

To find the chow
you have to work in the heat;
to find the chow
you have to work in the heat;
rather than bending your back
you have to bend your forehead.

De la caña sale azúcar,
azúcar para el café;
de la caña sale azúcar,
azúcar para el café:
lo que ella endulza, me sabe
como si le echara hiel.

From the cane comes the sugar,
sugar for coffee;
from the cane comes the sugar,
sugar for coffee:
Whatever it sweetens, tastes to me
as if it were sweetened with bile.

"West Indies Ltd."

The bile of a harassed and very poor life comes up again in Cuba, the "sugar container of the world";

Mi patria es dulce por fuera	My country is sweet from the outside
y muy amarga por dentro;	and very bitter inside;
mi patria es dulce por fuera	my country is sweet from the outside
con su verde primavera	with its green spring
con su verde primavera	with its green spring
y un sol de hiel en el centro	and a sun of bile in the center

"Mi patria es dulce por fuera" ("My Country is Sweet on the Outside")

At that time, in 1943, Cuba was suffering from Northamerican neocolonialism. Guillén reflects the popular rejection of this:

Aunque soy un pobre negro,	Although I am a poor Black man
sé que el mundo no anda bien;	I know that the world is not doing O.K.
ay, yo conozco un mecánico	I know a mechanic
que lo puede componer!	who can repair it!
Quien los llamó?	Who called you?
Cuando regresen	when you return
a Nueva York,	to New York
mándenme pobres	send me poor people
como soy yo,	like I am
como soy yo,	like I am
como soy yo.	like I am.
A ellos les daré la mano	To them I will give my hand
y con ellos cantaré,	and with them I will sing,
porque el canto que ellos saben	because they sing a song
es el mismo que yo sé.	that is the same one that I know.

Contemporary Black Poetry

"Black poetry" is the most original movement and among the strongest in the Spanish language. It survives like a live current within Latin-American poetry, even though its original stage was totally eliminated. It was produced in Cuba because that is where the *son* survived, the Cuban *son* that invaded the Antilles and America through orchestras, records, and the radio. Black Cuban poetry expanded rapidly. It influenced the great poet Palés Matos of Puerto Rico, where the national musical rhythm, called *la plena* belongs to the same family as the *son*. It influenced Solano Trinidade in Brazil; the Uruguayans Virginia Brindis de Salas and Paredo Valdes; the Ecuadorian poets Adalberto Ortiz and León Damas; Carew and Carter in Guyana; the poets of Jamaica, etc. It is impossible to enumerate all of its Latinamerican reverberations. The wide themes of Black poetry, as we have seen, were first based on the Black and Mulatto musical rhythms, mixed with the first Spanish rhythms. Today it reaches the most daring lyrical forms while still maintaining its rhythm.

It must be noted that in the other Antilles as well, Black cultural consciousness spread dramatically. It was enhanced by forces from the new, natural expression in the writings of Haitians, and of English-speaking Antillean Black poets, particularly the more "cultured." Aimé Césaire developed a concept of "negritude" that was rebellious and full of protest. Sometimes, above all in the dominant British Antilles, there was the Utopian theme of a return to Africa.

The influence of the words, euphonics, myths, proverbs, rhythms, dances, and songs, of the tense personality of the Black African, inherited and transformed by the descendants of those who had been slaves, is a creative force in present-day Latin America. Its destiny is unpredictable, since it is at the beginning of its history. Already conscious of its values and its achievements, it is ready to create and to survive in the Latin-American genre into which it has already been immersed, happily, and decisively.

8

Music and Dance in Cuba

Odilio Urfé

Introduction

With the conquest and colonization of Cuba, the island's small indigenous population disappeared. We will not enter into the human, political, and demographic considerations that brought about this occurrence, which has often been referred to as genocide. We only wish to stress that the indigenous population hardly counted in Cuba from the seventeenth century forward, and that its cultural influence was insignificant.

In the face of all historical and anthropological facts, the cultural and artistic circles in Cuba in the 1920s witnessed the development of a tense argument between Eduardo Sánchez de Fuentes* and Fernando Ortiz** on whether there were indigenous elements in Cuban music. Sánchez de Fuentes, a brilliant musician, maintained that there was an indigenous influence; Ortiz replied that ". . . Cuban music owes its identity to the integration of the African and Spanish roots, and contains no elements of Cuban indigenous music."

The indigenous thesis was more political than scientific, since it tried to hide what is known as the "Africanism of Cuban music." In a neocolonial atmosphere, one deeply prejudiced against the Black population, the cultural presence of an oppressed people disturbed the dominant class. The African presence was so obvious that the indigenous thesis on Cuban music would have been considered utterly ridiculous had it not had deculturation as its intent.

The truth of the matter is that the African slaves and their descendants, who were progressively Cubanized Creoles, developed their musical and dance activities within the constraints imposed upon them by their limited setting. This can be witnessed in rural areas in the *barracón* or semiprisonlike habitat of the sugar plantations; in areas of agricultural work, like the sugar cane fields, the coffee plantations, or the bush (where rites and ceremonies were celebrated); in the *batey* where sugar was manufactured; in the *palenques* (compounds); and, of course, in the *llanos* or plains, the Cuban symbolic name given to the site of the great slave riots and revolutionary struggles.

---

*Eduardo Sańchez de Fuentes (1874–1944): composer and Cuban musician, author of the world famous *habanera* "Tú."
**Fernando Ortiz (1881–1961): well-known Cuban cultural anthropologist, author of *Los instrumentos de la música afro-cubana.*

However, it was the urban slaves who—although fewer in number than the rural slaves, but living under far more favorable conditions for cultural expression—developed an art form kept alive through congregations, fraternities, and *cabildos,* or through informally organized groups that were hardly institutionalized. A particularly fascinating phenomenon is that of the bellringers at Cuban Catholic churches, who were traditionally Blacks, (usually Cuban-born), and either enslaved or freed Mulattoes.

The Cabildos of the Nation

The *cabildos* constitute an necessary reference for Cuban musical historiography, to uncover the roots of Cuban dance and music. These *cabildos* were organizations, usually of freed Blacks, Creoles, or Africans, who helped each other and participated in collective recreational activities. They usually maintained social cohesion among Africans of the same ethnic group or "nation." The colonial governments sponsored them as a useful divisionary tactic, to split the free Black population; however the *cabildos* became real centers of conservation of the African traditions and recreational activities corresponding to their original ethnic group.

These *cabildos* had gatherings to sing and dance in honor of Olofi, Abasi, and N'Zambi, respectively the Supreme Deities of the Yorubas, the Carabalís, and the Congos. We cannot really determine the degree of purity of the rhythm and harmony, the rich sounds and African dance heritage, of the songs that were performed at the *cabildo* festivities. We must always keep in mind that we have no written music from the time the Africans arrived in Cuba. Thus, any study of African influence comes to us with an "original gap," since no one has heard original versions. A comparison of what has been preserved by the *cabildos* with present-day African music could be both interesting and useful, as long as one does not believe that the current expressions are identical to those at the peak of the slave trade. On the other hand, an experienced musicologist could rapidly detect any European elements that have been incorporated into the African musical expression preserved and transmitted through the *cabildos*. But would it also be possible to detect any African elements incorporated after the music had arrived in Cuba?

Until 1900, January 6 was a very significant day for the *cabildos*. Among the Catholic saint festivities, this was the Day of the Epiphany or of the Adoration of the Three Kings; and on that day the *cabildos* were permitted to celebrate a special carnival. Although this essay will not consider any social aspects unrelated to music, it is particularly interesting to note that just like the classical European carnivals the "Black Carnival" on the Day of the Kings was used by the colonial government as a deliberate catharsis for the oppressed. On that day, in Cuba's main cities, various dance groups from *cabildos* representing different ethnic groups that had arrived in Cuba as slaves came out to dance and to compete with each other.

Written and graphic sources offer us a vivid image of these groups and allow us to know in detail the types of instruments that were used. These instruments were different from those used in private religious ceremonies of a sacred nature (whether esoteric or not). When they arrived in Cuba, the Africans had reconstructed both the objects and musical instruments necessary for their liturgy, and those to be used for their profane public activities. We have already identified the following musical instruments generally used by *cabildos* on their Day of the Three Kings parties: various types of drums, tambourines, *marugas,* multicolored maracas, *erikundis* of Carabalí origin, jingle bells, triangles, graters bells, *guiros* (type of gourd), trumpets or horns, whistles, *fotutos* or conchs (*strombus giga,* a large seashell), cattle bells, jugs, and bass drums. Obviously all the instruments were not used by every *cabildo* on the island; however their use was fairly generalized.

Incidentally, it must be pointed out that in the list of instruments just mentioned, there is one that was also used by the Cuban Indians: the large seashell called *fotuto* in Cuba, *guamo* or *cobo,* or simply seashell. This seashell, carefully perforated at the base of its spiral and blown by a trained player is the Cuban (or island) equivalent to the European shepherd's horn. Until quite recently (the tradition survived until the 1920s) groups of youths and adolescents would run around the streets of their villages on Christmas Day playing the *fotuto* and asking for tips, like waifs. Naturally, in the case of the Black Africans and their descendants, it must still be determined whether the *fotuto* was taken over from the Cuban indigenous population, or whether the Blacks, upon arriving on the island, recreated in Cuba a tradition of islanders all over the world who use seashells as musical instruments.

The *erikundi* is a sort of maraca that has been lined with cloth. It is an instrument used exclusively by the Carabalí efik *cabildos,* which is where the secret *abakuá* society originated. The *erikundi* is widely used in the western part of the island, although there is an eastern replica of the instrument known as *chachá.*

The festivities of the Day of the Three Kings gave Cuba, through the *cabildos,* four melodic rhythmic patterns: the *marcha,* the *saludo,* the *cuadros* (quadrilles), and the *tango.*

The marching song has prosodic accents, spontaneously blended with the polyrhythms set by the percussion instruments, to which the mass of dancers moves. The *cabildo* marches are in an antiphonal mode, and generally do not exceed four real measures. Few marching songs have survived. A good example of this type of rhythm and song is found in *El Cocoyé,* which helped to form, through a continuous evolutionary process, a variant of the *cabildo* march known today, both nationally and internationally, as the *conga*.

The salutation song, or simply, *el saludo* (the greeting), was, as the name implies, the song the *cabildo* used to greet the colonial authorities waiting for the carnival groups to pass by at certain locations. In Havana, the greeting took place in front of the Palace of the Captains General on the Main Square (Plaza de Armas). The words, sung in halting Spanish, were used to honor and to express good wishes to the authorities. No examples of these greetings remain. According to verbal descriptions, we know that percussion was reduced to a minimum so that the song, which was quite long, could be understood, and so that it could have the required invocational tone.

The *cuadros* or *cuadrillas* were a peculiar symbiosis of musical choreography. They combined African beats and songs with choreographic routines copied from European court dances and dances from southern Spain, particularly those danced on the feast of Corpus Christi. The songs and dances called *tumba francesa* (French drum) preserved in Santiago de Cuba and Guantánamo are live examples of these *cuadros*.

The *tango* was one of the favorite musical forms of the festivities of the Day of the Kings. Everything seems to point to its Congo origin. Because of its importance in Cuban music, we will refer frequently to the Congo *tango* in another part of this essay, when we discuss the *rumba*.

One of the most important people involved in the artistic direction, and thus, in the public success of the *cabildo* dances, was the choreographer. The musical and terpsichorean creativity of some of these choreographers, the manner in which they assimilated the European and the Creole dances, gave them the opportunity to work as dancing masters in the homes of upperclass families. Some even became teachers in dance salons and to direct the complicated dances in the mansions of the powerful city gentry.

This dual function of the choreographers who worked simultaneously at the top and at the bottom of a stratified society stimulated the dialectic play of the transculturation process and contributed to the formation and affirmation of the nation's identity in its dance.

Ritual and Profane African Music and Dance in Cuba

We pointed out earlier the relationship between the music and dance of Africans and their descendants and their restrictive environment. One extraordinary example of the work song, created in the heart of the sugar plantation, was collected by the Havana composer Eliseo Grenet (1893–1950) and was incorporated, with a few necessary adjustments into Ernesto Lecuona's musical play *Niña Rita*. We refer to the Congo *tango*

"Mamá Inés" that was traditionally sung on the first day of the sugar-grinding season, that is, the first day of the sugar harvest.

In Cuba, the musical art and dance of Africa was best expressed and conveyed through religious activity. Much has been said about religion as a means of conserving and defending the identity of an oppressed culture. Since most of African religion and liturgy are expressed through music and dance, it is clear that we find the greatest and most important artistic contributions of Africa to Cuba in this area.

African studies indicate that the Yoruba people of Nigeria had a very high culture in the sixteenth century, at the time when they were invaded and colonized by the Europeans. During the nineteenth century, the Yorubas constituted the largest African group living in Cuba. Because of their polytheistic religion, which, according to Frobenius, was "richer and more original and better preserved than any of the forms of classical antiquity," it is understandable that this religious force generated the complex beliefs popularly known in Cuba as *santería*. We will not discuss the fascinating aspect of religious syncretism of *santería,* the psychological mechanism that forced African believers to identify their *orishás* with the Catholic saints in Cuba. Nor will we discuss the economic mechanism, the domination and deculturation that induced the leaders of the Catholic Church that were serving in the colonies to identify their saints with Yoruba *orishás*. We shall limit our remarks to the musical aspects.

For each deity of the Yoruba-Lucumí-Catholic pantheon there are a variety of songs, rhythms, and dances that constitute the richest manifestations of art and religion in Cuba. From the melodic viewpoint, the songs of the *lucumí* cult, are characterized by their precise themes, their modal sequences, the development within the framework of their antiphonal liturgy, and, above all, their deep spiritual and psychological sense. The *santería* songs were sung in closed rooms, such as *cabildo* houses, the private homes of the *babalao,* the *santero,* the *santera,* and the *ahijados* (the initiated), or in the open (religious or funeral processions). The participants in the ritual were the interpreters of these songs. They were directed by a cantor called the *akpuón* who initiated the songs and controlled the antiphony with the chorus, called *ankorí,* and its synchronization with the instruments. Among the styles appearing in the *santería* songs, the most important is the *rezo,* or prayer, which, for its lyrical beauty and climax of sounds, is considered an artistic manifestation hard to duplicate.

The polyrhythmic mixture of *lucumí* music achieved through a variety of instruments, all in perfect harmony with soloists, vocal choirs, and dancers, has been noted by ethnomusicologists because of the complexity of its infinite *toques* or beats and the integrity it achieves through its melody, which shapes and identifies it. The basic group of instruments used in *santería* consists of four types: three double-headed drums called *batá;* three *güiros, aggües,* or *chekerés;* a *maraca* or *acheré;* and the cow bell or *agogó.*

The *batá* are the basic sacred instruments, which is why in every ceremony their use expresses hierarchy. Says Fernando Ortiz: "The three drums are of different sizes but of the same shape. To give them a precise definition, we would say that they are closed, hour-glass-shaped boxes made of wood kept permanently in tension by strips of animal hide. Inside, the drummers enclose a magic secret known as *aña* that the instrument builders, of course, do not wish to reveal." To Ortiz's description we add that hemp is sometimes used to tighten and to tense the membranes, but that drums with hemp tensors are known as *judíos* (jews).

Ortiz continues: "Each drum has the profane name of *ilú.* This type of orchestra and its music are known as *toque de batá.* Each *ilú* also has its own name. The smallest is called *okónkolo* or *omelé* and has the highest pitch. The medium-sized drum is the *itótele,* used to give the key note. The largest drum, which is in the center of the three-piece group is known as *iyá.*"

The *chekerés,* like the *batas,* are three in number. Their unmistakable sound was the most typical element of the semireligious festivities known as *wemileres* or *bembés.* Each *chekeré* has a different shape. The largest of the three is called *caja* (box). They are made of dried *güiros* (gourds) that are hollowed out and wrapped with a net whose cords are threaded with dried seeds of various fruits. When the player hits or shakes the *chekeré,* the seeds hit against the gourd and make a dry, rattling sound. As a result of the revaluation of African cultural elements transplanted to Cuba, the *chekerés,* once used exclusively for rituals, became an instrument used by popular musical groups.

The terpsichorean richness of the *lucumí* cult runs parallel to its musical wealth. Let us not forget that the Yoruba *lucumí* pantheon has more than four hundred gods, of which many appear in the Cuban *santería.* Since each god has one or more lyrical and rhythmic identities, we are left with a wealth of dances. Of these dances Fernando Ortiz has said: ". . . They are a kind of pragmatic ballets, created by an artistic people, the Yoruba, to whom we can attribute the best dance forms in Black Africa, and who have the most dramatic mythology, full of happenings and complexities, like that of the Greco-Romans. The allegorical movements are so stylized that the uninitiated often cannot understand their meaning if it is not explained."

Examples of the choreographic wealth can be seen in the dances of Eleguá, a mischievous god whose evocation dance involves a dancer with a small crooked stick or *garabato* that is moved from side to side, as though it were pushing aside evil or opening up a path in the jungle. The dances of Changó are erotic and warlike, the dance to Yemayá is the dance of the waves and the dance of Ochún is the dance of the fountain.

Many Cuban male and female slaves came from the Congo River basin. Among them were the Bantu Congos who brought valuable musical and dance expressions that were, however, of a development level far inferior to the Yoruba Lucumí culture we have just described.

The music and dance imagery of the Congo culture in Cuba has been preserved through a mythical religious system divided into two main branches: the *kimbisa* rite and the *mayombé* rite. *Zambia* is the directing deity or power for both cults and the *palero* or *tata ganga* is their supreme priest. The Congo musical and dance legacy can be found in the following present-day rhythms, dances, and instruments:

a. The Congolese originated the rhythm, instrumentation, and dance of the *rumba* complex.
b. They shaped the variants of the *rumba* complex such as the Congo *tango,* the *taona* (also *tahona* or *tajona*), the *guaguancó,* the *columbia,* and other minor variants;
c. The original Congo *tango* is the rhythmic base for such forms and national genres as the *contradanza,* the *habanera,* the first *danzones musicales* by Miguel Failde, and the Afro *son.* On an international level the Congos generated the Argentine *milonga* and *tango,* and the blues of the Black American composer William Christopher Handy; all of these assimilated the rhythm of the Afro-Cuban Congo *tango.*
d. With regard to instruments, the Congos have left us the *conga* drum, also known as *mambisa, tumba,* or *tumbadora;* the *bocú* drum, typical of the *congas* of the Santiago de Cuba carnivals; the *bongo;* the *guayo* (according to Fernando Ortiz); the *claves;* the *marímbula;* etc.
e. Their contribution to dance has been the *guaguancó rumba* and the *columbia.* These dances, embellished with the steps and gestures of the *iremes,* or little *abakuá* devils, are the original core of the Cuban *rumba,* spread around the world by professional dancers. We must also include the *changüí,* the more intricate forerunner of the Cuban *son* complex; the *mambo,* a syncopated variant of its Bantu ancestor, introduced by composer Orestes López into a *danzon* he called "Mambo," thus originating the rhythm launched and popularized by Dámaso Perez Prado; finally, we also have the world-renowned *conga.*

The Congo musical identity, both ritual and profane, is marked by a set of formal musical elements which include conciseness, the brevity of its melodies, isochronal rhythm patterns, martial tempi, and the loudness of its phrases. Congo dances are typified by vigorous steps and gestures and jerky movements, in keeping with the nature of the music.

Compared to the Yoruba *lucumí* group, the rhythmic units of the Congos are few. The main beats can be found in the *kimbisa* and *mayombé* liturgy, with its funereal sequences and its parallel expressions, such as the Congolese *tango,* the *palo-mambo,* the *palo-monte,* and the *yuka.* Another outstanding example is the *macuta* (also the name of a drum and a dance step.)

The beat or rhythmic unit of the *makuta* is martial and isochronal; the drums and the bells are counterposed to accentuate the two beats of the binary measure. The rhythmic pattern of the Congo *tango* has a basic three-beat configuration; (a dotted eighth note attached to a sixteenth, for the strong beat, and a sixteenth in the first half of the second beat of a binary rhythm). The *yuka* beat is set by three drums and is more elaborate with regard to rhythm and sound than the other forms.

The number of variants of original Bantu Congo instruments is relatively large. We will list the names of instruments that are still actively used in Cuban folklore, regardless of whether their African origin has been proven or not:

—*Yuka* drums known as *caja, mula,* and *cachimbo.*
—*Ngulero* drums.
—*Makuta* drum.
—*Kinfuiti* drum (esoteric).
—*Palo mumboma* drum.
—*Tumba* (also called *tumbadora, conga,* or *mambisa*).
—*Tumbadera* or *tingo-talango.*
—*Bocú* drum.
—*Bongó.*
—*Kimbilia* (a type of small hand *marímbula*).
—*Marímbula.*
—*Pianito, ginebra,* or xylophone (derived from the Guinean balaphone).
—*Claves xilofónicas* (small hardwood sticks beaten together).
—*Palitos percutivos* (Small percussion sticks) to play the *koko, chiva, wawa,* or *muela* beats on the *yuka* drums.
—*Garabato* or *lungowa* (a piece of a tree branch used to beat the ground rhythmically).
—*Nkembi* (small maracas that drummers place on their wrists).
—*Guayo* (a tin or sheet-metal food grater)
—Sheet metal *nkembi.*
—Battery of metallic artifacts (consisting of machine parts and domestic utensils, etc., such as train wheels, pieces of a plow, bells, spades, pans, etc.).

Both the ritualistic and the profane Congo dances have many elements relating to myths and symbols. Following the triumph of the Cuban revolution, the government's cultural departments were able to rescue many of the choreographic elements of the Bantu Congo culture, working with music that was based on authentic cultural components and presenting them for the first time in the history of Cuba as a public spectacle. This rescue operation, combining the recreation and transmission of the Bantu Congo music and dance legacy was accomplished with scientific and technical accuracy by the Conjunto Folklórico Nacional.

Music and Dance of African Roots used in Ceremonies of Profane or Semireligious Institutions.

The music and dance legacy of Dahoman Arará origins is far less significant than the two influences we have just described. The reason is quantitative. Forced migration of Dahoman Arará people, although significant in the seventeenth and eighteenth centuries, was practically nonexistent during the nineteenth century, which was precisely the century of the largest immigration. Nevertheless, the *cabildos* of the nation of Arará did achieve some importance and distinguished themselves by their dance groups on the Day of the Three Kings. Few Arará musical traces survive; most were lost during the deep transculturation process when they were fused with European and African cultures dominant on the island. Yet we are left with a beautiful collection of single-headed drums, a tangible, physical proof of the Arará's lost world of sound, which has been fused with so many other voices. Needless to say, the identification of Arará instruments has been difficult. *Agronika Babalú Ayé* rite preserves some Arará liturgy of direct African descent. This rite, according to some very old informants, was apparently influenced by the Lucumí culture.

We find some of the Dahoman Arará music and dance in the French *tumba* societies that were established all over the island, although they survived only in the eastern part. The violent revolutionary upheavals in the French colony of Saint Domingue brought about the massive emigration to Cuba of coffee and sugar plantation owners as well as technical and commercial classes. Many of them brought with them their slaves and trusted servants. It was this group of Blacks transplanted to Cuba who brought with them the music and dance of the French *tumba,* also known as the French rhythm or the French beat. The French *tumba* took root in Cuba: it was transmitted to slaves and Creole freedmen, was organized into *cabildos,* some of which even had French names like Lafayette, and it became a part of Cuban folklore.

The most typical *tumba* dances were: the *masón,* the *cocoyé,* the *fronté* or *de frente* (front), the *babul,* and the *manga silá,* all of which are danced by couples forming part of a choreographic group; and the *yubá* and the *carabiñé,* danced by male soloists. The dance style contrasts sharply with the melodic nature of the songs and the rhythmic language of the drums, the *marugas,* the *catá* and the largest drum, the *redoblante.* The melodies of the *tumbas* are very brief and rarely exceed four measures. The sounds of the refrains contain guttural inflections of unquestionable African origin. The *composé* is in charge of the choir, the rhythm, and also of the lyrical repertoire.

There are three types of *tumbas* or drums that participate in this art form. Generally they are of equal size. Their peg system and decorations are proof of their distant Dahoman Arará origins. Traditionally, these drums have always been engraved with Cuban and Haitian patriotic names. They are named according to their function. The main drum or tumba is known as *premier* and resounds freely within the framework of the rigorous traditional style; the second is called *second,* the third is the *bulá* or *bebé.*

The French *tumba*'s most interesting polyrhythmic aspect is the frequency with which the *tambuyé* or first drummer rolls his drum in the *redublé.* This routine has been handed down to the *bayao* or Dominican *merengue* and the carnival *conga* of Santiago de Cuba. Also important is the rhythmic unit known as *cinquillo Cubano* that is fundamental for the *danza* and Cuban *danzón* rhythms. The *catá* intermittently marks the *cinquillo* beat. In typical Cuban dance and *danzón* orchestras of the nineteenth and twentieth centuries, the *cinquillo* is performed by kettle drummers or *paileros.* At the time of the triumph of the Revolution (1959) only two French *tumbas* survived in Cuba, one in Santiago de Cuba, the other in Guantánamo.

Santiago de Cuba preserves another deeply rooted cultural group, the Carabalí Izuama *cabildo.* Contrasting with the groups we have surveyed so far, the songs of this group are sung in Spanish, although many of the words are Carabalí, Congolese, or Yoruba. The melodic framework of the songs is closer to Cuban standards than to Haitian ones. The dances are ceremonious.

Aside from the *chachá* (a kind of *erikundi ñáñigo,* but made of wickerwork or basketry), the instruments of the Carabalí Izuama *cabildo* consist of a group of double-headed drums played with mallets, sticks, metal pins, an iron plowshare, a pair of sticks used for beating on the sides of the wooden boxes of the drums, plus one or two pairs of *chachás.* The undeniable influence of the drums of the European military bands is proven in the system of tuning the drums with iron keys or pegs. These percussion instruments have existed since the end of the eighteenth century. The four basic Carabalí Izuama drums are the *quinto* (fifth), the *fondo* (or *fondeadora*), the *respondedora* and the *bajo* (bass). The measure of the Carabalí Izuama beat is $\frac{2}{4}$.

Almost everyone seems to agree that the Carabalí *apapá* dance music unit, developed within the *abakuá* secret societies, also known as Ñáñigo Powers, is the most original and suggestive of those brought over by the Afro-Cuban transculturation process. The history of *abakuá* societies is the most involved and fascinating of all the African-based organizations

that were established in Cuba and it is linked to fundamental social and
political events. Of course, the ruling class portrayed these societies in
the darkest of colors. Present-day historians and ethnologists, trained
after the Revolution, have begun to clarify the real past of the *abakuá*
societies, a task that is often difficult because of their secrecy. This essay
will only describe the *abakuá* dance-music legacy.

In a *plante ñáñigo* (initiation ritual) music and dance operate as organic
elements, although during the course of the ceremony they only occur
occasionally or as interludes. The *ñáñigo* drums, and therefore the drummers, are very important. Some of the drums have only a symbolic or
ornamental function, while others are active sound emitters, among them
the sacred *ékue*.

To begin with the symbolic and ornamental ones, we have a group of
drums called *eribó, sesé* (or *seseribó*), *enkríkamo, ekueñon* and *empegó*.
The last three derive their names from the positions they occupy. These
drums are decorated with light brown feathers called *beromo* or
achecheré. The *eribó* has four *beromos,* the others have only one each.
The *eribó* is shaped like a chalice, which is not coincidental; it was a result
of the strong transculturation process which began in 1863, when Whites
began to be admitted to these societies.

The *ékue* is not only a musical instrument, it also has a highly symbolic
significance. Since it is sacred, it is kept in a secret room belonging to the
Power, (a room called *fambá, batamú* or *butame*), and within this room it
has its special place called *fambayin*. The *ékue* is played in a special way
called *fragaya*. For this a *güin,* or very fine cane stalk, is rolled rapidly
from one side to the other of the drum head.

As the *son* septets became more popular in the 1920s, one could hear a
sound effect very similar to the *frayado* or rubbing of the *ékue* when the
bass drummers did their *glissé* with their middle fingers on the drum
membrane. Some popular musicians even had trouble with members of
abakuá societies because of their use of the *glissé* on the bass drum.

Among the actively sounding instruments we have: the drums, the
ekón, and the *erikundis*. There are four drums; three are of similar size
and called *obiapá, kuchi-yeremá* and *bin komé.* The fourth is larger and is
called *enchemí, bonkó-enchemi* or *enchemiyá.* All of them share the
same cord and wood wedge system that fastens the drum head and tight-
ens it for tuning.

The *ekón* is a bell without a clapper. Its origins could be Bantu Congo.
It is hit with a wooden stick. This instrument is used for rhythm in a large
variety of Afro-Cuban music, particularly in a ⁶/₈ meausre. Of course, its
pitch depends on its size, shape, and the thickness of its metal plate.

The melody of *ñáñigo* liturgy has strong prosodical accents that are
very appropriate for the narrative style. Melismatic inflections abound in
the funereal songs. Although most *ñáñigo* songs developed a short, anti-

phonal style, there are also many that are noted for the length of their melody. Some songs sound like elegies, although they are in a major key. The funereal rites are rich in lyrical recitatives. From a rhythmic standpoint we can observe two standards: the *toque Efik* and the *toque Efo* (Efik and Efo beats) Both are strong and cohesive beats in a ⁶⁄₈ measure. *Ñáñigo* polyrhythms have infiltrated various genres, forms, and styles of Cuban music: folk or popular, theater, symphonic, operatic, chamber, and choral.

African presence in Cuban music and dance

The following is a very important historic process. For many years almost all of the musical activity in Cuba (obviously we refer to music as a profession, not as a private cultural event) was carried on by Blacks, Mulattoes, and Creoles. Within a rigidly stratified society, the musical standards of the elite were imposed upon the Black musicians. These Blacks and Mulattoes, belonging to the lowest echelons of society, learned to play European instruments and to adopt European patterns; however, they were at the same time the transmitters of the patterns of the oppressed class. This permitted them to be simultaneously the source of and the vehicle for the creation of a new music.

The Spanish influence on this music was largely determined by the artistic values of groups of Spanish workers and soldiers who came to Cuba. The more developed and cultivated music and dance contributions of the upper class were much smaller. Thus, music and dances like the *zapateado* or tap dance, the *fandango*, the *romance*, children's songs, *seguidillas, polos, boleros,* and *zarabandas* were fused with the artistic expressions of the Africans who had been transplanted to Cuba. Of course, the dominant Spanish culture assimilated only some of the African elements. As we have seen, these African elements did not get lost, but remained as a part of the oppressed culture that lay at the base of the society, where they were preserved, recreated, diluted, or disappeared every time a traditional performer passed away. However, they always reemerged when the country was shaken by periods of social turbulence, at which time new elements of the oppressed culture found their way into the dominant culture. Thus, a new form with its own identity was created: Cuban music.

Two musical developments illustrate this creative process. The first was the Afro-Cubanization of the Spanish *zapateado*. In fact, the typical orchestras or wind ensembles, formed exclusively of Blacks and Mulatto Creoles, used the polyrhythmic formats of the *wemilere* or *abakuá bembé* as the base for the Spanish tunes, within the frameworks of ⁶⁄₈ time. This Afro-Cubanized version of tap dancing achieved its maximum intensity and vigor during the performances of the so called *chambelonas* of the

Liberal Party and the *congas* of the Conservative Party, political "clam-bakes" with a strong musical flavor. The author of this essay will never forget the vibrant interpretation of the Cuban *tap dance* by the Chambelona of Madruga, which is his birthplace. This orchestra performed most beautifully, paying attention to all details and to the rhythmic harmony of Afro origins.

An excellent example of Afro influence can be observed in the ringing of bells. The job of bellringer in churches was always performed by Black and Mulatto Africans or Creoles. There is ample information that confirms that the bellringers, in pealing out hosannas or hallelujah would use the rhythmic units of their own African religious liturgy. María Alvarez Ríos, a noted Cuban composer and musician, claims that the bellringer Joseato, who was Black, used to play the *conga* on his church bells at Sancti Spiritus and at the Tuinicú sugarmill. We personally remember the bell-ringing at the Madruga Church. It is possible that the basic rhythmic unit of the "Danza de los Ñáñigos" by Ernesto Lecuona is based on the *rumba*-like beat of the bells of Madruga. To conclude we should not forget that most of the slaves were brought to Cuba to work on the sugar plantations and that each plantation had several bells. A complicated sequence of changes called the slaves to work, another signalled the end of the workday, a third called the White employees. Each White worker had his own call which would vary with the degree of urgency. There were peals for giving instructions to cart drivers, peals for cane cutters, peals to signal danger, fire, an uprising, and peals to celebrate the beginning and the conclusion of the sugar season. Plantation bellringers were invariably Black slaves, so that, eventually, the sounds of bells had a special, symbolic significance to the slaves. Bells on sugar plantations were so important that the belfry at the Manacas plantation, near Trinidad, is taller than that of the Havana Cathedral. All this helps to explain the African influence on bellringing at churches.

The *rumba* complex originated among the Bantu Congo groups. With regard to the origins of the word *rumba* as used in music, it is possible that it referred to "the women of the *rumbo*," prostitutes linked to the dance houses. The first variant of the *rumba* group is a *danza* called "El Yambú" (the word *danza* is used here to refer to a specific Cuban dance form). After "El Yambú," composed around 1850, we have the following generic-stylistic categories of *rumbas:*

(a)—*rumba estribillo*
(b)—*rumba yambú;*
(c)—*rumba guaguancó*
(d)—*rumba* of the *bufo* theater
(e)—*rumba guaguancó* chorus
(f)—*tahona* rumba

(g)—Congo *tango*
(h)—*open rumba*
(i)—*Columbia rumba*.

According to this classification, which follows the chronological appearance of each variant, types (d) and (h) were recreated on the stage of the *bufo,* the vernacular theaters. The others have folk roots. Each variant has a basic style with tempo and melodic variations (for example the *guaguancó* has a slow tempo and the *columbia* a fast one), as well as different drum beats and different accents in the basic scheme. In every case three Cuban drums of Congo ancestry and claves are used. All variants, but particularly the *guaguancó,* have well-developed phrasing and are marked by African liturgical cadences and modes; however, the lyrical guidelines are undoubtedly Spanish. Choreographically, the *rumba* complex presents four different, well-defined styles: the *guaguancó,* the *tahona,* the Congo *tango,* and the *columbia.*

The choreography of the *guaguancó rumba,* or, more accurately, the refrain of the *guaguancó* song, since this is a genre for song, comes from the *yambú,* although it has symbolic variants. The *guaguancó* dance is very difficult to perform because of the economy of steps required by the dancing couple. The vernacular theater, the cabaret, and the movies have deformed the original version, by presenting it as a sensual and obscene dance. The *guaguancó* dance has a greater Spanish (probably flamenco) influence rather than it has African base.

The *tahona* variant was devised by the bakers of the Carraguao neighborhood of Havana to which it owes its name. It is a combination of martial movements and *cabildo* airs. The Congo *tango* is a Popular Creole group dance, devoid of any symbolic religious meaning. The colonial *rumba* is danced by only one person and represents a duel between the dancer and the *quinteador,* the drum soloist.

The *guaguancó rumba* choirs were formed in the last two decades of the nineteenth century at a time when Cuban Black activities were being institutionalized. The choral structure of *guaguancó* choirs is similar to that of the *coros de clave.* These consist of an Afrocuban assimilation of the Catalan choral societies of Havana. The name *coros de clave* is a corruption of the Anselmo Clavé choirs, named after the Catalán composer. The choir consists of cantors, intoners, soloists, the censor, and a mixed chorus, accompanied by instruments similar to those used in the *rumba yambú.* Some of the choirs have up to 150 voices. The songs and rhythms of every variant of the *rumba* complex are in ¾ time, and all the *coros de clave* are in a ⅝ time. Strangely enough there is no drum among the instruments. There are two keyboard instruments and one *viola,* similar to a bass fiddle, but without strings, that is lightly tapped by the violist. The fact that the choirs use *claves* has led some musicologists to erroneously believe that the use of the sticks is the reason for the *coros de clave* name.

The creation of carnival groups or *comparsas,* to succeed the role of the *cabildos* on the Three Kings Day is significant for Cuban music. This type of folk expression has three variants corresponding to the different regions of Cuba. Between 1886 and 1914 there were six very important *comparsas* in Havana: "La culebra" (the snake), "El pajaro lindo" (beautiful bird), "El gavilán" (the sparrow hawk), "El sapo" (the frog), "El alacrán" (the scorpion) and "El alacrán chiquito" (the small scorpion). The zoomorphic references relate to African ethnocultural elements. In Cuban folklore we still have symbolic characters of Congo origin, like Tata Cuñengue, or Cañengue, a magician who kills a snake, a scorpion, and all bad animals; and we have the *sun sun* bird or pretty bird, a hummingbird adored by the Congos. There were also dance groups without zoomorphic themes that were popular in Cuba and internationally, such as: "Mírala que linda viene" ("Look at how pretty she is"), "Quítate de la acera" ("Get off the sidewalk"), "Tira si va a tirá, mata si va a matá" ("Shoot if you are going to shoot, kill if you are going to kill").

As for choreography and rhythm, the *comparsas* are the creators of the world-famous Cuban *conga.* This beat or rhythm comes from Matanzas where it was first popularized by the "Los Turcos" ("the Turks") *comparsa.* Both "The Turks" and "Los Turcos de Regla" used the Turkish bass drum, to which they owe their name. Cuban composer Eliseo Grenet took the dance and the rhythm abroad, and Ernesto Lecuona was very successful with his *conga* hits "Panama," "Por Corrientes va una conga" ("A Conga Is Going Through Corrientes"), and "Para Vigo me Voy" ("I am going to Vigo").

Although the *comparsas* were forbidden by municipal legislation around 1937, they were reinstated soon thereafter by demand of the most noted members of the Cuban intelligentsia. In 1938, the *comparsas* were triumphantly reborn, and "El alacrán," organized by folksinger Santos Ramirez, known as "El Niño" (The kid), performed brilliantly. "El alacrán" employed as its themes the main socioeconomic elements of the Cuban past (some of which still exist). It showed slaves cutting cane, slaves being transported in carts to the sugar plantations, and familiar colonial characters such as the overseer, his assistant, the maroon boss, and the lottery-ticket seller. The focus was on the terrifying but venerated Tata Cuñengue. Various songs from this particular *comparsa* are internationally known, like the one that starts: "Listen, friend, don't get frightened when you see. . . ."

The most important *comparsas* include the *parrandas villareñas* of Los Villas province.

Santiago de Cuba displays some Haitian ethnoculture, as well as some Chinese elements (in the nineteenth century alone some 150,000 Chinese arrived in Cuba). The rhythm of the Santiago *conga* is quite different from that of the *comparsas* of the western parts of the island. Its percussion instruments are the *bocú* drum, which has already been described, the two-headed drum or *pilonera,* and the strident wheel or bell. The Santiago carnival achieves its typical color through the *corneta china* (Chinese cornet) called *sona* in Cantonese. While in Havana the people are merely spectators, they participate actively in the Santiago carnival.

Finally we must mention a musical group that was very popular in the first few decades of the twentieth century: *la chambelona.* The *chambelonas* served to brighten up political party gatherings. They were known as *chambelonas* only when they participated in Liberal Party affairs; they were known as *congas* when they played for the Conservative Party. The instruments used were quite complex. Brass instruments consisted of horns, trumpets, saxhorns, ophicleides, and tubas; among the percussion instruments were *claves, maracas, guayo, güiro, reja, guataca,* pans, *gangarria,* bells, bass drums, *redoblante,* cymbals, *caja* and the Turkish bass drum; in addition there was a choir. Sometimes the group had as many as a hundred men. This type of group emerged in the cities of Remedios and Camajuaní. As the music moved westward, the brass section, with the exception of one or two horns, was dropped.

African Presence in Popular Cuban Music

Earlier we noted how Blacks and Mulattoes became practically the only members of the popular Cuban orchestras of the nineteenth century. This was such a common practice that when at one point a White orchestra was formed, it became known as an extraordinary event. In our search for distant historical precedents for Black musicians, we go to the musical bands of the *Pardo* and *Moreno* (Black and Brown) batallions, which became the source of musicians who were to fill the demand for musical dance groups in the second half of the nineteenth century. This essay will not explain the nature of these batallions. Suffice it to say that they were a militia, organized by the Spanish colonial government, that was very active in defending the empire during the eighteenth century and the first two decades of the nineteenth. Once Cuba was transformed into a large slave plantation, the batallions were dissolved, as the former defenders of the empire were now a threat.

These musicians, who were taught by members of Spanish military bands or by "conductors" who lived on the island, were the composers of the first anonymous contradances, with Afro elements imitating the Saint Domingue models. These composers shaped the popular national music of Cuba by blending the rhythm of African music with Spanish and French as well as other elements that had been transcultured into Cuba. Juán de Dios Alfonso y Armenteros was typical. He was a distinguished composer of contradances and director and clarinetist of the "The Flower of Cuba" orchestra. The contradance generated an instrumental group called the "typical Cuban orchestra" or wind ensemble. The *danza* that succeeded the contradance accentuated the Afro elements, both in the music and in the dance. Raimundo Valenzuela (1848–1905) another conductor and trombone player, was a well-known *danza* composer. And Miguel Failde (1858–1921) created the *danzón,* a very Cubanized version of a German dance fashionable in Cuba since the 1850s. The 2/4 tempo is Cuban but its pace is slower than that of other groups, including the dances performed by the *comparsas* and the *cabildos*.

Like Raimundo Valenzuela and Rafael Landa, Miguel Failde wrote many *danzones* with African themes. This trend found a better expression when José Urfé (1879–1957) included the style and rhythm of the *son oriental* at the very end of Failde's *danzón* structure. Thus the A-B-A-C-A-D-A-G scheme was developed (it lost its C part around 1920). José Urfé's danzón, "El bombín de Barreto" (Barreto's bowler hat) was the first to display this innovation; it advanced the absorption of African-style songs and polyrhythmic units, particularly in the last part of this complex Cuban musical form.

In its second stage, the Cuban *danzón* was taken up by Octavio "Tata" Alfonso (1866–1960), who blended elements of Yoruba, Congo, and *abakuá* liturgy and songs into his *danzones* and *danzas*. Antonio María Romeu is responsible for the blossoming of the *charanga cubana,* an orchestra made up of a five-keyed flute with a violin, a double bass, a piano, and metal percussion pans *(pailitas),* Cuban *timbalito* drums, and a *güiro* scraper made of half a gourd.

From their titles we can see that numerous danzones were inspired by African themes, such as "Yayoé, "Yerefá Maniló," "Congos de Lubini," "El ñáñigo," "Ohún," "Yemayá,"Africa speaks," "Ireme maco Ireme," "Ireme," "Bozambo," "Nongo alive," "Africa alive," etc. Notably the African influence in these *danzones* is most marked towards the end.

As the creative process continued, a new *danzón* emerged, written by Orestes López, called "Mambo" (which means "to speak" in Congo), which very much altered the interpretations of the *danzones*. The *mambo,* popularized by the orchestra Arcaño y sus maravillas (Arcano and his Wonders), was an extraordinary hit. In the 1940s some arrangers like Dámaso Pérez Prado, began writing *mambos* for jazz orchestras with Cuban-style percussion. In short, the *mambo* was created by Orestes López and the Arcaño y sus maravillas orchestra, and Dámaso Perez Prado, with his personal style, launched it abroad.

The creator of the *chachachá* undoubtedly was Enrique Jorrín, a composer, violinist, and conductor of the orchestra that bore his name. Historically, "La engañadora" ("The Deceiver") is considered the first *chachachá,* even though Jorrín had already used some elements of his new style in an earlier *danzón*. Choreographically the *mambo danzón*, the *mambo* (as a structure that is independent from the *danzón*) and the *chachachá*, owe their dance arrangements to popular creativity.

The vocal arrangements of popular music, including songs and sung dances, took longer to acquire a national flavor. In the case of the *son* complex, which is a very Cuban music and dance form, the national character only appeared with commercial exploitation. The sixteen stylistic variants of the *son* include a number of works with an Afro influence. This is apparent in the following titles: "Clave Carabalí," "Palo mambo," "Papá Oggún," "Un toque de bembé," "Bilongo," "Chacumbele," "Bruca maniguá," "Quimbombó que rebala," "Burundanga," etc. Exceptional popular Cuban *son* musicians include Ignacio Pinëiro, Miguel Matamoros, Benny Moré, and the dance couple René and Estela. Nicolás Guillén, Cuba's national poet, developed the *son* into an exceptional lyrical form.

The vernacular theater also reflected Afro-Cuban musical inflections. We cannot dwell upon musical theater; however, it is worth mentioning that *zarzuelas* (operettas) like "The Wizard" (1896), "María the Mulatta" (1896), and "The Funeral of Pachencho" contain numerous Congo *tangos* and *rumbas* that were the great hits of that period. Jorge Ankerman was the composer who left the deepest Afro-Cuban imprint on the repertoire of the vernacular theater. He recreated folk forms with African content; and his play "The Little Creole House" (1921) was a very important contribution to the rise of the musical theater.

With the opening of "Niña Rita" (1927), musical theater in Cuba that had an Afro-Cuban context took a definite step towards consolidation. The play was written by Ernesto Lecuona; it included the famous *tango* "Mamá Inés" by Eliseo Grenet, and it also marked the debut of actress Rita Montaner. In addition to being an accomplished actress with an excellent lyrical voice and remarkable stage presence, she was also a great pianist. The people called her "La Unica" (the only one). Lecuona's *zarzuelas* were set among Cuban working people, like "The Coffee Plantation," "María la O," "Rosa the Chinese Woman" and "The Sugar Factory." Strangely enough, his one song dedicated to the extinct Cuban indigenous population, the immortal "Siboney," is a Congo *tango*.

It would be impossible to speak about the Cuban musical theater without mentioning Rodrigo Prats, who employed Afro-Cuban themes in his plays "María Belén Chacón" and "Amalia Batista," or Gonzalo Roig, whose "Cecilia Valdés" continues to be a hit of musical repertory theater.

Misés Simons is perhaps the most distinguished Cuban composer of Afro-Cuban songs because of his perfect blend of musical language and themes. Somewhat similar are the Eliseo and Emilio Grenet brothers, Gilberto Valdés, Obdulio Morales, Margarita Lecuona, and Ignacio Villa, "Bola de Nieve."

The African Influence on Cuban Musical Nationalism

Cuban musical identity was formed among the popular stratum of Cuban society, solidified by musicians of the working class and of the Black and Mulatto petty bourgeoisie. It was, however, the White middle class, or whitened middle class, and the artists of the upper class who took this music to the lyric theater and placed it the framework of so-called musical nationalism.

Manuel Samuel y Reboredo (1817–1870) was the forerunner of Cuban musical nationalism. A White musician with a petty bourgeois background, he lived the social life of the Creole upper bourgeoisie because of his high artistic achievements. Using the contradance as his base, he transcended its content through stylistic and rhythmic adornments of ¾ and ⅝ time. Samuel and some of his disciples, like Nicolás Ruiz Espadero (1832–1890) and Ignacio Cervantes (1847–1905) limited their nationalist work to the piano, an instrument that they employed with admirable skill. José White was the first to attempt the transfer of musical nationalism to the violin.

Except for a few passages from the work of the above-mentioned composers, the African influence on Cuban musical nationalism did not become apparent before the appearance of "La Compara," Ernesto Lecuona's Afro-Cuban dance. Lecuona himself, then only 16 years old, called this genre an "Afro-Cuban danza."

Ernesto Lecuona wrote a number of dances that overrode the traditional classical format of 32 measures, and that are also different because of one or two rhythmic units played by the left hand. We attribute this style to Lecuona's virtuosity at the keyboard and to his double role of composer and musician.

Lecuona is the bridge that ties the Afro-Cubanist work of Alejandro García Caturla to that of Amadeo Roldán. Alejandro García Caturla (1906–1940) who wrote three Afro-Cuban dances for the piano that were later orchestrated, was a talented composer who had a deep knowledge of the complexities of Afro-Cuban polyrhythms. Amadeo Roldán (1900–1939) began his Afro-Cubanist phase with his "Overture on Afro-Cuban Themes."

In addition to the artists we have already mentioned, Pedro San Juan of Valencia, Angel Reyes Camejo, Félix Guerrero, Enrique González Mantici, Pablo Ruiz Castellanos, and Alfredo Diez Nieto have all contributed or are still contributing to the strengthening of Cuban musical nationalism. This nationalism consists of the merger of Spanish and African sources, as well as, to a lesser degree, those of other cultures, a cultural profile that differs from its roots without denying them, which is, in fact, Cuban culture.

9

Music and Dance in Continental Latin America, with the Exception of Brazil

ISABEL ARETZ

Where and How African Music Is Preserved

To answer this question we must first be able to determine what we mean by African music as a whole, since, from an anthropological viewpoint, Africa has many cultures and each culture has various musical forms: music for rituals, profane music, music for entertainment, martial music, royal music, work songs, ceremonial songs, etc. We must also be able to establish the musical traditions of the slaves who came to our continent, for this would enable us to trace the path followed by African music, or, to be more exact, the various types of African music, in America.

None of these questions can be answered to our complete satisfaction since the science that studies oral and traditional music only developed in the twentieth century, when we became equipped with tape recorders that permitted us to capture music that had been orally transmitted. Moreover, we must assume that present-day African music is not the same as the music that was played at the time of the slave trade; at least, it is definitely not the same as that of the people who underwent the strongest acculturation process, who are, of course, the ones that have been best studied and who have therefore served as a point of comparison.

As regards the various musical forms performed in Latin America by the more or less mixed descendants of slaves, these cannot possibly be the same as the forms brought here by their forefathers, since their life-styles have changed, as has their ability to perpetuate their rites and their music.

Having thus outlined our problem we will analyze the music of the Black population of continental Latin America, without including Brazil, which will be the subject of a special study. We will refer here to musical instruments, songs, instrumental music, and contemporary dances performed by the descendants of slaves. We will begin with an analysis of the different types of music that are being transmitted, comparing this music with music of known European roots, and with identifiable Indian music that has been preserved by groups surviving on the edges of our civilization. We will have to separate the music, not by the skin color of its interpreters, but by its cultural characteristics, its function, ritualistic or profane, and by other anthropological elements.

African slaves already began to lose their tribal identity during their voyage to America. Later, the preservation of essential cultural traits, and the consequently greater or lesser adaptation, depended on their degree of isolation upon arrival. The adaptation took place initially with regard to language, which in many cases led to a new cultural expression known as Creole or *criollo*.* The slaves ate a mixture of Amerindian and African vegetables. Their homes were African in style, although sometimes they were built according to the models of their new environment. Their social organization was a product of their new circumstances: few women, plus the separation of the family and of tribal groups. In the midst of all this they developed their music, its literature, its dances, and its musical instruments, which acquired on American soil, with the passing of years, a new life, new forms, and new functions. The same process affected their religious beliefs and their gods, whose names are well known in some countries where priests and magicians still abound; in other countries they have been fused with Catholic saints and festivities through a syncretism that, though at first forced, we see today in new dimensions of music and musical instruments in countries like Venezuela.

Africans adapted their music and dance to the new circumstances in the Americas, enriching American music by creating an Afro-American music. With their extraordinary musical talents, Blacks also submitted to their new masters by placing their talent at the service of the music of European salons, which began to develop its own American characteristics. For example, the contradance was transformed into the *danza,* the *danzón,* and the *merengue,* to mention just one European genre and some of its well-known American descendants. Similarly, we also find European-trained musicians borrowing melodic and rhythmic elements and instruments from African musicians, which is the same thing Indian musicians did when they came into contact with African groups. The *marimba* is an outstanding example of this fusion; there is more than one American country that claims credit for the invention of this instrument, which was imported from Africa, name and all, as we shall see further on.

Rituals

The slaves attempted to continue their festivities to their divinities upon arriving in the new lands. In many places their religion and rites have survived to this day, with a few variants, but without losing their ancient meaning. Thus, among the Boni of French Guiana—a group of Black canoers and farmers descended from Blacks who fled the coastal plantations in the eighteenth century—the songs are meant for the worship of ancestral gods and appear to be linked to ceremonies of possession and to

*In Latin America we also consider folk music with no African elements as "Creole."

funeral rites. These Blacks continue their secret cult to the Kromanti jaguar gods using their *apinti* drums. But the God, their God, comes from Africa, they say, and has followed the paths of their forefathers. (The *apinti* drum is Bantu in origin and belongs to the Ashanti culture.)

Their songs are also, according to Herskovits, directed to Dagowe, a serpent deity; to the *apuku,* the small, good spirits of the jungle, capable of turning into demons when they get angry; to Aidowedo, the rainbow serpent; to Wata-winti, the spirit of water; to G'a Obia, the great magic spirit; to Towenu, the "strong name" of the *father god,* a serpent divinity; to Zambí, the great god of the Loango Congo, also venerated by the Saramaccans as Loango; and to the gods of the earth. They have ancestral cult songs that include the *Twins,* considered holy in the jungles of Suriname, just as the *Yorka* or spirits are sacred in certain regions of Africa. Other songs, harder to classify, include those for the *papa,* or the dead; secular dance songs like the *susa,* which is a pantomime dance where men fight wth shields and spears, the *saketi,* the more popular river dances, the *sungi,* which accompany the *djuka* dance; semireligious dance songs like the *asawa;* and the *banya,* the *alada,* and the work songs, sung as the Boni heave logs into the river.

Members of the San Basilio group in Cartagena, Colombia, still preserve the *lumbalú* ritual to the dead, celebrated, as they say, because death puts an end to all suffering. Thus, they cry at childbirth because the infant is born to suffer; this was explained to us by Batata, their chief, in 1956. Aquiles Escalante gives us a vivid description of the *lumbalú,* which we quote, since it is one of the few writings of this type to survive:

> When a person who belonged to Lumbalú during his lifetime dies, his family immediately announces the death to Batata, who convenes the Cabildo by beating on a drum, an instrument that remains in the home of the dead person for nine days. The drum is played and there is singing at various times a day: at dawn, at noon, at 6 p.m. and in the early hours of the night, for nine days.
>
> Batata places himself at the door of the bedroom or living room, at the head of the deceased, who remains in an uncovered coffin in the center of one of the two rooms of the house; to his left or right is a person who plays the *yamaró.* The head of the Cabildo sits at his drum and plays it. Sometimes a log is placed under the dead man's head to raise it. Between the head of the corpse and the Batata are the old women of the Cabildo; in their midst one of them dances with a Cabildo member. The women of the family of the deceased sing and dance around the coffin. There is always an instructor who initiates the songs, while other monitors and other participants form a chorus that repeats a refrain. The old women remain standing most of the time; they sit down once in a while, but only briefly to rest, and then they resume their dance and their songs. While they dance around the corpse, they touch each others' palms, turn, dance, moving their waists, and some-

times they slightly pick up their skirts when they pass close by the corpse. At midnight, once the alcohol has animated them, Batata gets up with his drum and leads the two lines of teachers in song and dance.

The meaning of many of these songs is unknown to the group members, who learned the words from their ancestors by word of mouth, which is how they were passed from generation to generation; the songs are very important, however, because they preserve the language used by the first rebels who broke away from slavery. The following is a group of songs:

Yantongo

Eee . . . moná mi pacasariáme
Mamujé
Yantongo, Yantongo
Moná mi pacasariáme
Mañane por la mañane
Me voy con mi compañera pacasariáme
Moñá ñapete loquiparí
A gobbé cabecite

The following song is usually sung in the early hours of dawn:

Juan Gungú

Chiman Congo
Chi man luango
Chi man ri luango de Angola
Juan Gungú me ñamo yo
Juan Gungú me a re ñamá
Cuando so ta caí mamé.

Sabangolé

Sabangolé, baile guiní cha Lora
Cuando cha Lora llegá
Cu monéle ahi homblo
A tie fue baile di Sabangolé

The Cabildos

At first the Blacks would get together and dance in the streets, a matter that was of some concern to the *cabildo* members (municipal authorities), as is apparent from this page, dated August 13, 1563, reproduced by Jiménez Borja in Lima:

At this Cabildo it was discussed that the Blacks dance and beat their drums in the public streets of this city. As a result one cannot use the streets, and horses are frightened, and other damages and inconveniences occur. It would be more appropriate for them to gather in public plazas. This is why we would like to have it publicly announced, that, from today on, they should not dance or play their drums or other dance instruments, unless it be in the public park of this city and in the Park of Nicolás de Ribera El Mozo, or the Blacks will be punished with 200 lashes and their drums will be broken, and the constable who caught them shall receive one peso for each Black man.

The Blacks then organized themselves into groups, but even so they caused major disturbances in the celebration of their ceremonies. So Viceroy Don Luis de Velasco, on September 18, 1598, signed a royal ordinance forbidding these congregations. The third chapter of the ordinance reads as follows:

No owner or tenant of a place will tolerate the dances and the playing of drums by groups, nor any other kinds of parties by the aforementioned people. The fine will be of 30 pesos for the first incident; and double for the second, to be paid in thirds to the chamber of his Majesty, to the judge and to the accusers; and the third time the same penalty will be paid, in addition to which the locale will be confiscated.

In Buenos Aires and Montevideo the Blacks also took refuge in their *cofradías* (fellowships), *hermandades* (brotherhoods), *cabildos* (councils or chapters) and *candomblés* (a name arising in the earliest days of slavery and also given to drum-accompanied dances). The most common name, however, was *cabildo*. *Cabildos* were real mutual aid societies, presided by a king and a queen, in charge of organizing the celebrations according to the rituals of their country of origin. Fernando Assução rightfully believes that it was the songs and dances that permitted the slaves to survive even the most adverse conditions, since behind an innocent façade they could hide

. . . pagan gods (sometimes transcultured to Christian saints); exorcisms; war incantations that preserved the bellicose spirit of ancient warriors; initiation rites; coronations or the rendering of homage to kings or chiefs; magicians and witch doctors disguised behind a jolly masquerade . . . (1969–1970, p. 16).

In Buenos Aires, in 1770, two centuries after the Lima prohibitions, the viceroy Juan José de Vertiz made a pronouncement against "those indecent dances of the Blacks accompanied by their drums" (Grenon p. 37). At that time each "nation" practiced its dances in different locations, accompanied by "the instruments they play with which they strengthen the beat of their lascivious songs" (in Vega, 1936, p. 61). In Montevideo, in 1816, the *cabildo* also banned, within the city limits, the "dances known by the name of *tangos* which are only permitted to be danced outside the city walls on holiday afternoons until sunset" (Ayestarán, 1953, p. 69). In

Paraguay, the procession of Blacks with their queen and banners was suspended in 1786 (Carvalho, 1961, p. 363).

In Lima, in the *Mercurio Peruano* of 1791, there appears an article entitled "A note on the Congregations of the newly arrived Blacks." We can appreciate the impression these festivities must have made on outsiders (and we can also see that the previous decrees had not been effective):

> . . . it is admirable how rapidly the Blacks go from extreme sobriety to shouting, noise and frenzy. Following their consultation hour, they begin to dance, until 7:00 or 8:00 at night. All the walls of their rooms, especially the inside ones, are painted with figures, that represent their original kings, their battles and their revelries. The sight of these grotesque images inflames and stirs them. It has often been observed that parties taking place outside of the groups and far from their paintings are dull and short lived. The dances really have nothing agreeable about them, and are, in fact, shocking to the propriety of our customs. When one person dances alone, which is most common, he jumps indiscriminately in all directions, turns and turns again with violence and without looking anywhere. The ability of the dancer is measured by his endurance, and the capacity to keep rhythm with his body, while following the pauses of those who are singing around the circle. If two or four dance at once, first the men will go by the women, contorting their bodies in the most ridiculous manner and singing, then they turn their backs, and little by little they separate; finally they all turn to the right at once, and run, suddenly, to meet with the others face to face (navel to navel). The resulting crash looks indecent to whoever thinks that the outward behaviour of the Blacks has the same meaning as our own. This simple and rude exercise is what they consider recreation, consisting in their dance and their contradances, and has little rhyme or reason. But they do have a good time, and once the party has ended, their revelry also comes to an end. Hopefully our own delicate French, English and German dances will bring us more than mere exhaustion and wasted time! . . . We have already expressed that the music of the slaves is very rough. The drum is their main instrument: and the most common drum is one made from a cylindrical container with a hollow stick inside. Those drums are not played with sticks, but they are beaten with the hands. They have some small flutes that they breathe into with their noses. They obtain a sort of musical noise by beating the dried, fleshless jawbone of a horse or ass, with its rattling teeth: they do the same thing by rubbing a smooth stick against another one with a grooved surface. The only instrument that seems to have some semblance of melody is the "marimba." It is made of long, narrow and thin strips of wood, set at a distance of four lines above the mouths of some empty dried gourds, all fastened to a wooden frame. It is played with two sticks, like certain Bohemian psalteries.

In Buenos Aires and Montevideo, the Blacks also continued to practice their *candomblés* despite prohibitions, while the authorities continued to persecute them. In 1879 the chief of police of Montevideo published an edict with the following articles:

1. All *candomblé* dancing with drums is forbidden in the center of the city; only those located in front of the Southern wall may continue for the time being.
2. The above mentioned *candomblés* with drums are only permitted to gather on holidays and their dances must end at 9 p.m.

These rules were loosened during the siege of Montevideo. By the end of the Pereyra presidency, the Black kings of the nations and their retinues, dressed in their colorful garbs, could display themselves. Later, in 1873, when Antonio Antuna, the Congo king of the Seven Flags died, the funeral cortege that took him to the cemetery sang to the sounds of African instruments.

Across the Plata River, Rosas revived the drums. "Black on red" is the "impressionistic vision of the Federation," wrote José Luis Lanuza (1937). Quesada (the Victor Gavez of *The Memories of an Old Man*) describes "a great African feast in the shadows of the pyramids":

Before noon they began to gather in the neighorhood of the drums, and, at a set time, the parade to the Plaza began, preceded by the kings and queens and their chiefs, all dressed up. Each group brought its own musicians, Blacks who had their originally-shaped drums. These drums consisted of a type of large gourd that was held between their legs. Seated, holding short sticks with a ball on one end, they would bang on a tighly stretched skin extended over both ends of the gourd: the beats had a rhythm and served as an accompaniment to the choirs that sang in their dialects. They were really barbarous songs: their recitations resembled the sounds of animals, and the choir would repeat each measure. These were dances with choirs, and I think there were also bells and reed flutes, but I am not entirely sure of that.

To those feasts, the Black women wore their gala garbs, generally made of muslin in light colors; colored beads were worn around their necks and on their arms; they had low necklines and bare arms. The Black men wore white, a red jacket and badges. They carried their flags and the banners of each nation and marched in an orderly fashion, dancing and singing. The plaza was filled with people and the drums thundered through the air. The crowds came from everywhere, and on Don Miguel Riglos' balconies and at the police headquarters there were men and women watching the spectacle.

In 1870 the drums died in Buenos Aires. In Montevideo, on the other hand, they are carnival participants to this day, still bearing the name of *candomblé*.

Today, in Venezuela, the "dance of the drums" is the dance practiced by the Afro-Venezuelan population. Here Whites mix with Blacks in an admirable cultural symbiosis; there are *cofradías,* but they are now dedicated to a saint: San Benito, or San Juan Congo, or San Pedro. In Venezuela, as in other countries, there existed at first a forced religious syncretism; the Blacks could perpetuate their own rites and festivities, but these were finally replaced by the Catholic saints. Time erased the memory of their African divinities, giving place to what we now call "folk religion," which mixes Catholicism or another official religion with indigenous or African beliefs and celebrations. As a final result, the music and the instruments of African origin were introduced into the Catholic ceremonial, as was observed by the historian Eugenio Pereira Salas in Chile.

In Panama, as in other countries, the Congo organization had a real and functional existence. But in our days, as Zárate said, it is more of a tradition and symbolism that is felt during the carnival activities: "But the spirit of the group is maintained all year round . . . furthermore, in his 'games,' the Panamanian 'Congo' can be credited with having linked his African heritage to the basic events of national history" (Zárate, pp. 118–119).

Musical Expressions

The abolition of slavery did not necessarily mean the cultural integration of Blacks with the dominant groups. Working in different jobs, the descendants of the slaves remained on the margins of the rest of the population isolated by European and American racism, until the rise of anticolonialism brought an awareness of their culture, in which religion and music are so very important. Here we will compare the music of different Afro-American groups and the musical instruments they made on American soil, all of which constitute the survival of ancient traditions.

As is true in Africa, the musical group that accompanies dancing consists of three essential elements: the musicians who play the instruments; the singing in which soloists alternate with a choir; and the participation of the spectators who clap their hands and shout. A fourth element can be a recitation that precedes the song or that alternates with it to develop the drama of the myth. One example is the song "to kill the snake," which becomes a game in Venezuela, as we shall see later on.

Musical Instruments

On our continent slaves discovered materials similar to the ones they had used in their own countries. They used them to make the instruments they had been unable to bring along. Like artisans, they made them one by one and always for a specific purpose. Their major instrumental wealth was in percussion instruments, but they also used musical bows and some wind instruments. Here we will look at the main instruments, since we consider them to be the most faithful and most genuine documents in the study of the survival of African culture in Latin American countries.

Idiophones

Among those instruments which produce sound by the vibration of their own bodies, we can find having African ancestry those of percussion, those that are used to hit each other, shaken, and rubbed. Almost all now form part of the national heritage.

Bamboo tubes

The *quitiplás* of Venezuela are four or more tubes that are banged together or hit on the floor. These tubes are also used on the Caribbean islands, and come from Africa, where they are often beautifully worked. (In Nigeria they are used in pairs. The Badouma in the Gabor region of the Congo also use them.*) The Venezuelan *quitiplás* are divided into "male" or *pujao*, which is the largest one, and "female" or *"prima,"* which is smaller; the remaining pair are called *quitiplás*, just like the entire set. Once they were employed in the Barlovento region in a dance similar to the *tambor redondo* (round drum) that we will talk about later.

Among the percussion idiophones, Romero describes the Peruvian *tejoletas*, little boards or little sticks (p. 53). And also the *cajón* (big box or drum) which is "one of the last remainders of the instruments brought here by grandfather Congo" (p. 51). Among the players of the Creole harp and sometimes the guitar, there can be a second musician who is said to *cajonear* (play on the wood of his instrument), but we do not know to what extent this is still related to the African *cajón*.

The *palitos* are little sticks though not as widely used as the Cuban *claves* that people from Barlovento sometimes hit together. There was once in Curiepe, Venezuela, a musician called "Tocapalitos" (player of *palitos*), and every time he used to play people would take him for the devil.

Within this group of instruments, but far more developed, is the African *marimba* played by Blacks, Indians, and Whites, depending on the region. The instrument's name even reveals its African origins: it is a Bantu instrument. In Southern Africa, as in America, there are *marimbas* with hoops, standing *marimbas* and hanging *marimbas*. Their construction technique came to America from Angola. In Mesoamerica, the Indian, the Ladino, and the Creole, in short, the "folk," adopted it to play folk and popular music of a Creole-European nature.

---

*This type of instrument is used outside the African continent, in Indonesia.

The pianist Albert Friedenthal has given us a description of the *marimbas* that he saw in Guatemala in 1891, and remarks that "Creole music is played on them, even though the players are Indians or Mestizos, because the Blacks are only found on the coastal regions of Central America; however, the presence of Zambos (a mixture of Blacks and Indians) in the interior indicates that there must have been an abundant African population there before." (Friedenthal, 1913, p. 79)

During a trip to Central America in 1966 we saw hoop *marimbas* and standing *marimbas* with one or two sets of keys, sometimes even put together in pairs. In the entire region, the instrument par excellence is the *marimba,* yet no one remembers where it came from.* The hanging *marimba* is used on the coast of Ecuador and in southern Colombia, where it is played by the population of African descent. Strangely enough, the *marimba* also appears among the Colorado Indians. At the Traversari Museum there is a collection of various antique *marimbas* made from bones and wood, but without vibrators, that belonged to the Colorado Indians; and there are also table *marimbas* that give the impression of being more developed.

The marimba was formerly used in Peru, as it was in other South American countries, by groups of African origin. According to the *Mercurio Peruano* of 1791,

> The instrument that helps to carry the melodic line is what they call the marimba. It is made up of long, narrow strips of wood, set a few inches above the apertures of dry, empty gourds, all fastened to a wooden framework. It is played with two little sticks, like certain Bohemian zithers. The decreasing diameters of the gourds make it possible to adapt them to the notes of the scale (quoted by Jiménez Borja, op. cit., p. 50).

In Buenos Aires this instrument was still played during the Rosas regime.

Another typically African idiophone used for a long time in America, is the *marimbola* or *marímbula* (it is the *mbira* of the Congos, of the Zambeze Wandas, and of the Kaffirs). Israel Castellanos identifies it among the African-born Blacks, citing Esteban Pichardo as his source. The *marímbula* first appeared in the Antilles, and perhaps only recently arrived in Venezuela; it has also been identified in Colombia. The instrument is a big box or gourd upon which wood or metal strips are fastened; they are played either directly with the fingers or with a piece of leather placed on the playing finger in order to avoid injury.

Iron percussion instruments in the shape of small bells are common in the Antilles and in Brazil. In our area of interest they are restricted to

---

*For a deeper understanding of the instrument see Chenoweth, Vida, *The Marimba of Guatemala* (Lexington: The University Press of Kentucky, 1964).

Guyana. In Suriname, the Bush Negroes and those living on plantations use the percussion of "iron against iron" or the *felu-kon-felu*.

Among African rattles we find *maracas* with handles, played both in Africa and in America and used singly in rites or ceremonies, above all for cures. The descendants of Africans in Venezuela shake them one at a time to accompany the "songs of the drum," and they play them in pairs—male and female—to accompany their folk music. In Ecuador, along with the *marimba,* the *bombo,* and two drums, one *maraca* is used, as well as the *guasa, guacharaca,* or *alfondoque,* which I observed on my trip to the area. This instrument is made from a piece of bamboo cane, closed at either end, pierced with nails made of hard wood; many seeds are placed inside the tube, making the walls of the instrument emit a sound when shaken. This instrument is usually played by women, while the *marimbas* and drums are played only by men. The *maracas* are played one at a time as among Venezuelan Blacks, and they are used to accompany singers.

Membranophones

In ancient days, drums resounded in all places where there was a Black population. On Sundays, according to Romero, a very "hot" drum "duel," a typically Congo game, announced the *cofradía* dances. Concolorcorvo, in his *Lazarillo de Ciegos Caminantes* wrote that Peruvians used a hollow log with a coarse skin at each end. "This drum is carried by a Black man on his head; another follows, with two little sticks in his hand, he wears stilts and beats on the leather end with his sticks . . ." (p. 326). African drums in America have a very specific function assigned to them in lay ritualistic ceremonies, as well as in religious processions and feasts. Often they are personalized. When we visited Caraballeda, a village on the Venezuelan coast, in 1947, a truck had driven over Burro Negro (black mule), as they called their large drum; the women mourned over it, and the men buried it. There, each drum had its own name: the most sonorous, for example, was called Campanita. However, the language of the drum, as in Africa, is unknown; at the most, the drum "declares," "speaks," or "rings," but this is not related to drum talk itself.

The drums are generally played in groups of two to five or six, and each has a specific function. Among the Bush Negroes of Suriname, for example, the *apinti* is the main drum, the tenor drum, on which the most intricate rhythms are played. The *apinti* calls the gods in the sky, the powerful Kromanti spirits, the ancestors. The *tumaco* is used to call on the spirits of the jungle, and provides the medium accompaniment rhythm. The *agida* is the bass drum of the Bush Negroes and the city Blacks, and dominates the other percussion instruments with its persistent rhythm. It is consecrated to the serpent gods and is used to call them.

In the following paragraphs we will describe the main types of drums in our area of interest.

Drums made of hollowed logs

These are present in the area we are studying either in the form of goblets or in their natural log shape. The goblet-shaped drum is prevalent among the Talamanca, the Chiriqui, and the Choco Indians, who play it with their hands while holding the drum between their legs. (Since there are also archaeological drums of a similar make in the Americas, it is quite possible that the ancient inhabitants of America were familiar with this type of instrument; some of them are exhibited at the Museum of Costa Rica.) The Capaya Indians of Ecuador also have similar drums. But in every case the Pre-Columbian drum had its head fastened to the body with glue, with wooden nails, or with a rope rolled over the head; as far as we know, tied ropes and wedges were never used.

Drums made of hollow logs (of the Loango type from the Congo) are presently built in different sizes; they can be up to two or three meters in length, and display fundamental variations in the method of affixing the membrane: either iron nails are used, as in the case with the *cumacos, tamunangos,* etc. (in which case the drum is tuned by heating) or cord or rope ties are preferred.* In this case there are different systems for attaching the ropes: these can be attached either to small or to large wedges incrusted in the body of the drum. (This first method was used in the *apinti* drums of Suriname; the second, is that of the *mina* drum of Barlovento, Venezuela, and is markedly Dahoman in origin, and of the *curbata,* a drum with legs, that is smaller, and that is used to give the rhythmic base). The cords can be attached to a loop of rope that encircles the log, and is tightened with wooden pegs, a system that is widely used among descendants of slaves and that has passed into the world of folk music particularly in Ecuador, Colombia,** Panama, and Venezuela. Or else they form a net, fixed to the inside of the drum while other ropes are threaded through some small holes in the bottom part of the log; this type is used in Travesía, Puerto Cortés, and Honduras. The long drums with their membrane nailed onto the log are played lying on their side in Venezuela: the player is seated astride the log and taps the membrane with his hands; two or three more players squat alongside the drum and

---

*Today, logs are often replaced by barrels, because it is so hard to get wood. This is true of the *candomblés* of Uruguay as well as of the coast of Venezuela.

**The Pechiche drum played at San Basilio for the *lumbalú,* was described by Escalanté: "The *lumbalú* or *pechiche* is a conical drum, 1.55 m high; the diameter of the upper mouth is of 40 cm, and of the lower mouth, 25 cm: it only has one membrane made of goat skin (which is played with the hands), five nails, and its body is made of balsa wood. In addition to the *lumbalú,* the *yamaro* is used, also shaped like a conical trunk, has one membrane, wedges, and is similar to the drum generally used along the Atlantic coast" (Escalante, p. 283).

hit it with sticks. The long drum, *mina,* on the other hand, is placed on two crossed sticks; while the main player hits the membrane with his hands, or at times with his fists, others stand at the sides and hit the log with sticks.

Many of the instruments we have briefly described belong to sets of two to six percussion instruments, including drums of various sizes to achieve different pitches, which can also be combined with a bass drum (generally of European type) with two membranes held in place by rings tied with a rope. With these combinations of drums the players produce percussion patterns that may be polyrhythmic and even heterorhythmic, always using as a base one drum beating a uniform rhythm. Because different places on the membranes and on the wooden edges are hit, and because drumsticks, thin sticks, the hand, and the fingers are all used, the drummers achieve many sound combinations that enrich the beat and avoid monotony. Some African tribes communicate through drums, using elaborate codes. This practice was lost in America, but from it stems the thought of Afro-Venezuelan drummers who say that their drums "declare" or "ring."

Drums with Two Membranes

The group of "round drums" of Barlovento, which Juan Liscano, a pioneer in Venezuelan musical research, found so well represented at the Belgian Congo Museum in Brussels, is also frequently seen in the state of Miranda in Venezuela. There are three drums of slightly different sizes made out of very light logs, with membranes that are attached with zigzag ties.

The Choco Indians of Colombia also have a small drum with two membranes tied in the form of a net. Karl Gustav Izikowitz mentions them in his valuable study of the Indian instruments of Latin America; he considers this drum "hardly of African origin," an idea that I do not share.

String Instruments

The most developed string instruments came to us from Europe, as is well known, and were adopted by Black musicians. From Africa, however, came different musical bows, generally used for the vibration of gourds. So far it has been impossible to establish whether the small musical bow with a mouth resonator is Pre-Columbian or African. That is also the case with the Peruvian *rucumbo,* a bow to which catgut is attached that is hit with a little stick, as it is with the *lunku,* a long mouth bow used by the Miskitos in Honduras and by Indians descended from slaves mixed with the natives, especially the Tawira (Agerkop, 1975). In Colombia, in the district of Bolivar, a long time ago the Black group members danced to the rhythm of mouth marimbas, two drums, and a guacho. The mouth marimba is a musical bow placed over the legs so that the cord takes advantage of the musician's mouth as a resonating box. Vibrations are achieved through a wooden stick (Escalante, p. 297).

In Brazil and in Uruguay (the latter having inherited it from Brazil) the musical bow is called a *urucungo, bobo, bucumba,* or *berimbau* and has half a gourd attached to it as a resonator. In Paraguay, the *gualambau,* a bow pierced by a small resonating gourd, appears among the Guaraní Indians. Max Boettner writes that the name is a "curious mutilation of Mbarimbau or Berimbau," since the Guaraní have no *r* sound and change it into an *l* (p. 31). These bows are thought to have come from the Bantu; however, in our countries everyone uses them for folk music, with the exception of the Guaraní.

In Venezuela and Colombia there is yet another type of musical bow, called *carangano* in the first country. The *carangano* is placed on a tray or a box to make it vibrate. This instrument is used by Creoles. The same can be said of the *caramba* or *quijongo* of Central America, which has been mentioned since colonial days. The Costa Rican type of bow that we studied is strung with either vegetable fibers or metal strings. A *sacaguacal* (the local name for a gourd or calabash of the *Crescentia* family) is hung from its top to act as a resonator. The string is hit with a small stick, and with the fingers of the other hand the mouth of the gourd is covered and uncovered, while the big toe is used to keep time at the bottom part of the instrument.

Wind Instruments

The *Mercurio Peruano* describes a nose flute used by the Blacks in Peru. This type of wind instrument can still be seen among the Chimbangueleros (Black dancers of San Benito, in some places of Zulia) of Venezuela. The players call them "whistles" and they can also be blown by mouth, as we saw on our trip to Shanga, Mali, in 1974.

Musical Phenomenology

Of the instruments we have described, the drums and rattles are still the bases of the rhythm and timbre of Afro-American music, while the *marimba,* the string instruments, and the wind instruments are isolated units, generally not played by Africans, with the exception of the *marimbas* used on the Pacific Coast. These instruments are usually used for different types of music.

With regard to the African characteristics of American music, the analysis must begin with the documentation of sounds found *in situ,* and it must be relatively technical in order to discover scales in the melodies, preferences for certain intervals and ornamentations, independence of the song from its accompaniment (often lost on account of the influence of western music), and the use of particular structures. To these are added what Carlos Vega called "the ways of doing it": responsorial songs, voices, vocal ornamentation, and even the use of particular timbre, all of which permit Zárate to write "little or nothing has been said about the voices of the Black groups, their physiological and tonal characteristics, which are quite different from those that appear in Hispanicized groups" (1962, p. 78). All this, added to the varied rhythm and tone of the drums and to the rhythm and timbre of the accompanying idiophones, forms what we can scientifically classify as Afro-American music.

Taking function into account, we can now separate songs pertaining to religious ceremonies from work songs, and recreational music. These include dance-songs with portions that are sung and various representations that stem from the ancient *candombes* and are passed on to the carnival, or used to accompany processions. Having begun as a product of religious syncretism, they are today the authentic expression of folk religion.

Ritual Music

Only in places where Blacks were the majority of the population or where they were able to remain hidden or at least isolated were they able to continue practicing ceremonies and rituals to their own gods. We have already mentioned the San Basilio *Palenque,* the maroon stronghold of the slaves who were led in their rebellion by Benkos Bihojo in 1608. Here the *toque,* the crying song, and the *lumbalú* dance were preserved (the latter is repeated during the nine nights of mourning). The musical example below (example 1) was taped by me in 1959 and was transcribed by Ramón y Rivera, who has the ability and patience to capture the essential characteristics, the rhythm and melody, as well as the expressiveness of difficult pieces, without which any scientific analysis is impossible.

This example demonstrates a typical responsory song in which a soloist alternates with a choir. The melody is made up of combined modal scales, and the *pechiche* and *llamador* drums specify the rhythms and staccatos.

Solo	
Hoy se acabaron las recetas	Today the remedies have ended
Hoy se acabaron las novenas	Today the novenas have ended
o le le le	o le le le
ya ta fin de a nana	ya ta fin de a nana
ji re na	ji re na
le re le re i re e	le re le re i re e

Example 1. Lumbalú, 1959, Palenque de San Basilio, Dto. Bolívar, Colombia,
Aretz-Ramón y Rivera.

tu alma termina	your soul ends
le a le i le	le a le i le (women)
a le ya ja le le o	a le ya ja le le o
van a poner el (burro)	They will place the burro
a e e le i le . . .	a e e le i le . . .

Drum Beat: Solo Variation

Drum Solo: How played

Example 2. Beat of the Drum, 1961, Guarenas, Edo. Miranda, Venezuela. Ramón
y Rivera, 1971, p. 157.

In Suriname there is a great wealth of basically African music, as some
of the Black groups still practice their ancestral forms of worship. However, so far it has been impossible to record the music of their secret
ceremonies, or at least the recordings have not been published. On the
other hand, the music of "open" services and lay songs, recorded and
published by the Herskovitses, transcribed and analyzed by Dr. Kolinski,
are well known, as are the songs of the Boni or Aluku of the Maroni River

on the border between French Guiana and Suriname, taped by Hurault in 1957–1958. Recently Terri Agerkop of INIDEF did some research among the Bush Negroes of the Suriname or Saramacca River, called Saramaccans after the river. Richard Price has also worked with the Saramaccans, but we are still not familiar with the results of his studies.

The adaptation of Blacks to their new life engendered a new type of accultured music, again without racial or color distinctions. The main variable was their participation in the ritual, although the musicians, drummers, and singers are mostly descendants of Africans. In Venezuela, the "round drum *toques* and dances" and those of the "large drum" in honor of San Juan in Barlovento, as well as the *toque* of the *chimbángueles* of the Black San Benito in Zulia, are good examples of this religious music. Our example 2 consists of a song and drum *toque* recorded and annotated by Ramón y Rivera, in his book *La Música afrovenezolana* (Caracas: Imprenter Universitaria, U.C. de Venezuela, 1971) in which the author points out how a series of melodic elements, all grouped together, not in isolation, constitute what we might call the African *melos*.

The *yancunú* we taped in Puerto Cortés, Honduras in 1966,* is another example of a dance song; it is sung by a group that maintains strong Afro traits, even in its music. The yancunú is played between December 25 and 31, when members appear "masked like Africans" (at the end of the dance the masks are given to the children, who destroy them.) The soloist alternates with the chorus, and is accompanied by two drums, whose basic rhythms we have transcribed (example 3).

Work Songs

Black men in America participated in three basic economic activities: mining, agriculture, and industry. They were also porters, and even carried pianos across the high Andes; today they load boats in many Atlantic, Caribbean, and Pacific ports. In agriculture they worked in two basic crops, tobacco and sugar. They also participated in the cacao harvest, a crop grown in the hot lands of Venezuela and Colombia. Later on they worked with pickaxe and shovel, or else, as was the case in Venezuela and Colombia, and earlier in Uruguay and Argentina, became the blood brothers of the *gaucho* or the *llanero* who herded the cattle. Their songs rang out in each activity, aiding them in their work and soothing the animals.

Black women, on the other hand, were porters and wet nurses; they nursed and soothed White children with their songs, and with every new

*The trip was made possible by Guggenheim scholarships shared by Ramón y Rivera and myself in 1966–1967, completed in 1968.

Example 3. Yancunú, 1966, Puerto Cortés, Honduras. 1. Aretz-Ramón y Rivera.

generation the nurses became another family member, sometimes a second mother. (The Liberator Bolívar's nurse was Black, and he decreed the freedom of slaves.)

These work songs and lullabies show African traces in their melodies and their forms of expression. They have come to us with Spanish words: some of them are couplets from overseas, others are couplets that reflect the feelings of Blacks. The example we offer is a unique rowing song that

Example 4. Rowing Song, 1968, San Lorenzo. Dto. Esmeraldas, Ecuador. I. Aretz-Ramón y Rivera, 1967–1968, p. 85.

Ramón y Rivera and I discovered in San Lorenzo, Ecuador, during our 1968 trip (example 4).

In this song one can appreciate the interplay of the 3rd and 4th intervals and the pentatonic Afro-influence, not at all similar to the Inca style that is dominant in this country, as it is in Peru and Bolivia.

There are many other songs of this type in Colombia, Panama, and Venezuela, not to mention Brazil or the Caribbean Islands. In many of them one hears shouts and falsetto ornamentations reminiscent of certain songs of the African pygmies.

ay ay a i a mi el capitán	ay ay a i a mi
pirata	the pirate captain
a mi el capitán pirata me convidó	Oh my! the pirate captain
a navegar	has invited me to sail
para que fuera maestriar	so that I can learn
lo que aseñalaba el mapa	what the map says
que me voy	I am going
que ya ha yay	I am go-go-going
que me vaha	I am go-go-going
que me voy	I am going
ya ay dijo dijo que me cuidaría	He said he would take care of you
a dijo que me cuidaría	he said he would take care of me
a con mucha delicadeza	with great delicacy
pagan de mi el mes cien pesos	Paying me 100 pesos a month
y tres comidas al día	and three meals a day
que me voy	I am going
que ya yay que me vaya lao lei.	I am going lao lei

Recreational Music

As Blacks entered popular life, they began to participate in the people's folk culture as poets, singers, musicians, and dancers. They followed the processions of saints, they danced *cuecas, bambucos, tamboritos,* and *joropos.*

Now the guitar or regional *guitarrilla* appeared, joining the drum in some Panamanian and Colombian dances; however, with this change, one can observe the tendency to "free" the vocal melody from the rigors of the rhythm, and even from the accents of percussion (Zárate, p. 78). Thus we note the entrance of the "chanty" style in the *tamborito,* together with certain other vocal effects, that are neither European nor Indian in origin. This style is also perceived in the Venezuelan *joropo* and in parts of the *tamunangue* (*chichivamos, juriminga, poco a poco* and *perrendenga*), as well as in the more "Creole" work songs; also in the *fulías,* that the Black man from Barlovento sings to the Cross, and which are very different from the eastern *fulías* of Venezuela.

In Colombia, the *cumbia,* the *mapale,* the *bullerengue,* and the *currulao* all preserve typical musical characteristics and names that are not Hispanic. The *cumbia* spread from Cartagena de Indias via the *bajeros* and miners and became the central focus of popular festivities. Its instruments are two drums, two Indian bagpipes, and two millet reeds, and the relatively new European accordion, plus a European box drum and a *caña de lata* or "tin can," a sheet metal instrument played by rubbing, called a *guacharaca* (Zapata Olivella, p. 193). Octavio Marulanda says that the *cumbia* rhythm is undoubtedly of African origin. I too, in analyzing the music of an example I obtained in Cartagena de Indias, find melodic ornamentations in thirds that are characteristic of Black music.

The *mapale* is another "most typical example of Africanism," in which "the song and the clapping of hands alternate, with drums acting as a chorus, with the final objective of attaining a very rich and exuberant choreography" (Marulanda, p. 87).

The *bullerengue* is considered by Delia Zapata Olivella "as one of the most important African legacies of the Atlantic Coast repertory." Zárate has the same to say about the *bullerengue* of Darién: "the most typically Black dance," within which "all the internal sap of sensuality is preserved." Of course Zapata and Zárate are referring to the choreography, which we will discuss later. But it is absolutely true that the dance is based on a music that determines its nature. One can also consider a minuet or a contradance and observe the correspondence between dance and music.

The marimba, two *cununos* or conical drums with one membrane, two bass drums (male and female), and two *guasas* or tubular idiophones that are shaken, are used to play the *currulao* of the Pacific Coast. "The choir, generally of women, repeats verses, refrains and phonemes, following the rhythm and permitting the melody of the song to dissolve without vocal modulations" (Marulanda, p. 90).

On the coast of Ecuador, among Black groups a *bambuco* very different from the well-known Creole Colombian *bambuco* is played and danced. It appears together with the *caramba,* the *torbellino,* and the *figa,* none of which are African names, but which, like so many other pieces, consist of a mixture of African and European elements. That is, at least, how Ramón y Rivera and I perceived it in San Lorenzo, in 1968, where we recorded the piece transcribed as example 5 in this paper. Here we see the typical song in thirds, that differs so dramatically from the European and Creole duos in thirds. Another Afro-Ecuadorian element here is the polyrhythmic nature, noticeable when the singer expresses himself with freedom and a rhythmic counterplay takes place between the singer and the music. The sound context is generally dissonant, with more or fewer intervals, to which is added the harmony of the *marimba,* played by two men, the *tiplero* and the *bordonero.* Ramón y Rivera analyzed the scale of the sung portion at the very end of the piece, which shows a peculiar similarity with the *vidalitas* that we recorded years ago in the provinces of La Rioja and Catamarca in Argentina. We have also transcribed one of these, having reached the conclusion that we are dealing with African vestiges in that southern country, where, during colonial times, Black slaves were taken to work on the sugar plantations of Tucumán. We would never have discovered these vestiges had it not been for our findings in Ecuador (Ramón y Rivera, 1967–1968, pp. 81–84).

In Suriname, assimilated Blacks today have a folk music known as "Creole," wherein African traits survive side by side with European traits. The songs are still responsorial, their construction following un-

cont'd →

complicated forms in which simple melodies are repeated with slight variations.

Dances, Dramas, and Comparsas

Whoever has witnessed African dances in Africa, or among descendants of Africans in America, must be well aware that they do not at all resem-

cont'd →

ble our Creole dances, European dances, modern dances in or out of
fashion, like the shimmy, the *conga,* or others whose names escape me
for obvious reasons. Africans dance, above all, according to their beliefs,
to get closer to their gods and to participate in a rite that may well end in
possession by a god or a spirit. Even when this ritualistic reason disappears, as in Venezuela, it would seem that a hidden mandate remains in
the background, and emerges in the drum dances. There is sometimes a

Example 5. Toque de Marimba, San Lorenzo, Ecuador. I. Aretz-Ramón y Rivera
(pp. 262–264).

certain difference between the dance of older people and that of youth.
However, in most cases, the elders still pass down the traditions, and so
the character of the dance is perpetuated. I was able to observe this
recently in Venezuela, where I witnessed a drum dance in the town of

Caraballeda, located on the coast, just across the mountains from Caracas. The beat of the drums and the songs were practically the same as those we had recorded in 1947. (In order to appreciate the real differences, a careful comparative study would have to be made.) But the dance changed with the dancing style of each couple. Some of the youngsters participated without much enthusiasm, almost mechanically, using the steps and motions of loose modern dances that contrasted noticeably with the dance style of the older people, or of the children who were being instructed by their elders during the dance. If this is the case today, the reaction of bishops and other authorities accustomed to the modest European salon dances of the period is easy to understand with regard to the ritual and sex dances of the slaves, who were experiencing some degree of freedom during their drum dances, whether it be the *calenda,* the *bambula,* the *chica,* the *candombe,* or the *tango,* at least in the south.

Today, within the area we are studying, there are Afro dances that maintain their original function—in Suriname, where secret and open sessions still take place, as in the cult of the Kromanti jaguar gods, which we have already mentioned; or in Colombia, at the San Basilio *Palenque* where the *lumbalú* or cult to the dead, is still practiced. In all other countries there has been a cultural symbiosis, and it is only on account of the strength of tradition, and the magnetism of the beat of drums, that ancestral dances have survived. It is this fact that permits Zárate to say that the *bullerenge* of Darién (Panama) is "the most genuinely black dance," wherein:

> . . . the internal sap of sensuality is preserved. . . . It is characterized, above all, by the concentration and introspective attitude with which the woman moves. She slides rather than walks, her clockwise steps are tiny, she sets down her entire foot at once and her feet are close together. Her legs are closed, giving the impression of inaccessibility of the lustful forbidden fruit. This movement is called "hacer plantillas" (to walk on the soles). This seems to excite the male, who employs his energy in acrobatic gestures, renditions and sensual provocations. The woman alternates the "plantillas" with more open movements, and reaches a convulsive state when she dances the "bosar," the typical movement of hips and belly, while her partner, as if in a solitary trance, takes this as a form of consent, tries to approach for the attack, but to no avail, because the woman dodges him and makes fun of him, pushing him away and turning away herself. Another female movement that is full of artfulness and charm occurs when the female dancer performs a sweeping backward motion, as the male approaches again, this time executing an acrobatic bow all the way to the ground. Acrobacy and sexual gestures of the male abound and heat up the dance and the crowd. One of the peculiar incidents that reveals the endless resourcefulness of the male dancer, is the test of the hat. When the woman is about to escape, the man throws a hat into the center of the circle and the woman stops her flight to perform "plantillas" in front of the hat. Then, the man,

coming from the opposite side, performs a stunt that can only be performed by a few, select dancers. Without ceasing to dance, the male, gradually opens his legs, holds up his pants, and with spasmodic backwards and forwards movements of his hips, staring and pointing his chin at the female, he slowly descends, until his rear end almost touches the ground; then, gradually, he leans towards the hat, his hands placed on his thighs, then, finally, with a brusque movement, he tries to catch, with his teeth, the wing of the long desired hat, then, throwing it backwards, he places it on his head. If he is successful, there is noisy rejoicing, the drums become louder as do the voices, and the "impossible" lady seems to become humanized and rewards with the gestures of a happy and amiable dance.

I have deliberately reproduced Zárate's entire vivid description, so that the specialist can perhaps, sort out the various elements appearing in this *bullerengue*—sometimes so African, at other times, so similar to other Creole folk dances, even to Spanish dances, for example the part where the man throws his hat at the feet of his partner for her to dance around it.

The *bunde,* was, according to Zapata Olivella, and also to Zárate, "the origin of all the drum dances of Colombia and Panama." But, in addition, and now we quote Zapata Olivella, "It is quite evident that a series of dances like the *bunde,* the *mapale* and the *bullerengue* evolved into the *cumbia*" (Zárate, p. 147). Actually, the *bunde* described by Zárate performed in Darién, has some similarities to our *tamunangue,* although not with regard to the slightly Afro figures of the same. But this could already be a result of acculturation, in this case of the choreography and of the music.

Marulanda mentions the *abozao* of the Colombian Choco region as another rhythm and dance "displaying the relationship between the ancient 'belly' dances, the 'landos' that were danced by the slaves (frequent cries accompany the *abozao*)" (p. 95).

The Congo drums of the Black groups who live along a large part of the coast of Colón, are also, like those of Darién, "the archetype of the primitive or most ancient drum dances that were danced in Panama." Zárate says that "They are also usually associated with a mime show, concerning a variety of historical episodes about the infamous slave trade, slavery, and the Black revolts that followed, during the days of the conquest and the colony" (p. 23).

Zárate gives us a graphic description of the drums that we have reproduced, and reminds us of scenes we witnessed in Kumasi and other Ghanaian villages in Africa.

We must however ask ourselves to what degree Blacks also suffered from acculturation over there? The African dramatized dance acquired new characteristics in America, to the point of becoming a real folk theater in some countries, or degenerating into a carnival *comparsa* in others.

In Venezuela, the *sangalamule* or *sambarambule,* first recorded by Juan Liscano, is like a short farce with dramatic and humorous moments, revolving around the ancient rite of the snake. Ramón y Rivera considers its origins to be strictly African, an assertion corroborated by Fernando Ortiz. This piece of popular theater has become a part of the carnival, together with the blackface *comparsas* that were once very common all over Venezuela.

In the southern part of the continent the *candombes* also survived due to the carnival *comparsas.* According to Ayestarán:

> There are three stages in the order of Afro-Uruguayan music. The first was secret: the African dance rituals known only to the initiates, it had no socializing function and it disappeared with the death of the last African slave. The second was superficial. Superficial in the sense that it emerged and spread so rapidly and is very colorful; in the eighteenth century it was expressed by the *comparsa* that accompanied the Sacred Monstrance during the Corpus Christi celebrations. Later it became organized into the "calenda," "tango," "candombe," "chicha," "bambula" or "semba" that were danced between Christmas and the Day of the Kings, around 1800. And finally it became transformed, at a third stage, into the carnival *comparsas* of Black societies, from 1870 to the present day.

That was when the "societies of Blacks" reappeared, and when, according to the same author, the strange music of the *comparsas* appeared. Strange because the Black societies went to Italian musicians living in Montevideo to have their carnival music written. In Uruguay there are still societies that preserve the *candombe* tradition, including its typical instruments and dance forms. One of them, of the *negros lubolos* was studied in great detail by Carvalho Neto, during his stay in Uruguay in 1954 (1963).

In the San Basilio *Palenque* of Colombia, the group members seem very happy during their carnival, according to Escalante:

> A very typical Carnival comparsa is that of the Carabalí-Mondongo Blacks, formed of ten to twelve men, one of whom is disguised as a woman. Their pants are tucked up and held up by rope belts; they wear sandals, no shirt, and their bodies are made to shine by a mixture of powdered coal and honey. In their hand they hold a wooden sword, and their head is covered with a decorated hat.
>
> They begin their dance at the house of the police chief, and then go through the village in two lines, headed by the drummer, the chief and the person dressed up as a woman. The chief holds a large stick and a sword that is larger than that of the other participants. The *"negritos"* dance from home to home, and form a circle. The drummer places himself in the center of the circle, so that each participant of the comparsa can dance with the "Black woman."

The Chief is the soloist, the others form the choir. On this occasion the *palenqueros* prove to be excellent improvisors, and this becomes the occasion to criticize the most important events that have disrupted the daily rhythm of the life of the community. In the following quartets we see the reaction against mixing with persons who are *palenqueros*:

En la caya e la niña Mecce	On young girl Mecce's street
Ay un niño cororao	There is a colored child
Ni la niña Mecce sabe	Not even young girl Mecce knows
Quien ej ec pae ec pelao	Who is the child's father
Guillebmina ejtaba alegre	Guillermina was happy
Pocque tiene mario blanco	Because she had a White husband
Se la yeban se la yeban	They are taking her, they are taking her
Se la yeban pa ec Banco.	They are taking her to the bank.

[Escalante, p. 295]

The name *negrito* refers today, in all of Latin America, to *comparsas* that have White members and sometimes Indians who dress up in blackface. Most of the time they appear during the carnival, but sometimes they also come out for the celebration of their saint, as is the case with the Paramero *"negritos"* of San Benito in Mérida, or the Tundiques I filmed in 1942 accompanying the procession of our Lord of the Great Power in the center of La Paz. These were Indians imitating the Blacks of Yungas. Other Bolivian *comparsas* are called *morenos* (Blacks) and also parody the Blacks. They wear masks, or paint their faces, and use wigs. They play a wooden rattle or shake fish-shaped maracas, and are accompanied by a band called "Amaikatatis," which in Aymara means "those who drag along the dead" (information from Marta López, 1942). They dance alone and independently.

In Peru the dancing *"negritos"* of Huanuco and of San Mateo, Department of Lima, are well known, as is the *"negrería"* of Junín (Jiménez Borja, p. 52). Also, on December 24 the *Atajo de negritos* (*negrito* group) of El Carmen appears, which has been practicing since the month of October. On that night, at the crossroads of "San Regis," groups of *pallas* and *negritos* render their first homage to the patroness of the district and to the Infant Jesus. After which they continue to dance until January 6. Francisco Iriarte Brenner neglects to inform us whether these *"negritos"* are Indians, painted Creoles, or real Blacks. We are satisfied to point out that they are a *comparsa* remnant with the name *"negritos"* (Iriarte Brenner, 1974).

In Ecuador, Carvalho Neto discovered that "Folklore is interested in the Blacks for displaying certain masked figures . . ." (1964, p. 313). We found *"negritos"* in Central America in Santiago de la Conchagua, El Salvador. In Guatemala, in Palin, for the celebration of Santa Teresa there is an entire folk show called "dance of the negritos" (*Guatemalan Traditions*, 1974). And there are many others that we need not list here.

A la Mazoma no voy, no voy	I am not going to Mazoma, I am not going
yaya porque no tengo	ya ya, because I don't have,
Porque se me acabó la plata.	Because I have run out of money.
Ay ya yay o yia o in o o ho ho	Ay ya yay o yia o in o o ho ho
ha o ho ho ho	ha o ho ho ho
Also	
Scale	
Chorus: Play of thirds in both melodies	
Range of the high voice	

Vidalita

Mixed chorus:	
Salí lucero brillante	Come out bright morning star
salí si sabis querer	Come out if you know how to love.

Example 5. Marimba Music, San Lorenzo, Ecuador. I. Aretz-Ramón y Rivera (pp. 262–64).

Tangos

The name *tango* became synonymous with *candombe* in Uruguay and in Buenos Aires around 1800. A century later, in Curiepe, Venezuela, the most famous Black settlement of Barlovento, there lived a composer called Juan Pablo Sojo R., who created a series of farces or street satires that he called "Los negritos," as well as several *tangos,* some of which are available in their original form. These are real farces, to be presented during carnival season on Holy Innocents Day (December 28) and on Candlemas, that have become a regular tradition. Sojo's characters, although most of them were Black, would paint their faces with charcoal. Both the traditionally sung music and the music annotated in Sojo's compositions has a *tango* or a *tango-merengue* rhythm. (The *merengue* changes the Argentine *tango's* classical 2/4 accompaniment in 5/8). We must point out, however, that neither these performances, nor those of the southern *candombes* or *tangos* of 1800, are at all similar to the rich, Argentine folk music later also known as *tango*.

Stories with Songs and Sung Stories

This type of literature with African roots, reminiscent of the *griot* still existent in some parts of Africa, consists in an alternation between narrative and song. In Venezuela, we have heard narrations both in the Afro region of Barlovento (such as "the typical story of the sword fish") and on the plains from a famous singer, whom we taped in 1947. He narrated the "Story of the Cows." The main character, the stranger, was called "The Negrito," and was the personification of the devil. (This syncretism of the Black man and the devil was not only used by this singer; it is quite widespread. In Argentina, the famous triumphant minstrels were either Blacks or *morenos*. Because of their magical powers they were identified with the devil, to whom they had sold their soul, according to fearful individuals hastily crossing themselves.) The tale of the cows was unique; we never again heard anything like it. Its development is very Venezuelan, and typical of the *llanos,* the plains; the melody is a real work song, with Afro ornamentations and forms of expression (example 6).

At the San Basilio *Palenque* I taped a "Story of the Mohán" or of "María Catalina Luango," with a billingual text and a clearly African melody.* This does not necessarily mean that the myth, well known throughout the Tolima region, is African, although in many places the protagonist is Black.

Song of the Story of the Cows

Example 6. Song of a Story, Parapara, Edo. Guárico, 1947, Venezuela. I. Aretz-Ramón y Rivera.

*I call it African when no European or Indian characteristics can be observed.

Por a quel banco e sabana	On that bank and savannah
se pasea, se pasea, se pasea.	is walking, is walking, is walking
La ra, la la ra, la la la la va la.	Tra-la-tra-la-la-tra-la-la
Primero cojo el paltó	First I pick up the jacket
despues cojo el pantalón	then I pick up the pants
ahora cojeré las tetas	Now I will pick up the teats
para ordeñar a Garzón Garzón.	to milk Garzón, Garzón.

The Black Folk Musician

The Blacks became enthralled with Creole instruments, such as guitars and harps, as is shown in a notice published in the *Gaceta de Caracas* in 1809.

> The priest, don Manuel Faxardo, of the Village of Santa Cruz del Escobar, in the Aragua Valleys, has been missing a slave since the month of January, 1807. He is a single Mulatto slave called Hermenegildo who can play the harp, the guitar, he sings, and paints, and sculpts, but badly. [Ramón y Rivera, 1953]

In Peru, Luis E. Valcárcel says that in the dance called *marinera* for no apparent reason (known as *cueca* in Chile and Argentina) "the music of guitars and drums, and the song and dance itself, achieve their best interpretation, when the musicians are Blacks, or have some Black blood . . . ." And he concludes: "The Black man is the most Spanish thing we have left" (1942).

As a folk musician, the Black became a *payador,* a troubadour or wandering minstrel. In Chile, don Javier de la Rosa sang with the Mulatto Taguada in 1886.* José Hernandez also had his Martín Fierro singing with a Black man. Santos Vega sings with the devil himself, who is Black, because he represents the evils of society that triumph when the devil defeats Santos Vega. Gabino Eseiza (1858–1916), the invincible *payador* was Black. When he was a child, Creoles and Blacks would gather in the neighborhood of San Telmo (Buenos Aires) to practice counterpoint, which is how he learned his music (Moya, 1959, pp. 308 ss).

Integration of the Black Man in Latin America Musical Life

Since the beginnings of slavery, the masters recognized the musical abilities of the Blacks. In Buenos Aires, Vicente Gesualdo wrote about a Black violinist called Josesito, who arrived around 1745 and was

---

*There is a reconstructed recording of this song at the University of Chile, 1969.

the slave of a Buenos Aires family of the time. . . . Chronicles of that period say that upon arriving in Buenos Aires on a slave boat, he already had a remarkable knowledge of music. The praises of this Black musician reached the ears of Governor Andonaegui, who wanted to hear him; thus, an audition was organized at the Cabildo, where, before all the high city officials, Josesito, the Black man, played with admirable mastery, a prelude, a gavotte, and a Corelli concert. [Gesualdo, I, p. 105]

The director of the orchestra that performed at the Buenos Aires cathedral in 1777, Ignacio San Martín, was a "freed Black man." Teodoro Hipólito Guzmán, another "freed Black," was the violinist at the Buenos Aires Cathedral, and later played in Chile. Pedro Contreras, another excellent freed Black violinist, played with Joseph Basurco (a freed Black man) in 1780 (Gesualdo, op. cit., pp. 103–4).

In the nineteenth century, during the siege of Montevideo, one could hear the voices of Black men singing songs of pain, but also of happiness, because the Black man, in spite of his condition, could laugh and express a fleeting happiness. Also, in Montevideo as in Buenos Aires and in other places, the Black, because of his musical talents, begins to perform in bands. Thus in Montevideo, "on quiet afternoons, when the siege seemed to ease, their musical bands cheered the passing people" (Lanuza, 1938). Blacks also formed the bands that accompanied General San Martín on his liberation campaigns. It is said that he arrived in Chile with a band of African Blacks and Creoles wearing "Turkish" uniforms (Pereira Salas, 1941, p. 69).

Gesualdo mentions the African Domingo Lara, who "was the trumpeter of San Martín's orders in Chacabuco and Maipo, and went along to Peru and Ecuador." He died in Buenos Aires at the beginning of the century. And "a Black man," Cayetano Alberto Silva (1868–1929) was born in San Carlos (Uruguay), became the conductor of various Argentine bands, and in 1902 wrote the famous "San Lorenzo March" (Gesualdo, III, pp. 750 and 786.)

After the liberation of slaves in Buenos Aires, almost all piano teachers were Blacks or Mulattoes, like Remigio Navarro and Roque Rivero, who had very good manners, according to Wilde; and he adds that "all the little Creole Blacks had an excellent ear and one could hear them whistling in the streets at all hours whatever the bands were playing, even operatic arias" (Wilde, p. 170).

Blacks in the Theater. Popular Music

With the appearance of "fake" Blacks on the stage, we witness the beginning of an era of commercialization and deformation of African cultural elements. Gesualdo cites a Spanish operetta and comedy troupe in the

Argentine theater around the middle of the century that sang the "American Tango." Its actors, in blackface, "dance typically Black dances," while the "newspapers make reference to the acrobatics and jumps that actors Ramos and Giménez perform on stage" (III, p. 851). In 1868, according to the same historian, "the North American singer, Albert Phillips, arrives in Buenos Aires, sings songs by Foster, accompanying himself with a banjo, an instrument typical of Blacks in the United States South, and he ridicules their customs." Actors [in a U.S. troupe] "delight the theater-going public of Buenos Aires with their perfect imitations of Blacks" (Gesualdo, op. cit. p. 851). The group also traveled to Chile, and Eugenio Pereira Salas, having traced their prior appearance to 1860, tells us that this was a White group, directed by E. P. Christy in New York, where "the genre was deep-rooted," and he adds:

> It consisted of a mixed spectacle of songs and dances, inspired by Black melodies. In center stage, the first performers would form a semicircle. On the ends were the drums and percussion instruments, while the "interlocutors" ingeniously presented a variety of acts. The program was put together harmoniously. In the first portion they sang some "Spirituals" like "Mother Dear," "I Am Thinking On," "Black Smoke," "Wasn't That a Pull Back?" In the second part they dramatized scenes from celebration days at the cotton plantations, interspersed with ballades accompanied by the banjo. The bright program ended with merry dances, that we haven't been able to classify. [Pereira Salas, 1957, p. 120]

This is the beginning of what later was to become quite common, the performance by pseudofolk groups, of the art of a group that they do not represent at all—although sometimes, one must admit, they were fine artists, able to recreate what they had learned from the people, or from recordings, which is not an uncommon occurrence even in our days.

The case of the Black men who became composers and salon musicians is the same, but in reverse. It is their spirit, or, to be more accurate, their expressive talents and interpretations, that modify the insipid and rigid music, of European contradances, transforming them into syncopated *danzones,* into 5/8 *merengues* and other well-known dances. This is how the Black man expressed his *rochelera* happiness,* enriching its rhythms, adding tones and ornamentation, and superimposing the richness of percussion onto the music that he received from the White man, changing it into the "hot" music that is so popular with our youth today. However, when the White man used the Black repertoire, he felt he had to "square" the music, to "rationalize" it, as I once read in a paper pre-

---

Love for festivities and an attitude of "I don't care," expressed by this very Venezuelan and Colombian term.

sented at a congress (whose author I do not know so I cannot tell whether he was Black or White). Be this as it may, when Africans study in Europe they can apply any White theory and are convinced that this is technical, universal, academic, and the best way to become a part of the modern world. So far I know of no White innovations in African music and dance, with the exception of a few good jazz instrumentations.

On the other hand, I think that Black musicians had a very favorable influence on the development of popular and folk music in America. Pianist Albert Friedenthal, born in Pomerania, who traveled through Latin America toward the end of the nineteenth century, was a careful compiler of music and customs and made excellent observations about the influence of Black musicians. He even attributed to them the creation of the Habanera, which he considers one of the most widespread musical forms on the continent. Friedenthal claims that Blacks had their greatest influence in the Antilles, on the Caribbean coast, and in Brazil, but that, even in areas where there were never any Blacks *(sic),* such as in the Mexican highlands, in Argentina, in Chile, and on the Altiplano, we encounter the Habanera and songs that share its rhythm (Friedenthal, 1913, p. 38).

In Colombia, the *merengue* synthesizes what Marulanda considers "a regionalization of neo-African rhythms that spread along the coast of South America with the coming and going of merchant vessels." This music "shows no relationship to other themes of Colombia's Mulatto regions," and now invades piano and violin orchestras (p. 99).

Popular Afro-Antillean music only arrived on the mainland a little over fifty years ago, and in Venezuela it took root where its carriers settled, in the mining town of El Callao, in the state of Bolívar, as well as in some other eastern towns, where it generated what Ramón y Rivera calls in his book *La Musica afrovenezolana,* a neofolklore. It also took root on the coast of Costa Rica, Nicaragua, and Honduras, creating some very particular songs that we taped during our 1966 trip. Yet, in these, no trace of African music remains, just as there are no indications of African music in the music played on the *marimbas.* Just the opposite is true in Suriname, where saxophones and clarinets play a music called *Kaseko,* genuinely "Creole"* in its Afro and other mixtures. This music is played for "old dances" and it is even used in "city homes that are not Hindu" (a published recording called Naks exists).

In Argentina, perhaps through the *zarzuela* (Spanish-type operetta), some "Black urban" music and verses survived, like the ones I collected

---

*In countries with deep-seated Afro roots, this type of mixture is called "Creole." The rest of Latin America refers to the local development of Spanish or European roots as Creole; the existence of Indian or African elements is not a prerequisite.

from a children's round thirty years ago in Tucumán, which seems to be the last Black musical redoubt (which it is for African-based *comparsas*) (Aretz, 1946, p. 414—see example 7). The lyrics, according to Ismael Moya, were sung by "olive and corn soup vendors who walked the Buenos Aires streets, advertising their merchandise in their Afro-Spanish dialect" (Moya, *Romancero,* t. I, p. 341).

Yo soy el negrito fino	I am the fine little Black boy
que siempre paso por acá,	who always comes by
vendiendo escoba y plumero	selling brooms and feather dusters
y nadie quiere comprar.	that no one wants to buy.
Lara lala lara lala.	Lara lala lara lala.
Será porque soy tan negro	Is it because I am so black
que a nadie le va a gustar;	that no one likes me;
será porque soy finito	is it because I am so polite
que me pongo colorado	that I turn red.
Lara lala lara lala.	Lara lala lara lala.
Señor de la concurrencia;	Gentlemen here present
La fiesta ya se acabó;	the party has ended already;
mande los hijos a su casa,	send your children home,
y el negrito saludó.	and the little Black boy has said goodby.
Lara lala lara lala.	Lara lala lara lala.

Example 7. Children's round, Siete de Abril, Tucumán, 1942, Isabel Aretz.

Obviously, we are dealing with an imported text and perhaps even music, of Spanish origin, based on a Black theme. To conclude, we will mention the adaptations made by the Black to Hispanic poetry. There are innumerable couplets, Spanish stanzas of ten octosyllabic lines, *cielitos,* and other Spanish and Creole combinations, used by Blacks, such as the beautiful example that Professor Zárate found in Panama, which depicts a social situation:

Los blancos no van al cielo	White men don't go to heaven
por una solita maña	for one little vice,
les gusta comer panela	they like to eat brown sugar
sin haber sembrado cana.	without having sowed the cane.

[1962:130]

Other cases involving Afro-American themes in Spain with regard to text and music go beyond the framework of this essay; nor will we discuss the return of Afro-American music to the African motherland.

APPENDIX: INCORPORATION OF AFRICAN MUSICAL
ELEMENTS INTO ACADEMIC MUSIC

Black music has little influence on the work of academic composers in the area I have studied. This is largely the case because the heyday of the Black ended in the last century in the southern countries and in the Andean countries Indian and Western music seemed to establish itself with greater vigor. The same occurred in Central America and Mexico, where Afro music became diluted with Americanized versions of salon music, where the *marimba* ruled supreme, and where Afro music did not engender new types of music. Only in Colombia, Venezuela, and Panama does African music preserve its individuality, and thus can exert some influence on the works of academic composers. Nonetheless, I am not familiar so far with that type of composition in Colombia. In Venezuela, on the other hand, Antonio Lauro has composed an interesting symphonic suite called "Giros negroides" ("Black Ornamentations"), consisting of three movements in which he develops elements of Afro music. Antonio Esteves in his "Creole Cantata" (although I do not believe he is attempting to develop African themes), uses work songs that contain Black melodic elements; but his work, as a whole, should be included among the compositions of Creole inspiration. I, myself, am author of "Tres Preludios Negros" ("Three Black Preludes") for piano (recorded by Lia Cimaglia in Argentina); I have used African rhythms and instruments for parts of my ballet "Movimientos de Percusión" ("Percussion Movements"), and I have composed a cantata entitled "Simiente" ("Seed") based on Juan Liscano's poem "Los Negros" ("The Blacks"), in which I use three round Barlovento drums, with their typical form of percussion. In several portions of the work, I use typical Afro-Venezuelan ornamentations. In Panama, Roque Cordero, one of today's most important composers (now living in the United States), projects a sense of nationalism in his music. It would be interesting at some point to look at his score to analyze the elements he uses and to establish to what degree these contain an Afro influence.

In conclusion I would say that there is nothing further from the minds of today's composers, who study ten or more years in musical conservatories, than the study of ethnomusicology; yet without it they will never be able to acquire an in-depth understanding of African musical techniques, nor of any other oral music to incorporate into their creative process. It would be different if a musician who had inherited the African culture of one of our countries were to study composition and then create within his or her ancestral style.

DISCOGRAPHY

Colombia–Ecuador
Whitten, Norman. *Afro-Hispanic Music from Western Colombia and Ecuador.* Ethnic Folkways Library, FE 4376.
Chile
Contra-Punto de Tahuada, with don Javier de la Rosa, *Antología del folklore Chileno,* Universidad de Chile, RCA, CM 2739.
Suriname
(Folk group) Naks: This is Suriname. (Duuwoort, R. F.) Omega International, 444-020.
Hurault, Jean. *Musique Boni et Wayana de Guyane.* Enregistrements de Collection Musée de l'Homme, LVLX-290. D. Paris, 1968.
van Rouselaar, H. C. Suriname Song and Sound the World. Recording produced with the cooperation of Phillips, 831-231 PY. Holland.
Venezuela
Aretz, Isabel; Ramón y Rivera, Luis Felipe; y Fernaud, Alvaro. *Música folklórica de Venezuela,* International Folk Music Council, OCORA OCR 78.
Laffer, Barlovento. Vol. 1. *Folklore de Venezuela,* Vol. 5. 1971.
Liscano, Juan, and Lomax, Alan, *Venezuelan Folk and Aboriginal Music.* Edited with notes by The Columbia World Library of Folk and Primitive Music. Vol. X. SL-212.
Liscano, Juan, y Seeger, Charles. *Folk Music of Venezuela.* The Library of Congress, AFS L15.
Ramón y Rivera, Luis Felipe. *Autóctono: Auténtico folklore de Venezuela.* 1967.

10

Music of African Origin in Brazil

José Jorge de Carvalho

The first steps to be taken by any student of Afro-American culture are to attempt to identify historically which ethnic groups were brought over from Africa, and to discover what their cultural characteristics were upon arrival in the New World.

Such knowledge would permit us to evaluate to what degree the social norms (including music, dance, and ceremony) molded during the colonial era under the social situation of slavery, reproduced, transformed, reinterpreted, or countered African rules of conduct and cultural standards. We could then establish criteria that would help us understand African influence on the formation of present-day American society.

In our specific case, a close look at Brazil's most important musical forms that originated in Africa will permit us on the one hand, to determine their traditional character, and, on the other, to place into perspective their main currents of development and transformation.

The usual procedure is to divide the slaves who arrived in Brazil into two large groups identified by their linguistic roots: the Sudanese and the Bantu. The Sudanese arrived mainly from the coastal regions of the Gulf of Guinea, particularly the so-called Slave Coast and the Gold Coast in West Africa. Among them, the most important in number and culture were the Yorubas or Nagôs of Nigeria, and the Gêges (Ewes) of Dahomey. They settled mainly in Bahia and in some northeastern states like Alagoas and Pernambuco. In addition, in the very south of the country (Rio Grande do Sul), there was another nucleus of Yoruba culture, possibly descendants from Africans who came from Oyo. The Yorubas of Bahia are traditionally linked to the Kêtu (Ibadan, capital of the Yoruba kingdom) and Ijeshá regions. From Western Sudan came the Moslem Blacks; their four main groups were the Hausas, the Tapas, the Mandingas, and the Fulas. Although fewer in number than the Bantu, according to some authors, the social institutions of the Sudanese were better preserved in Brazil.

The Bantu, who came from the Congo, Angola (São Paulo de Luanda, São Jorge de Mina, Benguela), and East Africa (Mozambique) are usually divided into the following groups: the Angolas, the Congos or Cabindas, the Benguelas, the Macúas, Angicos, Cassanges, Quiloas, Minas, Bandas and Igesis. Initially they spread into the states of Rio de Janeiro, Bahia, Pernambuco, and Maranhão; from there they redistributed throughout the whole country to Rio Grande do Sul, São Paulo, Mato Grosso Goiás, Minas Gerais, Alagoas, and Prá.

One must remember that this historical picture does not correspond, by any means, to Brazil's present-day ethnocultural picture, since racial mixture was always intense and varied in this country.

We will be using Roger Bastide's original theoretical framework, which we think is more typical of Brazil than of any other country in our continent: "America offers us the extraordinary picture of the rupture between ethnic groups and their culture."[1] Thus we recognize *African cultural groups* (Yorubas, Ewes, etc.) but not ethnic groups.

One of the first great problems that emerged in Afro-American studies is that we only have a disorderly and clearly prejudiced mass of information, from the days when there were still easily identifiable ethnic groups and cultural groups. Some of the oldest reports on Black music in Brazil, for example, are documents revealing colonial policy with regard to prohibitions or control of slave dances and the playing of drums.[2]

The second stage of Afro-American studies consisted of an attempt to identify and to isolate cultural elements of the already mixing ethnic groups in order to show how different they were from the official (European) culture of the republics. (This phase coincided historically with the independence of the colonies and the formation of national republics according to the imported model of the Old World.)

The third phase, which is barely beginning, must confront the problem of Black acculturation. Obviously we shall be tracing its reflections in music. Here the job of the student of culture would not be restricted to the cataloguing of phenomena and characteristics, but would highlight the significance and foreshadow the interplay of consequences, whereas formerly each thread was separated by its origin, be it Indian, African, or European.

Through this last form of analysis, it follows that a study of African contributions to New World cultures should not emphasize differences viewed through a microscope, nor a vision of the phenomenon as a whole, whose survival could possibly be explained as a mere accident. One should understand instead the *structure* into which the African traits we are pursuing were inserted. Thus, we will try to follow an analogous route to that chosen by Andrew Pearse in his methodological treatment defining musical typology according to *social institution*.[3] This type of reasoning will try to prevent our study from becoming exclusively "an account of selected aspects of Afro-Brazilian music." We realize that this path presents many risks, since the role of Blacks in Brazilian society was limited mainly on account of slavery to restricted behavior within the social structure imposed by the colonial government. Their social institutions could only reestablish themselves in a fragmentary fashion within the surroundings of the *senzala*,[4] where Blacks of the same ethnic background were not even permitted to get together. Attempts at flight by slaves, who hid in the jungles, where they formed Black settlements or communities *(palenques)* in Brasil called *quilombos,*[5] were foiled, unlike those of the groups of Suriname and French Guiana maroons (Bosh or Bush Negroes)[6] who survived the persecutions of the colonizers and formed clans whose living patterns survive to this day.

We must also take into account that Africans arrived in America at the very beginning of the formation of its nations. In Brazil, the first load of slaves arrived in the captaincy of San Vicente (which today is São Paulo) in 1538, at a time when the Portuguese population consisted of only a few settlements along the coast; the prohibition of the slave trade took place in 1850, which is to say that slavery thrived for over three centuries. It is thus accurate to accept that Black cultural influence ran so deep that many African elements were transformed to the point of nonrecognition. At the same time it is also hard to isolate certain Portuguese elements within Brazilian culture; they are the heritage of a society formed in the New World.

This is exactly why it becomes so very difficult to analyze Black music in Brazil, since its presence becomes apparent at such a deep level (although at present it has not been studied in depth) as in the ritual music of Yoruban *orixás* in Bahia that is still sung in African languages. It is also evident in almost all traditional Brazilian musical forms, whether of European or of Indian origin, both of which, to a greater or a lesser degree, have been colored by some aspect of African music.

We therefore have a very wide selection of criteria to choose from. Some musical forms, like the *vissungos,* attract our attention because they are among the few remaining archaisms. The Afro-Bahian cult music exemplifies an entire repertory of songs within a body of coherent and functional tradition, typifying what Bastide calls "preserved religions." Umbanda displays the importance of syncretism, that is, the impossibility of picking out only the Black element of an institution created in America that is still in a state of flux.

Parallel to this breadth of cultural reference with regard to preservation, dissemination, and transformation, we also have various ways of focusing on African contributions to traditional Brazilian music that vary with the musicologists and anthropologists who work with them.

We realize that in an essay of this nature it is not to our advantage to expand upon critical considerations, but instead to emphasize the factual information and objective data; however, there are times when we find that a pure phenomenon or musical trait that can be associated with African music[7] becomes compromised during the determination of its origin, since this can depend on the author's conceptual position or theoretical approach. Thus there are authors who will barely admit the presence of African music in Brazil, perhaps because they give an exaggerated importance to the tonality, which is evidently European, as a musical trait. On the other hand there are others, like myself, who find many African and Afro-American characteristics when analyzing the same music.[8]

Finally, we alert the reader to the question of methodology, since it is not always enough to enumerate phenomena, forms, and musical types. These enumerations are by themselves often insufficient to supply information that can be interpreted in just one way, nor are they valid for a comparative study, due to the presence of subjective elements in the points of view of each author at the very moment of expounding them.[9] Generally we will be chosing types of music within Brazilian culture that have a pronounced degree of "Africanism." Of course the study does not claim to be exhaustive; our purpose is merely to offer examples.

Music of Afro-Brazilian Cults

Bahian Candomblés

Undoubtedly the most important displays of Afro-Brazilian culture always revolved around the complex structure of the *candomblés*. This African term was first used to refer to the large annual religious feasts of the Yorubas in the city of San Salvador, capital of Bahia, and later became identified with all Afro-Bahian cult ceremonies. The Yorubas, in successfully restructuring their religious-mythological system in America, exerted great influence on other ethnic groups (Dahomans and Moslems) among whom they lived, whether in their theology, their ceremonies, or their main festivities. Thus the general structure of the Afro-Bahian cult adopted the main traits of the rituals of the *orixás* (gods) of the tribes from the Slave Coast of Africa.

This cultural dynamic occurred in various regions of Brazil, and the syncretisms that resulted obviously varied, according to the composition of the groups that came in touch with each other. Thus, we have structures analogous to those of the *candomblés* of the Nagô (a Fon term used to identify Yorubas) both in the north and the south of the country: *Babassué* (Pará); *Casa-das-minas*[10] (Maranhão); *Xangô* (Pernambuco and Alagoas); *Candomblé* (Bahia); *Macumba* (Rio de Janeiro and Espiritu Santo); at present they are expanding through the south central part of the country); and *Batuque* (Rio Grande do Sul). It is fair to assert that the Yoruba cult is the best preserved in Brazil.

With regard to mythology and ritual practices, the contact of the Yorubas with the Ewes, who also had a very complex religious symbolism, resulted in a wide array of Brazilian *orixás*.[11] These we will describe, since the role of music cannot be understood without that information, and few ethnomusicological studies offer a very complete description of *orixás.* In addition, one can also compare the music of the Brazilian cult to the Yoruba divinities with that of the Afro-Cuban cult and the *shangó* cult in Trinidad, both of the same Nigerian origin. The *orixás* are as follows:

Oxalá (Orixalá or Obatalá): The most important *orixá,* symbolizes the productive forces of nature. A bisexual divinity. Fetish: a lead ring, cowrie shells *(buzios).*

Xangô: Lightning and thunder *orixá,* one of the most popular African divinities in Brazil; the name became the name of the cult in Pernambuco and Alagoas. Male. Fetish: lightning stone, identified with Saint Jerome and Saint Barbara.

Ogum: Masculine *orixá* of war, identified with Saint Anthony. Fetish: iron, a spade, a hoe, and a machete.

Omulu (Xapanan) *Obaluaié:* Male god of the plague, particularly small-pox. Associated with Saint Benedict and Saint Roque. Fetish: *piacava* (palm fiber) and *buzios.*

Exú: The Elegbara of the Dahomans; Loba of the Gége Brazilians; Zumbi or Cariapemba of the Bantu. Somehow associated with evil or the Christian devil. His fetish is mud, iron, and wood.

Iemanjá, Mae d'agua (mother of the water), the sea. Identified with Our Lady of the Rosary, Our Lady of Piety, and Our Lady of the Conception of the Beach. Fetish: a seashell.

Oxum: The personification of fresh water. In Africa she is the goddess of the River Oxum. She is identified with the Immaculate Conception and Our Lady of the Candles.

Iansan: The *orixá* of the wind and the tempest and the wife of Xangô. She is identified with Saint Barbara. Fetish: a meteorite.

Oxumaré or *Oxum-manre:* The rainbow. Fetish: a stone.

Ananburucu, Nananburucú or *Nanan:* The oldest of the mothers of the water and the oldest *orixá;* she personifies rain and is identified with Saint Anne. Fetish: a stone.

Obá: The goddess of the earth; the wife of Omulu.

These are the principal *orixás.* As for the music of the Bahian *candomblés,* it became well known through the recordings made by Melville and Francis Herskovits in 1941–1942 that were studied by Alan Merriam and Richard Waterman.[12] In other states, no specific ethnomusicological study has been performed to this date on Black cults. Depending on their ethnic composition, the *candomblés* are known by their "nations"; at present we have the Kétu nation (with the largest number of *terreiros* or cult houses), Ijeshá and Nagó, all three of Yoruba roots; the Géges of the Dahoman Ewes; the Gége-Nagós, formed by groups of Yorubas and Ewes, which, according to some authors, are "totally" Brazilian; the Congo-Angolans; the *Caboclo* and *Candomblé de Caboclo,* that include Amerindian divinities.

Caboclo Candomblés

We know that these *candomblés* were formed more recently, and display differences regarding the beings that are invoked and the cult music. Tupinamba, Saint Juremeiro, Forte e Valente (Strong and Brave), Iara are some of the mythical figures of *caboclo candomblés.* For musical accompaniment the three *atabaques* (drums) and the *agogó* (rattle) of the *candomblés* are no longer used; instead a large gourd and a *chocalho* or maraca (reminiscent of the Indians) are substituted, and sometimes a *violão* (guitar) is played.

In the Caboclo *candomblé,* because of its spiritualist background, the people who came from the Congo, Angola, and Mozambique were able to revitalize ancestor worship, as well as worship of the gods of West African rivers. Because these were not a part of a system like that of the Blacks of the Slave Coast, there had been a tendency to lose this aspect altogether.[13]

We find variants of the *caboclo candomblé* in various northern states, where the Indian elements are more predominant than the African. Such *candomblés* include the *cantimbó* in the northeastern states, the *tambor de criolo* in Maranhão and *pagelança* in Piauí, Pará, and Amazonas.

Macumba

The *macumba,* the Afro-Brazilian cult of Rio de Janeiro, Espiritu Santo, and São Paulo, is far harder to recognize and to interpret than the African *caboclo candomblé* or the Indian *pagelança,* in which the components from the two races are juxtaposed. The fusion of fragments of institutions and rites existent in the *macumba* does not always present a clear, functional picture. According to Roger Bastide: "The Macumba of Rio and of the State of Guanabara (now the state of Rio) is a crazy round, into which *eshús, orishás,* bodyless souls and *caboclos* enter, responding without rhyme or reason to the calls and trances of the faithful."[14] Arthur Ramos had already pointed out, without dwelling specifically on the role of music, the formidable agglutinizing background of the *macumba.*[15]

In a *ponto de macumba* without accompaniment that we transcribed we noticed that Xangô is called John the Baptist, although in Bahia he is identified with Saint Jerome.[16]

The Umbanda

In no other type of Brazilian religious institution has there been so pronounced a syncretism as in *umbanda* spiritism. This religion has developed in various states throughout the country over the past hundred years. In it one can identify, although not without difficulty, certain traces of Kardecism, of Bantu religions, the veneration of Catholic saints and ancient Amerindian superstitions and animist cults. All of these could only survive their own original social units, which had disintegrated through increasing acculturation, by becoming attached to the African rituals.

For our own purposes the *umbanda,* like the *macumba* that derives from it, is a Brazilian cult; for historic reasons, however, it has been associated with Black rather than European culture, since its ritual continues to resemble that of the cults to the Yoruban *orixás.*

We will offer Bastide's simple description of *umbanda:* "The spirits of the dead, particularly the ancient Blacks who have died and the Caboclos, constituting the spiritualized forces of nature, form enormous armies called *phalanges.* At the head of each "phalanx" there is a general, an *orixá* who bears an African or a corresponding Catholic name. Thus Oxóssi leads the Urubatão troops; Ararigboia (a famous Indian chief), leads the caboclos of the Seven Crossroads, the legions of redskins, the tamoios, and the Jurema Caboclos; Xangô or Saint Jerome leads the legions of Intiasan, of the Sun, of the Moon, of the White Stone, of the winds, of the waterfalls, of the tremble-tremble, and of the dead Kuenguele Blacks; Omulú, in his Quimbanda or Black magic phase of Umbanda,[17] leads the troops of the souls, the skulls, the Nagós, the evils, the Munurubi (Moslems), and of the Quimbanda *caboclos,* that is, the scum of Indian warlocks, plus a mixed troop."[18]

As for *umbanda* music, so far it has not been much studied by Brazilian ethnomusicologists; however, its Black traits are not very hard to identify. The accompaniment of *atabaque* drums, the *agogó* bells, *chocalho* and the *reco-reco* are similar to that of the *samba.* The use of response singing is maintained, although the versification does not seem to display an African influence. The melody develops within one tonality, thus the juxtaposition of the rhythm and Black accompaniment to the European melody satisfied those researchers who believed that the function of the Black was "the job of adding color to the material that came from Europe."[19] However, a simple comparison of these melodies with well-known Portuguese songs *(modinhas, cantigas de ronda, fandangos)* will show that, actually, the tonality was due to the acculturation that occurred when African music was being transmitted.

Musical Instruments of African Origin

To this day there has not been a satisfactory catalogue of African musical instruments brought to Brazil, which represent about three-quarters of the popularly used instruments in the country. On the one hand, the lack of intensive collecting only permits us to guess how widespread certain instruments are;[20] on the other hand, the comparison with African sources is still incomplete and not very technical. Until recently the four main references for the study of Bantu dances and musical instruments in Brazil were those written in Portugal during the course of this century and their authors were not specialists.[21]

We will try to present a provisional list that will group and organize the material described in various places by specialists, since the study of instruments is very important for a comparative analysis. We are excluding instruments for which we do not have credible information regarding their African origins; but we include those instruments that surely did exist, although they are currently not in use.[22]

Idiophones

Chocalhos. This generic term encompasses a variety of Afro-Brazilian musical instruments, all of which are rattles or maracas. Some of them also have in addition to the loose stones inside, a bead-strung net covering the body of the instrument.

Caixixi, mucaxixi. A small, closed and elongated wicker basket, sometimes with a gourd bottom and full of seeds. It is used as an instrument at *candomblé* rites, and together with the *berimbau,* it provides the musical accompaniment for the game of *capoeira.*

Angóia. A type of *chocalho* used in the *jongo* dances of Rio de Janiero and São Paulo, similar to the *caxixi.*

Guaia. A variant of the *chocalho* used in the São Paulo *batuque* dance.

Ganzá, canzá, xeque-xeque. A *chocalho* consisting of a small, closed, tin-plated tube; it is the main instrument for all varieties of the *coco* dance, typical of the northeast. It is common for *coco* singers to play the *ganza.*

Maraca, xére. A *chocalho* used in the Xangô cult, made of two brass cones joined at their bases, with a handle.

Permanguma, prananguma. A variant of the *ganzá* used for the *mozambique* dance of São Paulo. It consists of a round, flat, can with pieces of lead inside; it has two handles that serve as a support for the instrument.

Piano-de-cuia, age, obe. A type of *chocalho* made of a gourd covered with a cotton thread net, to which are attached, at the intersection of the threads, small seashells or seeds known as *cuentas* or "tears of Our Lady." There may be pebbles inside the gourd. Argeliers Leon[23] mentions that the *piano-de-cuia* is an instrument also found in Cuba *(chequeré, obwe* or *güiro)* and in Haiti *(asón).* In the Recife *xangô,* the *obe* is played by hitting the base of the instrument against the palm of the hand or by transferring it rhythmically from one hand to the other.

Paiás. The origin of this type of jingle bell has still not been well documented;[24] it is a shoulder strap with brass bells tied to it, or with a small, cylindrical, closed tube containing little stones that is also tied to the body. Apparently it is used by *mozambique* dancers. We have no information about the corresponding dance, but it is interesting to compare the *paiá* with the *jiuáua* of the Angolan Lundas, described by Arthur Ramos: "It consists of a wire thread that children wrap around their bodies, and from which hang small strips of thin iron that clash against each other with the movement of the dancers, marking the rhythm of the dance and of the percussion instruments."[25]

Agogó. An iron instrument consisting of a double bell with a handle that the player hits with a stick of the same material. It is used by the Bahian cults in Rio and Pernambuco as well as in the samba schools. This double bell of iron is called *longa* in the Congo; among the Angolan Lundas it is known as *rumbeque*. The *gongue* is a single bell *agogó* used for the *xangô;* it is also called *adjá* or *ga* in Bahian *candomblés*.

The *marimba* is another musical instrument that originated in Africa and is widely used in America. Although it was very popular during the last century in Brazil, it is now seldom seen, since its use is confined to the Saint Sebastian and Caraguatatuba *congadas* (folk dramas) along the southern coast of São Paulo. It consists of a series of wooden strips of different sizes, placed over different sized gourds that operate as resonators. The keys are hit with little sticks. In some places the instrument can hang from the neck of the player by a cord tied to the ends of the base of the boards. The Brazilian *marimba* came from Angola.

Another instrument, still widely used on the African continent but no longer played in Brazil is the *sansa* or *quincangue,* called *quissanje* by the Lundas of Angola. It is made of a small wooden box (in Brazil they were also made of a *cuia,* the longitudinal half of a gourd, or of the shell of the *jabuti,* which is a type of armadillo); its concave top portion has a series of curved iron strips of different sizes that form a keyboard played with the thumbs, while the other fingers hold the body of the instrument. Some time back, in Pernambuco, a *cuia* made of iron strips called a *matungo,* was used.

There are also historical references to a pair of African instruments, the first of which consisted of a wooden box at the edge of which were fastened, by means of small clasp, four little tongue-like pieces played by hand. Another player would hold an eight-inch stick with a gourd at one end, containing seeds that were rattled around. Meanwhile, the other end would be hit against the box of the first instrument.

Membranophones

Atabaques. This term, whose origins may be Portuguese-Oriental (from the Persian *tablak* or the Arabic word *atal,* meaning drum) refers to three different drums used for Bantu dances *(batuque, samba),* at *candomblés* or *xangós. Generally the atabaque* or *tabaque* is an oblong drum with only one skin, which employs tension wedges in the case of the Nagó and Gêgé people, and a set of cords extending from membrane to membrane for the Angola or Congo nations.

The *atabaques* used by the first Yorubas in Bahia were made of large gourds; their names used to be *batá, ilú* and *batácoto* (the war drum). Nowadays their most common names are *rum* (large), *rumpi* (medium) and *lé* (small). In addition there are giant *atabaques* more than two meters long, which are only used on special occasions. In Nagó *candomblés*, the *atabaques* are played with thick lianas called *aghidavis* (a Dahoman term). The *atabaque* is called *ronco* in Caboclo *candomblés*.

Jongo drums. This Afro-Brazilian dance, the *jongo*, is accompanied by four *atabaques*. The largest is the *tambu*; then comes the *angona ocandongueiro*; a smaller one is called *junior*, and the smallest of them all is the *guzunga*. The players straddle the first three drums; the *guzunga* hangs by a leather strap from the shoulder of the musician. They are all beaten with the hands.

Mina drums. In Maranhão three different drums are used for the *batuque* dance: the largest or *resingueiro* rests on the floor and is tied around the musician's waist with a rope; the *meao* or *tucador* and the *perengue* or *crivador* also rest on the floor, but longitudinally, and the musician straddles the drum. The African cults of Maranhão call the three drums by their Dahoman names: *hun, gunpli* and *humpli;* the drumsticks are the *oghidavis* also used in Bahia.

Quinjengue or mulemba. The *batuque* of São Paulo is played on the *tambu* that we have already mentioned, and the *quijengue*, a closed, one-membrane drum shaped like a funnel.

Samba drums made of Piqui. They preserve the generic name *tambor* (drum), and they are three, carved out of the trunk of a *piqui* or *jenipapo* tree. The large one and the *socador* (medium sized) are played with the hands, and the *quirimbador*, which is the smallest is played with two drumsticks.

Coxambu. A drum used in the states of Goiás and Rio de Janeiro to accompany the dance of the same name.

Ilú. This is the general name given to the three drums that are used in Afro-Pernambucan cults. They used to be made of a wooden barrel and tensed by cords; today they are made of brass, and tension is achieved through screwed-in metal rods. They have two membranes. The largest is the *ilú-chefe, mestre,* or *inha;* the medium-sized one is the *omele-ago* or *mele-ankó* and the small drum is the *marcação, omele,* or *mele* (the most frequently used name). In Bahia, the Ijesha nation *candomblés* also call their three *atabaques ilús*. This is a Yoruban term. The *ilú* played with wooden drumsticks is called *birro*.

Batás. Yoruban term used for the three wooden drums with two skins, played at the Nagó nation *xangôs* of Recife. The drums hang from the neck by a cord and are played with the hands.

Ingono, ingome. In Pernambuco and other northern states large, one-membrane drums are given this name. They are the same as the *ngomba* or *angomba* of the Congo and the *angoma* of the Lundas.

Zambé, zambe. A small, one-membrane drum used in the Xangós; in Rio Grande do Norte this term refers to small drums played between the legs for the dance known as *bambelo*. *Zambe* refers to a small drum in the *quimbundo* language of Angola.

Cucumbi. A drum used for *cucumbis,* ancient Black rites of Bahia that come from the Congo, for which the participants decorate themselves with feathers and animal pelts and bows and arrows.

Pererenga, mugangue, mangongu: Little research has been done on this instrument; our only information is that the name was given to the smallest of three Black drums.

Carimbó, curimbó. The only information we have on this instrument is that it is found in the state of Pará.

Mulungú. Large, flat, one-membrane drum, formerly used by the Blacks in Alagoas.

Cuica, puita. A drum with a wooden staff inside it attached to the stretched skins. It is widely used in Afro-Brazilian music. When the membrane is rubbed with a wet hand or cloth, it vibrates and produces a type of snoring sound. Its origin is Congo-Angolan (the name derives from *fuita* in Ambundo, or from *puita* in the Angolan languages). It is typical of the Rio de Janeiro samba schools. One variant of the *cuica* used in Minas Gerais is the *angono-puita,* which accompanies the *vissungos.* In Maranhão, Pará and other northern states the *cuica* is referred to as *roncador, fungador,* or *socador.*

Adufe. This is another Bantu membranophone, a type of large, square *pandeiro* or tambourine, used in the *boi-bumbá,* a variant of the *bumba-meu-boi* of Amazonas and Pará. There is also an *adufe* without bells around its body. An instrument of this type, but smaller in size, is used at the samba school, and is called *tamborín;* its source may be the *ndembo* of the Congo.

String Instuments

The only originally African string instrument we know of is the *berimbau, urucungo, gobo, bucumbumba,* or *gunga.* It is a musical bow made of wood, with a wire string. A small, globular gourd with a circular opening is attached to one of its ends, or more towards the middle of the bow. The instrument is held vertically with the left hand, which also modifies the acoustics of the string by means of a coin or a small perforated disc held between the thumb and the index finger. The string is hit with a small rod held in the right hand. The gourd acts as a resonator when placed over the chest or the stomach of the player. The *berimbau* is usually accompanied, especially when playing the Bahian *copoeira,* by a *caixixi,* which hangs from the little finger of the left hand. The *urucungo* is a traditional Angolan instrument found among the Bangalas and the Lundas; its Bantu name is *humbo* or *rucumbo.*

Finally we will mention the *afofie,* a small reed flute, used by the Blacks of Bahia, and the *canga,* which is made of cane, with its ends closed off by the knots in the cane, and with holes. It was played last century by the Pernambucan Blacks. These are the only known wind instruments in Brazil that definitely have African roots.

From this list of musical instruments we can see that most have Bantu roots (mainly from the Congo and from Angola). One may therefore wonder at the absence of Nigerian and Dahoman instrumental contributions to the New World, in contrast to the tremendous influence of the Bantu, and of the Yorubas and the Ewes with regard to the structure and practice of Brazilian festivities and religious rituals. In answer to this, we must bear in mind that we always find relationships established between the sources of our African traits and regions in Portuguese Africa, possibly because material on these regions is what has been most accessible to Brazilian researchers up to now.[26] Only a comparative study between Afro-Brazilian instruments and those of the Sudanese tribes we have mentioned would give us complete certainty that the origins we have attributed to certain instruments are accurate.

Dances, Religious Plays, and Ceremonies

In the field of dance it is more difficult to recognize the African elements and to place them in ethnomusicological perspective, since these have become more fluid and partially disintegrated with regard to ritual or communication. The fact is that in Brazil Portuguese dances become Africanized, while African dances became more European; in addition, where the Indian influence was strong, we find the product of a triple contact. On the other hand, the music did not display much fusion between the Indian, the African, and the European.[27] It is quite apparent that the first process took place in the medieval Iberian plays that were brought to America, the *Nau Catarineta,* the *cheganças de marujo* (Portuguese seafaring adventures), and the battles between Christians and Moors, all now marked by a Black tint. Of the second process, the most perfect examples are the *batuque* and the *samba,* both originally from Angola. The *samba* (Angolan *semba* that came about when the *batuque* dancers let their turn to dance go by),[28] is the most widespread dance in the country. It was initially characterized by the pelvic contact of the couples, called *umbigada* (navel touch), which had to be toned down in Brazil to be danced by Blacks and Whites. Thus Edison Carneiro says: "As long as the samba was the dance of the slaves, the real *umbigada* was the rule; however, as it was passed on to other ethnic and social groups, this figure, which was the most typical and unique trait of the dance, was gradually replaced by equivalent gestures, like waving a handkerchief, a mimicked invitation, a simple touch on the leg or the foot. . . ."[29]

With the change in the behavior of the colonizer, due to his ethical-social attitudes, we achieve the first degree of transformation leading to syncretism, later to attain a new, self-sufficient form. In fact, this is our idea regarding a large part of those Brazilian festivities, dances, and plays that still bear some African traits. On the other hand, the information we have on many Afro-Brazilian dramatic and choreographic varieties are relatively rare, incomplete, and above all, obsolete.[30] Most of them were described by Mario de Andrade, Luciano Gallet, Oneyda Alvarenga, and other researchers of the 1920s, 1930s, and 1940s. Unfortunately, this first round of interpretations remains virtually unchanged.

Of the third case we mentioned (the Euro-Afro-Amerindian fusion, with the outward appearance leaning towards the Black), there is no better example than the *bumba-meu-boi*. This is a very ancient religious drama found all over the country, based on the resuscitation of a dead totemic ox. There are regional variants of it with names such as *boi-bumbá* in Amazonas and Pará, *bumba-meu-boi* in the northeast, *bo-de-mamão* in Santa Catarina, etc. It is a thorough synthesis of theater, dance, and music, which, according to general opinion, is the most complete example of this phenomenon in Brazil.

Edison Carneiro finds samples of the *samba de umbigada* with regional differences in the following places: *tambor de crioulo* (Maranhão), *tambor* (Piauí), *mambelo* (Rio Grande do Norte), *coco* (the entire northeast), *samba-de-rada* (Bahia), *samba* (Rio de Janeiro), *batuque* and *samba-rural* (São Paulo), *jongo,* a variant without the *umbigada* (Rio de Janeiro, São Paulo, Minas Gerais, and Espiritu Santo) and *caxambu* (Rio de Janeiro).

We have yet to discuss the *maracatú,* a peculiar "dramatic dance" reminiscent of the corteges and royal coronations of the Bantus;[31] today it is almost exclusively restricted to the Pernambuco carnivals, especially to that of the capital city, Recife. Formally related to the *congos* and *congadas,*[32] various characters participate in the *maracatú*—the king, the queen, the ambassador, pages, and a *dama-del-paso* (the pace-setter), who carries in her hands a black doll called *calunga* (sometimes *catita*), a religious symbol undoubtedly of Congo and Angolan origins, as is its name, whose religious symbolism is hard to determine.[33] A ceremony precedes the cortege, and this is the profane aspect of the drama. The musical accompaniment of the *maracatú* includes *gongues, ganzás,* bass drums and the *agogó*. It was curious to observe in a *maracatú* text that we transcribed, the use of the term *kétu,* originally Sudanese, right next to Luanda, the legitimate source of the *calunga,* the *boneca preta* (black doll).

There is also a rural version of the *maracatú,* restricted to sugar mills and plantations, called the *samba matute,* where all references to Bantu coronations are excluded.

The *congos, congadas, reisados o Reis do Congo* (Congo kings) present an extensive cycle of entertainments that are found from Ceará to Rio Grande do Sul, displaying noticeable variations of interpretation in both choreography and music. At present the main performance is the cortege of the king of the Congo. At first these popular dramas presented an historical event: the ambassadors sent by the queen Ginga Bandi to the Portuguese governor in Angola in the seventeenth century. The *congadas* changed their nature dramatically as they were encouraged by slave-owners (and may even have been recreated by them) as a means of dominating their slave workers.[34]

"In the days of slavery, the police initiated the custom of electing governors and judges of the *nation,* who were responsible for the good behavior of the slaves. Above these they instituted the Kings of the Congo, crowned in ceremonies that included the participation of the Catholic Church. Parades were organized to take them to be crowned in the church."[35] "The kings were elected annually or preferably for life, and were chosen by the Brotherhoods of Our Lady of the Rosary of the Blacks."[36]

Finally, to give an idea of the enormous Black contribution to dance and popular ceremony in Brazil, we transcribe two lists prepared by Luciano Gallet,[37] reproduced by Arthur Ramos and Flausino Rodriguez Vale.[38] We only include in this list forms that have not been mentioned in any other part of our essay. We must, however, warn the reader that a portion of this material may have already fallen into disuse.

Dances

1. *Sarambéque* (Minas Gerais)
2. *Sarambu* (Minas Gerais)
3. *Quimbete* (Minas Gerais)
4. *Sorongo* (Minas Gerais and Bahia)
5. *Alujá* (fetishist)
6. *Jeguedé* (fetishist)
7. *Caxambu* (Minas Gerais)
8. *Lundu* (old-fashioned parlor dance)
9. *Chiba* (Rio de Janeiro)
10. *Coco-de-zambe.*

Ayres de Mata Machado Filho mentions the *canjere,* a dance of African roots, found in the mining region of Minas Gerais.

Edison Carneiro[39] describes the *maculele,* a dance that includes a rhythmic game with sticks that can still be found in Santo Amaro, in the state of Bahia. The *mosambique* of São Paulo is another dance that includes a stick game; formerly it was a part of the *congadas,* but now it has become an independent dramatic dance. The same author also refers to the *catopes,* groups of dancers about whom we have little information, but who probably participated in the festivities of the Brotherhood of the Rosary in the region of Diamantina, Minas Gerais, together with the *caboclos* and the *marujada.*

José Ribeiro[40] describes the *bangule,* that was danced to the sounds of the *cuica,* accompanied by the clapping of hands; the songs supposedly contained "obscenities ad nauseum."

Maynard Araujo[41] studied the *jongo* in São Paulo, a round, with songs improvised by singers in the form of a competition. The singers are known as *jongueiros.*

Festivities and ceremonies

1. Dances and festivities of the *quicumbres* and *quilombos,* dating back to the days of the Palmares *quilombo.*
2. Festivities of the Holy King Balthazar, that were celebrated in Rio de Janeiro until about 1740, for the coronation of the Cabunda Kings.
3. Official dances of saddlers and carpenters, where participants dressed up in Moorish attire.
4. Reign of the Congos, where the titles of king and queen were disputed.
5. The magic *soba,* where participants disguised themselves as animals.
6. The twelve lions, who brought a Hercules as their guide.
7. *Colastros, aubacás,* and *moleques,* with twelve participants for each group.
8. Dances of the *negritos* and *malandritos* (little hobos) of Angola.
9. Dances and songs of the *taieiras* at the festivities of Our Lady of the Rosary.
10. The *catupes.*
11. Festivities and processions of Saint Benedict and Our Lady of the Rosary attended by Black queens, Congos, and *taieiras.*
12. *Jongo* and *samba* rounds, circling fires, during the festivities of Saint John Peter.
13. Festivities of the dead, where ceremonies were divided into three parts: fasts and prayers; sacrifices; and banquets and dances. The *batuque* and the *coco-de-zambe* would be danced for several days

in a row to the sound of *atabaques, puitos, ganzás,* and tambourines.

14. Dances and funeral festivities, on the occasion of the burial of African kings.
15. *Entrudo* festivities, an archaic form of carnival.
16. Ceremonies and festivities at the plantations after the sugarcane had been processed, at the end of the coffee harvest, at fetishist ceremonies, etc.
17. Festivities in honor of Iemanjá, the Goddess of the Water, lasting for fifteen days.

The Vissungos

In 1928 African songs using words in a Bantu dialect were discovered in a Black community living in the interior of Minas Gerais. Their themes were related to work in the diamond mines and to funerary rites. The importance of these archaic forms of Congo-Angolan culture have already been pointed out by their discoverer.[42] Dulce Martins Lamas has pointed to the purely melodic nature of the *vissungos*[43] and Correa de Azevedo compares them to several South African songs.[44] Yet we still lack a deeper analytical study of this valuable material.

"Generally the *vissungos* can be divided into the *boiado,* a solo by the lead singer without accompaniment, and the *dobrado,* with a responsory by the rest acting as chorus, sometimes accompanied by the noises emitted by mining instruments. Some were particularly appropriate as work songs and would be sung at certain phases of work in the mines. Others seem to be religious songs that have been adapted to the occasion, whether as a part of fetishist practices, or because their original meaning had been forgotten. The Blacks used to sing all day while they worked. They had special morning, noon, and afternoon songs."[45]

Since the literary value of the *vissungos* is so significant, it is worthwhile to become familiar with some of their lyrics. In some portions the dialect has remained isolated from the Portuguese; in others, the presence of Portuguese words generates some very interesting poetic effects.

The following is the text of the second *vissungo* of the sixty-five that are known:

Pae Nosso ("Our Father," sung on the way to work)

Ai! ai! Ai!
Pade-nosso cum Ave-Maria,
qui ta Angananzambe-opungo
Ei! curiete
Ai! ai! ai! ai!
Pade-Nosso cum Ave-Maria
Qui tá Angananzambe-opungo
Ei dundarie e.

Let us take a look at another *vissungo,* where the singer boasts of his abilities:

> XX
> Eu memo é capicovite
> Eu memo é cariocanga
> Eu memo é candandumba serena.

It was forbidden to tell the researchers the *"fundamento"* (translation into Portuguese) of certain *vissungos,* as their meaning was reserved exclusively for initiates. The following is one of these, supposedly in pure dialect:

> Onuma aue, numa aue
> re re a
> numa tara pipoque,
> numa tara angue rezá
>
> tue iá . . . tue iá
> numa tara qui zombá,
> tue, iá tue, iá,
> numa tara angue rezá,
> tue, iá . . .

Final Observations

We believe that the critical and systematic bibliographical compilation presented in our essay gives a general idea of the current conditions of African ethnomusicology in Brazil. As we mentioned earlier, there has been no constant, increasing progress made to date in the field of Afro-Brazilian musical studies. Neither has there been such progress in Afro-Brazilian anthropology, and it is precisely in the appendices of anthropological research that we find a large portion of the information on the musical behavior of Blacks in this country.

The dynamic, syncretic, acculturating, or patchwork reality we find today in the Afro-Brazilian cult groups has surpassed the possibilities of the conceptual approach started by Nina Rodrigues at the beginning of the century and developed by the Arthur Ramos school in the 1930s and 1940s (where one can see the results of the comparative method, based on tracing parallels with the African cultures from which Brazilian Blacks originated). The continuity of these studies was provided by the deep influence that the work and thoughts of Melville Herskovits had on the anthropologists of the period, particularly with regard to the concepts of cultural tenacity, cultural focus, and reinterpretations, etc.[46] This cycle, as we might call it, ended approximately in the 1950s.

There is much less to say about Afro-Brazilian musical studies, since the old studies of Luciano Gallet, Mario de Andrade, and Oneyda Alvarenga were interrupted almost fifty years ago. One must still either confirm or correct, by comparing them to reality, the systems worked out by these authors.

That is why we alerted the reader that certain terms employed in our study should be viewed within the context of the time frame when they were used. The term *candomblés-de-caboclo,* for example, is far less definite today than it was thirty years ago.

In Pernambuco, the differences between the *xangôs* of the Nations (Nagô, Gêgê, Kétu, Ijeshá, Shambá, Mozambique, Congo, and Angola) are becoming increasingly less significant, at least from the point of view of their music, and we are basically left with a Nagô complex, with slight traces of the other nations. The dominating expansion of the Umbanda throughout the country accounts for the fact that very few Recife *xangôs* are without *mestre, caboclo,* or *jurema* rites; the *ingeme,* a drum that belonged originally to the Shambá, Congo, and Angolan nations is already used to set the beat for the *caboclos;* in many cult locations the lyrics of the songs to the *orixás* or "saints" are now sung in Portuguese and many popular urban musical elements have been introduced, mainly the *samba*-style songs of Rio de Janeiro.

The fact that in the 1930s, texts and possibly also melodies of the songs to the *orixás* of Bahia were found in Recife,[47] was formerly explained by the influence of Afro-Bahian cults in Pernambuco, or by the possibility of a cultural divergence in Africa itself, within the predominant cultures that formed the Afro-Brazilian cults. Today this similarity is becoming increasingly stronger, and can only be understood by employing convergence as a criterion. This phenomenon is occurring due to the expansion of the Umbanda, which serves as a point of acculturation between units of the main groups of Afro-Brazilian cults in Rio Grande do Sul and São Paulo, where they were recently formed, and in Rio de Janeiro, Bahia, Recife, São Luis do Maranhão, Belem do Pará.

There are books written by members of Umbanda sects wherein many of the Afro-Brazilian rituals are codified (like catechisms), including lyrics in Gêgê, Nagó, Congo-Angolan, the names of the instruments that are used, etc. Such manuals gather elements from all the converging lines.[48]

There are also many recordings made by famous *pais-de-santo* (cult leaders), particularly of the *umbanda,* which serve to spread the "Afro-Brazilian religious songs that are the least orthodox," much like the spreading of the popular music of certain isolated sectors, such as the peasants.

It is not for us to evaluate these phenomena; they are merely the characteristics of a new phase in the process of acculturation of African music in Brazil.

In order to study them, one must elaborate new ethnomusicological criteria that can deal with the complexity and the accelerated dynamics of this stage of the process.

NOTES

1. Roger Bastide, *Las Américas Negras* (Madrid: Alianza, 1967), p. 14.

2. Bastide, (ibid., p. 87) presents an analysis by the Count of Arcos showing how dance was used to ease social tensions generated by slavery. It was through this bread-and-circus imperial policy that a great part of African culture was preserved in the New World.

3. Andrew Pearse, "Aspects of change in Caribbean folk music," *International Folk Music Journal* 7 (1955), 29.

4. A building used for the collective housing of slaves in the *hacienda* patio. See Gilberto Freyre, *Casa Granda & Senzala* (Rio de Janeiro: 1973).

5. Bantu term used for the "republics" of slaves who fled the plantations of their masters. The Palmares *quilombo* in Alagoas became famous. Memories of that *quilombo* survive in Alagoas through popular theater pieces dealing with the Battle of Palmares. See Arthur Ramos, *O folklore negro do Brasil* (Rio de Janeiro: 1954), pp. 35–67.

6. These are the Saramaccan, Auca, Boni, Matawaai, Quinte Matawaai, and Paramaccan tribes, who live in isolation in the jungle. Bastide, *Americas Negras*, pp. 54–70; Arthur Ramos, *As cultures negras no Novo Mundo* (Rio de Janeiro: Civilização Brasileira, 1937), p. 238.

7. For a description of the characteristics of African music, see Richard Waterman, "African influence on the music of the Americas," in *Proceedings and Selected Papers of the XXIXth International Congress of the Americanists,* (Chicago: 1949); Maria de Lourdes Borges Ribeiro, "A música africana," *Revista Brasileira de Folclore* 12, no. 37 (1973); E. M. von Hornbostel, "La Música de los negros africanos," *Revista Musical Chilena,* 17 (September 1952).

8. This seems to be the reasoning behind Luis Heitor Correa de Azevedo's assertion that "Black music, on the other hand, of exclusive national formation as we have seen, without apparent roots in the primitive songs of the African continent, is very docile in submitting to European tonalism and displays in its rigorous musical tempo, although subtly divided by an apparent instability in the syncopation, its most typical and marked appearance." *Música e músicas do Brasil* (Rio de Janeiro: 1950), p. 22.

9. Oneyda Alvarenga offers us a good example of a mistake caused by subjectivity: "It is well known, for example, that African music employs only a short melody, that its melodies generally evolve by degrees, that other intervals that are found are short, and that the rhythm is usually fixed during the course of each melody. These characteristics can be found in Brazilian popular music, but they should not be attributed to African influence because they also appear in the rest of the world. They are therefore universal characteristics of popular music." "A influencia negra na música brasileira," *Boletím Latinoamericano de Música* 6 (Rio de Janeiro: 1946), 358. Alvarenga mentions certain African traits, but classifies them as non-African; what is important to the Brazilian is that these elements *did come from Africa* and from no other place in the world.

It is interesting to note that this same methodological error (which is sometimes ideological) even exists today, as we can observe in the following discussion by Renato Almeida concerning the melodies of Afro-Brazilian cults: "Could the defective scales characterize them? No, because we can also find them among the primitives. The intervals? The tonality? The free discursive rhythm? None of these are exclusively Brazilian, none of them are exclusively African, all of these elements can also be found in other cultures." *Vivencia e projecão do folclore* (Rio de Janeiro: 1971), p. 104. The mistake occurs again because of the incompatibility between the concern for the origin and the neglect of the historical criterion.

10. The *casa-das-minas* shows strong similarities to Haiti's *vodú rada,* because the Dahoman element is so strong in this *candomblé* variant: Bastide, *Americas Negras,* pp. 127–128. One can assume that there are also similarities between the *casa-das-minas* and the *rada* cult of Trinidad (see Andrew Carr, "A Rada Community in Trinidad," *Caribbean Quarterly* 3, no. 1, 35–54 and Alan Merriam, "Songs of a Rada Community in Trinidad," *Anthropos* 51 (1956), 157–174. For a description see Octavio da Costa Eduardo, *The Negro in Northern Brazil* (Seattle: 1966).

11. Mediating spirits or divinities of Olorum, a formless primordial entity, accessible to men, for which there are special songs and dances that lead to possession. Etienne Ignace, "Le fetichisme des negres du Brésil," *Anthropos* 3 (1908), 881–904.

12. Melville Herskovits, "Tambores e tamborileros no culto Afro-brasileiro," *Boletím Latinoamericano de Música* 6 (Rio de Janeiro: 1946), 99–112; Alan Merriam, "Songs of the Ketú Cult of Bahia, Brazil," *African Music* 1, no. 3 (1956), and no. 4 (1957); Alan Merriam, "Songs of the Gêgé and Jesha Cults of Bahia, Brazil," *Jahrbuch für musikalische Volk und Völkerkunde* 1 (1963); Richard Waterman and Melville Herskovits, "Música de culto afrobahiana," *Revista de Estudios Musicales* 64–127.

13. Bastide, *Americas Negras,* pp. 103–104.

14. Ibid., p. 85.

15. Ramos, *As Culturas negras,* p. 175.

16. It is really difficult to follow closely this correspondence. For a systematic account of the *orixás* and their syncretisms with Catholic songs see Valdemar Valente, *Sincretismo religioso afrobrasileiro,* (Rio de Janeiro, 1952), pp. 153–159.

17. Bastide does not clarify the difference between the two "lines" very well: *umbanda* is the positive white magic; *quimbanda* is its black, negative side.

18. Bastide, *Americas Negras,* p. 85.

19. Alvarenga, "Influencia negra," p. 370, quoting Mario de Andrade, asserts paternalistically, "No one can deny that they have colored it well."

20. We still are not very familiar, for example, with the instruments of African origin used at the Pôrto Alegre dances (see M. Herskovits, "Os pontos mais meridionais dos africanismos no Novo Mundo," *Revista do Arquivo Municipal,* 95, [1944], 94) or even in the north of the country (Piauí, Maranhão and Pará), if we compare what is known with the detailed informations we have on the *candomblé* drums of Bahia or the *xangôs* of Pernambuco.

21. Edison Carneiro, *Folquedos tradicionais* (Rio de Janeiro: 1974), p. 37.

22. To make up this list we consulted, in addition to the studies we have already cited, the following works: Edison Carneiro, "Vocabularios negros de Bahia," *Revista do Arquivo Municipal,* 99 (São Paulo: 1944), 45–62; Leopoldo Bettial, *O batuque na Umbanda* (Rio de Janeiro: 1963); Pereira da Costa, *Folclore pernambucano* (Recife: 1974); René Ribeiro, *Cultos afrobrasileiros do Recife* (Recife: 1952); José Ribeiro, *Candomblés no Brasil* (Rio de Janeiro: 1972); Octavio da Costa Eduardo, *The Negro in Northern Brazil* (Seattle: 1966); Gonçalves Fernandez, *Xangôs do nordeste* (Rio de Janeiro: 1937); Vicente Lima, *Xangôs* (Recife: 1937); Pierre Verger, *Orixás* (Salvador: 1951). We also rely on our own research to correct certain mistakes or obsolete information as well as for additional information (as, for example, our knowledge of the Afro-Pernambucan cults).

23. Leon, "Música popular de origen africano en America," *America Indígena* 39, no. 3 (Mexico: July 1969), 627–664.

24. There is a drawing of a *paiá* in Alceu Maynard Araujo's *Cultura Popular brasileira* (São Paulo: 1973), p. 137; see also *Folclore Nacional* 2, (São Paulo: 1967), 426.

25. Ramos, *As Culturas negras,* p. 142.

26. Edison Carneiro suggests the following explanation for this problem: "We say that, of the African tribes that arrived in Brazil, only a few (Angolan, Congo, and those from Mozambique) contributed to Brazilian folklore; and that, on the other hand, the comparative study of these people can be accomplished very easily, given the similarities of language, historical traditions, customs, and habitat among them in Africa." *A sabeduria popular* (Rio de Janeiro: 1957), p. 86.

27. Richard Waterman, "African influence," p. 207, says that "there is a great deal of similarity between Amerindian, African, and European music."

28. Edison Carneiro, *A sabedoria popular,* p. 36; also in Minas Gerais, in Diamantina, the word *semba* is still in use (Ayres da Mata Machado Filho, *O negro e o garimpo em Minas Gerais* (Rio de Janeiro: 1943), pp. 137–38.

29. Edison Carneiro, *A sabedoria popular,* p. 63.

30. See, for example, the interpretations of the *candomblé* dances by Arthur Ramos *(O negro brasileiro)* based on Lévy-Bruhl's ideas of the emotional behavior of primitive people; also the concept of the "dramatic dance" is developed by Mario de Andrade *(Boletím Latinoamericano de Música* 6, Rio de Janeiro: 1949, 49–97), is seriously and rigorously criticized by Edison Carneiro, *A sabedoria popular,* pp. 155–175.

31. According to Ascenço Ferreira, "O maracatú," *Boletím Latinoamericano de Música,* pp. 130–132, and also Oneyda Alvarenga, *Música popular Brasileña,* (Mexico: 1947), 364.

32. "In both cities (Recife and Salvador) the congadas and the corteges of the Congolese king disappeared, they became profane, and turned into the Pernambucan *maracatú* and the Bahian *afoxé,*" Carneiro, *A sabedoria popular,* p. 83.

33. Ayres da Mata Machado Filho, *O negro e o garimpo,* pp. 123–125, discusses the term at length. It can also be found in the so-called "Auto dos Congos."

34. Edison Carneiro, *Dinámica do folclore* (Rio de Janeiro: 1965), p. 38.

35. Edison Carneiro, *A sabedoria popular,* pp. 81–82.

36. Carneiro, *Dinámica do folclore,* p. 38.

37. Luciano Gallet, *Estudos do folclore* (Rio de Janeiro: 1934), p. 61.

38. Ramos, *As Culturas negras,* p. 126; Flausino Rodriguez Vale, *Elementos do folclore musical brasileiro* (São Paulo: 1936), pp. 71–83.

39. Carneiro, *A sabedoria popular,* p. 84.

40. Ribeiro, *Brasil no folclore* (Rio de Janeiro: 1970), pp. 383–84. It must be noted that this work deals almost exclusively with secondhand information that is generally incomplete.

41. "Jongo," *Revista do Arquivo Municipal* 128 (1949), 45–54.

42. Ayres da Mata Machado Filho, *O negro e o garimpo.*

43. "Vissungos," *Relação dos discos gravados no estado de Minas Gerais,* (Rio de Janeiro: 1956), 75–77.

44. Correa de Azevedo, "Vissungos," in *Music in the Americas,* Indiana University Research Center in Anthropology, Folklore and Linguistics (The Hague: 1967), pp. 64–67.

45. Ayres da Mata Machado Filho, *O negro e o garimpo,* p. 61.

46. Mentioned in René Ribeiro, "Significado dos estudos afrobrasileiros," *Revista do Instituto Historico de Alagoas,* (Maceió: 1952), 7–16.

47. See, for example, in Gonçalves Fernandez, *Xangôs do nordeste,* pp. 103, 106, the lyrics to songs to Exú that were taped in Bahia by Herskovits. (The transcription can be found in Waterman and Herskovits, "Música de culto afrobahiana.")

48. As an example of *umbanda* "musical catechism" see N. A. Molina, *3777 Fon-cantados e riscados na Umbanda e na Quimbanda* (Rio de Janeiro: undated); for the Nagô texts of the songs to the *orixás,* see Ribeiro, *Candomblé no Brasil.*

Socialization and Development

11

Hello and Goodbye to Negritude

RENE DEPESTRE

Why did we choose such an ambivalent title for this essay? First of all we must stress the ever-increasing imprecision of the connotations and the content of the concept "negritude." This term initially referred to a form of revolt of the spirit against the historic vilification and denaturalization of a group of human beings, who, during the colonization process, were baptized generically and pejoratively as "Negroes."

However, as it developed into an ideology, and even an ontology, the concept of negritude began to adopt one or various meanings, all of them ambiguous, until it presented the following paradox: formulated to awaken and to encourage self-esteem and confidence in the strength of the social groups that slavery had reduced to the status of beasts of burden, negritude now makes them evaporate into a somatic metaphysics.

Far from arming their class-consciousness against the violence of capitalism, negritude dissolves its *negroes* and *African negroes* into an essentialism that is perfectly inoffensive to a system that strips men and women of their identity. Currently, the "negrologists" of negritude present it in the form of an exclusively Black worldview within American or African societies, independent of the position they occupy in production, property, and the distribution of material and spiritual goods. We have, in fact, a *Weltanschauung* of antiracist origins, which, retrieved by neocolonialism, attempts in its shadow, and through sophistry, to separate the oppressed Blacks from the conditions that would fertilize their liberation struggle. Negritude, formerly a literary and artistic protest movement, now transformed into an ideology of a colonial state, is not, however, a spontaneously generated phenomenon. Negritude has a past: it is, in effect, tightly linked to the history and to the social structures shaped by the scandalous New World slave trade and the plantation system.

It is therefore necessary to go back to the origins of negritude, to the various paths that lead to it and to its equivalents in colonial society, in order to show that, during its life, it has been, in literature and in art, the modern equivalent of cultural marronage with which the masses of slaves and their descendants opposed deculturation and assimilation to the colonial West.

Questions Regarding Method

The original sin of negritude and the misfortunes that debased it derive from the fairy godmother that supported it at its baptismal font, namely anthropology. The crisis that has shaken negritude coincides with the winds that revolution has blown over the fields upon which anthropology, be it cultural, social, applied, or structural (and with a Black or a White mask) used to carry out its wise research. The first charge against the various schools of anthropology is to have given preference to the European contribution in the analysis of cultural elements that specify the metabolism of our societies. This contribution has always been the ideal reference model, the measure, par excellence, of all ferment of culture or civilization. This basic Eurocentrism even postulated an identity of divine right between the typically colonial concept of "White" and that of the universal human being. The creative expressions of Africans and their descendants were isolated and became a heterogeneous heap of *africanisms,* morbidly encased in the immaculate organism of the Americas. Given this racist point of view, slave revolts, political and cultural marronage and the participation of Blacks in peasant struggles, were rarely considered decisive contributions to the formation of societies and national cultures in Latin America.

In 1941, Melville J. Herskovits dedicated a famous study to the "Black heritage" of the American continent, and devised a scale of "intensities of African survival." He never worried about offering a correlative "scale of the intensity of European survivals." African influences were mechanically juxtaposed to modes of feeling, thinking, and acting that were supposedly inherited from the Christian West by the mixed, Creole nations of our hemisphere. Herskovits and his disciples lost sight of the fact that within the geographic and socioeconomic space between the southern United States and the north of Brazil, even though there was an historic rupture between ethnicity and culture, between infra- and superstructure, such a dissociation was not exclusively characteristic of the African heritage. It could be a double or even a triple rupture if we were to include the Indian ethnic groups and cultures. The elements inherited from Europe, Africa, and the Precolumbian world were restructured and remetabolized (and not unilaterally reinterpreted by the Blacks), due to the effects of material living conditions and of the emancipation struggles that were the origins of our various national structures. More than a quarter of a century after the Herskovits hypothesis, the influence of Africa is still being studied as though it were a racial plankton, eternally suspended in the waves of the national liberation process, of the *sui generis* societies of America. When dealing with the problem of nationalism, setting aside the singular experience of Haiti, it has only been in analyses and studies performed in Cuba since 1959 that one can clearly see the historical role of the descendants of African slaves, both during the political emancipation movements and in the structure of sociocultural values.

In their ethnocentric hunt for African "isms," anthropologists and ethnologists have not included the European heritage in their inventories, when, actually, the mixture of races has equally conditioned private and social behavior and the formation of a conscience and psyche of the descendants of Europeans. There is no such thing as an ethnology of the "White strata" of our population: their specifically Creole American relationship to work, religion (Latin American Catholicism), collective festivities (carnival), magic, culinary traditions, art, music, and body movement—including their gait, dance, copulation—and various other types of behavior that display the reciprocity of the phenomena of syncretism and transculturation. The African presence in the cultures of the New World is talked about as though, before the slave trade, in addition to the Amerindian cultures, there would have existed in America well-structured Greco-Roman or Anglo-Saxon cultures, onto which, much later, well or badly, the African savage was grafted. The scandalously segregating, terrorist role that racial dogma exerts on our countries, be it in its negrophobic form or under more refined disguises, has accustomed people to consider the African contribution as a strident note in formerly well-organized sociocultural groupings.

When one studies the objective dynamic of our national cultures, there is a tradition of distinguishing, from the Caribbean to Brazil, the *Hispanic, Iberian, Latin, Anglo, Gallic, Batavian, Indian,* and *Afro-American* cultures. This logic of separating and mechanically juxtaposing our common heritage, far from being innocent, presents close ties of cause and effect with the racist adventures of colonialism and imperialism. There exists a sociohistoric determinism within the Western hemisphere that, since the "discovery," within very particular economic, cultural, religious, psychological, and ecological conditions, acts dialectically upon the life of various social types that have molded, through antagonisms of class and "race," our national realities. Historical creativity has not been the exclusive privilege of one social group considered in isolation. America, unilaterally termed *Latin* or *Anglo-Saxon,* arbitrarily proclaimed *White* or *Black,* is actually, the simultaneous social creation of multiple ethnic groups, aboriginal or originating in various African and European countries. It is the ethnohistoric result of a painful process of racial mixture and of symbiosis, that has transformed or even transmuted, with the rigor of a nutritional phenomenon, the original social types, the multiple African, Indian, and European substances and contributions, to produce absolutely novel ethnic groups and cultures within the world history of civilizations.

Under the plantation system, and under the equally oppressive national systems that succeeded it, what were initially Africanisms, Indianisms, and Europeanisms, have ended up, transmuted through the metabolic confrontation of their own singularly vital elements, into a heterogeneous *Americanism* that has been reciprocally advantageous for all the people of our original family of societies. The value scales brought from abroad and those that ruled locally, at levels that varied from one society to another, have been the object of a universal process of American *Creolization*. The study of this dialectic development must break with arbitrary cuts and ethnocentric classifications. This requires the revision of postulates, methods, and conventional anthropological concepts, which, since the eighteenth century, have been concerned with our identities.

In the first place, why should Africanology shed light on the *mutations of identity* of the European and African heritage in the Americas? Within the framework of an anthropology that would scientifically unify cultural and political practices, we feel that there would be material for autonomous discipline that would simply and plainly be Americanology. Its methods of analyzing our global societies should then omit generic denominations, always loaded with racism or ethnoeurocentrism, which, beneath the apparently innocent terms *Hispanic, Iberian, Luso, Latin, Anglo, Indian, Batavian,* and *Gallic,* unilaterally prefix the description of our intrinsic American identities.

Towards the end of his life, the eminent professor Roger Bastide proposed methodological tools that were more appropriate for the evaluation of our sociohistorical situations and junctures. He, however, considered it useful to maintain the prefix *Afro* before the word Americanology. By preserving *Afro* he rendered inevitable the correlative preservation of the other erroneous meanings that the old, racist ethnocentrism traditionally attributes to the form and content of our Americanness. Only plain Americanology, without the prefixes of Afro, Indo, or Eurocentrism, could free the analysis and reevaluation of our sociocultural phenomena from the conceptual and methodological imperialism that has divided, dismembered, fractured, "epidermized," and racialized our knowledge of the laws of our history.

This having been said, one should not underestimate the research findings on popular religion, familial ties, customs, musical expressions, and folklore, all of which describe the originality of the popular cultures of this continent. Some scientists, particularly Ortiz, Price-Mars, Arthur Ramos, Alfred Metraux, Roger Bastide, Edison Carneiro, Aquiles Escalante, Acosta Saignes, Frazier, Leiris, Aguirre Beltrán, etc., who have studied the African influence on the New World (some unilaterally as was the case with Herskovits), have accumulated over more than half a century a prodigious number of observations and analyses that will permit scientific anthropology, once it has been liberated from all its ethnocentrism, to correctly identify our people within the history of the national societies they have formed in this hemisphere.

The obvious ties between imperialism and anthropology are not always direct ties. In the same manner the links between negritude and neocolonialism are not necessarily reciprocal expressions. There is, nevertheless, an overwhelming disproportion between the considerable knowledge anthropology has harvested and the derisible tools of action it has finally placed in the hands of those social groups that have been the subjects of their field study.

In the first studies conducted by anthropologists (frequently of high scientific value) one is struck by the scarce connection of the data to the question of nationalism, that is, the liberation struggles that our people were involved in, in order to unify democratically, for their exclusive benefit, the historic components of their identity. There is no anthropology that studies the original types of resistance to slavery, such as *cultural marronage,* that was practiced on this continent by Africans and their descendants. Neither are there, at present, field projects, which would be highly significant, on mining societies, on the sugar industry, fruit companies, coffee plantations, etc. Anthropology has wisely compartmentalized the map of the Caribbean and Latin America, without bumping into the flamboyant imperialist installations on the way. In using a fine-tooth comb to go over each nook and cranny of Latin America, ethnology has frequently stopped to reveal, at times quite brilliantly, the mythology, family ties, racial prejudices, oral literature, sexual and culinary mores, musical and artistic creations, eternal folkore, without ever adequately showing the historical relationship between capitalism and this original and contradictory crucible of cultures and civilizations. Where are the anthropologists or ethnologists who had the idea of taking as their field of study the boards of management of neocolonial banks and exchanges? Where is the anthropology of the military caste, of so-called Inter-American economic and political institutions, of pseudolegal mechanisms, of "Papadocracies" and military dictatorships? To summarize: How long should we continue to rule into squares the elementary structures of imperialist power, which, together with the indigenous oligarchies, continues to underdevelop our societies?

Origin of the American Social Types

The human essence of the Blacks, Whites, and Mulattoes within the region of America that concerns us, encompasses, historically, all of the social and racial interactions from the sixteenth century to our day, among colonists, slaves, freed slaves, and their descendants on this continent. This slave society "epidermized," somatized, and deeply racialized the production interrelationships, thus adding to the innate contradictions and alienations of capitalism a new type of class conflict that acquired its own characteristics within the specific framework of the American colonies: namely *passionate racial antagonism.*

This racism or class egotism reduced the human essence of imported labor from various African ethnic goups to a fantastic *inferior Black essence;* and the human essence of the owners who came from various European nations became a no less extravagant *superior White essence.* This double mythological reduction on the one hand shaped the erroneous good conscience of the colonizers who voluntarily left Christian and "White" Europe, and on the other hand served to downgrade, deform, and dismantle the social conscience of the slaves forcefully brought from pagan "Black" Africa. Even though the racial problem is the psychological aspect of the socioeconomic structures of colonialism, the secret of "White" racism, as well as the antiracism or antiracist racism of the "Blacks," must not be looked for in the psychological makeup of these social types, but in the objective analysis of their interactions, as determined by slavery and colonization.

The "peculiar institution" of slavery, as a way of dominating both economically and physically, shaped at the level of superstructural relations, aided by the dominant and deforming myth of "antagonistic races," a type of cultural aggression and terrorism that functioned efficiently, although frequently with the help of a separate economic structure and with the operational strength of a vital contradiction. Colonization locked African labor into the double trap of economic and psychological vassalage, thus doubly alienating the consciousness of the plantation workers. The African human being, thus submitted to this twofold deculturating pressure, was transformed into an invisible man, a nameless bone in history, exposed day and night to the peril of irreversibly losing the remains of his human identity. Often the concept of alienation is used to qualify the fantastic loss of identity inherent in slavery. This concept only inadequately covers the sterilization that threatens the cultural personality of the colonized Black man. In this case the concept of "zombification" is a more appropriate one. It is no coincidence that the myth of the *zombi,* which originated in Haiti, is equally well known in other American countries.

Within the many-sided irrational relations of slavery and colonization, the fetishism of the merchandise served as a model for the genesis of the racial dogma. Just as money and skin color became an abstract, passionately powerful symbol, the color *white* became the universal symbol for wealth, political power, beauty, and social well-being inherited from the "Greco-Roman miracle"; the color *black,* became a symbol for poverty, political impotence, physical and moral ugliness, the congenital characteristics of "African barbarism and primitivism." The color of the human beings dominated them, obsessed them, and miserably clouded their consciousness and their perceptions, until color became a kind of generalized equivalent, of a biological nature, to productive relations. Thus fetishism, extrapolated from an essentially economic setting, was *colored* (and it is important to use this term) with somatic, ethical, aesthetic, and ontological meanings. The Black man as merchandise had his own intrinsic value, with the sole difference that the African slave could not be valued like a metal coin, because of his irreversible aging process. Nevertheless, in addition to property, production tools, labor, and capital, African slaves provided their European masters with supplementary "capital": the white color of their skin, the mask and sign of proprietorship and political and cultural power that accrued automatically to the colonizing class.

The African human being baptized as "Negro" by the triangular trade pattern, turned into the "mineral man" who guaranteed primitive accumulation within a capitalist economy. This absolute depersonalization inherent in servile labor brought with it a complementary form of alienation, the pure and simple assimilation of the colonized, the disappearance of their psychological being, in short, their zombification. The colonial system wished to transform the Africans and their descendants into Anglo-Saxon and Latin subproducts of Europe in the Americas. The capitalist West made sure that the dependent labor force would lose not only its freedom but also its collective and imaginative memory that permits people to transmit the truths and particular experiences of their social and cultural vitality from generation to generation. In the case invented by the plantation economy, the famous "Je est un autre" of Arthur Rimbaud, became: "*I* am an inferior model of the white European." "*I*" was a production instrument, an exchange value, a value of usage, an animal and motor work force, in short, a subhuman-biological-combustible, transformed by external hostile powers into colonial merchandise, who, in addition, before the use of electricity and steam, was also the creator of wealth that unknowingly enabled the first industrial revolution of the modern world. Thus colonization robbed the Africans who were deported to America of their past, their history, their elemental confidence in themselves, their legends, their family patterns, their beliefs, and their art. Even the beauty of their skin became an eternal source of frustration, an unsurmountable obstacle between the prefabricated condition imposed upon them and the taking of their rightful places in history and society. Depersonalization and alienation surpassed the limits of the economic and social course of servile labor, to penetrate through the pores of Blacks, even the visceral structures of their demolished personality. This threatening, deculturing pressure is responsible for the poor opinion "colored" men and women of the Americas had, for a long time, of the role of their bodies, their spirit, and their identity in the history of civilization.

Cultural Marronage: Genesis of Negritude

How did the African slaves and their Creole American descendants react
to the social and racial oppression that depersonalized their lives? What
did they do to restructure the disembodied components of their historic
identity in this unfamiliar world? Marronage was the process by means of
which some slaves abandoned their plantation and sought refuge in the
mountains, to preserve, as best as possible, their identity. Analogously, in
the cultural area, it can be said that they attempted to escape the
hegemony of the colony, endowing it with their own values, "marronag-
ing" wherever possible the horrible deculturing and assimilating mechanisms of the civilization imposed on them. The sociocultural history of the
downtrodden masses of the western hemisphere, is, in a global sense, the
history of ideological marronage that permitted them not just to reinterpret Europe with its sword, its cross, and its whip through their "African
mentality," but to demonstrate heroic creativity, in order to painfully
reprocess new ways of feeling, thinking, and acting. This prodigious effort
of self-defense became manifest in religion, magic, music, dance, and
popular medicine, in Creole jargon, cuisine, oral literature, sexual life, the
family, and other expressions of the wisdom and optimistic genius of
these people. With the exception of Haiti, the slave rebellion failed on the
political level. The majority of the heroic armed movements that marked
the history of slavery between 1519 and the end of the nineteenth century,
were sooner or later totally wiped out. From the Caribbean to Brazil (not
counting the groups of Bush Negroes of Guyana and the Jamaican maroons), the *palenques, cumbes, quilombos,* or maroon republics, did not
evolve, as they did in Haiti, into a real liberation war and a nationally
independent society.

In its sociopolitical form, marronage, according to some sociologists,
was a very healthy collective self-defense mechanism. Also, on the cultural level it proved to be healthy, for, by searching for the new truth of
their lives, the American slaves took from the anguish of their "Black
condition" its deepest dynamism to maintain and to stimulate in them the
universal feeling of liberty and human identity. This was the cognitive
process that in the popular plantation cultures often transformed the
existential drama from the status of servitude into a healthy creative
explosion.

In the case of religion and mythology the marronage of the slaves'
forceful evangelization program led to extraordinary results.

It created on plantations and in maroon communities a clandestine and
fruitful network of correspondences and mythical and ritualistic interrelationships between the representations and the gestures of Catholicism and
the African Yoruba, Fon, Fanti Ashanti, Bantu, Congo, etc. cults.

These mental and motor replies to a crisis situation that threatened to destroy or to zombify their social consciousness, reveal a very sane attitude of the slaves, both in resisting and in creatively adapting to the ferociously hostile conditions of the American socioeconomic scene. The concrete demands of the struggle against slavery and colonization drove the slave to an obstinate search for a new psychological and cultural equilibrium. The marronage of the dominant values permitted them to rework their shredded African traditions. Thanks to the power of their collective and imaginary memory they could create new rules of life in a society that restructured their personality. This vital creativity could be seen in the most varied areas, from methods of agriculture to matrimonial and family standards, from religion to folklore, from language to modes of cooking and eating, from funerary rituals to bodily expressions through dance and copulation, from magic to popular remedies, from music to oral literature and social games, from the manner of carrying children to female hair styles, and from mythology to armed resistance.

Marronage did not express itself with the same efficiency in all the areas of culture and life. The language of the masters could not be marooned, even though there is a certain influence of African languages in Latin-American Spanish and Portuguese. Aside from the Creole languages of Haiti, Guadalupe, and Martinique, the Papiamento spoken in Curaçao and Aruba, and the Antillean and Guyanese pidgins, marronage of European languages was not very generalized. Nor did the legal traditions of West Africa; and the political and economic thought of the precolonial societies of the African continent disappear. In the same fashion, the technology, iron work, spinning, statuary, and wood and ivory sculpture, as well as other expressions of the creative intellect of the African people, were submerged by the purely "socioeconomic" sensitivity of colonial America. Marronage, a legitimate self-defense movement, contributed to a limitation of the mental devastations. It saved from zombification all that could be saved in religion, magic, plastic arts, dance, music, and of course, the ability to resist oppression. Historically, marronage could not conspire against the attitudes of "Uncle Tomism," the fear and shame of being Black, the inhibition and cultural dualism, the replacing of being by seeming, psychic bipolarism, the inferiority complex, compensating aggression, the denial of the self, intellectual "Bovaryism," imitation, forms of social ambivalence, and other psychological disorders that still characterize the behavior of many Blacks and Mulattoes in our society. Slavery, colonization, and imperialism with their triple impact on America have seriously marked the social types. Stereotyped images, mythical portraits that the descendants of Africans find of themselves in the "White mirror," as well as the narcissistic opinion that descendants of Europeans discover in the "Black mirror" of their interrelationships, are echoes of racist myths of the past. They are manifestations of the spiritual misery of the various stages of the expansion of capitalism.

The Twentieth Century in America: Identity Crisis with the Will to be Born Again

The African heritage reevaluation and identification movements can be traced directly to Haiti between 1791–1804 and the end of the nineteenth century. These movements would find their way into the various social sciences (history, sociology, ethnology, and anthropology) as well as music, literature, and the visual arts. This general renovation of the oppressed spirits within the continent naturally had to distinguish itself and to differentiate itself according to the national structures of each of our Mestizo societies. The historic, exotic, and indigenous factors that have led to a Cuban, a Haitian, a Jamaican, a Dominican, a Brazilian, and an Antillean identity, as well as our common American or Caliban identity, do not coincide with each other simply and plainly at any level. In Latin America and the Caribbean there is no social awareness or a literary or artistic sensitivity that constitutes an organized, homogeneous, uniformly American bloc, without frontiers or peculiarities, that is interchangeable or can be superimposed upon its expressions. One observes, instead, an historical family, shaped by its people and its national cultures. People and culture have been dialectically shaped, both by the diversity and the harmony of the material and spiritual conditions of colonization and the struggles that put an end to the colonial period. Even though our national lineage globally experienced the same ethnohistorical adventures of an antidevelopmental world capitalism, each nation that emerged from the popular fight against the colonial conditions has its own very original system of contradictions of class and race. In spite of a doubly common origin and social situation, at the economic level (underdevelopment, plantation system) and at the superstructural level (mutation of institutions, religions, traditions, and Euro-African idiosyncracies), the four national cultures of our insular and continental countries' linguistic groups each present very precise characteristics upon analysis, due to the sociohistoric sedimentation imposed by the economic and political policies of seven different empires (six European powers, plus the ascending imperial United States). Among the islands, Cuba, Puerto Rico, and the Dominican Republic speak Spanish; Jamaica, Trinidad-Tobago, Barbados, Santa Lucia, etc. are English speaking; Haiti, Martinique, and Guadalupe are Francophone; and Curação and Aruba are Dutch speaking. On the continent Brazil speaks Portuguese; Suriname, Dutch; Guyana and Belize, English; French Guyana, French; and Venezuela, Colombia, Panama, etc. are all Spanish speaking.

Of the colonizing countries, although they belong to the same western civilization of Greco-Roman, Anglosaxon, Germanic, and Scandinavian cultures, each has its own history and pronounced national traits, and each has practiced its own colonization policies according to its level of development and the expansionary tactics of its capitalism. All these factors, be they of diversification or of association, in addition to the intercolonial rivalries and contradictions, determined the variety of historical class and race relations in our societies. All these levels of differentiation and heterogeneity, however, did not manage to destroy within the insular and continental Caribbean the existence of a very real civilization. Historical unity depends upon multiple sociological, anthropological, psychological, linguistic, ecological, and geographic realities that translate into similar behavior patterns within social groups; similarity between the tough, past work experiences on the plantations as well as present-day industrial and agricultural enterprises; similarities in popular religious forms, psychological peculiarities, and types of alienation; similarities of folklore, mythology, dance and song rhythms, games, cooking, feelings, and movements expressed in the street, in the home, in public festivities, and in intimate lovemaking. There are, in short, a variety of Antillean and Latin American ways of "marooning" socioeconomic oppression, cultural colonialism, and racism; there is an historical similarity in our Calibanesque ways of dreaming, feeling, having fun, thinking, acting, working to the south of the Rio Bravo. The diverse conditions of social existence of our people before the slave trade and during slavery, in national societies that only indigenized the methods and values of colonization, have structured an intolerable lifestyle, *serious identity crises,* that have reached a global scale, in the century of the great socialist October Revolution and of decolonization, and have triggered a *general will to be reborn* observable in syndical and political struggles as well as in literary and artistic emancipation. This universal process of self-determination in economics, politics, literature, music, and art that can even be seen in the oppressed people, had various names after the First World War. But behind the multiplicity of names, postulates, concepts, schools and *vanguardisms,* we discover from a distance, a vast general phenomenon of a search for an identity. Among the Blacks in the U.S., this identification process, initiated in 1895 by William E. B. DuBois, is correctly known by the name—which is equally valid everywhere—of *renaissance.* This concept, according to Littré, "is used upon occasions to identify a supple mental movement, following a period of oppression."

Is this not exactly what occurred among the people of our hemisphere and its political and literary intelligentsia, after centuries of slavery, colonization, and sociocultural hibernation? The first signs of this "supple movement of the minds" began to show before this century in Haiti, with Firmin, H. Price, Janvier, O. Durand, and others; in Cuba the eminently synthetic genius of José Martí propelled it, with an intensity that had no precedents, leaving an impact on the islands and on the continent linking it tightly to the second independence struggle of America on a political, literary, and anthropological level. In a much less visceral form, the renovation of intellectual and artistic activities in Latin America can be observed in the originality of Rodó and Rubén Darío, and the modernists in general, such as Enrique José Varona, Justo Sierra, Manuel Díaz Rodríguez, José Vasconcelos, Antonio Caso, Alfonso Reyes, B. Sanin Cano, J. García Monje, and other intellectuals of the area within America that concerns us. With the Mexican Revolution this new spirit was revitalized both on the islands and on the continent with the work of essayists, novelists, and poets of the country of Benito Juarez, and also, significantly, by the great neo-Aztec muralists which Siqueiros has called "the first artistic manifestation in Latin America that deserves a front-row seat in the concert of universal culture." Also, during the 1920s and 1930s, at least six vanguard movements, which suffered different fortunes and vicissitudes, emerged on the literary and artistic scene of Latin America and the Caribbean, some following the example of the European vanguard, others surviving independently. Among this half dozen of *isms,* which were discussed by our friend Oscar Collazo, we are missing one ism: *negrism,* which has a legitimate right to a place in the sun of Americanisms "in search of our expression."

Negritude in the midst of this identity crisis?

Could it have been a mask of an *American ism* without a doctrine in the midst of the effervescence of spirits?

Has it shown signs of a renaissance, like the "Black and White" vanguards of the United States, of Mulatto Brazil, and of the rest of America of "one color or another?"

We have followed the historic roads that lead to negritude, in order to present it better, at this time when we are bidding it hello and goodbye, to present it, alive or dead, flaming body of the future, or a celebrated corpse, both in its structure and in its literary, artistic, and social function.

In Search of the Formula for "Americanism" or Americanness

The year 1928 symbolically witnessed the birth of Che Guevara and three works that offer (just like the author of *Man and Socialism in Cuba*) decisive points of reference within the "history of the spiritual organization of our America." They are, *Ainsi Parla l'Oncle,* by the "Black" Haitian Price-Mars; *Seven Interpretive Essays of Peruvian Reality (Siete ensayos de interpretación de la realidad peruana),* by the Peruvian "Indian Mestizo" José Carlos Mariátegui; and *Six Essays in Search of Our Expression (Seis ensayos en busca de nuestra expressión)* by the "Creole White man" of the Dominican Republic, Pedro Henriquez Ureña. These three great works reflect the converging Creole aspects of the descendants of Africans, Indians, and Europeans in Latin America.

I have purposely brought together these three great minds, all connected to José Martí, to show the triple historical complexity of the road taken by our people, sometimes in the midst of contradictions and solitude, to arrive from Toussaint L'Ouverture to Fidel Castro, from Simón Bolívar to Che Guevara, from Tupac Amaru to Salvador Allende, from Tiradentes to Sandino, and to reach the level to which the Cuban Revolution has brought Latin American consciousness. In none of the great books that we have just mentioned can we find the entirety of sociohistoric roots of our Americanness. In them we find, planted in parallel rows, Mariátegui's "Indian" trunk, the "Black" trunk of Price-Mars, and the "White Creole" trunk of Henriquez Ureña. In each one of three studies the historically Creole unity of the American trunk of our common identity was absent. It was through this trunk that the knowledge and the tenderness of the creator of the idea "Our America" was supposed to be grafted upon the knowledge of the world. The descendants of Africans, who had become Creole and Americanized in the midst of the atrocious conditions that we are already familiar with, could not in 1823, identify with the *Alocución a la poesía* and other admirable *Silvas americanas* by Andrés Bello; nor could they identify in 1845 with Domingo Sarmiento's *Facundo,* or in 1872 with *Martín Fierro,* and in 1879 with *La vuelta de Martín Fierro* by José Hernández; nor could they later identify with the law-abiding, philanthropic and jocular *negrism* of Rubén Darío, the modernists and the postmodernists; or with José Enrique Rodó, whose Americanism was inclined more towards the aerial aestheticism of *Ariel* than towards the solid reality of the people of Caliban. Of the six great names mentioned in Henriquez Ureña's essay, Bello, Sarmiento, Montalvo, Martí, Darío, and Rodó, the suns around which "the literary history of Spanish America" turns, none, with the exception of José Martí, has offered a definition of the self, an emancipation of the spirit and the sensitivity, useful *at once* to all the social types that have emerged from our common colonial tragedy.

The fact is that although the declarations of cultural independence within the hemisphere between 1823 and 1928 were just, brilliant, and well-received, they continued to be, with the exception of Haiti, unilateral, Eurocentric, and always sacrificed one or two of the trunks of our multinationality.

Since the 1920s, the wind of renaissance has begun to blow simultaneously in the spirits of the United States, the Caribbean, Brazil, and Latin America in general. There was never a pan-negrism or a pan-negritude as the sole vanguard, with manifestations of the romantic school. The anthologies gave the illusion of such structures by amalgamating and superimposing the most diverse authors in the same books under a generic racial title. In the francophone countries of the American and African Third World, the vision of a "zionist" negritude began to emerge, with the anthology by Léopold Sedar Senghor, with a famous prologue by Jean-Paul Sartre, "Black Orpheus" ("Orphée Noir"), and during the 1950s and 1960s, with the writing of university theses destined to recapture academically and politically, for the sake of neocolonialism, the spiritual tempests and cyclones of Caliban. But our great brother William Du Bois had already said it: "The Blacks do not have a Zion, nor an ecumenical meeting point such as 'Next year in Dakar!' " These were parallel movements without any type of linkages, which in each country were molded to the national cultural contents and contours, as well as to the diversity of class origins, talents, and individual tastes.

In the western hemisphere the first was the "Black Renaissance" movement of the U.S., more precisely located in Harlem, which revolved around the main figures of the new intelligentsia that included Frederick Douglass, Paul Lawrence Dunbar, Booker T. Washington, as well as W. E. B. DuBois, James Weldon Johnson, Alain Locke, Claude McKay, Langston Hughes, Countee Cullen, Jean Toomer, and Sterling Brown. The majority of these creators, particularly DuBois, Langston Hughes, and Claude McKay came directly from the people, and from expressions of cultural marronage like jazz, the blues, and Negro spirituals. This "colored" intelligentsia took from the people the vitality and the innovative beauty of their productions. The vanguard movement of these North American intellectuals was not at all bourgeois, elitist, or aristocratic. Although this essay does not concern itself with North America, it is necessary to evoke for the sake of analogy the extraordinary reevaluation effort of U.S. Blacks, their forms of cultural self-defense, fertilized by the vanguard of poets, musicians, and essayists. This process of identification became as or more valid than the renovation that took place in the "White" arts and letters in the United States led by such brilliant men of the "lost generation" as Hemingway, Faulkner, Fitzgerald, Tom Wolfe, Dos Passos, etc. The "Black" Renaissance constitutes a prodigious "tomorrow that shines like a flame"—and an immense rainbow over the still long road that the citizens of the country that produced John Brown and Frederick Douglass, Gabriel Posser and Walt Whitman, Emerson and DuBois, Faulkner and Bessie Smith, Hemingway and Langston Hughes, must still cover together.

Jacques Roumain, in his work as a novelist, poet, essayist, ethnologist, and political leader, maintained up to his premature death a very revolutionary interpretation of the class and race issues in Haitian social history. He was able to establish, as was done after his death by Jacques Stephen Alexis and other heirs to his ideology, the real historical relation between economic oppression and racial inequality. In 1939 Roumain published an essay on the "Complaints of the Black Man" ("Quejas del Hombre negro"), that seems to indicate that, had he not died prematurely at the age of 37, he undoubtedly would have founded, upon rigorously Marxist foundations, a scientific anthropology of the Caribbean, and perhaps of all of Latin America. He writes:

> The slogan of the protection of the White woman, the unavoidable inferiority of the Black race, the mission of the White man, this mission that Kipling used to call, with his imperturbable imperialist humor, a burden, the *white man's burden* [Roumain's italics], hide the egotism of the rapacious and unscrupulous class; and finally racial prejudice, which, directed at once like a divisive instrument and a pushing aside, permits the domination of a wide strata of the White population in the United States.

It is perhaps Roumain who has given the best definition of racial prejudice we know:

> It is impossible to see in color prejudice something other than the ideological expression of the antagonism of classes, which, at the same time reflects the contradictions within the production system. It is this double overlapping in the economic infrastructure that makes it difficult for the superficial observer to analyse a phenomenon that, at first sight, seems to relate solely to psychology.

At the end of this brilliant anthropological study, Roumain invited all the oppressed, the Black and White peasant workers, to prepare together, on top of the discriminatory ruins fomented by capitalism, a new *Abolition of Slavery* (racial and salaried) for the "reconstruction of the world." That same year, 1939, so fruitful in the history of his spirit, he expressed similar ideas in verse form, in a poem of epic dimensions entitled "Ebony Wood." In this capital text, having lyrically reviewed the terrible adventure of the slave trade and colonization, and having overcome the affective givens of the "Black condition," Roumain drops the bow and arrow of the *negritude* of Philoctetes and Pyrrhus, to surpass the morbid enchantment of a bad conscience, and to proclaim in body and in soul, to be of the "universal race of the oppressed":

> Africa, I have guarded your memory, Africa
> you are within me
> like a splinter in a wound,
> like a tutelary fetish in the center of the village
> make of me the stone for your slingshot
> of my mouth, the lips of your sore
> of my knees the broken columns of your humiliation.
>
> HOWEVER
>
> I only want to be of your race
> peasant workers of all countries
> . . . .
> As the contradiction of features

results in the harmony of the face
we proclaim the unity of suffering
and of revolt
of all the people on the entire surface of the world
and we beat the mortar of fraternal times
into the dust of the idols.

(Brussels, June 1939)

Only the revolutionary fighter with a perfect understanding of the dialectics of colonial history, could, in one of the most beautiful lyrical expressions of the twentieth century, express and philosophically go beyond the racial concept. In one same gesture of pride and generosity, Roumain was able to synthesize in "a song of all and for all" (Sartre) the oppressed men of the world, the tragic class and racial experience that international capitalism imposed upon the West Africans and their descendants on the American continent.

These general considerations on Americanness as a triumphant movement among the best authors of our world, lead us directly to the man who has assumed, with the greatest precision and original grace, the Creole essence within the Caribbean and Latin America: Nicolás Guillén. There is no negrism in Guillén (as there is none in Martí). Fernández Retamar was correct when he declared that the racial sentiment is integrated by Guillén into the Cuban identity, into the historic essence of the country. It is not a *literary fashion,* but a *manner of being* Cuban, Antillean, American. In fact, what pertains most precisely to the art of Nicolás is the constant felicity with which he has been able to project into the orbit of the social revolution a way in which to live fully, clearly, and lyrically the radical values of our Americanness. At the level of great poetic creativity, Guillén drew on the resources of Góngora and Lope de Vega, the secret metabolism of the *son,* and the flavor and knowledge of popular genius. Alfred Melon has called Guillén, the "poet of synthesis." In his work, Melon has done a masterly job at understanding this sovereign poet. We are dealing with an exceptional feat, quite extraordinary with regard to Marxist criticism, and not easy to accomplish following the essays that Marinello, Augier, Noël Salomon, Mirta Aguirre, E. Martínez Estrada, Reemar, Claude Couffon, Robert Marquez and other critics have dedicated to the work of Guillén. In 1931 Emilio Ballagas had the right idea: "With the original, sincere, and strong poetry of Guillén, we began to be America . . ." Six years later, in 1937, Juan Marinello also arrived at the essence of Guillén's poetry; "an American happening," par excellence: "The poetry of Guillén fulfills this desire, it is part of our flesh because in it we find our yesterday, our present, and our tomorrow. This poetry, this strange and adjusted expression, is an American happening of the widest significance because it is a definitive triumph of the 'mestizoized' Antilles."

It is at this level that we must read and listen to the American words of Guillén. In his case it is not a question of *isms*. Romanticism, modernism, negrism are all transformed into the lyrical becoming of a Cuban identity. The renewal brought by Guillén into the lyrical work of the continent can only be compared, *mutatis mutandis,* to the profoundly innovative Americanness of Neruda and Vallejo, of Carpentier, of João Guimarães Rosa or of Gabriel García Marquez. Guillén himself is a "vanguardism," a day and night school, to whom all the social types of Cuba and of the Caribbean refer to quench their thirst for justice and beauty. The poetry of Nicolás Guillén, beginning with the famous "Here we are!" from his poem "Arrival," is an effort crowned with the success of rehabilitating the body and the spirit of our America. Guillén was able to accomplish this double transmutation of identity because he comes from the same country as José Martí. In Guillén's motherland the *Cuban quest for nationalism* followed a social process of transmutation of ethnic and cultural values from *mambismo* between 1868–1895 to the worker's movement of Mella and Martínez Villena, from Céspedes to Jesús Menéndez, from Máximo Gomez to Lázaro Peña, from Antonio Maceo to Fidel Castro, despite one hundred long years of vicissitude, until the decisively unifying action of the present-day socialist revolution, wherein the people of Martí and those of his continent have begun, not only at the level of poetry but also in their real life, to "be America."

Negritude in the French-Speaking Antilles

The Martinican, Guadalupan, and Guyanese negritude movement, more or less contemporaneous with the Haitian renaissance of 1928 that took off with *Ainsi parla l'oncle* and *La Revue Indigène,* constitutes a vanguardism that does not, however, coincide with that of Haiti. This movement was organically formed in Paris, where its initiators attended university. They included Étienne Léro, Jules Monnerot, René Menil, Aimé Césaire, Léon Damas, Léonard Sainville, Aristide Maugée, the Achille brothers (the only Haitian of the Antillean group was Doctor Sajous of Cayes, Haiti); these were joined, two years later, by the African students Léopold Sedar Senghor, Osmane Sosé and Birago Diop, all from Senegal. At the beginning, and possibly until its dismemberment by World War II, this group was ideologically very heterogeneous, and included the strict Marxist René Menil, a man of exemplary loyalty, and Jules Monnerot, who was to lose himself in the desert of low-grade anticommunism. These young intellectuals started—aside from the *Revue du monde noir,* a bilingual publication with Andrée Nardal and Sajous with the collaboration of Price-Mars, A. Locke, C. McKay, Félix Eboué and René Maran—two equally ephemeral publications: *Légitime défense* (1932) and *L'Etudiant noir* (1934), which, with various arms (Marxism, surrealism, Freudianism, not counting the ethnology of Frobenius, Delafosse, George Hardy, Robert Delavignette, Théodore Monod) opened heavy artillery fire on both the "bourgeois, Christian, capitalist world and upon colonial oppression and racism." Facing the absurdity of a world where the fascism of Benito Mussolini for ten years had villified the Italy of Dante, Giordano Bruno, Leonardo, and Antonio Gramsci, and where Adolph Hitler was at the verge of launching Nazi bestiality upon Germany and Europe, eight young Martinican intellectuals published an explosive text, entitled *The Manifesto of Legitimate Defense,* where they openly took a political and cultural position.

This manifesto, easily traceable to the francophone colonized Caribbean, was rapidly stifled by the French police, but was to reemerge two years later in *L'Étudiant noir* published by Césaire and Senghor.

Within this context, so well analyzed by André Lucrèce (with the three mortgages: ethnology, Freudianism, and surrealism, in which negritude would be stuck until it reached a crisis within the confusingly paired concepts of master/slave, White/Black, reason/emotion, class/race, culture/civilization, Prospero/Caliban, Senghor/Césaire), an Antillean and African vanguardism would be articulated by the "racial" troika of Aimé Césaire, Léon Damas and Léopold Sedar Senghor.

From where does the fortunate word-concept *negritude* come? Césaire, who used it for the first time in *L'Étudiant noir,* answers:

> Since the Antilleans were ashamed of being Negroes, they looked for some kind of circumlocution with which to refer to a Negro. They talked about "the man with the tanned skin" and other similar stupidities . . . so we adopted the word *nègre* (Negro) as the *challenge word.* This was a name of challenge. It was somewhat of a reaction of an angry young man. Since they were ashamed of the word *nègre,* we then decided to use the term *nègre.* I must confess that when we founded *L'Étudiant noir,* I really wanted to call it *L'Étudiant nègre,* but there was too much resistance in the Antilles. Some considered the word *nègre* too offensive, for this reason I took the liberty of talking about negritude. There was within us a will to defiance, a violent affirmation of the word *nègre* and of the word *negritude.*

On another occasion, and in answer to the precise question of Lilyan Kesteloot: "I would like to know what is your exact position with regard to *negritude?*" Césaire subjected himself for the first time to public self-criticism in which he was careful to dot all his *i*'s:

> . . . There is an obvious fact: negritude has brought with it certain dangers. It has had the tendency to transform itself into a school, to transform itself into a church, to transform itself into a theory and into an ideology. I am in favor of negritude from a literary point of view and as a personal ethic, but I am against an ideology based on negritude. I am posi-

tive that negritude cannot resolve everything; I am particularly in agreement with the viewpoint of those who criticise negritude because of certain ways it has been used. When a theory, for example a literary theory, begins to serve a certain policy, I believe it becomes very controversial . . . On whether negritude acts as a forecaster . . . well, not really, because I believe there are other elements, that there are philosophical elements, etc., that must define us. I absolutely reject that idyllic type of pan-negrism based on confusionism; I tremble to think that it could be confused with negritude. . . .

One must also point to the work of Henri Bangou, a Guadalupan historian and essayist. The following are a few of his critical evaluations of negritude:

It is absolutely impossible to separate the work of Césaire and his negritude from a total compromise on the political level, both with regard to decolonization in general and with the liberation of the oppressed people. From this point of view Senghor's negritude is totally different. It is formal and mystical, and thus equally racist, since it makes one believe that there are essential Black traits that are different from distinctive White traits. We find nothing similar in Jacques Roumain or Price-Mars or Depestre. . . . There is another misunderstanding that must be dissipated; Césaire's negritude has nothing to do with masochistic self satisfaction, with that type of beatific return to the past, that type of primitivism that would not hesitate to make of the liberated people new victims of the developed world, if these would have the time to sing to the Black soul and to primitive agrarian communism.

Ideological Role of Negritude

In speaking about negritude and Sartre's *Black Orpheus,* let us make it clear that it was not Sartre who originated all the misunderstandings we have pointed out. It is not for nothing that Jean-Paul Sartre, in addition to having written his famous preface to Senghor's "Anthology" and another hundred well-known texts, was the author of a study entitled *The Critique of Dialectical Reasoning.* In *Black Orpheus,* written in 1948, one could already see, in spite of his serious struggles with historic materialism, that there was nevertheless no incomplete or hasty understanding of Marxist dialectics. Sartre's discourse was based upon three fundamental premises that almost thirty years ago clarified the class content of the anthropological notion of negritude, before its pure and simple retreival by Prospero (as opposed to Caliban):

1. The Black man, just like the White worker, is the victim of the capitalist structure of our society; this situation is revealed in his close solidarity, that surpasses skin pigmentation, with certain classes of Europeans who

are as oppressed as he is; he is encouraged to project a society without privileges where skin pigmentation is considered a simple accident. But although oppression is only one, it is shaped by history and by geographical conditions: the Black man is the victim because he is black, because he is a colonized native or a deported African. And because he is oppressed on account of his race he must thus gain awareness of his race. . . . Insulted, enslaved, he rises, he picks up the word "negro" that has been hurled at him like a stone, and he proudly becomes revindicated as a "negro" before the White man.

2. In fact, negritude appears like the weak point within a dialectic progression: the theoretical and practical affirmation of the supremacy of the White man is the thesis; the position of negritude is the antithesis. But this negative moment is not sufficient in itself, and the negroes who use it, know it very well; they know that it points to the preparation of the synthesis or the realization of the human being within a society without races. Therefore, negritude must be destroyed, it is a transition, not a point of arrival, it is the middle and not the ultimate end.

3. What will happen if the "negro" casting aside his negritude in favor of revolution only wishes to consider himself as master? What will happen if he will only permit himself to be defined by his objective social condition? . . . Will the source of poetry stop? Or will the great black river color, in spite of everything, the ocean into which it flows.

The truth of Jean-Paul Sartre's *Black Orpheus* revolves around three axes. In discussing them in 1948, in a West infected by racism, the author of *The Words* expressed as well as his ideology would permit him to, the historical drama of the West African ethnic groups and of their descendants who had been dispersed throughout the Americas. He was right in asserting that the achievement of class awareness and the solidarity of the colonized people had been prepared ideologically from the 1920s to the 1940s by parallel identity movements of the cultural or political pan-African conferences, which had given an important place to the *notion of race*. Sartre showed how the Black proletariat was doubly alienated: as human beings whose work power is confiscated and as human beings whose pigmentation is viewed pejoratively, thus making color an object of change of genetic history, a social fetish, an evil essence of human relations. In reading the lyrical productions of the francophone descendants of Africans, Sartre saw that the awareness of this double alienation—and the obsessive preoccupation to overcome them with their dual class/race aspects—had fostered the creativity of the most important poets of Léopold Sedar Senghor's *Anthology*. In 1948, wherever one looked in the West, what could one see? Black workers taking the chestnuts destined for the "White" colonial oligarchies out of the fire. Both in America and in Africa, the vast majority of Blacks were cane cutters, cooks, street cleaners, fire tenders, agricultural workers, or factory laborers, whose arms and muscles only counted for the services they rendered to the insolently oppressive minorities. In 1948, save for Haiti and the United States, there still weren't any bourgeois Blacks on the historic scene who were accomplices to the colonialist activities of the West. From reading the sixteen poets whose work had been compiled by Senghor, Sartre concluded that negritude would be called on sooner or later to make common cause with the socialist October Revolution and the liberation movement of the colonized people. His study therefore had other merits. He accurately analyzed, for example, what Léon Laleau wanted to express in his poem "Treason."

> This obsessive heart that does not correspond
> to my language or to my clothing
> and on which bite, like on a hook,
> sentiments and habits
> borrowed from Europe. Do you feel the suffering
> and this unequalled exasperation
> to dominate with words from France
> this heart that came to me from Senegal?

Thus Sartre offered an analysis acceptable by a Marxist, with regard to the difference between Christian "pain," which invites the oppressed to morose and masochistic resignation, and the suffering of the slaves of America, which was dynamically incorporated into history through *voodoo*, music, dance, which transformed the anguish of the "Black condition" through a state of healthy and legitimate defense, into a creative sociocultural factor. This we have humbly called "sociocultural marronage." Sartre also understood the importance of the "colored" intelligentsia in the rehabilitation of black skin, the physical beauty of Blacks, and the rationalization of the socioeconomic concept of race, which was accomplished by Roumain, Guillén, DuBois, Langston Hughes, Fanon, Césaire, Claude McKay, Paul Niger, Morisseau-Leroy, Damas, Regino Pedroso, Gui Tirolien, Jean F. Brierre, Emilio Roumer, etc.*

Let us now briefly refer to Senghor's negritude. Léopold Senghor, with his vital, mystical, and neoromantic perspective, considered one of the

---

*Other very subtle aspects linked to the psychoaffective consequences of colonization have been philosophically explained by Sartre. But this great text, *Black Orpheus*, contains errors that are as glaring as its emeralds of truth. For example, for Sartre, the racial consciousness formation "is differentiated *by its nature* (my italics) from that which Marxism tries to awaken in the White man . . . . The awareness of race is thus fixed upon the Black soul, or, better said, since the term recurs in the *Anthology*, on a common thought and conduct of Blacks that is called "negritude." Here a Marxist cannot agree with Sartre. The Africans who were deported to America were forced to form a *racial consciousness* not because they had a "Black soul" or a negritude that was consubstantial to their nature, but because of the specific colonial capitalist mode of production. The condition of enslaved Africans has been defined by the American plantation system of production and the distribution of goods. Racial consciousness is imposed upon the plantation workers by strictly dated circumstances.

historic forms of alienation (racial dogma) that emerged out of the bourgeois work ethic, out of the production and distribution of goods, as an eternally intrinsic objectivation of the "Black African man" (at least since Grimaldi's little negroid statuettes). He made of negritude a timeless, a historical phenomenon headed for a passionate and irrational return towards the vital, towards "Black emotion."

Historic circumstances have not selected, however, one sole nation or one particular "race" to advance the New World renaissance. A universalizing class, the proletariat, with its natural allies, is irreversibly on the road towards this qualitative jump that Lenin and his people forced history to take in 1917. The passion and the sacrifices of the Blacks have been consummated. Black and White, as well as all other "racial" categories of capitalism, are disappearing from the historic scene. The cursed pair class/race will be erased more and more in the laws, constitutions, customs, and ways of dreaming and acting of human beings. Black and White, as social types of a bygone social structure, only maintain a mythical existence within the delirium of the Old South or within the colonial insanity known as Apartheid.

Recently Cuban troops crossed the South Atlantic, following the inverse route of the slave trade and its slave boats. For the first time since the fifteenth century, an African country, formerly plundered by the raiders that fed upon the market of "pieces of ebony," witnessed the arrival on its shores and the penetration in its air space of the caravelles that came from the Caribbean. What did the Angolans discover onboard? Raceless brothers, plain Cubans, of the type of José Martí, Antonio Maceo, Mella, and Fidel, carriers of the good news of a well-armed solidarity. The American brother did not come to pick up a knife or a rifle against his African brother, but he came to help him expel from his invaded home the agents of Prospero, traitors to his nation and to Africa. This is no tempest in a literary glass of water, but an alliance of free men that cuts off the arms of colonial violence. The *route to Angola,* constitutes in 1976 a sea and air trip of sheer humanity, aware of its internationalist rights and duties; it is the crossing of a Caliban who can pilot the modern boats and airplanes. It is a success without precedent in the history of the African/American couple.

The fact is that there is no negritude of tomorrow not even on this December night. This morning, in rising before the cocks of Havana, the Black Orpheus of my youth has discovered a lifeless fairy between the blue sheets of this essay. It is time to say hello to our Mother America and to the revolution that it has started here. It is time for good Cuban coffee and to say goodbye to negritude!

12

Latin America in Africa

PIERRE VERGER

It was not the Latin Americans themselves who had an influence on Africa, but instead, the old freed slaves and their descendants returning to their original continent after having remained involuntarily in the Americas for some time.

One exception to this generalization is the case of certain White Brazilian families, who, during the anti-Portuguese movement that followed Brazil's declaration of independence in 1822, left Pernambuco over a period of several years and settled in Mossammedes. They took with them all their belongings, including their African slaves, so that they could rebuild large agricultural plantations, patriarchal in nature, similar to the ones they had abandoned in Brazil.[1] However, this phenomenon comes closer to Portuguese colonization than to Latin American influence.

The real Latin American influence, transmitted via the freed slaves, was a consequence of the slave trade. But this return movement of some thousands of freed slaves did not arise in all Latin American countries. Its point of departure was limited to Brazil, and Bahia in particular, within the first few decades of the nineteenth century. It was not until the second half of the century that the movement extended to Cuba. We know very little about it with regard to other Latin American countries.

Likewise, the places they returned to were also limited, including certain regions along the coast of the Gulf of Benin, such as Agoué, Ouidah, Porto Novo, Badagry, and Lagos, which were then the main slave export ports. The slave trade ended in Brazil around 1851, and some fifteen years later it also ceased in Cuba.

In this study we will refer to the Brazilian influence along the Gulf of Benin, since it is the most visible influence that still exists.

The ports that the Cuban and Brazilian freed slaves returned to are located now in Nigeria and the People's Republic of Benin, the same territories they had come from. But once they had returned, the repatriates could not return to their native inland villages without running the risk of being imprisoned again and sent back as slaves, due to the war that the Dahoman King had been waging for many years with his neighbors, and because of the intertribal conflicts that were devastating the Yoruba nation.

This was the sad fortune of forty passengers aboard the Portuguese ship *General Rego,* who, backed by a letter written by the British consul in Lagos on January 2, 1856, "Should be, according to the contract, permitted to disembark in Lagos with all of their goods. However, these unfortunate people were forced to disembark in Ouidah, where their property was embargoed, and, under the pretext that they were from Egbá (a village in the interior of Abeokuta), they were sent back to the King of Dahomey, who condemned the adults to death and saved the children as slaves."[2]

The king of Dahomey in vain tried to reconquer Abeokuta. This was the only village in the interior of the Yoruba country where numerous slaves freed from the repressive slave trade by the British fleet had been brought from Freetown, in Sierra Leone, to be regrouped under the influence of Protestant priests to form a society with a far stronger British than Latin American influence.

On the other hand, the freed slaves who were returning from Brazil had been strongly influenced by their long stay in that country. "They had no ties with 'Africans' other than the fact that they had arrived as such in Brazil," writes Gilberto Freyre. "Rather than Brazilians, one could say that they were 'Brazilianized Africans' due to their contacts with nature, the environment, and the culture of this part of America, which already had a strong mestizo coloration. These Africans and descendants of Africans who had lived in Brazil, particularly in Bahia, returned to Africa bringing along customs and habits that they had acquired in the foreign land, and to which they were tied forever."[3]

In fact, if they had been marked by the lifestyle imposed upon them in the New World, they, too, impressed their own African influence on Brazil. The contact of African slaves and freedmen with the Portuguese who had come from Europe or who had been born in Brazil had generated a double transculturation process that, according to Roger Bastide: "Produced at the same time Mulatto children and a Mestizo culture." The more or less pronounced "de-Africanization" of Blacks brought about, on the other hand, a certain Africanization of the White population.

The Africans imported by Brazil through the slave trade, their descendants who had also been kept as slaves, and even those who had succeeded in gaining their freedom, were members of the poorest class of Brazilian society at the end of the nineteenth century. Nevertheless, in spite of their low social level, their influence on the culture of the country is far from insignificant.

"Bahia is becoming Africanized," wrote Luis Vianna Filho, "everywhere we find the Black man with his culture, his customs, and his unconscious. It is as though he was unconsciously transmitting them to the new society into which he had been forcibly integrated. And this society was assimilating everything without perceiving that the Black slave was the transmittor. Organized society, following Portuguese standards, was unaware of this transmission. This society did not consider it possible that an influence generating from such base conditions and with such different and far away roots could have an impact. Nevertheless, slowly and insidiously, in a manner so much more efficient than if it had shown a concerted and deliberate effort that would undoubtedly have provoked a strong opposition, the Black influence made itself felt."[4]

This influence was initiated during the tender infancy of the Whites, who were nursed and taken care of by the Black wet nurse who would rock them to sleep to the tunes of African lullabies, amused them with her stories, and soothed or frightened them with African beliefs. Slowly they would become conditioned to African cultural values. Roger Bastide points out that on the large estates and sugar plantations the wife and children of the master rarely left their mansion, where they lived surrounded by a multitude of African and Creole slaves; they would work together on their sewing and embroidery, singing songs from Portugal and Africa, chatting together about African and Portuguese beliefs and superstitions, mixing the ideas, the proverbs, and the sayings that contained the knowledge of the two cultures. The young boys ran around the fields with Black peers who served as their scapegoats as well as being their play and study mates. Thus they learned and acquired African reactions and forms of behavior. Later they would have their first love experiences with Black women who worked at their ancestral home or in the fields, mingling elements of sexual attraction with understanding, in relationships with those conventionally considered people of a different race.

But Brazilian society was dominated by Whites, their culture and their religion. To advance in this environment, the freed slaves were obliged to succumb to the standards established by their ancient masters, and in order to be tolerated and to be admitted into the society, however marginally, they had to adopt its lifestyle and manners and to follow, at least outwardly, White principles.

Often, after they had been freed, they would form Catholic religious brotherhoods, grouped according to their ethnic origins.

The Brazilian custom that permitted slaves to obtain their freedom if they could repay their masters the amount for which they had been purchased, resulted in the early liberation from their servile condition of numerous slaves. Slaves working in the fields or in mines rarely had the opportunity to buy their freedom; but those who were sent by their masters to make money in the streets, as porters, salespersons, street vendors, errand boys, etc., and who had the right to keep a portion of the money that exceeded the sum stipulated by their masters, could easily gain their freedom.

In Bahia, once they were free, the Africans of Bantu origins, from the Congo and from Angola, became members of the *cofradía* (society or club) of Our Lady of the Rosary of colored people, established in the church of the same name in the Pelourinho neighborhood. The Dahomans, called Gêgê in Brazil, gathered around Our Lord of Necessities and Redemption in the Corpus Santo chapel in the lower part of the city; the Nagô-Yorubas, got together in two *cofradías* in the little church of Barro- quinha, in the heart of the city; the men gathered around Our Lord of the Martyrs and the women around the Virgin of Good Death.

All this was part of the process of 'de-Africanization,' stronger in appearance than in reality, for, among the members of the *cofradía* of Barroquinha were the founders of the first *terreiros* (cult centers) or Afri- can temples, where the cults to the various Nagô-Yoruba divinities have been faithfully perpetuated to the present.

African slaves had all been baptized when they arrived in Brazil or in Cuba, but some of them found it difficult to participate fully in the Catho- lic religion, which had been taught to them in a language that was not their own; in fact, most of them preserved their faith in the efficiency of the control of the forces of nature by their traditional gods, and they believed in the soothing protection offered to them by their ancestors.

Since these African religions had to be hidden behind the mask of the religion of their masters, there resulted a syncretism between the African gods and the Catholic saints. This syncretism was based on the degree of approximation between the religious imagery of the latter to certain char- acteristics of the former.

After some time, adherence to the religion of the masters became more sincere. Among the descendants of Africans—Creole Blacks born in Brazil—educated to equally respect the beliefs of their African ancestors and the teachings of the Catholic Church that came from Portugal, the two religions mixed and became confused without provoking major problems.

As we said earlier, the freed Brazilian and Cuban slaves, upon return- ing to Africa, were often unable to reestablish themselves in their home village in the heart of the continent and could therefore not become rein- tegrated into their traditional milieu. Isolated from their families and liv- ing in coastal villages, where they were considered strangers since they were members of different ethnic groups, they formed a coherent Latin American society; the cultural and religious traditions they had all ac- quired in the New World was what tied them to each other. Thus they formed a relatively small group inserted into an African world that was no longer their world.

If in the New World they had preserved their African peculiarities, it was their non-African side, their Latin American originality, that they cultivated and tried to highlight upon returning to Africa.

In some cases their birthplaces had been destroyed by wars, and they ran the risk of repeating the adventures of the freed Black man of Bahia who had been found by John Duncan in Adofobia in 1845, deep in the heart of Africa: "Once he returns he finds that his birthplace had been burned twice by the enemy and that it was largely inhabited by foreigners of a far away country. Now he was a stranger, looked at suspiciously, and his land, that he had desired to return to for so many years, was no more than a desolate place. With a lonely heart, the old freedman took the long journey back to the coast, so that he could return to Bahia, if that were possible."[5]

The importance of Bahia among the people who returned to the shores of Africa is made obvious in a text published by Elysée Réclus in 1887: "The name of the Brazilian city Bahia was the most important since they eyes; it served to designate, in a general manner, all countries located outside of Africa."[6]

The same John Duncan, who observed the departure of a slave expedition at Ouidah, wrote: "The freedmen who had arrived from Brazil had all lined up to watch the procession [of slaves who were about to embark on a slave ship], which gave them a great feeling of satisfaction, in this maintained that their happiest days were those that they had spent in Bahia. I asked many why they had left such a pleasant place, and they assured me that it was because of a revolt that had been organized by some slaves in Bahia that had ruined many owners and large sugar plantations, which meant that they could no longer be employed. However, in all probability, these men had been among the revolutionaries and had been expelled from the country."[7]

The opinion expressed by this British traveler was perfectly sound. There had been a series of slave and freedman revolts in Bahia between 1807 and 1835, on the inland plantations and in the city itself. The nature of these revolts had not been understood by the government at the time. This had not been a general revolt of Blacks against Whites like in Haiti, but a Bahian repercussion of the *jihad,* or holy war, of the Fulanis, that had been declared in Africa in 1804. The impact of the Islamic religion to the north of the Yoruba country led to the arrival in Bahia of war prisoners of the fighting tribes: Fulanis, Haoussas, and Yorubas, some of these recently converted to Islam. This holy war continued in Bahia in the form of slave and freedman revolts, all by Moslems fighting against a world of infidels. These attacks were also directed against their enslaved comrades who were not Moslems, and against their White masters.

After the last revolt in 1835, the police had persecuted the freed slaves without great discernment, not making any distinctions between Moslems and Catholics; they had also conducted a series of inquiries that sometimes resulted in the expulsion of freed Catholic slaves who had not participated in the seditious movements. These investigations, often conducted without any sort of understanding, resulted in the return to their homeland of many African Catholics, so that, paradoxically, as a consequence of the *jihad* (the holy war that was to spread Islam throughout Africa), the Catholic faith was expanded in Africa.

It was thus that, in 1835, a freed slave from the Azima family of the

Hoko region in the country of Mahi, north of Abomey, returned to Africa under the name of Joaquim de Almeida, after having spent many years in Bahia as a servant of navy captain Manuel Joaquim de Almeida.

Having obtained his freedom, Joaquim de Almeida established himself in Agoué, to become a slave trader! Being a good Catholic did not inhibit him in his profession; in fact, with his own money, he was able to build one of the first Catholic chapels in this coastal area of Africa, long before the arrival of missionaries. He brought with him from Bahia a statue of Our Lord of Necessities and of Redemption, similar to the figure in the left nave of the present church of Corpus Santo in Bahia, which was the meeting place of the Dahoman Gêgê *cofradía*, of which Joaquim de Almeida was a member.

Although he was Catholic, Joaquim de Almeida had maintained the African custom of polygamy, and displayed a remarkable desire to perpetuate himself through a large number of descendants. He had a respectable number of concubines. His children were baptized in the chapel he had built in Agoué, in groups of fifteen and twenty at a time, by Catholic priests in transit to the island of São Thomé.

The first Catholic missionaries, arriving in 1863 to successfully evangelize this part of Africa, were surprised to find the presence of Christians for over thirty years on the shores of present-day Dahomey and Nigeria. But because they were not familiar with the flourishing syncretism (which still exists) of Brazil, they expressed their indignation in sharp terms.

The Reverend Father Francisco Borghero wrote in 1864: "We were very sad to see those Portuguese Blacks and Whites, who called themselves Christians, for the most part living exactly like pagans. Their religion consisted of a monstrous amalgamation of paganism, Christian practices, and fetishist superstitions."[8]

Abbot Laffite said in 1876: "Some of them never had more connection with Christianity than their baptismal name, and they didn't feel guilty in invoking Black gods."[9] And he added: "Due to an innocent pride, these Brazilians do not want to be treated as Black." It is true that the Catholic religion in those days tried to link the Whites, who had certain privileges, to the faithful of other colors. The various professions of faith by "Brazilians" and other Africans who had been recently converted sought more to erase the disadvantages determined by social privileges than to show their sincere and profound devotion to the dogmas of the Church.

Under the energetic direction of the missionaries, both Protestant and Catholic, and motivated by their desire to climb the social ladder, they had to give up their traditional religious practices. It was thus, in Africa itself, that the returned Africans lost their African identity.

As for the "Brazilians" who had become Moslems in Brazil, they were not always well received by their African coreligionists, who reproached them for not being familiar with the teachings of the Koran. Many of the conversions to Islam that had taken place in Bahia had been provoked by rebellious sentiments against the White masters. These emotions had been toned down and calmed after the return. Furthermore, almost all of them had names related to Christianity, such as Cruz, Calvary, Nacimiento (Birth), de las Llagas (of Thorns), la Concepción (Conception), etc., and displayed a greater tolerance and understanding of it, since they felt closer to the Brazilian Catholic lifestyle than to African Moslems, which is why they had closer ties with the "Brazilian" community.

To reinforce their "Latin American" social status, so different from that of the natives, they maintained the nutrition and dress habits they had acquired on the other side of the Atlantic, and built houses similar to those that they or their masters had lived in. These were houses with windows cut into small squares, surrounded by a white molding, contrasting with the vividly colored African façades. In some cases, these houses also had wrought-iron balconies that had been brought from Brazil. The interior was furnished with seats, beds, and jacaranda trunks.* The living room had a glass case containing porcelain dishes and crystal glasses, which were the pride of the homeowner. The walls were decorated with family portraits and religious images; a picture of the Last Supper was exhibited in the best location.

The furnishings also included, to the exasperation of Richard Burton, music boxes. "These articles, he wrote, were one of the afflictions of the West African. The Whites would honor a visitor by activating one of these abominations, and the Blacks, who had a half dozen, would make them all play at the same time."[10]

A doorway decorated with lions, or a carved lintel, flanked the house and gave access to an inside patio and the gardens that surrounded the main building.

Everything was reminiscent of the home of the master, whom the "Latin Americans" who had returned to Africa, had served for many years in America.

According to Elysée Réclus, "the Brazilians" went into business as intermediaries or as importers. They proved to be stiff competition for European merchants, and because of their family ties with the natives, they acquired an increasing advantage over the foreigners. Without any state intervention, as in Sierra Leone, and without the presence of philanthropic societies, as in Liberia, the African coast was being peopled by freed slaves and sons of slaves in this part of the Black continent, and the results of this voluntary immigration did not seem inferior to that of the British colonies or the North American companies."[11]

*Brazilian rose wood.

The only possible line of business upon return was to join the slave trade, which was what some of them did with great financial success. Having been the merchandise they now became the merchants. Later on, when the European markets opened up to cotton and palm oil imports, the "Latin Americans" were able to become involved in more innocent commercial activities.

Together with the old slave traders, who had sent them across the Atlantic, they now formed the wealthiest group of this Latinamerican society.

They maintained a grand lifestyle. The Prince of Joinville, having passed through Ouidah in 1843, referred to Francisco Félix de Souza, known as "Chacha," in his memoires: "In the afternoon, I ate with him on silver plates, lit by church candelabra and candlesticks. We toasted to the king and to the queen, and to the prosperity of France. Each toast was saluted by twenty-one cannon shots, since Chacha's factory was a veritable fortress, protected by cannons. Chacha gave me a box of tobacco from Havana, such as no king of Spain had ever smoked."[12]

Forbes, who had been invited by the Souza family in 1850, declared that during the course of a picnic "a tablecloth as white as milk had been spread on the grass, covered with delicacies, French, Portuguese, Spanish and German wines, and all the china, from the coffee cups to the gravy dishes, was of solid silver."[13]

Relations with Brazil were very close, and the means of communication were plentiful: for some years, Ouidah and Bahia were tied by more than a hundred trips, an average of one boat every three and a half days. The children of the former slaves had studied in Brazil, and their slaves had learned a profession.

"The slave trade was a very profitable investment," wrote John Duncan, "and the merchants were able to import all they needed from Brazil."[14]

The same traveler also wrote: "The countryside surrounding Ouidah is very interesting. The land is good and many places are cultivated by the people who came from Brazil. These are the most industrious people I have encountered in a long time. All of their beautiful estates, six to seven miles from Ouidah, are well cultivated. Their clean and comfortable houses are located in the midst of the best one's imagination could ever describe. It is really agreeable to unexpectedly find a home where one is greeted in European style and invited to have a drink. Later, I always found proof that these people had been slaves."[15]

Various aspects of everyday Latin American life (particularly of Brazil and especially of Bahia), are still visible in the villages along the coast of the Gulf of Benin, as we pointed out earlier.

A mass is celebrated each year on the third Sunday of January in honor of Senhor do Bomfin (Our Lord Bomfin), a very popular Bahian festivity brought to the African coast by the Brazilians. After the religious ceremonies a picnic is organized in a rural area in the vicinity of the city.

All the resources of Brazilian cuisine are conjured up in the preparation of dishes such as: *feijoada, cousido, caruru, mocoto, feijão de leite, cocada,* * and other delicacies cooked according to the recipes learned long ago in Brazil.

After the meal, the Brazilians dance the Samba de Roda (Samba round), where male and female dancers alternately display an orgy of complicated steps, with frills and acrobatic skills, dancing alone in the center of a circle of people who accompany their steps with the clapping of hands and with Brazilian songs.[16]

Samba eu quero samba	Samba, I want samba
Cajueiro Cajuá	Cashew nut tree, Cajua
Samba eu quero samba	Samba I want samba
Eu vou ver minha Sinhá.	I will go see my mistress.

Some of these songs express the feelings of nostalgia of these repatriate Africans for the land to which they had been sent as slaves:

Corre meu cavalo	Run my horse
Na maior alegria	With the greatest happiness
Vai dizer meu Brazil	Go tell my Brazil
Que não se esqueça de mim.	That it should not forget me.

or else the following, that humorously reflects religious prejudices:

Minha mãe que me pariu	My mother who gave me birth
Me bota tua benção	Give me your blessing
Que eu vou na terra dos negros	For I am going to the land of the Blacks
Vou morrer sem confissão.	Where I will die without confession.

Others refer to the feast of Senhor do Bomfin:

Papai eu quero casar	Father I want to marry
Mamãe eu quero casar	Mother I want to marry
Hoje, hoje, hoje	Today, today, today

---

*Feijoada: stew of black beans, dried meat, ham, sausages, pig's feet and tail
Cousido: a stew
Carurú: dish with okra, shrimp, fish, peppers and palm oil
Mocotó: ankle bones of pig or cow, the inside of which is eaten
Feijão de leite: a white bean
Cocada: coconut sweet meat dish [translator's note]

Na festa do Bomfin
Hoje, hoje, hoje
Domingo do Bomfin
Agora Deus vou me casar
Agora Deus vou me casar.

At the feast of Bomfin
Today, today, today
Sunday of Bomfin
Now, God, will I marry
Now, God, will I marry.

Or else:

É a festa do Bomfin
É o dia do Bomfin
Olêlê prima Chiquinha
Vamos sambar
Na terra d'areia.

It is the feast of Bomfin
It is the day of Bomfin
Olele cousin Chiquinha
Let us dance the samba
On the sandy ground.

Themes of everyday life in Brazil are also evoked:

Papai cadê minha mãe
Tua mãe foi na feira
Foi na feira comprar quiabo
Para cozinhar para meninha
Para comer comida
Junto da minha filinha.

Father, where's my mother?
Your mother went to the market
She went to the market to buy okra
To cook for the little girl
To eat food
Next to my little daughter.

or:

Acenda luz Maria
Eu quero alumiar
Água de beber
Goma de gomar
Acenda luz Maria

Turn on the light Maria
I want to light up
Water to drink
Tapioca to eat
Turn on the light, Maria.

and even more:

Suba na mangueira
Ora suba na mangueira
Não jogue manga no chão

La darriba respondeu
Não tem mais manga
Não tem
Suba na mangueira

Climb up the mango tree
Now go up the mango tree
Don't throw the mango on the
    ground
The one at the top answered
It has no more mangos
It has none
Climb up the mango tree.

or this drinking song:

Carro não puxa sem boi

Eu não canto sem beber
Quem tem só a boca fala
Quem tem só oho vem ver.

The cart does not get pulled with-
    out an ox
I don't sing without drinking
Whoever only has a mouth will talk
Whoever only has an eye comes to
    see.

Or this one about the popular street in Bahia:

Vamos na Baixa dos Sapateiros	Let us go to the Baixa dos Sapateiros
Vamos rabaixar o colarinho	Let us unbutton the collar
Do Sinhô Galinheiro.	Of Master Chickencoop

This last song was sung to me one day by Epifânio Olimpo, grandfather of a former president of the Republic of Togo:

As creoulas da Bahia	The female creoles of Bahia
Todas andam de cordão	All walk around with gold chains
Ai violão, violão, violão	Ai violin, violin, violin
Ai violão, violão, violão.	Ai violin, violin, violin.

On Christmas Eve and Epiphany, the Brazilian societies of these African villages organized parties called *burrinha,* similar to the *bumba meu boi* of Brazil. They included a horse, a cardboard ox, and various disguised people, all of which are part of the folklore of the Brazilian northeast:

Vem a ver, vem a gostar	Come see, come have fun
A burrinha está na rua	The little donkey is in the street
Vem a ver, vem a gostar.	Come see, come have fun.

In cities like Lagos, where the British influence was felt in the homes of the freed slaves who had come from Sierra Leone and who had been converted to the various Protestant sects, the Latin American identity was strengthened by belonging to the Roman Catholic Church, and by the splendor of the baptismal, marriage, and funerary ceremonies.

In other essays we have published some comments on these practices:

> The weddings were announced with simplicity or pomp depending on the social position of the parents of the young couple and their attitude towards the mundane.
> The marriage of Mr. Júlio Martins, who teaches at the Roman Catholic school, to Miss Victoria Pinto, first daughter of Mrs. Felicidade Maria de Jesus of Bamgbosche Street, on September 27, 1890, was celebrated at the Roman Catholic Church with great pomp.[17]

On October 8, in the same church, Mr. Ignacio Pinto was wed to Miss Angela R. da Silva, daughter of Mr. F. R. da Silva. The ceremony was officiated over by the Reverend Father Pied. The bride was given away by her cousin, Mr. F. Medeiros.

On December 10:

> The marriage ceremony of Miss Eugenia Margarita de Carvalho and Mr. Jeronimo W. Medeiros, took place at the Roman Catholic Church; the

Reverend Father Pelley officiated. The bride wore a thin, white, silk dress, decorated with orange flowers, with a long, white, silk veil, held by two beautifully dressed pages; each one carried a silver chain and medal, gifts of the husband. After the ceremony all the guests went to Carvalho Hall, home of the mother of the bride, where a buffet was served. The couple left at noon to spend their honeymoon at Victoria Beach. Best wishes for a long life and happiness to the newlyweds.

On April 1, 1896, the *Lagos Standard* published the following notes:

In spite of its being Lent, the elegant season of Lagos is at its peak. At the Roman Church of Santa Cruz, the wedding celebration of Mr. L. A. Cardoso, the well-known merchant of Bamgbosche Street, to Miss Juana G. Bastos, daughter of Mrs. Felicidade M. de la Concepción, has already taken place. The young lady is without a doubt one of the most important people of the Brazilian quarter.

In May, Miss Julia Campos, a young and very affable lady, will take as her husband Mr. Maximilano A. Lino of Porto Novo. This wedding will certainly be a wedding that will attract a large number of attendants. Mr. and Mrs. J. A. Campos are well known and well respected in the community. And furthermore, Mr. Lino de Porto Novo, is a friend of Mrs. W. W. Lewis and of Mrs. George Smith of Carvalho Hall.

In other sections of the newspapers we can read that on April 8, 1896:

Miss Maria Francisca Ramos wishes to acknowledge that through their letters and visits, they have helped her overcome her sadness due to the recent death of her mother, "Madame" Luiza Antonia de la Purificación.

There was a certain hostility between Protestants and Catholics in Lagos (Anglo-Saxons versus Latin Americans), according to an article that appeared in the *Lagos Times* on August 18, 1891:

The selection of Father Chausse as Bishop of the Yoruba diocese, recently formed by the Pope, has been announced. The Protestants of the Yoruba mission, who have faced grave difficulties with regard to the resurgence of Mohammedanism and stubborn paganism, must also fight against the invincible enemy, the aggressive Roman Catholic. Unless we stop being Protestants, our attitude toward Roman Catholicism cannot be other than a declared hostility.

This rigid and sectarian attitude was in total contrast with the spirit of understanding that continues to exist, despite the strong position of Catholic missionaries in Africa, among the "Latin Americans," freed slaves who came from Brazil and Cuba, in whom religious syncretism had produced an equal respect for the teachings of the Catholic Church and the beliefs they had inherited from their African ancestors. This tendency to accept various religions was so ingrained that it continues to this day. Such was the case with the Bahians who attached themselves simultaneously, and with equal sincerity, to Catholicism and Islam.[18] This same juxtaposition of the two religions, intransigent and mutually exclusive, is found again in the descendants of the "Latin Americans" who came from Africa, where some families bear Brazilian names, and are in part Catholic and part Moslem. Their children, at birth, were given names deriving from both religions, and to these they themselves added names inspired by their traditional beliefs, thus giving the world a lesson in wisdom and tolerance.

NOTES

1. Gilberto Freyre, *Problemas brasileros de antropologia* (Río de Janeiro, 1959), p. 27.

2. Pierre Verger, "Influence du Brésil au Golfe du Bénin," *Memoire de L'IFAN,* num. 27 (Dakar, 1953), p. 614.

3. Freyre, *Em torno de alguns tumulos Afrocristãos* (Bahía, 1960), p. 267.

4. Vianna, p. 105.

5. John Duncan, *Travels in Western Africa* (London, 1847), vol. 2, p. 176.

6. Elysée Réclus, *Nouvelle geographie universelle* (Paris, 1887), p. 470.

7. Duncan, vol. 1, p. 201.

8. Francisco Borghero, "Relations sur l'établissement des missions dans le vicariat apostolique du Dahomey," *Annales de la Propagation de la Foi* (Lyons, 1864), p. 440.

9. Abbé Laffite, *Le pays des nègres,* (Tours, 1876), p. 46.

10. Richard F. Burton, *A Mission to Gelele, King of Dahomé* (London, 1864), p. 72.

11. Réclus, p. 471.

12. Prince de Joinville, *Vieux souvenirs, 1818–1848* (Paris, 1894), p. 345.

13. F. E. Forbes, *Dahomey and the Dahomans* (London, 1851) vol. 1, p. 124.

14. Duncan, vol. 1, p. 137.

15. Duncan, p. 185, vol. 1.

16. Verger, "Influence du Bresil," pp. 25–27.

17. Verger, "Flux et reflux," p. 627.

18. Ibid., p. 520.

13

Africa *of* Latin America:
An Unguarded Reflection

SIDNEY W. MINTZ

Against the continuums of time and space, scientists and humanists alike project their constructions of reality, dividing what is really indivisible, and thereby labeling and freezing an elusive and particular truth with their invented categories. We speak of "the Old World" and "the New World," of "feudalism" and "capitalism," of "free labor" and "slave labor," and of "the past" and "the present." At the same time, we concede at the outset the arbitrariness and artificiality of our procedures, seeking to employ considered judgment in interpreting events, in the hope thereby of revealing more of a complex reality, rather than of concealing it. Our reifications of that reality ought to make things clearer, precisely because we recognize them as artifices, as stratagems of research. Interpretations of the past and present of entire societies, economic systems, or cultures are, in these terms, never complete or definitive, but only more or less useful, to the extent that they make sense of "the facts" by establishing or demonstrating relationships among those facts. Such, at any rate, is the perspective used in the following presentation.

To address in general terms the theme of "Africa in Latin America" is to confront one of the most massive, dramatic, and tortured chapters in human history. Any serious attempt to summarize or to interpret this total phenomenon, which involved millions of persons, whole continents, and deeply disturbing economic, political, and social transformations affecting hundreds of different societies, would be the work of many lifetimes. The present paper does not pretend to more than a sketchy and personal overview of certain limited aspects of this grand theme.[1]

Between the first years of the sixteenth century and the final abolition of slavery in Cuba (1886) and Brazil (1888), an estimated 9,200,000 enslaved Africans (Curtin 1969: 268) and perhaps 50,000 free or emancipated Africans (Laurence 1971: 14; Aimes 1907: 236–37) reached the New World. The estimate of more than nine million imported African slaves is based on Curtin's careful examination of available published sources; he readily admits that all such figures are subject to substantial error, and he expects them to be revised in the future, in accord with the findings of other scholars.[2]

This unimaginably vast movement of peoples across the Atlantic was incident to one of the clearest turning-points in world history: the first of the classic divisions with which the present article intends to deal. The so-called "Discovery" of the New World is as much a benchmark in the chronicle of humanity as was the control of fire, the domestication of plants and animals, or the mastery of fossil fuel or nuclear power. When López de Gomara, addressing himself to Charles V in 1552, asserted that, after the Creation and the coming of Christ, the most important event in history had been the discovery of the New World, he was only proclaiming what most informed Europeans of that epoch would have freely conceded (Hanke 1959: 2–3, 124).

The incorporation of the New World into European consciousness had, among many others, two major dimensions which require our notice immediately. First of all, it marked the emergence of what Konetzke (1946: 9) called "planetary" empires, spanning whole oceans, and a shift from the "thalassic" (Mediterranean) orientation of Europe to the "oceanic" (Atlantic) orientation that was to dominate the external expansion from the European heartland for centuries after. Second, the Discovery coincided with—indeed, facilitated—the beginnings of what Wallerstein (1974a) has aptly named "the modern world-economy." In Wallerstein's formulation, it was not the political enlargement of the European imperium that marked the change, so much as the emergence of a single economic system that could exceed and transcend political boundaries. That economic system was capitalism, and its appearance, spread, and consolidation, beginning in the sixteenth century, has been a many-sided and intricate phenomenon. It seems impossible to this writer to discuss the meaning of Africa in the Americas without attending the significance of these two dimensions, expressed both geographically and historically upon an immense canvas, one that encompassed not only the whole New World itself, but Europe and Africa as well (Mintz 1977).

The guiding institution embodied in the capture, sale, transportation, and exploitation of more than nine million persons and their descendants, stretching over nearly four centuries, was slavery, and the political, military, and economic conditions for its institutionalization and perpetuation. The relationship of the slaves to the means of production is easily differentiated—at first glance—from those relations of production conventionally associated with the capitalist system. The existence of a labor force with no access to the means of production other than by the sale of labor power—a proletariat, in short—is regarded as a keystone in any adequate description of the capitalist mode of production. Marx himself was very explicit on this point, and his view has been accepted by many distinguished students of European history. The "secret" of primitive accumulation consisted of ". . . nothing else than the historical process of divorcing the producer from the means of production" (Marx 1938 [1867]: 738).

But the expansion of European capitalism involved the assimilation to homeland objectives of societies and peoples not yet part of the capitalist system, by a variety of techniques that do not fit easily within a definition of the capitalist mode of production. Though his interest in the world outside Europe was of necessity secondary to his objective of demystifying and unmasking the evolution of capitalism in Europe itself, Marx was aware of this problem:

> The discovery of gold and silver in America, the extirpation, enslavement and entombment in mines of the aboriginal population, the beginning of the conquest and looting of the East Indies, the turning of Africa into a warren for the commercial hunting of Black-skins, characterized the rosy dawn of the era of capitalist production. These idyllic proceedings are the chief momenta of primitive accumulation. . . .
>
> The different momenta of primitive accumulation distribute themselves now, more or less in chronological order, particularly over Spain, Portugal, Holland, France, and England. In England at the end of the seventeenth century, they arrive at a systematical combination, embracing the colonies, the national debt, the modern mode of taxation, and the protectionist system. These methods depend in part on brute force, *e.g.,* the colonial system. But they all employ the power of the State, the concentrated and organised force of society, to hasten, hothouse fashion, the process of transformation of the feudal mode of production into the capitalist mode, and to shorten the transition. Force is the midwife of every society pregnant with a new one. It is itself an economic power.
>
> Whilst the cotton industry introduced child-slavery in England, it gave in the United States a stimulus to the transformation of the earlier, more or less patriarchal slavery, into a system of commercial exploitation. In fact, the veiled slavery of the wage-workers in Europe needed, for its pedestal, slavery pure and simple in the new world" (Marx 1938 [1867]: 775–785, *passim*).

The slavery of Africans in the New World, then, was neither a harking-back to Rome or Carthage, nor merely "slave society" (Genovese 1965) or "plantation economy" (Mandle 1972). In the present writer's view, it was an essential, *intrinsic* component of European capitalism:

> The point is that the "relations of production" that define a system are the "relations of production" of the whole system, and the system at this point in time [the sixteenth century] is the European world-economy. Free labor is indeed a defining feature of capitalism, but not free labor throughout the productive enterprises. Free labor is the form of labor control used for skilled work in core countries whereas coerced labor is used for less skilled work in peripheral areas. The combination thereof is the essence of capitalism. [Wallerstein 1974b: 127]

Such an assertion, with which the present writer finds himself in substantial agreement, derives some justification textually in Marx:

> Freedom and slavery constitute an antagonism. . . . We are not dealing with indirect slavery, the slavery of the proletariat, but with direct slavery, the slavery of the black races in Surinam, in Brazil, in the Southern States in North America. Direct slavery is as much the pivot of our industrialism today as machinery, credit, etc. Without slavery, no cotton; without cotton no modern industry. Slavery has given their value to the colonies; the colonies have created world trade; world trade is the necessary condition of large-scale machine industry. Before the traffic in Negroes began, the colonies only supplied the Old World with very few products and made no visible change in the face of the earth. Slavery is thus an economic category of the highest importance. [1968 (1846): 675]

But if slavery was indeed an economic category of the highest importance; if world trade is *the necessary condition* of large-scale machine industry; then what is the origin, *within* capitalism, of a subsystem of production typified by forced, rather than "free" and proletarianized labor? The answer to this question lies in the peculiar form of relationship between the New World colonies, where slavery would flourish, and the European metropolises. That relationship grew upon the basis of the land-labor ratio particularly typical of the subtropical, coastal regions of the New World.[3]

Students of comparative slavery institutions have sought the origins of slavery in the nature of the land-labor ratio (*e.g.*, Nieboer 1900, Thompson 1932). Other scholars have asserted with reason that this ratio does not explain the *origins* or *presence* of slavery, so much as reveal a basic relationship within which slavery could constitute a "solution" (Domar 1970, Engerman 1973). In the case of those parts of the New World of preliminary concern to us here—the Atlantic coast from Mexico to Brazil, the Antillean islands, and also the southern colonies of North America, in particular—pioneer settlement by the Europeans occurred under conditions either of sparse aboriginal populations, or of the swift genocide of the aborigines. Production by slaves was not an inevitable consequence of the low land-labor ratio, but of that ratio in situations where (1) an effective closure of the frontier to pioneer settlement by free persons was not feasible; (2) police power adequate to the legal-military containment of population was unavailable; and (3) "surplus" population for labor power was obtainable at an acceptable market price elsewhere.

Under different conditions, the European entrepreneur had been able to employ free but needful and landless workers as wage earners in order to garner a profit; or to purchase and resell commodities produced by peasant cultivators at a profit, by turning the terms of trade against the peasantry; or to rent or to lend at interest scarce resources (land, capital, tools, etc.) to independent producers, both agricultural and nonagricultural. But these entrepreneurial alternatives ultimately depend upon either an effective artificial scarcity of needed resources, such as land; the real scarcity of such resources, due to a prior primary accumulation of capital in the region itself (keeping in mind that "capital" *ultimately* is ". . . not a thing, but a social relation between persons, established through the instrumentality of things" (Marx 1938 [1867]: 791); and/or the presence of a large landless and free population competing in the sale of its labor. It is in the presence of the conditions enumerated in the preceding paragraph, and in the absence of the conditions just mentioned, that slavery may become a "natural" or "expectable" solution for the capitalist investor (cf. Mintz 1977).

Though enslaved Africans and their descendants were employed in a very wide spectrum of activities in the New World situation, the primary use made of their labor was in the production of basic commodities for European consumer markets. It is in the nature of those commodities, and in the classic form of agrosocial organization by which they were produced, that the intimate linkage between urban European factory proletarians and rural American plantation slaves is to be found. The growth and expansion of the plantation system was unmistakably linked, from the very first moments of its establishment in the New World, to mass European markets. To take but a single illustration, both the prices and the absolute quantities of sugar produced in the colonies of the Americas by slave labor between the sixteenth and nineteenth centuries reveal the transformation of sugar from a medicine and preservative of European royalty into a fundamental food substitute of the European masses (Mintz 1966, 1979). Sugar, however, was but one such item; a full list would certainly include tobacco, rum, cocoa, and coffee. It is no accident that sugar from the Antilles, the Guianas, and Brazil, as well as elsewhere in Latin America, should have become combined with tea from India in the "food" *par excellence* of British factory workers and miners; they were chained to their machines and their coal pits as firmly as the Indian tea-pickers to their tea-groves, and the Latin American and Antillean slaves to their canefields and sugar mills. Between 1700 and 1809, the *per capita* consumption of sugar in the United Kingdom rose from *four* pounds to *eighteen* pounds (Deerr 1950 [II]: 532), even while its population was increasing by nearly two thirds. During almost the identical period— 1700–1800—tea consumption in the United Kingdom rose from 167,000 pounds to more than 23 *million* pounds (Sheridan 1974: 21)! To note that neither of these productions, one in the New World and the other in the Old, was accomplished with proletarian laborers should not permit us to ignore that they were *consumed* by proletarian laborers, and that the profits from such production helped to fuel in many different ways the engines of capitalism in the European heartland.[4]

A backward glance at Europe of the fifteenth century reveals, however, that the plantation system itself was not a New World innovation, so much as part of the untrammeled expansion of a form of production already tested and proved in the European periphery. Malowist (1969), in an excellent study of the Portuguese sugar plantations of São Tomé, off the Guinea Coast, demonstrates that these enterprises embodied all of the essential characteristics (as well as many of the ancillary features) of the New World plantation economy: European capital, seized or ceded land, substantial estates, enslaved African labor, European processing technology and management, monoculture, iron control of the slave population, and production destined for European consumer markets.

The plantation system, and slavery with it, went through a progression of developmental stages in the Americas; and while the system as a whole—and even slavery itself—may be treated as homogeneous, undifferentiated phenomena, particularistic historical studies (*e.g.*, Mintz 1953, Stein 1957, Moreno Fraginals 1964) reveal considerable diversity, both in time and in space. Among those many attempts to analyze differences among slave systems, some special attention may be given in passing to the now-famous Tannenbaum thesis (1947) that Catholicism, unlike Protestantism, granted a moral personality to the slave. The Tannenbaum argument rested upon ideological and institutional constraints, which were believed to have protected the slaves in the colonies of the Catholic powers.[5] His critics have often seen the major differences, however, in terms of the varying levels of capitalistic development of the metropolitan powers (and, accordingly, in different epochs, of their colonies), correlated with differing intensities of the slave systems themselves. The present writer's view is embodied in the following citation from earlier work:

> Especially important is the degree to which a particular mode of slavery is primarily economic, or embedded within a code of behavior such that the economic rationale is submerged or secondary. All slavery may be slavery, but not all slaveries are the same, economically or culturally.
>
> Through slavery, human beings, their labor, their lives—that is, their production and reproduction—are transformed into things. In capitalistic societies these things are commodities; in part-capitalistic societies they are part-commodities. Where the kind of social and technical organization is such that it is not possible readily to appropriate a worthwhile portion of the product of others by enslavement, the goals of slavery, when it occurs, will not be directed to the maximization of profit. Where servitude is total, the kind and degree of appropriation will vary, according to what the level of technical development and accompanying institutional apparatus, including the economic system, make possible. [Mintz 1961: 580].[6]

Each New World colony in which the labor of enslaved Africans figured importantly was tied politically and economically to a European society, in particular to sectors of its capitalist classes. After the Haitian and North American revolutions, such ties continued to influence significantly the nature of productive relations even in those New World societies; only Haiti—and by a long and tortuous process—was able to eliminate coerced labor before the legal abolition of slavery itself. The slave trade was abolished by Denmark in 1802, by England in 1808, by Sweden in 1813, by Holland and France in 1814, and by Spain in 1820; it continued "illegally" until after the middle of the nineteenth century. Slavery itself ended by revolution in Haiti, 1791–1804 (though plantation production on European-owned estates continued until substantially later); in the British colonies in 1834–1838; in the French islands in 1848; in the Dutch islands in 1863; in Puerto Rico in 1873–1876; in Cuba in 1882–1886; and in Brazil in 1888.

It would be premature and misleading to claim that the various slavery systems of these and other New World colonies can either be analyzed best by treating them merely as variants of a single definable institution, or by asserting that the differences among systems are so great as to preclude any effort to generalize about their functioning. In fact, it is not difficult to identify significant differences in the slavery institution at different periods in the history of a single colony; or among different slave groups in the same colony at one point in time. A presentation of the sort attempted here can do no more than point to some of the generalizations which, while commonly proposed, usually appear to crumble when tested against historical particulars. It no longer seems useful, for instance, to divide slavery systems into "Catholic" and "Protestant," or "North European" and "South European," categories (cf., for instance, Mintz 1961). It does not appear to follow that so-called "benign" slaveries necessarily led to enlightened race relations after emancipation, nor that so-called "malign" slaveries led to difficult race relations after emancipation (cf., for instance, Hoetink 1973). While the relative proportions of enslaved Africans and free Europeans undoubtedly influenced significantly the particular forms taken by slavery in specific colonies, the nature of that significance is not yet fully understood (Mörner 1973). In fact, most generalizations of these kinds must still be tested against historical particulars, and it may be expected that this will eventually result in sweeping revisions of nearly all such generalizations.

The slave trade had its heaviest impact in Africa itself on the peoples and societies of West Africa, broadly defined. But both the volume and the locus of the trade shifted, according to the policies of the slave-trading powers, the waxing and waning of particular plantation colonies, and the diplomacy of the trade itself. Immense difficulties face that scholar of the slave trade and of slavery in the Americas who is interested in cultural continuities and discontinuities. Earlier and more general interpretations of continuities of the African tradition, which held that particular New World colonies and societies could be linked unmistakably to specific

African civilizations, have not been easy to sustain. In the case of Saint Domingue, for instance, it has often been contended that Dahoman culture formed a core around which Haitian culture took on its characteristic shape (Herskovits 1937: 25 *et seq.*, Hall 1971, Hurbon 1972), while Jamaican culture has sometimes been seen primarily as a rendering of Akan-Ashanti civilization, merely reordered in a new form.

Such tribal-specific attributions constitute a questionable solution to the problems of Afro-American culture growth (Mintz and Price 1970), and seem to suffer from two principal difficulties. First, they tend to be ahistorical, to the extent that they contain an implicit assumption that African cultures of the twentieth century have not changed significantly since the heyday of the slave trade, such that similarities revealed by comparisons between contemporary Afro-American and African societies can be treated as certain evidence of historical connection. Second, they pay too little attention to the processes of culture change, to the immense importance of the innovativeness and adaptability of enslaved Africans in the New World, and to the special challenges posed by enslavement, transportation, and the needs for adjustment to completely unfamiliar settings.

An alternative approach to the problems of Afro-American culture growth, rather than imputing culture-specific continuities between African and Afro-American societies, takes as its starting point the concept of a common (West African) cultural substratum (Herskovits 1941), upon which the specific cultural manifestations of any particular African people or nation—Dahomey, Ashanti, or whatever—may be seen as a local variant built upon deep common unity or, as Herskovits himself once put it (1941: 81), that there is a genuine analogy between the "similarities in the grammar of language over the entire West African region . . . [and] what may be termed the grammar of cultures." If we are prepared to assume that significant but nonetheless subtle, even unconscious, *common* patterning of values and beliefs underlay the cultures of the majority of those millions of enslaved Africans brought to the New World, then the task of retrieving those patterns for analysis and comparison is a serious and important one. It is made even more serious because the presence of easily apprehendable links between an African and an Afro-American culture—as in the use in Haitian culture of unmistakably African lexical items, such as *marassa, akasan, afiba,* etc.; tribal and place names, such as *Congo* and *Guinée;* and gods' names (Shango, Legba, Damballa, etc.)—may predispose the scholar to pass over or ignore features that are at once more fundamental, but more disguised and more difficult to elicit. To offer but one illustration, Price and Price (1972) have demonstrated in the case of Afro-American naming systems that surface manifestations (*e.g.,* specific "African" names, such as Cudjoe, Quashie, or Quaco) and subsurface manifestations (*e.g.,* the use of names to epitomize events, character and values) may both be attributable to the African past, but do not necessarily travel together in a single Afro-American culture. Their argument is relevant enough to deserve quotation at some length:

> . . . it may be necessary to stress that a system with a relatively high proportion of "African" names can be less similar to West African systems on a fundamental level than a system which retains fewer such names. We would argue that even the Gullah [Georgia and South Carolina] system, in which locally used names are "nearly always a word of African origin" (Turner 1949: 40), may be less "African" in an important sense than the Saramaka [Suriname] system, in which only about one-sixth of names are lexically African. Might it not be that the dynamism and creativity of a cultural tradition developed with minimal Western influence have allowed the Saramaka to be mildly prodigal with their gradually declining pool of lexically African names, yet more faithful to West African naming principles at a deeper level? [Price and Price 1972: 362]

It is the determination of those "deeper" principles that poses for the student of Afro-American civilizations one of the most difficult problems in methodology and in theory. Surface manifestations of African origins are no less African by virtue of being obvious. But they have too often been used as the only measures of the degree of "African-ness" or as sufficient evidence in themselves that deeper-lying and more fundamental features were necessarily present. In fact, surface manifestations (such as the presence of provably African lexemes) may or may not be the "most African" of surviving features; *their absence* may distract scholars from the presence of much more fundamental, but subtler, materials of African origin.

As Price and Price have pointed out, this line of argument resembles that advanced by Bastide (1967: 133–135), in dividing Afro-American religions into those he calls *"en conserve"* (such as *candomblé* and *santería*) and those he calls *vivants* (such as Haitian *vodū*). The former seem to involve a commitment to the total preservation of some African cultural segment, for fear that any change may destroy the integration of the subsystem; the latter leaves room for greater modification, without fear that progressive changes will erode the more fundamental African orientation of the subsystem as a whole. Price and Price conclude (1972: 362–63):

> If students of the African heritage in the Americas were to turn their attention more fully to the delineation of higher-level cultural rules or deeper structure, it might be found that the more dynamic, "African" systems generate forms in some domains which are less readily traceable to specific West African sources than do the more defensive, retentive ones. But, of course, the identification of such "rules" has barely begun.

Thus the question of Africanisms, though it has long attracted the attention of scholars of Afro-America, is now being reopened on a new and more sophisticated level of discourse. The "obviously African" may eventually turn out to demonstrate less about the retention of tradition than the more modified and less immediately identifiable aspects of culture. As in the case of names and religious usages, Afro-American language study is entering a new phase as well. Creole languages, once regarded as mere "simplifications" of European idioms (as revealed in their metropolitan labels, such as *Sklavensprachen, petit-nègre,* "jargon," and *Kauderwelsch*), with some concession to the possible presence of some African syntactic forms, are now being reexamined with much more care and reflection and, in some clear instances, the presence of even more telling features of African provenance than words is being demonstrated (*e.g.,* Taylor 1956, Allsopp 1970, Hymes 1971, Alleyne 1980).

These research trends attest to the innovative vitality, the creativity and strength of the African past. What they add to previous studies of the Afro-American heritage is a deeper respect for care and prudence in research, a more conscious historical orientation, and an understanding of the importance of the comparative approach in reconstructive analysis. They also add a fuller understanding of the toughness and intelligence of those millions of enslaved people who built their new ways of life under conditions of almost unremitting repression.

We who are Americans in the hemispheric sense rarely experience our common destiny, as contrasted to Old World peoples. But we of this hemisphere are peoples whose ways of life share the common quality of a foreign past (Mintz 1974a). We live in societies and bear cultures whose origins are elsewhere, transformed by the migrations of our ancestors and by the novel challenges imposed upon them by a world which became, in complete ethnocentric innocence, "new" in 1492. Today, the consequences of transplantation and of adjustment during nearly five full centuries define us, even those of us who are descended from Native Americans.

But the special meaning of being American has never united all of the peoples of the Americas. Instead, other priorities of consciousness—of region, of nation, of language, of "race," of religion, of class—have always laid first claim upon our identities. A major distinction that has consistently intruded upon any generalized American identity is that between what is called "Latin America" and what may be called—for convenience only—"Anglo America" or "Anglo-Saxon America." For convenience only, because there is no convincing criterion—even geography—according to which we can confidently refer to Jamaica or Haiti, for instance, as parts of either "Anglo-Saxon America" or "Latin America." In fact, the major basis for dividing the Americas in two is economic and political, not social and cultural: since the start of the nineteenth century, the grossest division has been between the United States on the one hand, and the rest of the Americas on the other.

It has been the habit of some North American historians of Latin America to view the history of that culture sphere as consisting of four periods: the aboriginal or preconquest period; the conquest and colonial period; the so-called republican period; and the modern period. Contained within this deceptively commonsensical formulation, however, is an important feature of the North American bias. If Wallerstein's conception of the world-economy is accepted, then the so-called "colonial" period is differentiated from the so-called "republican" period by the fact that North American political and economic power made their most telling penetrations into Latin American life *after* political independence was achieved in Latin America. The retreat of Spain (and, to a lesser degree, of her European competitors) from Latin America was not the unexpected creation of a vacuum of power, but rather the yielding of the weakened European metropolises to North American expansionist pressures. That these pressures were not fully felt until after the Civil War in the United States does not alter the fact that the Monroe Doctrine, which underlined North American claims on the hemisphere, was promulgated within twenty-five years of the founding of the North American republic. Accordingly, the study of any aspect of Latin American history and culture must involve a recognition of the satellite geopolitical status of most of Latin America. More tellingly demonstrated in the Caribbean region than elsewhere, perhaps, the overwhelming presence of the United States has been felt by her neighbors throughout the hemisphere for two hundred years.[7]

But the North American presence is simply a background feature of the Latin American cultural landscape. The place of Afro-Americans is not defined by that presence, so much as by the particular social and economic histories of the societies within which they live. The present character of hemispheric Afro-America represents the end-product of lengthy centuries of sociocultural change, in which Afro-Americans were not simply the unwitting and passive subjects of external processes, but often, and instead, active agents of change themselves. We have already stressed the creative character of the evolution of Afro-American cultures. In the study of Creole languages, syncretic religions, or other cultural subsystems, too little attention has been paid to the analysis of specific processes of change, and rather too much to a simplistic identification of the historical origins of particular elements. What is intrinsically more interesting scientifically (and perhaps aesthetically, as well) than the "blending" of African and European elements in Afro-Cuban belief, for instance, is the system of underlying values and perceptions, and the particular local conditions, according to which that particular "mixture," rather than some other, took on its characteristic form. The same may be true of studies of material culture, art, folklore, and all else that is definably Afro-American.

Such an emphasis may be judged ahistorical or even anti-African, in seeming to put more weight upon the mechanisms of change than upon cultural continuity. Such a judgment, however, misses the point of inquiry. Social groups the members of which define themselves as Afro-American, or who are so perceived by others in the same society, may be allocated socially according to physical traits, cultural features (including linguistic features), or both physical and cultural traits, seen either as interlocked or as separate. The particular position of such groups within any New World society is an historical product; in some cases, their members may be arranged within a socioeconomic subsystem that is parallel to—and may overlap with—the subsystems for European and other groups of the same society. But we are still far from being able to identify common or differentiating characteristics among these different whole systems. Hence, the attempt to describe the socioracial structures of American societies as belonging to a single class—as in claiming that economic features take precedence over physical traits, making a "Black" person White and a "White" person Black—appears to be a fundamental misunderstanding of the variety, changing character, and symbolic complexity of systems of social allocation.

Much as the origins of Afro-American culture cannot be properly studied without attending to the *particular integration* of its elements and the *symbolic significance* of cultural content in each case, so the position of Afro-American groups within American societies cannot be grasped without specifying the characteristic features of each social system, and the peculiar symbolic integration of such features for those concerned. In spite of the broad common characteristics that we may interpret as characteristically Latin American, each Latin American society has its distinctive identity. In much the same way, the groups that might be called Afro-Latin within Latin America express in each instance something of the national socioracial structure within which they are located. Little useful purpose is served by ignoring their distinctive characteristics in order to posit generalities which, however great their breadth, quite lack historical depth. The same distinctiveness and peculiarity typifies, of course, the United States and its Afro-American citizens. Hence an objection is advanced here of the sort that was earlier raised against the blanket distinction between slaveholding Catholic and Protestant powers. While that distinction has a preliminary classificatory utility, and indeed may express a deeper difference, it is probably best laid aside for the moment, in order better to examine specific historical periods. The changing position of Afro-Americans in a society such as Mexico or Cuba, over time, reveals more of social process than does any assertion about the common character of Afro-American culture.

Whatever the details in particular historical periods and in particular American societies, the discriminatory exclusion of persons of African origin from the mainstream of national life has been a depressingly consistent theme in the history of the New World. The recognition by social scientists and writers alike of this exclusion has led, over time, to the development of a theory of marginalization, which seeks to take into account the adaptation of Afro-Americans to continuous discrimination (*e.g.,* Whitten and Szwed 1970, and the essays in Gräbener 1971). That persons and groups of African origin are the targets of discrimination, subtle or overt, throughout the Americas, hardly needs to be proved; the theory of marginalization seeks to deal with this discrimination as a part of social reality.

But it is perhaps worth stressing that some risk is run in viewing the position of Afro-American peoples as defined by their marginality. Such peoples are marginal from the point of view of their access to full participation in society, or to the benefits of citizenship. They are not, however, marginal from the point of view of their contribution to the economic order. In fact, their marginality as citizens is a function of racist politics; their disproportionate economic contribution to their societies is a function of the very same politics. The role of Afro-American peoples in providing shamefully cheap labor (for instance, the bulk of plantation labor and of domestic labor) to others of greater privilege represents an enormous saving to members of other classes in the same society. Their confinement in manual labor makes available many better jobs for others. In these and in other ways, the role of the poor Afro-American is not in the slightest marginal, but is instead an important, at times even essential, feature of the economic organization of racist societies.

No better illustration of this thesis can be provided than the immense migration of Caribbean peoples to the urban centers of North America in recent decades. The development of an international, "portable" supply of cheap labor has accompanied the growth of relatively inexpensive air transportation. In fact, this labor now pays for its own transportation. The movement of Haitians, Jamaicans, Dominicans, Puerto Ricans, etc. to the mainland United States has simultaneously intensified the struggle for work in that country, while reducing the overall average cost of labor at the lowest levels of skill. That many of the migrants are "illegal" entries increases their accessibility and defenselessness, and lowers their price. The same process (though usually less extreme) can be seen in many Latin American countries; and the same rules which apply to Afro-American persons in one country may be applied equally well to persons of Amerindian (or other non-White) origin in another.

It is for these reasons that the concept of marginalization deserves to be employed with some care. The assertion that persons of African origin in the United States are of little economic value to that economy—predicated on the movement of Afro-Americans to the cities, their presence on the relief rolls, their fecundity, etc.—while usually advanced with an air of compassion, should not be permitted to conceal the intense economic exploitation of which these same persons are the prime targets. Anthropologists and sociologists in particular need to remember that marginalization has not meant the exclusion of Afro-Americans from their role either as victims or as creators of surplus value.

This essay has sought to enumerate several characteristics of the history and study of Afro-American peoples that have not always been taken into account. Though impressionistic in character, it may indicate some research directions of use to others. The study of Africa in Latin America, and *of* Latin America, forms an important part of the saga of the modern world, with particular reference to the creation of planetary empires, the expansion of Europe, and the appearance and maturation of capitalism as an economic system transcending national boundaries. The principal motive force behind the enslavement and transportation of African peoples—while by no means the only such force—was the development of the plantation system in the American colonies for the production of staples for the mass consumer markets of Europe. A central problem in the study of the role of Afro-American peoples in this development is that of the relationship between European overseas enterprise based on forced labor, and the heartland of European capitalism.

Afro-American peoples were forced to reconstitute their social forms and their cultures for the most part—though not always—while living as forced laborers.[8] The role of the African past is that reconstruction was—and remains—vitally important. But a simplistic tracing of elements of African origin, or a mere reasoning by analogy with the cultures of contemporary African societies, is less important scientifically than the study of the particular integrations and symbolic forms developed by New World peoples in the consolidation of new societies.

Africa in Latin America, and of Latin America, has taken on its differentiated and complex character in the shadow of North American power. What is more, Afro-American peoples have always had to cope with the particular disadvantages imposed upon them by local codes of discrimination and exclusion. At the same time, this exclusion has not diminished, but has instead increased, the proportionate economic contribution they have perforce made to the well-being and wealth of the racist societies of which they have been a part. Indeed, Afro-American peoples have had to adapt themselves to their oppression; but this has neither meant that their role as a source of profit has declined, nor that their creativity has reduced their oppression. In the modern era, the countries of Latin America, like those of Africa and Asia, have increased their contribution to the developed world by migrating to its centers. Thus, in New York as in Paris, London, and Amsterdam, the poorest segments of the colonial social structure are now contributing anew and more immediately to the easement of life for others in the metropolis.

The ultimate political implications of this demographic movement, now assuming substantial proportions,[9] are not yet fully grasped, and cannot be wholly predicted. Nonetheless, in the case of Afro-American peoples, it is already clear that the United States is undergoing a process of urban "Afro-Latinization" on a substantial scale, with no indication of a reversal of the trend in the near future. This subject, however, exceeds the concerns of the present paper. It is hoped that students of Africa in Latin America will keep in mind, however, that the cultures of those whom they study are vibrant, inexhaustible phenomena; if five centuries of direct oppression have not crushed them, it will take more than the modern world to erase their distinctive character.

NOTES

1. Among the works essential to the study of this subject, one can mention Herskovits 1941, Ramos 1943, Franco 1961 and 1968, Bastide 1961, Davis 1966, and Price 1973. Papers by Herskovits 1930, Bastien 1969, Mintz 1970b and 1971, and Unesco 1970, throw some additional general light upon the problems of the study of Africa in Latin America, as does Mintz and Price 1976. It is not feasible, however, to include more than occasional bibliographical references of this kind in the present paper.

2. Of the risks of such calculations, Curtin (1969: xviii) writes:

> One danger in stating numbers is to find them quoted later with a degree of certitude that was never intended. This is particularly true when the percentages are carried to tenths of 1 percent, whereas *in fact the hoped-for range of accuracy may be plus or minus 20 percent of actuality. Let it be said at the outset, then, that most of the quantities that follow are wrong.* They are not intended to be precise as given, only approximations where a result falling within 20 percent of actuality is a "right" answer—that is, a successful result, given the quality of the underlying data. It should be also understood that some estimates will not even reach that standard of accuracy. They are given only as the most probable figures at the present state of knowledge" [italics added].

To which we may only say that this issue, like many to be raised in this paper, has an important political coefficient. Curtin suggests that the scholar whose estimates he finds most persuasive (Deerr 1949) was seriously overestimating importations to the United States. Deerr believed that the total importation was 2,920,000; Curtin thinks it was 399,000; for the period 1800–1861, Deerr estimated *one million,* while Curtin believes it was *54,000!* We may be sure that Curtin's downward revisions will be employed for political objectives at least as eagerly as were many earlier and much higher estimates, and this in spite of Curtin's own very great caution (Mintz 1972).

3. In this interpretation, I am stressing—and perhaps exaggerating—the extent to which the institution of slavery in the New World, which had its post-Columbian origins in Europe itself, was revealed in particular relationship to the development of the plantation system in the Americas. As we shall see, African slaves and their descendants were employed in many other ways, for many other purposes, and not solely in commercial agriculture. Nonetheless, the basic, essential and most important goals of the enslavement of Africans had to do with the development of that agriculture, to which even the use of slaves in mining enterprises, militias, as personal servants, as subalterns to the conquistadores, etc., were all secondary. The institution of slavery was *perfected* in the core area stretching from the south of what became the United States through what is today northern Brazil. Its expressions in other forms, and elsewhere in the hemisphere, while very important, were nonetheless peripheral, in my view, to this development.

4. This is not the place to review the now-lengthy and voluminous controversy concerning the specific contribution of the colonies to the economic development of the metropolises. The argument goes back to Smith 1937 [1776], Merivale 1841, Wakefield 1914 [1849], and Marx 1938 [1867], among others. Recent contributors have included Williams 1944 and, even more recently, Sheridan 1974, Anstey 1975, and Engerman 1972. While the *direct* contribution of the plantation economy to European economic growth may have been as modest as Engerman contends, it is not possible at this time to evaluate convincingly the indirect contribution (*e.g.*, through reinvestment, the freeing-up of the labor supply in nonplantation areas, etc.), nor to refute the argument I am presenting here: that plantation slave labor provided high-energy, low-cost, food substitutes to the European proletariat, and thus constituted an immense saving to European capitalism.

5. Like many other issues, this cannot be treated with the seriousness it deserves in a paper of this sort. Interested readers may wish to examine some part of the substantial literature that has accumulated concerning the relative importance of "ideological" and "economic" factors in affecting the treatment of slaves and freedmen. Among the most thought-provoking books and articles, we may mention Genovese 1967 and 1968, Harris 1964, Davis 1966, and Lane *et al.* 1971.

6. This formulation has been received with varying degrees of enthusiasm or criticism. Genovese (1968) is attracted; though a more extreme rendering by me elsewhere (Mintz 1974a) has made him more critical (Genovese 1975). Tolentino, who cites this passage (Tolentino 1974: 143), inclines to the view—at least by implication—that "systems" can be either capitalistic or not. But it is not clear from his interpretation, however, how the problems of transition from one mode of production to another are to be handled conceptually, nor how to interpret Marx's construction of a "dominant" mode of production. Bagú (1969) takes a position that this writer finds somewhat simplistic, but more congenial; see also Williams 1944, Wolf 1966, and Frank 1966.

7. Bryce Wood writes:

> On no less than twenty separate occasions between 1898 and 1920, United States Marines or soldiers entered the territory of states in the Caribbean area. It should not be surprising that a certain sense of the normality, and even of the propriety of calling on the Marines, should have persisted beyond 1920, independently of the nature of the formal justification for such action; it was an habitual, nearly automatic re-

sponse to "disturbed conditions" or "utter chaos" in a Caribbean country. [Wood 1961: 5]

To which one can add only that the situation can hardly be said to have improved significantly since 1920—with the very important exception that socialist Cuba has withstood repeated attempts to subvert its government by force.

8. Because no sketch of this kind can deal with many different themes, the whole issue of resistance by Afro-Latin peoples has been omitted, even though it is of course extremely important. The author has dealt with this theme at substantial length elsewhere (Mintz 1971 and 1974a). The literature on runaway slave communities and on slave revolts has been growing rapidly. Especially useful for an overview of the maroon saga is Price 1973.

9. Relatively little of an anlytical kind has been published on the movement of non-White Latin Americans to the United States, but cf. Bryce-Laporte 1972. For a useful contemporary summary on non-White Caribbean migrants, cf. Domínguez 1975; the theme is touched upon as well in Mintz 1974b.

BIBLIOGRAPHY

Aimes, Hubert H. S. *A History of Slavery in Cuba*. New York, G. P. Putnam's Sons, 1907. iv, 298 p., bibliogr., index.

Alleyne, Mervyn C. *Comparative Afro-American*. Ann Arbor, Karoma, 1980.

Allsopp, Richard. A critical commentary on the *Dictionary of Jamaican English*. *Caribbean Studies* (Río Piedras, Puerto Rico), vol. 10, no. 2, July 1970, pp. 90–112.

Bagú, Sergio. La economía de la sociedad colonial. *Pensamiento Crítico* (La Habana, Cuba), vol. 27, abril 1964, pp. 30–65.

Bastide, Roger. *Les Amériques Noires*. Paris, Payot, 1967. 236 p.

Bastien, Rémy. Estructura de la adaptación del negro en América Latina y del afroamericano en Africa. *América Indigéna* (Mexico City), vol. XXIX, no. 3, julio 1969, pp. 587–626.

Bryce-Laporte, Roy Simon. Black immigrants: the experience of invisibility and inequality. *Journal of Black Studies* (Beverly Hills, California), vol. 3, no. 1, September 1972, pp. 29–56.

Curtin, Philip D. *The Atlantic Slave Trade: A Census*. Madison, Wisconsin, The University of Wisconsin Press, 1969. xix, 338 p., tables, bibliogr., index.

Davis, David B. *The Problem of Slavery in Western Culture*. Ithaca, New York, Cornell University Press, 1966. xi, 493 p., index.

Deerr, Noel. *The History of Sugar*. 2 vols. London, Chapman and Hall Ltd. [vol. 1, 1949], vol. 2, 1950. xiv, pp. 259–636, tables, illustr., index.

Domar, Evsey. The causes of slavery or serfdom: a hypothesis. *Journal of Economic History* (New York), vol. 30, no. 1, March 1970, pp. 18–32.

Domínguez, Virginia. *From Neighbor to Stranger: The Dilemma of Caribbean Migrants in the United States*. New Haven, Antilles Research Program, 1975. (Yale University Antilles Research Program Occasional Papers, 5). In Press.

Engerman, Stanley. The slave trade and British capital formation in the eighteenth century: a comment on the Williams thesis. *Business History Review* (Cambridge, Mass.), vol. 44, no. 4, winter 1972, pp. 430–43.

Engerman, Stanley. Some considerations relating to property rights in man. *Journal of Economic History* (New York), vol. 33, no. 1, March 1973, pp. 43–65.

Franco, José L. *Afroamérica*. La Habana, Publicaciones de le Junta Nacional de Arqueología y Etnología, 1961. 204 p.

Franco, José L. *La Presencia Negra en el Mundo Nuevo*. La Habana, Cuba, Casa de las Américas, 1968, 135 p. (Cuadernos de la Revista Casa de las Américas, 7).

Frank, A. Gunder. The Development of Underdevelopment. *Monthly Review* (New York), vol. 18, no. 4, September 1966, pp. 17–31.

Genovese, Eugene D. *The Political Economy of Slavery*. New York, Pantheon, 1965. xiv, 304 p., bibliogr., index.

Genovese, Eugene D. Materialism and Idealism in the History of Negro Slavery in the Americas. *Journal of Social History* (London), vol. 1, no. 4, fall 1968, pp. 371–394.

Genovese, Eugene D. *The World the Slaveholders Made*. New York, Pantheon, 1969. xii, 274 p., index.

Genovese, Eugene D. Class, Culture, and Historical Process. *Dialectical Anthropology* (Amsterdam), vol. 1, no. 1, pp. 71–79.

Gräbener, Jürgen, Hg. *Klassengesellschaft und Rassismus* [Class society and racism]. Düsseldorf, Bertelsmann Universitätsverlag, 1971. 342 p., bibliogr., indices.

Hall, Gwendolyn M. *Social Control in Slave Plantation Societies*. Baltimore, The Johns Hopkins University Press, 1971. xiii, 166 p., bibliogr., index.

Hanke, Lewis. *Aristotle and the American Indians*. London, Hollis and Carter, 1959. x, 164 p., appendices, index.

Herskovits, Melville J. The Negro in the New World: the statement of a problem. *American Anthropologist* (Menasha, Wisc.), vol. 32, no. 1, Jan.–Mar. 1930, pp. 145–155.

Herskovits, Melville J. *Life in a Haitian Valley*. New York, Knopf, 1937. xvi, 350, xix p., illustr., glossary, index.

Herskovits, Melville H. *The Myth of the Negro Past*. New York, Harper and Bros., 1941. xiv, 374 p., bibliogr., index.

Hoetink, Harry. *Slavery and Race Relations in the Americas*. New York, Harper and Row, 1973. viii, 232 p., bibliogr., index.

Hurbon, Laënnec. *Dieu dans le Vaudou haïtien*. Paris, Payot, 1972. 268 p., glossaire, bibiographie.

Hymes, Dell, (ed.). *Pidginization and Creolization of Languages*. Cambridge, Cambridge University Press, 1971. vii, 530 p., appendices, amp index.

Konetzke, Richard. *El Imperio Español*. Madrid, Ediciones Nueva Epoca, 1946. 298 p., illustr., ports., maps.

Lane, Ann, (ed.). *The Debate over Slavery*. Urbana, Illinois, University of Illinois Press, 1971. vi, 378 p.

Lawrence, K. O. *Immigration into the West Indies in the Nineteenth Century*. St. Lawrence, Barbados, Caribbean Universities Press, 1971. 83 p.

Malowist, Marian. Les débuts du système des plantations dans la période des grandes découvertes. *Africana Bulletin* (Warsaw), no. 10, 1969, pp. 9–30.

Mandle, Jay. The plantation economy: an essay in definition. *Science and Society* (New York), vol. 36, no. 1, Spring 1972, pp. 49–62.

Marx, Karl. *Capital*. London, Geo. Allen and Unwin Ltd., 1938 [1867]. xxxi, 882 p., bibliogr., index.

Marx, Karl. Letter to P. V. Annenkov, Dec. 28, 1846. In: *Karl Marx and Frederick Engels. Selected Works.* New York, International Publishers, 1968, pp. 669–679.

Merivale, Herman. *Lectures on Colonization and Colonies.* London: Longman, Orme, Brown, Green and Longmans, 1841. xv, 329 p., index.

Mintz, Sidney W. The culture history of a Puerto Rican sugar cane plantation, 1876–1949. *The Hispanic American Historical Review* (Durham, N.C.), vol. XXXIII, no. 2, May 1953, pp. 224–251.

Mintz, Sidney W. Review of Elkins, S., Slavery. In: *American Anthropologist* (Menasha, Wisc.), vol. 63, no. 3, June 1961, pp. 579–587.

Mintz, Sidney W. The Caribbean as a socio-cultural area. *Cahiers d'Histoire Mondiale* (Paris), vol. IX, no. 4, 1966, pp. 912–937.

Mintz, Sidney W. Foreword. In: Whitten, Norman E.; Szwed, J. (eds.). *Afro-American Anthropology.* New York, The Free Press, 1970 [1970a]. ix, 468 p., bibliogr., index.

Mintz, Sidney W. Creating culture in the Americas. *Columbia University Forum* (New York), vol. XIII, no. 1, Spring 1970 [1970b], pp. 4–11.

Mintz, Sidney W. Toward an Afro-American history. *Cahiers d'Histoire Mondiale* (Paris), vol. XIII, no. 2, 1971, pp. 317–332.

Mintz, Sidney W. Review of Curtin, P., *The Transatlantic Slave Trade: A Census.* In: *Caribbean Studies* (Rio Piedras, Puerto Rico), vol. 11, no. 4, January 1972, pp. 112–115.

Mintz, Sidney W. *Caribbean Transformations.* Chicago, Aldine, 1974 [1974a]. xii, 355 p., bibliogr., index.

Mintz, Sidney W. The Caribbean region. *Daedalus* (Cambridge, Mass.), vol. 103, no. 2, Spring 1974 [1974b], pp. 45–71.

Mintz, Sidney W. The so-called world system: local initiative and local response. *Dialectical Anthropology* (Amsterdam), vol. 2, 1977, pp. 253–270.

Mintz, Sidney W. Time, sugar and sweetness. *Marxist Perspectives* (New York), vol. II, Winter 1979–80, pp. 56–73.

Mintz, Sidney W.; Price, Richard. An anthropological approach to the study of Afro-American history: a Caribbean perspective. *ISHI Occasional Papers in Social Change.* Philadelphia, Pennsylvania, Institute for the Study of Human Issues, Inc., 1970. i–iii, 64 p., bibliogr.

Moreno Fraginals, Manuel. *El Ingenio. Tomo I (1760–1860).* La Habana, Comisión Nacional Cubana de la Unesco, 1964, xii, 196 p., indices.

Mörner, Magnus. Legal equality–social inequality: a post-abolition theme. *Revista Interamericana* (Hato Rey, Puerto Rico), vol. III, no. 1, pp. 24–41.

Nieboer, Herman J. *Slavery as an Industrial System.* The Hague, Martinus Nijhoff, 1900. xxvii, 480 p., bibliogr., index.

Price, Richard S. *Maroon Societies.* Garden City, New York, Anchor Press, 1973. 429 p., bibliogr., index.

Price, Richard; Price, Sally. Saramaka onomastics: an Afro-American naming system. *Ethnology* (Pittsburgh), vol. 11, no. 4, October 1972, pp. 341–367.

Ramos, Arthur. *Las Culturas Negras en el Nuevo Mundo.* Mexico City, Fondo de Cultura Económico, 1943. 390 p., glosario.

Sheridan, Richard. *Sugar and Slavery.* Eagle Hall, Barbados, Caribbean Universities Press, 1974. xiii, 529 p., appendices, bibliogr., index.

Smith, Adam. *An Enquiry into the Nature and Causes of the Wealth of Nations.* New York: Modern Library, 1937 [1776]. lx, 976 p., bibliogr.

Stein, Stanley J. *Vassouras. A Brazilian Coffee Country, 1850–1900.* Cambridge, Mass., Harvard University Press, 1957, xv, 316 p., illustr., appendix, bibliogr., glossary, index.

Tannenbaum, Frank. *Slave and Citizen.* New York, Knopf, 1947. xi, 128, xi p., index.

Taylor, Douglas Macrae. The origin of West Indian Creole languages: evidence from grammatical categories. *American Anthropologist* (Menasha, Wisc.), vol. 65, no. 4, August 1963, p. 800–814.

Thompson, Edgar T. The plantation. A part of a dissertation for the degree of Doctor of Philosophy, Dept. of Sociology, University of Chicago. Chicago, The University of Chicago Libraries, 1932. 41 p.

Tolentino, Hugo. *Raza e Historia en Santo Domingo.* Tomo I. Santo Domingo, República Dominicana, Editora de la Universidad Autónoma de Santa Domingo. 233 p., indice.

Turner, Lorenzo D. *Africanisms in the Gullah Dialect.* Chicago, University of Chicago Press, 1949. vii, 317 p., bibliogr., index.

Unesco. *Introducción a la cultura africana en América Latina.* Paris, Unesco, 1970, 181 p., anexos.

Wakefield, Edward G. *A View of the Art of Colonization.* Oxford, Clarendon Press, 1914 [1849]. xxiv, 510 p., appendix.

Wallerstein, Immanuel. *The Modern World-System.* New York and London, Academic Press, 1974 [1974a]. xiv, 410 p., illustr., bibliogr., index.

Wallerstein, Immanuel. The rise and future demise of the world capitalist system: concepts for comparative analysis. *Comparative Studies in Society and History* (Ann Arbor, Mich.), vol. 16, no. 4, September 1974 [1974b], p. 387–415.

Whitten, Norman E.; Szwed, J. Preface. In: Whitten, N.E.; Szwed, J. (eds.). *Afro-American Anthropology.* New York, The Free Press, 1970. ix, 468 p., bibliogr., index.

Williams, Eric. *Capitalism and Slavery.* Chapel Hill, North Carolina, 1944. ix, 285 p., bibliogr., index.

Wolf, Eric R. *Peasants.* Englewood Cliffs, N.J., Prentice-Hall, 1966. xii, 166 p., illustr., map, table, bibliogr., index.

Wood, Bryce. *The Making of the Good Neighbor Policy.* New York, Columbia University Press, 1961. x, 438 p., index.

14

A Case Study: The Problems of Slavery and the Colonization of Haiti

Jean Casimir

To understand how Haitians have resolved or confronted the problems resulting from slavery and colonization, we will attempt to establish ties between, on the one hand, the cultural picture, with its African roots, that has determined Haiti's political patterns, and, on the other hand, the material conditions that explain the persistence of these patterns.

We will thus present a theory of Haitian society. Ours is an effort to build a model that attempts to establish relationships among the greatest possible number of events. It runs the risk of being rejected as new historical elements are taken into account or are discovered, although it does offer the advantage of dealing with empirical data.

We must warn the reader that, given the objectives of the present study—that is, to research the responses to certain problems within the framework of the "African" presence in Haiti—we will only be focusing on one aspect of the country's national history: the presence of slaves and maroons in colonial society, and the appearance of a peasantry as of 1804. Thus, we will barely make reference to the relationships that the great powers imposed upon the country.

The "Counterplantation" as a Response to the Slavery Problem

The fact that a western cultural heritage took root within the societies of the American continent is easily explained. The logical expressions of behavioral norms, along with their original source, present serious problems, since the American social and economic scheme was designed in the West and was adapted to the peculiar transatlantic conditions.

The presence of African culture in colonial society is undeniable, although the subject merits some thought. A culture does not flourish in a vacuum, without material support, that is, without a group of relationships that determine these ideological expressions and are guided by it. It is thus essential to ask how the African perceptions of the world are incorporated in a medium that revolves around a capitalist production mode, and, in addition, to inquire how Africans of various origins could create a relatively unified vision of the world.

If we consider the coercive migration characteristics of Africans to the colony of Saint Domingue, we must recognize that the expression of a particularly Black society constitutes an exceptional example of social harmony. The behavioral patterns which the transplanted African brought along were unhinged from the environment where they originated, and without which these behavioral patterns lack meaning. If we accept that each adult is a microcosm in whom the fragments of relationships and ideological contents that define a given culture are reflected, the Black immigrants can be seen as anthologies of isolated and diverse histories launched into a new harmony. Each individual curriculum vitae has to give under the strain of orientation and other colonial components.

Every African cultural reconstruction in America will only be African with regard to a series of potentials encompassed within the logic of how individual behavior deals with a new reality. The unity of such a reconstruction will not, from then on, be classified as African other than by virtue of those logical potentials that served as raw material. For the Black immigrant, the newcomer, this is a new empirical/reality that is born and restructured as he reconstructs and/or adopts the cultural universe.

Thus, for the recreation of "Africa in Latin America," that is, for the external reality (social or other) to acquire an African meaning, it is crucial for the material, existential conditions to permit the total development of the latent norms that determine the individual practices and behaviors of the immigrants. It is vital for the formation of an African-style consensus to have certain basic social relations.

Africa was not recreated in America, except in areas where the plantation system permitted modifications based on the institutionalization of new customs and the formation of new habits regarding food, the family, religion, and others, as well as political and legal relationships in the case of a breakdown of the plantation system. In a general way, the material conditions of existence in the plantation system and the means of socialization tended to reduce the range of behavior based on an African conceptualization of things; and, with each new generation some elements of identification with the ancestral land are disappearing. Thus, we witness the break between Creoles and new arrivals.

There are two types of "African" presence in America: one consists of fragmentary and isolated traits, and the other consists of total and integrated cultural groups. The presence of African cultural traits in the heart of the plantation society can only be explained by the persistence, in the private life of Blacks, of certain traits that were able to survive under the protection of Western socialization. It is legitimate to study this survival of cultural traits; but we do not have the right to talk about adaptation, unless we can prove that the conduct of political and economic affairs within the development of a society is as important as are culinary matters.

The colonial political and ideological structures all corresponded to the main production cell: the plantation. All social or individual behavior that escaped this pattern is not important for the analysis and understanding of a colony as a territorial, organizational system.

The culture that emerged from the plantation system (referred to as Creole culture in the English-speaking Caribbean), was for the proper functioning and the perpetuation of the system based on metropolitan norms and values. The colony followed a European scheme that maintained its purity because of its successful execution. It is based on this principle that we must analyze the socialization process of people of African origin, prisoners of a configuration of fixed relationships, that was a function of the preservation and the development of plantations.

There is an ideological continuity that goes from the Creole slave who worked in the fields or as a domestic servant all the way to the "colored" planter. They both viewed and lived their lives according to the same rules, although their means of expression may have varied, but not with regard to the meaning and the direction of their behavior. It is unnecessary to add that we refer to the Creoles as a social category, not as individuals. We shall see that two Creoles, Toussaint and Dessalines, came up with development projects that corresponded, in the case of the first, to the ideological framework of the plantation, and for the second, to village society.

The African cultural traits that were inserted in the functional and developed cosmic vision of the plantation (Creole culture), were by no means a reconstruction of the African ones in America, since we are dealing with isolated and fragmented elements.

There are two ways in which the plantation as a basic production unit could disappear: either the plantation gives way to more complex, capitalist forms, or it is destroyed. The latter was the road followed by the Haitian revolution. In analyzing its process of destruction we will discover the explanation of the vitality of African culture in this country, a vitality that originated precisely from the fact that it formed a complete, cultural complex.

If, during the colonial period, what was African survived only as a substratum, the organizational process of the "counterplantation" was essential so that Africanism could surface to a more significant level. The "counterplantation" was the maroon society of Saint Domingue that continued in the form of a village society as of 1804. Research on Haitian maroon societies, which were the equivalent of the Cuban *palenques,* the Brazilian *quilombos,* the Jamaican "free villages," and the "Bush societies" of Guyana, was born from a logical imperative, since, in contrast to the above-mentioned societies, no special name was even created to refer to them. As far as we know, this fact has never been the subject of systematic research. Recent studies by Jean Fouchard add strength to this logical imperative, but the author is unable to perceive the structure of the "counterplantation."

Maroon society on the Island predated the plantation economy. Chief Henri, who lived in the beginning of the sixteenth century, deserves the title of founder of a maroon society. Historical evidence seems to indicate that the maroons had liberated a vast stretch of land prior to the unrest that led to independence. Two facts point to the quantitative importance of these maroons. In the midst of the crisis, while the French armies were being defeated by the joint British and Spanish forces, the general declaration of freedom, although also directed at the slaves, basically addressed itself to "Africans." The lengthy proclamation of Polveral, of October 13, 1793, serves as an excellent illustration of this fact. It contains an appeal to the new arrivals, maroons and potential maroons. The problem is that today many historians continue to consider the fugitive slave as a regular slave.

The importance of the maroon societies was also noticeable in the demographic makeup of the island at the time of independence. As has been pointed out, the French plantation of Saint Domingue lacked an internal reproduction dynamic for the work force. The high proportion of males, and thus, the absence of family units, made for a negative reproduction rate. However, the balance of percentages of each sex was never considered a problem during the nineteenth century in Haiti, and the mortality rate of males during the wars, which varied in degree throughout the country, was not significant enough to explain this phenomenon. Maroon society was an immediate negation of the plantation system but in no case did it offer a solution to the contradictions inherent in the latter. Its economic organization was very simple, as we shall see when we talk about Goman. Plantation and village society were parallel forms of production, and their members kept up a constant state of warfare.

Thus, contrary to the traditional version, what we call Saint Domingue did not constitute one social formation, but two or more. Those who lived in an organized milieu as maroons were not a part of the colony. The colonists referred to them as fugitives, but, unless we acknowledge a right of property of French society over these maroons, there is no reason for us not to consider them as members of independent nations. The fact that the state that controlled these nations was not Western is not to the point. We cannot doubt its African roots. But, in view of the circumstances that led to its creation and its reproduction and survival mechanisms, these states are local creations, as is their culture and their economic system.

It is this point that leads us to the ambiguity of the revolutionary processes that brought about the early independence of Haiti. Even the most superficial comparison between these processes and those that followed in the rest of America, highlights some significant differences. In Haiti, neither the manumission of slaves nor the declaration of independence were the work of a small commercial bourgeoisie with industrial aspirations. There was no political compromise between the rebels on the one hand and the planters and port merchants of France on the other. Therefore Napoleon had given his brother-in-law Leclerc instructions to exterminate the island's population and to repopulate it with new Africans, in order to ensure the normal operation of a slave economy.

It is essential to distinguish two currents within the independence wars. The maroon liberation wars, crowned with partial victories, of which the village societies that predate 1804 were a legacy; and the participation of "colored" planters in (1) the civil wars occasioned by the colonists' disregard for city orders; (2) rivalry and insubordination wars among them; (3) defensive wars against the British and Spanish invaders.

The Creole movement took off directly from the French Revolution. However, it only had the external traits of the bourgeois revolution that originated in the center, precisely because Saint Domingue was a colony that served as a jumping board, or route towards France's industrial capitalism. Thus, the coming of Napoleon Bonaparte to power, and the recovery of power by the port merchants, the slavers, and the Antillean planters, immediately led to the reversal of the favorable emancipation orders. Consequently, the colored planters and other Creoles faced a difficult situation. Abandoned by Bonaparte's policies and isolated from the mass of new freedmen, they had to fight the battle for their political rights totally on their own.

Their options were civil war or to maneuver within the new context created by the proconsul. To fight against France was the Creole's last recourse. Toussaint was aware of this as can be seen by the chronological development of battles. The Creoles' armed confrontation for emancipation occurred in two stages; in the first, Toussaint and Rigaud were prominent. Toussaint beat Rigaud, but was himself defeated by Napoleon's armies. The second stage was a last-minute change of mind in October of 1802, when both agreed to join the August rioters against Leclerc's policy of restoring slavery.

Both in the first uprising (August 1791), and in the second (August 1802), the Creoles played a secondary role, either because Toussaint thought it best to offer the front ranks to Boukman, Jn. François, and Blassou, or because Dessalines, and, mainly, his staff, joined the rebel forces three months late. It is clear that the revolutionary torch remained lit among the new arrivals from Africa, whether they were maroons or not, and that the ease with which the Creoles capitalized on this revolt was due to international complications produced by the independence process. The Creoles tried to gain a gradual political independence without being isolated, and without regressing towards simpler forms of economic organization. The policies of Toussaint and Christophe (who had a firmer strategic position than Petion or Boyer) show that the greatest effort was made to create a "modern" state.

It is not our purpose to determine who was wrong and who was right, whether the new arrivals or the Creoles. However, it can be determined that the only social groups that emerged victorious from the independence wars were those who were a part of, or at least potentially a part of maroon societies—namely, the maroons themselves and the "new arrivals" portion of the army. Later we will see how the "colored" planters who did not flee the island witnessed what we could euphemistically call a socially descending movement.

Expansion of Village Society: Independence and Isolation

The Transition

No "father of the country" emerged out of village society. The gang leaders who came from the villages were replaced by Creole leaders, and were thus eliminated from the ranks of illustrious men. Why this society spawned numerous nationally prominent personalities as of 1804, such as Dessalines, Acaau, Soulouque, Salomon, Nord Alexis, Antoine Simon, Rosalvo Bobo, Charlemagne Péralte, and became the predominant economic organization, is a process we will discuss. We can divide the years between 1804 and 1915 into two periods. The first half of the century, until approximately 1860, was the expansion period of village society. The second stage was one of violent struggles between the rural and the urban population, between merchants and agricultural producers. The first of these two periods was one where village production expanded, and where African culture provided the ideological framework; the second looked towards a new dominant class, one that was responsible for the relationship between this production mode and imperialist capitalism.

To prove that Haitian social and economic development of the nineteenth century revolved around village production, we must look at the Toussaint-Dessalines opposition. After praising the former, Jean Price-Mars observed that the ruling class during his regime was formed of White and Black planters and former Black slaves. He then added the following paragraph on the subject of the "enslaved," which we transcribe in its entirety since it illustrates what we could call bourgeois and Creole development policies:

> The L'Ouvertourian reform had divided the Saint Domingue population into two different categories: the one we have just described that formed the *ruling class* and the one made up of the large rural masses, the *majority class of slaves* upon which *rested* the economic structure of the new soci-

ety. The daily life of this class of rural workers was carefully legislated by a work code that was strangely reminiscent of the projects designed by various urban representatives following the solemn freeing of slaves. In fact, they were declared "free" with the condition that these "new freed men" would be obligated to work on the properties of their old masters for a ridiculous salary, to be paid in kind. The L'Ouverturian code thus superseded its predecessors. It provided, among other things, for the worker to remain on the property of his former master for a period of five consecutive years, instead of the three years decreed by General Hedouville. The worker had no right to leave his obligatory residence for any reason whatsoever without the authorization of a pass, signed by his boss. If he was found outside the property without the above-mentioned authorization, he could be whipped and jailed.

From this text by Price-Mars it becomes apparent that the Toussaint scheme was based on the presence of a dominant planter class, unable to execute its development plans without the use of physical violence. There was no social cohesion based on a dominant ideology. We can thus understand T. Lepowsi's discovery which serves as proof of what we have just said: under the government of Toussaint, the number of maroons was larger than under preceding governments. Toussaint's strategy achieved only partial success, as the repressive apparatus was formed, in large part, of newly imported slaves.

Following independence, Dessalines, without rejecting Toussaint's policies, decided to distribute the land of the former owners to their respective slaves. This resulted in a land reform rather than in a reform of the labor system. What is truly interesting is not that the "rulers," the same ones (with the exception of the White planters) who had surrounded Toussaint, assassinated Dessalines, but that his body was mutilated by the people of Port-au-Prince, who had been domestic slaves (largely Creole) and freedmen.

We must therefore take into account the implications of Dessalines' urban development policies. In the first place, the Emperor moved the capital to his estate at Marchand, on the Artibonite plains. He immediately decided to reconstruct the coastal towns, including Port-au-Prince. This urban policy was unlike Boyer's idea of founding Petionville some miles from Port-au-Prince. Dessalines' idea was to displace the urban center to the Derance plantation, located in the heart of the most inaccessible mountains of the western region of the island, which owes its name to Lamour Derance, a former gang leader who was the scourge of the planters of the Cul-de-Sac plains. These urban and rural development plans disguised a concept that we could call "the least possible foreign trade," which we will return to later.

We must now ask ourselves which social force the Emperor relied upon to confront the other "leaders." It seems as though only the former rural slaves, who had held on to the ideology of new arrivals, forced into village societies or eager to consolidate themselves in towns, could have benefited from the Dessalinean strategy and would therefore have given it their support. It was between the government of Toussaint and the Dessalines regime that the victory of the revolutionary forces and the destruction of the planter class took place.

If the dismemberment of the plantations, abandoned by expatriate or massacred colonialists, could not be achieved by following Dessalines' plans, and if village society lacked the importance that we attribute to it in this study, once the author of this socially unpopular strategy had been physically eliminated, one would have expected that nothing could have prevented the rebirth of the plantation system. In this hypothetical case, the ruling class would have had in its hands all that would have been necessary to reorganize the land according to its own interests in order to arrive at least to Toussaint's formula.

In the southern and western departments this was not attempted. The Toussaint formula was revalidated in the north, a region that was not dominated by the Mulatto planters, the eventual heirs of the plantations that had been abandoned by their fathers. King Christophe created a class that could have become an agrarian bourgeoisie. "The fall of Christophe . . . in Autumn of 1820, was caused not only by the hate professed by a considerable majority towards the dictatorship and despotism. It was a rebellion of the army that originated from the agricultural class as well as from the peasantry, to which a number of dignitaries from the kingdom's aristocracy attached themselves. It is significant that work on the large plantations ceased almost immediately. . . . It is also typical that the king's model plantation, Duplaa, was destroyed by the peasants during the rebellion against Christophe." We can thus legitimately conclude that the plantation economy was bankrupted by the simple, mercantile production system. "Separate the plantations from the slaves, and, until the slaves engage in some other activity, no type of economy will survive."

The Peasantry and the Soldiers

At this point we should analyze the production means within the heart of village society, as well as the characteristics of the social classes to whom the dynamics of this type of production can be attributed. We will not describe here all the strata and classes of Haitian society of the nineteenth century, we just wish to establish the relatively stable framework within which developed an apparently anarchic political and economic practice.

Since the contemporary interpretations of the sociology of Haitian development have not highlighted our current thesis, we will base our subsequent thoughts on numerous quotes, in an attempt to prove that our thesis is present in the writings of the majority of the intellectuals of the period we are dealing with.

In his references to the division of Haitian society into social classes, Madiou wrote the following text that has never been refuted but has frequently been omitted. In writing about the government of Emperor Dessalines, he said:

> The citizens were divided into two classes: workers and soldiers. The former, who had given the signal for the independence war, had been concentrated on the large estates: they kept their arms and were militarily organized, they were always ready to obey government orders. The latter, recruited in the fields and the cities, performed a more active service. Civil servants such as administrative and customs employees, made up this second class, and were responsible to the armed groups to which they had to attach themselves if their country was in danger.

These social groups did not disappear with Dessalines, since it was not a policy that had been devised by the Emperor. In order to become convinced that this was so, it suffices to recall the organization of the villagers under Goman, "this man who had spent a part of his life in the mountains as a maroon."

> Goman [organized] his followers into two classes: one class waged war, the other cultivated the land to obtain the necessary products for clandestine interchanges and for the maintenance of the troops. It is impossible to imagine the order that was thus established: he [Goman] had in fact created a small state in the mountains where he was the absolute monarch. Thus it was so easy for him to resist for thirteen consecutive years, not with great gains, but at least without having to submit."

This social structure lasted until 1915, according to S. Vincent: "We cannot escape our essentially military and peasant origins with regard to the organization of our government. . . . All of our constitutions, between 1805 and 1888, established and confirmed the military system as an essential governing mechanism. They dictate that all Haitians between the ages of 18 and 50 (inclusive) who are not members of the active army, must belong to the national guard, which was to become integrated with the army in case of mobilization." Thus, "the peasant is condemned in perpetuity, to render horrible military service, and only returns to his land from time to time, depending on the good will of some general or other. In the cities and towns, Haitians who are not civil or military functionaries, await their turn to join. . . ."

Consequently, continuing our analysis at the production level, and using the restricted sense of the term, that is, production and distribution means, we can conclude that the peasants, or, to be more exact, the maroons who had been organized into village societies (the only structured social unit to survive the 1804 revolution) constitute a unique unit, from which will emerge the structure of the national economic and social classes. The presence of farmers, their power and the role they played within the political structure were an obstacle, until 1915, for the power *of the state* (and the power *within the state*) to be employed directly and in a manner compatible with capitalist evolution during the nineteenth century.

We can understand one of the elements of peasant presence in the political field by observing the mobility within the military heirarchy superimposed upon the recruitment process mentioned by Madiou. Spencer St. John refers to this fact in his book *Haiti or the Black Republic,* but quotes Vincent on this matter: the latter, however, cannot avoid the expression of the prejudices and of the impotence of the Haitian elite. These prejudices and impotence in fact obscure the perception of the control mechanisms of the government apparatus:

> In some brave peasants, the rank incentive and the ambition of command, sometimes triggered such acts of valor that in themselves helped in the success of their actions. They were compensated with military honors. They were given money. They easily attained the highest ranks. As they received honors they aspired to even higher ones, and soon they became division generals of the army of the Republic. Thus, one would suddenly hear about a general who was unknown only yesterday, who had performed wonders in some important battle, or of a general Z who had taken some unconquerable villages. They became municipal commanders, district commanders and everything else. These ordinary people were assigned to rule communities of ten, twenty, and thirty thousand souls. They imposed their whims, their grossest fantasies, and terrorized without mercy in order to show and to enforce their recently acquired and irresponsible authority. How many Exaus and Pierrimes, coming from the plains or the mountains, totally illiterate, superstitious, and violent, guided above all by their instincts, won the booty they deserved for a rapid military action or a more difficult campaign in which they became involved by invitation of the city dwellers or of a neighboring town. And it is thus that we gradually became a country of generals.

This army that emerged out of village society could only maintain its institutional characteristics by ensuring the reproduction of the society. The resulting measures that were taken, independent of the good or evil intentions of the officers, all led to the same purpose: the defense of village society. This does not mean that its role was to provide for the well-being of each peasant and for the transition of village economies into more complex and efficient production means. On the contrary, it can be observed that the position of the army, as a depository of state power, and its organization as a government arm, would have decayed if the peasantry had lost its particular structure, formed of independent and autonomous units. The army would guard, to the very end, this isolation and this autonomy, as a base for its dominant role within the state. It is with the purpose of such vigilance that the army began to control the peasantry through oppression, and ensured its reproduction as a social class.

Louis Joseph Janvier, in his treatise *Du Gouvernement Civil en Haiti*, has the following thought that is the key to the country's political structure: "The Haitian nation has been exclusively governed by the military. . . . Many of the military attained power without having received any form of civilian culture, and consequently, without having the vaguest idea about the existence of totally civilian governments." From this fact to the despotic production means within the village there is only one step. Compare the following paragraphs by George Sylvain and Frederick Engels. In 1904 Sylvain wrote: "Quite on the contrary, there are few people who displayed such tolerant, such simple, and such amiable customs as our own. . . . However, it is undeniable that certain acts within our public life display a total absence of interest in the preservation of the human being. This is basically due to our conception of political power." Engels states: "This absolute isolation among the various communities, that has created equal but not common interests, constitutes the natural base for oriental despotism."

The army and public administration are paid for with the excess, discounted from the payment of peasants, as we shall see later. Furthermore, these peasants are subject to personal loans. The nature of rendering personal services implied such arbitrariness and such obligations that one intellectual defined them as "earthly forced labor for the innocent." The peasant could be forced either to repair a road or to clean the stables of an important leader. Spencer St. John also writes: "The department general or the district general are the officers who have all the power, and generally have the absolute mandate over their respective regions." At the lowest level, the peasant has contact with the "section chief," who also has an "almost absolute authority." The relations between the city residents and the police remained under the same scheme, and whoever became a prisoner, particularly for political reasons, would never be able to forget.

One can therefore understand how M. Bird and J. B. Dehoux in 1867 were able to pose the following questions, and why they did not hesitate to come up with answers: "What does (the presence of) an army rationally show? Are they afraid of being attacked by foreigners? If this is not the case, we have the right to assume that their objective is to oppress the people. Certainly, protests against the military system have been frequent in Haiti, but they have invariably failed and attempts to overthrow the military have only managed to make it stronger."

This contradiction between the peasantry and the army explains the dynamics of Haitian society of the nineteenth century, or, to phrase it more accurately, its immutability. It is not a matter of rediscovering the phenomenon: "If the nation is indifferent to the State, we can say that the State is acting against the nation, since the individual (the *national*) is not guaranteed the necessary freedom to develop his faculties to accomplish his own destiny . . . *This occurred for one hundred years*. The State does not fulfill any of its functions. The most essential security function is left to chance. . . . In general, the rulers have no confidence whatsoever in the governed and vice versa. A totally abnormal situation emerges from this: the Haitian rulers are isolated from the nation."

Within this context it is easy to understand the relationship that bound the civil servants to the chief of state. They confirmed their loyalty to the Emperor Dessalines by swearing this oath that many presidents could have used to their advantage: "We swear to blindly obey the laws issued by his authority, which is the only authority that we recognize. We give him the right to make peace, war, and to name his successor." Price-Mars believes the chiefs of state who succeeded each other after 1804 to have been monarchs.

The Dissolution of Village Society: The Road towards Occupation

Village society declined around the 1860s with the opening of the country to international life. The lack of communications phenomenon ended, thanks to the deep transformations that modified the international system. The former Haitian attempts to establish external contacts had failed miserably, without even producing changes within the internal structures on the economic, political, or ideological levels. We can thus affirm that it is not Haiti that drew closer to the international system, but that the international system penetrated Haiti, in spite of the resistance of village society. In large part, the roads, the means, and the consequences of the capitalist, imperialist penetration into the country can be explained through this resistance.

To understand the peculiarities of the retreat of village society when faced with the imperialist push, it is necessary to analyze the characteristics of the beginnings of commerce in Haiti; or, more accurately, the process by means of which the merchants became the dominant class. We are talking about a two-dimensional process that asserted itself during the second half of the nineteenth century. The two dimensions should not be confused. The first of these dimensions penetrated the dynamics of village society; we are referring to the background and the bankruptcy of Haitian merchants, who, as a fraction of a class, did not become differentiated as a unique village unit. The second dimension penetrated the course of international economics and concerned the history and success of foreign merchants established in Haiti.

We thus maintain that the Haitian merchants were a mere fraction of the class in charge of the economic structures and practices. The ideological rupture we can observe between the rest of the population and this fraction of a class, whose expressions and pronouncements were articulated within a French frame of reference, gave it an importance that it did not really merit. Returning to the words of R. T. Smith, "They just cannot live that old life anymore." Commerce became the refuge of the "colored" people and particularly of those who during colonial times owned slaves and plantations.

The odyssey of Haitian merchants was inscribed, so to speak, in the conditions this fraction created under Alexandre Petion. The political economy of this statesman, and particularly, his successive land distributions, took place within the framework of a village economy, as can be inferred from the work of L. F. Manigat. This historian analyzed, among other things, the structural causes for Petion's policies. We can highlight, among others, the problem of the disappearance of the main source of private wealth. Thus Manigat cites the following phrase by one of the main representatives of the former freedmen: "As agriculture became less profitable *for those who could not cultivate or administrate their properties themselves,* commerce became a refuge for all industries: everywhere one could see stores, in the towns, the villages, the important road crossings, even the plantations were filled with stores."

The use of the attached lands by the former planters was no different from the use the small owners had for their plots. The former planters had not set aside their lifestyle and love of wealth, but they could not recreate the plantation system. S. St. John wrote at the beginning of the second half of the nineteenth century: "The prejudice against sugar-making is still strong . . . A friend of mine tried to persuade one of his cultivators to aid him in a sugar-making project, but the man answered sulkily 'Moue pas esclave' ('I am not a slave')." Further along, with regard to cotton, the same author wrote: "Field hands, however, were scarce, and in order to get in their crops the proprietors had to offer half the amount to those who would come and gather it for them."

Generally, scholars readily accept the fact that the large landowners subjected the peasants to the yoke of partnership. With regard to this, one would have to ask oneself who, in the nineteenth century, would impose partnership on whom (as suggested by the quote from S. St. John with regard to cotton). The production of this commodity increased from 689,000 pounds to 4,000,000 pounds between 1860 and 1865 because of the Civil War in the United States. It would be difficult to show that, if the planters had been able to establish acceptable salaries, they would have preferred partnership. And if this was the case in the 1860s, what could be said of the Petion or Boyer years? We can conclude that the "large plantations" of the plains rapidly became territorial wealth because of the requirements deriving from the establishment of a village society, and that commercial activity did not derive from the growth of an economic surplus destined for the marketplace, but due to an adjustment within the structure of social relations among members of a destitute class.

The habit of referring to a "national bourgeoisie" and of generating polemics with regard to this class is so great that one is naturally driven to research this class within the Haitian context. However, the meager information we have seems to point to the fact that Haiti never had a national bourgeoisie until the second half of the twentieth century. We will see how it originated.

A large group of Haitian merchants thrived under Boyer. But shortly thereafter, under the long reign of the peasant Emperor Faustin I, Similien was in charge of assassinating the Mulattoes who lived in the capital, among them, the merchants. The historian Benoit Joachin observed: "This merchant bourgeoisie was profoundly antinational, above all because of its cosmopolitan nature. The names that decorated the façades of the most important stores of the port were British, German, French, and North American. The Haitian establishments only seemed more numerous (70 out of 125 in 1853–1856) if one did not differentiate between the retail stores, the large stores belonging to wholesalers, and the coffee export stores."

Under Geffrard commerce witnessed a remarkable expansion. And, although some Haitians were able to make their fortune, this fortune did not survive the three years of the Salnave government. Salnave decreed the embargo of all internal and external commerce in favor of the state. The government imported priority products and sold them through its own distribution chain, at a "price that was lower than half the commercial price." The government also had the monopoly of foreign trade for the major exports, such as coffee and cotton. Under these conditions, private merchants had no other option than to abandon their businesses. To leave no doubt as to his intentions of controlling commerce, Salnave ordered that if any merchants "be it out of fear, or with the intention of obstructing the progress of things, were to keep his store closed, he would be considered an enemy of the government, and would be treated as such."

During the last quarter of the century, the Haitian merchants were becoming progressively scarcer. Armand Thoby pointed out that "around 1880, Port-au-Prince did not have one important Haitian merchant. Around 1903, small-scale business had also escaped Haitian hands. The foreigner who for many years owned the only bank of Haiti, then controlled all the financial resources. . . ." Stenio Vincent goes even further; according to him, almost all the nonagricultural activities were controlled by foreigners.

It is difficult to find Haitians during that period who belonged to a category above that of mere retailers. They were stifled to such a degree within urban society that the governments, which best defended business interests, did not dare to clearly advocate a policy of annexation to a large power, as could be observed in other republics within the Antilles. We are not trying to praise them for it, nor to reprimand those who sighed later for a North American invasion, but are merely trying to establish the situation within which they developed. Drowned by the urban masses, they did not have enough strength to successfully accomplish an annexation policy. Neither they nor the intellectual elite that represented the interests of the peasantry (the "nationals") were in a position to adequately organize, be it the defense of the nation or the less violent penetration of imperialism upon Haitian affairs. The possibility of an intervention was already forseeable as of 1873: ". . . I wish for my fellow citizens to understand that, if the country does not initiate its road towards prosperity, it will soon be exposed to the *greatest of dangers*. This is a fact that is obvious to every thinking man . . . And we must know that the enemies of our nationalism blame us for the current lack of productivity of our soil in order to deny us our autonomy and to question our ability for self government."

As is well known, monopoly of the tertiary sector by foreigners was not accomplished without the aid of gunboats, all bearing the flags of "our friends." It remains to be seen, however, how it was possible for the tertiary sector to achieve such importance within a village economy for it to serve as a jumping board for foreign penetration, particularly because such an economy is not open to investments. In the following paragraphs we will set out to describe this mechanism, which was also responsible for the creation of a dominant social class in charge of ensuring the participation of Haiti within the concert of modern nations.

In a society of the type we are analyzing, the government apparatus lives off the "nation," and the functionaries, by some means or another, absorb a part of village production. Within the Haitian context, it was soon necessary for this portion of production to be transformed into money. With the beginning of the isolation period, under the Petion government, the State was the largest landowner on the island, thus the executive paid its employees by appropriating a portion of the national patrimony for this purpose. And there was more; public employees were compensated by being paid directly in land. That is, currency was no longer necessary to cover their salaries.

However, under Boyer, the Haitian merchants who emerged within the above-mentioned structural framework played two separate cards in their efforts to establish a different and autonomous position with regard to the village masses. They became involved in the negotiations aimed at gaining the recognition of Haitian independence by France, and they encouraged a policy of monetary recovery. On the one hand, Haiti reestablished its foreign relations, since various European powers followed the French example; on the other hand, since a good part of the lands were in the hands of the state or of public employees, the only viable means of financing the administration of the military sector was by levying export and import taxes. In other words, as E. Paul would point out later, government revenues came almost exclusively from customs duties, meaning that ultimately, it was the farmer who paid for all the official expenditures.

However, this strategy, particularly due to the vast expenditures caused by the recognition of the country's independence, could not function unless foreign trade expanded. Otherwise, greater or lesser crisis conditions would emerge, depending on internal conflicts affecting the balance of the village system. L. F. Manigat shows an interesting correlation between the political crises of nineteenth-century Haiti and the drop in the price of coffee on the international market. Between 1842 and 1846 prices went down; there were peasant wars and general Faustin Soulouque came to power. This was the date of the first massacre of the embryonic Haitian bourgeoisie. It was accompanied by large issues of paper currency and an inflation that was accelerated by the abundance of false notes.

There followed a remarkable growth of trade between the end of Soulouque's rule and under the Geffrard regime. However, in 1865–1869, there was another fall in export prices, new civil wars, and the assassinations and pillagings of the S. Salnave regime. The devaluation of the currency at that time, reached unprecedented levels, stimulated by the work of forgers. The Haitian merchants in particular bore the brunt of popular outrage. No institutions protected them, while consulates and warships came to the defense of the foreign merchants.

At the beginning of the twentieth century there was a new price drop, with prices reaching their lowest level in 1909–1911. Popular fury was even more violent. To the political conflicts that followed one must add the rivalries among the different groups of foreign merchants, the Haitian version of the struggle between the great empires. Furthermore, the Haitian elite formulated its own diagnosis of the causes for the backwardness of the country. Measures were taken to deport the entire Syrian colony, among whom there were numerous Mideasterners who had become naturalized North Americans. Financial disorder increased progressively until the landing of the Marines.

This degradation process revealed an important fact. As political instability and civil wars grew, there were more peasants enlisted in the warring armies; there were more governors and "revolutionaries" in need of currency, who were therefore printing it; there were currency forgers with freedom of action; and the position of foreign merchants and their consulates grew progressively stronger. Thus, intervention in Haitian commerce became more and more blatant. This process and its relationships with the commercial and financial sector did not escape the intellectuals of the period. In 1892, Edmond Paul wrote:

> The government is mortgaging itself on short term to the usurious interest rates of private individuals, or for the purpose of giving equivalent benefits. Thus, little by little, *the millions of a floating debt concentrated in foreign hands* build up and uncertainty increases in these disastrous days during which some cannot control their desires to confiscate our land as a guarantee. . . . Although the Republic has a Bank and a national currency that is so costly to print, the rate of the currency on the market has been so unstable that the exchange rate has fluctuated in price between 20, 30, and 50%, which *impoverishes and disorients our national commerce.*
>
> Thereby, the merchants of all nationalities serve as intermediaries in the process through which peasants pay the salaries of soldiers. They perform this role without hurting their mercantile activities, which certainly also helps to increase their control over the administration.

While rivalries between the large powers were not defined in favor of one nation or the other on the international level, disorder and anarchy prevailed in Haiti. Order was reestablished, and maintained, in large part, up to our days, as soon as the United States consolidated its hegemony over the Americas (World War I) and when, within the country, the First National City Bank displaced all of its competitors with intermediary roles between the soldier administrators who had now become bureaucrats and the peasants.

In fact, from the point of view that interests us now, the achievements of the occupation resulted in ensuring the gradual acquisition by foreign merchants of a Haitian citizenship card. To this Haitianization of what we call "le bord de mer" (the port), one must add the formation of some plantations; we are thus left with a total absence of productive capital that could have multiplied and achieved some type of integration of the peasantry into contemporary trade. Since the productive means in the hands of peasants were not an inexhaustible resource, migration to towns or the urbanization process accelerated, as did the emigration to neighboring countries; that is, depopulation was occurring. During the nineteenth century it was impossible to find a single social group formed of salaried employees. Today a large market for inexpensive labor is attracted to Haiti by the light assembly industry, which produces exclusively for export.

The most powerful Haitian class between 1915 and the present continues to be that of Haitian merchants of foreign origins. We must therefore remember Dobb's phrase:

> Even though a dominant class can originate from commerce or can establish links with merchants, it is improbable that a merchant class, that has as its main activity that of being an intermediary between producer and consumer, could become a dominant class in a radical and exclusive sense . . . With their fortunes [the merchants] will tend to attach themselves to the existing production mode. It is more likely that they will feel compelled to preserve this production mode without transforming it, and it is likely that they will fight to become a part of the existing means of obtaining the surplus productive value of labor, but that they do not attempt to change the structure.

We can also add the words of Fleury Féquiere: "We cannot be surprised that the Haitian capitalists have always disdained agricultural and industrial enterprises, displaying their preference for incredible transactions. . . ."

Conclusion

The people of the colony of Saint Domingue resolved their problems of slavery by starting from the basic principles within their cultural and ideological framework. They created a "counterplantation," a village society formed by a majority of new arrivals from Africa and an indeterminate number of maroons. In other words, those who wanted independence in 1804 were an overwhelming majority of former Black slaves who had not been imbued with Creole culture, and freedmen who lived outside of the socializing reach of the plantation system. At the beginning, the country witnessed a period of real political and economic independence, at which time village society and the African culture were consolidated. Gradually the country, like all other societies at that time, was attracted into the orbit of the world capitalist economy, towards the end of the nineteenth century. The commercial and financial sectors served as the link. The country never had a national bourgeoisie or an industrial bourgeoisie, nor did it have a social force that was able to alter the unchangeable village society.

To prove the above-mentioned points, we have put aside all references as to why African groups were brought to Saint Domingue. We ignored the goings-on between the colony and the center. We did not mention the policies that were implemented by the large powers once the adventure of the slaves and maroons was crowned by success nor the unfavorable trade relationships between the new country and the capitalist world. We barely referred to the interimperialist struggles, and if we did mention the United States occupation, we did not question why it occurred.

Haiti did not choose to become isolated. As an American country populated by Blacks who had been slaves, it could only evolve in isolation during the nineteenth century. However, this isolation of rural society broke at the beginning of this century on account of the United States occupation. How this occurred, that is, how the economic, political, and ideological structures corresponding to the development of capitalist monopolies were created, is particularly significant for the understanding of the subject matter we are analyzing.

As the newly arrived Africans were seeking refuge in the mountains to create and to defend a non-European life style, they could not forsee the difficulties caused by the French Revolution and the changes that had occurred at the heart of British capitalism, which would eventually make for favorable conditions for political and economic independence in the Caribbean. Likewise, at the turn of the century, there was no way that the armed peasants could have guessed that the North Americans would fall upon them. Therefore, the prolific warnings by groups of intellectuals during these turbulent times produced no effect, as they themselves confessed. Their views were not inscribed within the basic framework of peasant thought, which was not built upon a series of structural exchanges with the capitalist world. This is the essential point in understanding the role of African culture and in the formulation of a response to the problems that once confronted and still face the country.

After the North American occupation, in the mid 1930s, when Herskovits visited Haiti to work on his well-known book *Life in a Haitian Valley,* he wrote that at that time "the second independence" of the country was being celebrated, in commemoration of the day when the Marines left our country. Today the anniversary of the day of the departure of the Marines is known as "army day." And let it be known that this army, trained by the Marines themselves, did not participate in the conquest of the second independence.

It thus happened that the isolation of the maroon peasant society, which was at first an endogenous defensive condition, became, after independence, an exogenous condition, imposed during the nineteenth century by the current powers. Later, once the structures of dependency had been formed, isolation turned into a condition mediated by certain Creole social classes.

If, during this project, we have insisted exclusively on internal conditions to explain the vitality of the African culture in Haiti, it is because a culture lives and develops by "looking inward" towards its productive and reproductive conditions. The question we have tried to answer is how a culture of African origin could develop while the problems presented by slavery and colonization were being resolved. We maintained that the

Haitian case is explained by the expression of a despotic, village production mode, with its roots going back to eras that predate the plantation system.

In view of the characteristics of the political system and the despotic village production system, and the position of the country's intellectuals with regard to its ideological structure, we must conclude that those intellectuals never gave their full and sincere support to the lifestyle inherited from the African maroons. They were never able to formulate a strategy that would ensure the participation of the peasantry within a politically viable system. Jean Price-Mars wrote:

> Therefore, given that the Haitian nation does exist, it so happens that it is infantile, which prevents it from displaying its political existence. It is not just for the North American to judge this state by calling us: 'an inarticulate people'! *Inarticulate people,* a term . . . that would indicate a people unable to express their thoughts, deprived of the ability to articulate their will and to assert it, thus reduced to be nothing more defined than a 'confused heap of individuals,' stultified by ignorance, a flock ready to follow the orders of a leader, no matter who he is, just so he is clever enough to assert himself. That was the situation between 1870–1880, which, by the way, has not changed much since then. . . .

This case study, in a way, goes back to the concept of "inarticulate people," by defining the organization of the Haitian nation as a juxtaposition of villages. From here we derive a similar conclusion to that of Price-Mars, namely, the inability of the peasantry to express its own idea or political will, and consequently, its versatility in facing national and international conditions. Therefore, in a book on "Africa in Latin America," we thought it appropriate to describe an array of relationships that would explain the vitality and persistence of African culture. In our day, when research on ethnic identity is at the base of social struggles in a large number of countries, this type of study is very important. It permits us to show that the culture of African origins involves a conception of politics and economics that can be empirically observed.

The despotic village production system, which confers its uniqueness and longevity to African culture, is devoid of an internal dynamic of economic development. Thus, its ideological baggage is unable to advance towards a greater understanding and a superior control of assymetrical relationships wherein the position of production that remains in the hands of the transmitters of this production system is determined. The culture of village society is an oppressed culture, that is, an assemblage of norms and values articulated around a system with little knowledge, created and dispersed by isolated parochial institutions that remain separated from the rest of the world.

It is under these conditions that we find an "Africa in Haiti," a Haitian version of Africa, involved in itself, unable to express itself and to demand its place under the sun; nevertheless its vitality and its universality are undeniable. It is a *national* culture that is not *official,* in the same way that its *national* language is not *official* either and that Haiti's religion is not *official.*

We have tried to show in this essay that a number of Haitian intellectuals in the nineteenth century and the beginning of the twentieth century have formulated in-depth analyses of the country's situation which made it easy to consolidate their interpretations into a coherent model. Among the names we have mentioned, and taking into account only their analysis, it would be impossible to separate the defenders of the peasantry from the artful advocates of annexation to the United States. One can say that within the framework of the dominant Creole culture, such as it was expressed before the North American occupation, problems that faced village society have been researched, although with varying success; and that it is at the level of development projects that we can catalogue the intellectuals.

In view of the political versatility of the peasantry, it would be necessary, some day, to put an end to the distinctions between the national and the official spheres; one must thereby resolve not only the problem of the dialogue with the peasants and of their participation in the political arena that seems to have been relatively easy in the past, but one must also resolve the problem of participation and of a dialogue in the exclusive defense of the interests of the country.

It is at this level that "Africa in Haiti" has, not withstanding the limitations typical of all oppressed cultures, a very important place in the future of the country. Because of the efforts of deculturation that occurred throughout the entire history of public instruction in Haiti, which for more than a hundred years became confused in large part with a "religious" history that did not retreat in light of open persecution, there are few spokespeople capable of ensuring a dialogue in the sense that we mentioned earlier.

Therefore, the problems inherited from colonization, problems of political relationships between Haiti and the outside world, have not been resolved, given the structure of the state in a village society. The power relationships in Haiti derive directly from the types of solutions found for the problems of slavery. They are radical solutions based on a rupture between slave society and peasant society. Given the radical nature of this rupture, the Creole unit, with bourgeois potential, was never able to develop, so that one of the main legacies of colonialism, namely the distinction between new Black arrivals and Creoles, remained alive. This dichotomy was apparent in many ways during the course of the country's history and according to various points of view: in the division between the countryside and the city, between *voodoo* and Christianity, between those who can read and write and those who cannot, between those who speak French and those who do not, between those who can discharge the functions of representatives and those who cannot, between the national and the official sphere.

Beyond the response that has been given to colonization and slavery, the problem today hinges upon the response given to the presence of "Africa in Haiti." It is here that one can make a distinction between those who respect and those who do not respect their own country and their ancestors.

About the Contributors

Allsopp, Richard
   Guyanese philologist (b. 1923). Studied at the University of London. Author of numerous linguistic essays on Caribbean speech, such as: *Some Problems Facing the Lexicography of Caribbean English,* 1971; *Caribbean English and the Problem of Communication,* 1969; *Expression of State and Action in the Dialect of English Used in the Georgetown Area of British Guyana,* 1962; *Pronomial Forms in the Dialect Used in Georgetown and its Environs by People Engaged in Non-Clerical Occupations,* 1958. Professor at the University of the West Indies, Cave Hill Campus, Barbados.

Aretz de Ramón y Rivera, Isabel
   Argentine/Venezuelan ethnomusicologist, folklorist, and composer, (b. Buenos Aires, 1913). Graduate of the National Conservatory of Buenos Aires, doctorate in musicology. Main writings: *Música tradicional Argentina,* 1946; *El folklore musical argentino,* 1952; *Música tradicional de La Rioja,* 1967; *Cantos navideños en el folklore venezolano,* 1962; *Instrumentos musicales de Venezuela,* 1967; *El tamunanque,* 1970. Principal musical works: "Simiente," 1965; "Yekuana," 1972; "Argentino hasta la muerte," 1975. Director and founder of the Instituto Interamericano de Etnomusicología y Folklore (INIDEF), of Venezuela.

Brathwaite, Edward Kamau
   Barbadian poet, critic, and historian (b. Bridgetown, Barbados, 1930). Principal works: *Rights of Passage,* 1967; *Masks,* 1968; *Islands,* 1969; *Folk Culture of the Slaves in Jamaica,* 1970; *The Development of Creole Society in Jamaica 1770–1820,* 1971; *The Arrivants,* 1973; *Other Exiles,* 1975; *Our Ancestral Heritage,* 1976. Studied at Cambridge, and later lived in Ghana. He is a professor at the University of the West Indies, founder of the Caribbean Artist Movement and of the magazine issued by this movement, called *Savacou.* Member of the editorial board of the magazine *Bim.* In 1976 he received the *Casa de las Americas* prize for his work *Black & Blues.*

de Carvalho, José Jorge
   Brazilian musician (b. Ipanema, Minas Gerais, 1950). Degree in musical composition at, and director of the orchestra of the University of Brasilia. He later studied ethnomusicology at the Instituto Interamericano de Etnomusicología y Folklore (INIDEF). He conducted research of narrative musical forms in the Northeast of Brazil. He is now working as a researcher for the Consejo Científico y Humanístico of the Universidad Central de Venezuela.

Carrera Damas, Germán
   Venezuelan historian (b. Cumaná, 1930). Main writings: *La dimensión histórica en el presente de América Latina y Venezuela,* 1972; *El culto a Bolivar,* 1970; *Boves, aspectos socioeconómicos,* 1968; *Historiografía marxista venezolana y otros temas,* 1967; *Temas de historia social y de las ideas,* 1969. Professor of history at the Universidad Central de Venezuela. He is currently coordinating, within the framework of the Departamento de Investigaciones Sociales del Centro de Estudios del Desarrollo (CENDES), a prediagnostic sociohistoric study of Venezuela.

Casimir, Jean
   Haitian sociologist and historian (b. Port-au-Prince, 1938). Main writings: *De la*

sociología regional a la acción política, 1970; *Los bozales: el supuesto de una cultura oprimida en Haiti,* 1973; Professor of sociology of development, and of geopolitics at the *Facultad de Ciencias Políticas y Sociales* of the Universidad Nacional Autónoma of Mexico (UNAM). He is currently living in Trinidad, where he is responsible for social affairs for ECLA.

Depestre, René

Haitian poet (b. Jacmel, 1926). Studied at the *Institut de Sciences Politiques* of the University of Paris, at the Sorbonne, and at the Louvre Museum. Main writings: *Etincelles,* 1945; *Végétation de clarté,* 1951; *Traduit du grand large,* 1952; *Mineral negro,* 1962; *Journal d'un animal marin,* 1964; *Un aracoiris para el occidente cristiano,* 1967; *Pour la poésie, pour la révolution,* 1968; *Poète à Cuba,* 1972; *El palo ensebado,* 1975. His poems and essays have appeared in various American, African, and European publications. At present he lives in Paris, where he works at UNESCO.

Dos Santos, Deoscóredes Maximiliano

Specialist in religious studies. Brazilian (b. Bahia, 1917). Main writings: *Yoruba, tal qual se fala,* 1950; *Contos negros de Bahia,* 1961; *Axé Opô Afonjá,* 1962; *Contos de Nagô,* 1963; *Porque Oxalá usa Edodidé,* 1966 (with Juana Elbein Dos Santos). He was initiated in the Nagô religion at age 7, and is currently *asogbá* (high priest) of the cult of Obaluaiye in the traditional community of Axé Opô Afonjá; and also *alápini,* (high priest) of the ancestral cult of Egún. He has carried out field work in Brazil, Nigeria, Dahomey, Togo, and Ghana.

Dos Santos, Juana Elbein

Argentine/Brazilian ethnologist (b. Buenos Aires, 1928), wife of the above. She has written numerous articles in her field and has coauthored with Deoscoredes Maximiliano Dos Santos *West African Rituals and Sacred Art in Brazil,* 1967; *La religión Nagô,* 1972; *Esú Bara Láróyè,* 1971. She received her doctorate in ethnology from the Faculté de Sciences Humaines at the Sorbonne. She has done research and field work in Brazil, the Caribbean, Mexico, the United States, Dahomey, Nigeria, and Ghana.

Feijoo, Samuel

Cuban poet, essayist, and painter (b. Las Villas, 1914). Main writings: *La alcancía del artesano,* 1958; *Diario de viajes,* 1960; *Diario abierto,* 1960; *El pájaro de las soledades,* 1961; *Caminante montés,* 1962; *El girasol sediento,* 1963; *Ser fiel,* 1964; *Juan Quinquín en Pueblo Mocho,* 1964; *Sobre los movimientos por una poesía cubana,* 1966. He was managing editor of the magazine *Islands* of the Universidad Central de Las Villas for several years. He is presently editor of *Signos,* a Cuban literary magazine.

Ianni, Octavio

Brazilian sociologist and ethnologist (b. Itu, São Paulo, 1926). Main writings: *As metamorfoses do escravo,* 1962; *Raças e classes sociais no Brazil,* 1966; *Estado e capitalismo,* 1965; *O colapso do populismo no Brasil,* 1968; *Imperialismo y cultura de la violencia en América Latina,* 1970; *Imperialismo na América Latina,* 1974; *Esclavitud y capitalismo,* 1976. For thirteen years he was professor of philosophy at the Universidade de São Paulo. Since 1969 he has been a member of the Centro Brasileiro de Analise a Planejamento and visiting professor at the Universities of Columbia, Oxford, and Mexico (UNAM).

Mintz, Sidney W.

U.S. ethnologist and anthropologist (b. Dover, N.J., 1922). Main writings:

Worker in the Cane, 1960; *Caribbean Transformations,* 1974; *The People of Puerto Rico,* 1956 (coauthor). Ph.D., Columbia University (anthropology), M.A., Yale. He has taught at Columbia and Yale Universities and at the École Practique des Hautes Études in Paris. He is currently teaching anthropology at Johns Hopkins University in Baltimore, Maryland.

Moreno Fraginals, Manuel
   Cuban historian and economist (b. Havana, 1920). Main writings: *El ingenio. El complejo económico social cubano del azúcar,* 1964–1976 (3 vols.); *José Antonio Saco: estudio y bibliografía,* 1960; *Misiones cubanas en archivos europeos,* 1953; *La Habana,* 1963. He has simultaneously conducted research in social science and has done practical work as a marketing and business analyst. He is professor and lecturer at the universities of La Habana, Las Villas, Caracas, Maracaibo, Los Andes, Mexico, Madrid, Oxford, Ibadan, etc. In 1981 he was awarded the Clarence H. Haring Prize of the American Historical Association. He has been visiting professor at Columbia, Johns Hopkins and the University of Florida, and a Fellow of the Wilson Center for Scholars in Washington, D.C. He is currently an advisor to the Ministry of Culture in Cuba.

Urfé, Odilo
   Cuban musicologist, pianist, flutist, and conductor of a popular Cuban band (b. Madruga, 1921). In 1949 he founded the Instituto Musical de Investigaciones Folklóricas (IMIF), the most important center of musical classification and of popular and folk music in Cuba. He has organized festivals of popular Cuban music. Currently, among numerous other assignments, he is professor of history and of Cuban musical appreciation at the Instituto Superior de Arte, director and pianist of the Charanga Nacional de Conciertos, and executive secretary of the Comité Nacional Cubano of the International Music Council (IMC).

Verger, Pierre
   French/Brazilian historian and ethnologist (b. 1913). Main writings: *Fiestas y danzas en el Cuzco y los Andes,* 1945; *O fumo da Bahia e o tráfico dos escravos do Golfo de Benim,* 1966; *Flux et reflux de la traite des nègres entre le Golfe de Bénin et Bahía de Todos os Santos, du XVII au XIX siecle,* 1968. For many years he lived in Bahía where he has studied the folklore and the ethnology. Currently he is doing research in Africa, particularly in Ghana and Nigeria.

Bibliography

Adams, Richard N. *Encuesta sobre la cultura de los ladinos en Guatemala.* Guatemala: Centro Editorial "José Pineda Ibarra," 1964.

Aguirre Beltrán, Gonzalo. *Cuijla. Esbozo etnográfico de un pueblo negro.* México: Fondo de Cultura Económica, 1958.

Aimes, Hubert H. S. *A History of Slavery in Cuba.* New York: G. P. Putnam's Sons, 1907.

Alexandre, P. *Languages and Language in Black Africa.* Chicago: Northwestern University Press, 1972.

Allsopp, Richard. *Dictionary of Jamaican English.* Rio Piedras, Puerto Rico: Caribbean Studies, 1970.

Ardouin, Beaubrun. *Études sur l'histoire d'Haiti.*

Aretz, Isabel. *Música tradicional argentina.* Tucumán, Buenos Aires: Universidad Nacional de Tucumán, 1946.

———. *El Tamunangue.* U. C. O. Barquisimeto, Venezuela, 1970.

———. *Instrumentos musicales de Venezuela.* Cumaná, Venezuela: La Heredad, U. de O., 1967.

Armstrong, R. *The Study of West Africa Languages.* Ibadan U.P., 1964.

Ayestarán, Lauro. *La música en el Uruguay.* vol. 1. Montevideo, 1953.

Bailey, B. L. *Jamaican Creole Syntax.* Cambridge: 1966.

Bartlett, C. J. *Chapters in Caribbean History 2.* University of West Indies, Caribbean University Press, 1973.

Bartra, Roger. *El modo de producción asiático.* México: Editorial Era, 1969.

Bascom, W. *Yoruba Food and Cooking.* Oxford University Press, 1951.

Bastide, Roger. *Les Amériques noires.* Paris: Payot, 1967.

———. *Les religions africaines au Brésil.* P. U. F., 1960.

Bastien, Remy. *Religions and Politics in Haiti.* Washington: Institute for Cross-Cultural Research, 1966.

Beckford, George L. *Persistent Poverty: Underdevelopment in Plantation Economies of the Third World.* Oxford University Press, 1972.

Bellegarde, Dantes. *La nation haitienne.* París: J. de Gigord.

Benoist, Jean *et al. L'archipel inachevé. Culture et societé aux Antilles françaises.* Presses de l'Université de Montreal, 1972.

Best, Lloyd. *Un modèle d'économie pure de plantation.* Fort-de-France: Cahiers du CERAG, 1971.

Boettner, Juan Max. *Música y músicos del Paraguay.* Asunción: Ed. de Autores Paraguayos Asociados (s. f.).

Borghero, Francisco. *Relation sur l'établissement des missions dans le vicariat apostolique du Dahomey, Annales de la propagation de la foi.* Lyon, 1864.

Brathwaite, Edward. *Contradictory Omens: Cultural Diversity and Integration in the Caribbean.* Kingston, 1974.

Brutus, Edner. *Instruction publique en Haiti, 1492–1495.* Port-au-Prince: Imprimerie de l'Etat, 1948.

Burton, Richard F. *A Mission to Gelele, King of Dahomé.* London: 1864.

Cabrera, L. *El monte.* La Habana, 1954.

———. *La sociedad secreta abakuá.* La Habana, 1958.

Carneiro, Edison. *Candomblé en Bahía*. Río de Janeiro: Ed. Conquista, 1961.

Carvalho Neto, Paulo de. *La comparsa lubola del carnaval montevideano*. Caracas: Archivos Venezolanos de Folklore, 1963.

―――. *Diccionario de folklore ecuatoriano*. Quito: Ed. Cultura Ecuatoriana, 1964.

Cassidy, F. G. *Jamaica Talk*. London: Macmillan, 1961.

Castro, Josué de. *Geopolítica del hambre*. Buenos Aires: Ed. Solar, 1962.

Césaire, Aimé. *Toussaint L'Ouverture*. Paris: Le club français du livre, 1960.

Chenoweth, Vida. *The Marimbas of Guatemala*. University of Kentucky Press, 1964.

Christaller, J. G. *A grammar of the Asante and Fante Language Called Twi*. Basel: Gregg Reprint, 1964.

Clarke, Edith. *My Mother Who Fathered Me: A Study of the Family in Three Selected Communities of Jamaica*. London: George Allen and Unwin, 1957.

Comitas, Lambros. *Caribbean 1900–1965*. Seattle: Washington University Press, 1968.

Concolorcorvo. *El lazarillo de ciegos caminantes*. Buenos Aires: Ed. Solar, 1942.

Corvington, G. *Port-au-Prince au cours des ans. La métropole haitienne du XIXe. siècle, 1804–1888*. Port-au-Prince: Henri Deschamps (s. f.)

Courlander, Harold. *The Drum and the Hoe*. Berkeley: University of California Press, 1960.

―――. *Religion and politics*. Washington: Institute for Cross-Cultural Research, 1966.

Curtin, Philip D. *The Atlantic Slave Trade: A Census*. Madison, Wisconsin: The University of Wisconsin Press, 1969.

David, B., y Jardel, J. P. *Les proverbes créoles de la Martinique*. CERAG, 1969.

Davis, David B. *The Problem of Slavery in Western Culture*. Ithaca, New York: Cornell University Press, 1966.

Deerr, Noel. *The History of Sugar*. London: Chapman and Hall, Ltd. 1949.

Domínguez, Virginia. *From Neighbor to Stranger: The Dilemma of Caribbean Migrants in the United States*. New Haven: Antilles Research Program, 1975.

Dos Santos, Deoscóredes M. *Axé Opô Afonjá*. Río de Janeiro: Instituto Brasileiro de Estudos Afro-Asiáticos, 1963.

―――, *West African Art and Rituals in Brazil*. Ibadan: Institute of African Studies, 1967.

―――. *Nagô et la mort*. Paris: Université de Sorbonne, 1972.

Drummont, J. C., y Wilbraham, A. *The Englishman's Food: Five Centuries of English Diet*. London: Jonathan Cape, 1964.

Eduardo, Octavio Da Costa, *The Negro in Northern Brazil*. Seattle: University of Washington Press, 1966.

Fanon, F. *Peaux noires, masques blancs*. Paris: Editions du Seuil, 1952.

Fernandes, Florestan. *Brancos e negros em São Paulo*. São Paulo: Companhia Editora Nacional, 1959.

―――. *A integraçao do negro na sociedade de classes*. São Paulo: Dominus Editora, 1965.

Freyre, G. *Maîtres et esclaves (Casa Grande e Sanzala)*. Paris: Gallimard, 1947.

―――. *Azúcar*, Brasil: Colección Canavieira, núm. 2, 1969.

Franco, Jean. *The Modern Culture of Latin America*. New York: Penguin Books, 1970.

Franco, José L. *Afroamérica*. La Habana: Imprenta Nacional, 1961.

Frazier, E. F. *The Negro Family in the United States*. Chicago: Chicago University Press, 1937.

Friedenthal, Albert. *Musik, Tanz und Dichtung bei den Kreolen Amerikas*. Berlin: Hans Schnippel, 1913.

Gaillard, N. *Recettes simples de cuisine haitienne*. Port-au-Prince, Haití: La Phalange, 1959.

Genovese, Eugene D. *The Political Economy of Slavery*. New York: Pantheon, 1965.

———. *The World the Slaveholders Made*. New York: Pantheon, 1969.

Gesualdo, Vicente. *Historia de la música en la Argentina*. Buenos Aires: Ed. Beta, 1961.

Gräbener, Jürgen, Hg. *Klassengesellschaft und Rassismus*. Düsseldorf: Bertelsmann Universitätsverlag, 1971.

Grenon S. J., P. *Nuestra primera música instrumental*. Buenos Aires: Libr. E. Perrot, 1929.

Groot, Silvia W. de. *Djuka Society and Social Change*. Assen: Van Gorcum, 1969.

Guerra y Sánchez, R. *Sugar and Society in the Caribbean*. New Haven: Yale University Press, 1964.

Hall, Gwendolyn M. *Social Control in Slave Plantation Societies*. Baltimore: The John Hopkins University Press, 1971.

Hanke, Lewis. *Aristotle and the American Indians*. London: Hollis and Carter, 1959.

Hauser, Philip M. (ed.). *Urbanization in Latin America*. Paris: UNESCO, 1961.

Herskovits, Melville J. *Suriname Folklore*. New York: Columbia University Press, 1936.

———. *Life in a Haitian Valley*. New York: Alfred Knopf, 1937.

———. *Trinidad Village*. New York: Alfred A. Knopf, 1947.

———. *The New World Negro*. New York: Minerva Press, 1969.

Hobsbawm, Eric. *Formaciones económicas precapitalistas*. México: Ediciones Pasado y Presente, 1971.

Hoetink, Harry. *Slavery and Race Relations in the Americas*. New York: Harper and Row, 1973.

Hurbon, Laënnec. *Dieu dans le Vaudou haitien*. Paris: Payot, 1972.

Hymes, Dell (ed.). *Pidginization and Creolization of Languages*. Cambridge: Cambridge University Press, 1971.

Ianni, Octavio. *As metamorfoses do esclavo*. São Paulo: Difusão Europeia do Livro, 1962.

Ker, M. *Personality and Conflict in Jamaica*. Liverpool: Willmer Brothers and Haram Ltd., 1952.

Knight, Franklin W. *Slave Society in Cuba during the Nineteenth Century*. Madison: Wisconsin, University of Wisconsin Press, 1970.

Konetzke, Richard. *El Imperio español*. Madrid: Ediciones Nueva Época, 1946.

Lacombe, Robert. *Historie monétaire de St. Dominque et de la République d'Haiti, jusqu'en 1874*. Paris: Ed. Larose, 1958.

Lane, Ann (ed.). *The Debate over Slavery*. Urbana, Illinois: University of Illinois Press, 1971.

Lawrence, K. O. *Immigration into the West Indies in the Nineteenth Century*. St. Lawrence, Barbados: Caribbean University Press, 1971.

Leiris, M. *Contacts de civilisation en Martinique et en Guadeloupe.* Paris: Unesco, 1955.

Le Riverend, J. *Historia económica de Cuba.* La Habana: Instituto del Libro, 1967.

Lewis, Gordon K. *The Growth of the Modern West Indies.* New York and London: Modern Reader Paperbacks, 1969.

Leyburn, J. G. *El pueblo haitiano.* Buenos Aires: Ed. Claridad, 1946.

Marcelin, Milo. *Mythologie vodou.* Port-au-Prince: Les Editions Haitiennes, 1949–1950.

Mars, J. A., and Tooley, E. M. *The Kudeti Book of Yoruba Cookery.* Lagos, Nigeria: Nigeria Bookshops, 1961.

Maximilien, Louis. *Le vodou haitien.* Port-au-Prince: Imprimerie de l'Etat, 1945.

Merivale, Herman. *Lectures on Colonization and Colonies.* London: Longman, Orme, Brown, Green and Longmans, 1841.

Métraux, A. *Le vaudou haïtien.* Paris: Gallimard, 1958.

Mintz, Sidney W. *Caribbean Transformation.* Chicago: Aldine, 1974.

Moreno Fraginals, Manuel. *El ingenio, tomo I (1760–1860).* La Habana: Comisión Nacional Cubana de la Unesco, 1964.

Moya, Ismael. *Romancero.* t. I. Buenos Aires: Imprenta de la Universidad, 1941.

———. *El arte de los payadores.* Buenos Aires: Ed. Berruti, 1959.

Nieboer, Herman J. *Slavery as an Industrial System.* The Hague: Martinus Nijhoff, 1900.

Numa, Edgar N. *Antoine Simon et la fatalité historique.* New York (s.f.).

Nurrauit, Jean. *Les noires réfugiés Boni de la Guyane Française.* Dakar: IFAN, 1951.

Ortiz, Fernando. *Cuban Counterpoint: Tobacco and Sugar.* New York: Alfred A. Knopf, 1947.

———. *Hampa Afro-Cubana, los negros brujos.* Madrid: 1906.

———. *La africanía de la música folklórica de Cuba.* La Habana: Ministerio de Educación, 1950.

———. *Los instrumentos de la música afro-cubana.* La Habana: Ministerio de Educación, 1952–1955.

Pereira Salas, Eugenio. *Los orígenes del arte musical en Chile.* Santiago: Imprenta Universitaria, 1941.

———. *Historia de la música en Chile.* Santiago: Universidad de Chile, 1957.

Poulantzas, N. *Poder político y clases sociales en el estado capitalista.* México: Siglo XXI, 2ª ed., 1970.

Price-Mars, Jean. *Ainsi parla l'oncle: Essais d'etnographie.* Paris: Imprimerie de Compiègne, 1928.

Price, Richard S. *Maroon Societies.* Garden City, New York: Anchor Press, 1973.

Querino, Manoel. *Costumes africanas no Brasil.* Río de Janeiro: Civilização Brasileira, 1938.

Ragatz, L. J. *The Fall of the Planter Class in the British Caribbean 1763–1833.* New York: Octagon Books, 1963.

Ramón y Rivera, Luis Felipe. *El joropo, baile nacional de Venezuela.* Caracas: Ed. Ministerio de Educación, 1953.

———. *La música afrovenezolana.* Caracas: Imprenta Universitaria, Universidad Central de Venezuela, 1971.

Ramos, Arthur. *O negro brasileiro.* Río de Janeiro: Civilização Brasileira, 1937.

————. *Las culturas negras en el Nuevo Mundo*. México: Fondo de Cultura Económica, 1943.

Rodrigues, Nina. *Os africanos no Brasil*. São Paulo: Companhia Editora Nacional, 1922.

————. *O animismo fetichista dos negros bahianos*. Río de Janeiro: Civilização Brasileira, 1935.

Sheridan, Richard. *Sugar and Slavery*. Eagle Hall, Barbados: Caribbean University Press, 1974.

Smith, M. G. *West Indian Family Structure*. Seattle: University of Washington Press, 1962.

————. *Kinship and Community in Carriacou*. New Haven: Yale University Press, 1962.

Stein, Stanley, J. *Vassouras. A Brazilian Coffee Country*. Cambridge, Mass.: Harvard University Press, 1957.

Steward, J. H. (ed.). *The People of Puerto Rico*. Urbana: University of Illinois Press, 1956.

Tannenbaum, Frank. *Slave and Citizen*. New York: Alfred A. Knopf, 1947.

Taylor, Douglas. *The Black Caribs of British Honduras*. New York: Viking Fund Publications in Anthropology, 1951.

Thieme, F. P. *The Puerto-Rican Population: A Study in Human Biology*. Ann Arbor: University of Michigan, 1959.

Thompson, Edgar T. *The Plantation*. Chicago: The University of Chicago Libraries, 1932.

Tolentino, Hugo. *Raza e historia en Santo Domingo*. Santo Domingo: Universidad Autónoma, 1970.

Turner, Lorenzo D. *Africanisms in the Gullah Dialect*. Chicago: University of Chicago Press, 1949.

Turnier, Alain. *Les Etats Unis et le Marché Haitien*. Montreal: Imprimerie St. Joseph, 1955.

Unesco. *Introducción a la cultura africana en América Latina*. Paris: Unesco, 1970.

Valldejuli Aboy, C. *The Art of Caribbean Cookery*. New York: Doubleday and Co., 1957.

Vincent Adebesi, Mrs. *A Cookery Book for the Tropics*. London, Allen and Unwin Ltd., 1962.

Wakefield, Edward G. *A View of the Art of Colonization*. Oxford: Clarendon Press, 1914.

Wallerstein, Immanuel. *The Modern World-System*. New York and London: Academic Press, 1974.

Whitten, Norman E. and Szwed, John (eds.). *Afro-American Anthropology: Contemporary Perspectives*. New York: The Free Press, 1970.

Wilde, José Antonio. *Buenos Aires desde setenta años atrás*. Buenos Aires: Imprenta La Nación, 1908.

Williams, Eric. *Capitalism and Slavery*. London: Andre Deutsch, 1964.

Wolf, Eric R. *Peasants*. Englewood Cliffs, N.J.: Prentice-Hall, 1966.

Wood, Bryce. *The Making of the Good Neighbor Policy*. New York: Columbia University Press, 1961.

Index

342   *Africa in Latin America*

Soulouque, Faustin, 311, 321
Souza, Francisco Félix de ("Chachá"),
    280
Sparrow, 128
Stein, Stanley J., 291
Stewart, W. A., 90
Suárez y Romero, Anselmo, 151, 157
Sylvain, George, 316
Szwed, John F., 298

Tallet, José Z., 162–63, 166
Tannenbaum, Frank, 39, 291
Taylor, Douglas, 88, 89, 92–93, 95, 295
Tempels, Placied, 126
Thaly, Daniel, 113
Thoby, Armand, 319
Thompson, Edgar T., 289
Thompson, Virgil, 66
Tiradentes, 263
Tirolien, Gui, 271
Tolson, Melvin, 133
Toomer, Jean, 264
Trinidade, Solano, 168
Túpac Amaru, 263
Turner, Lorenzo D., 85, 294
Turner, Nat, 108

Urdermann, J., 14
Urfé, José, 186

Valcárcel, Luis E., 220
Valdés, Gilberto, 187
Valdés, Paredo, 168

Valdman, Alberto, 92
Valentín, 160
Valenzuela, Raimundo, 186
Vallejo, César, 267
Vargas, Getúlio, 53
Varona, José, 262
Vasconcelos, José, 262
Vega, Carlos, 193, 203
Vega, Lope de, 165, 266
Velasco, Luis de, 193
Velázquez Rogerio, 149
Vértiz, Juan José de, 193
Vianna Filho, Luis, 274
Villa, Ignacio "Bola de Nieve", 187
Villaverde, Cirilo, 151, 157
Vincent, Sténio, 315, 320
Voorhoeve, Jan, 84–85, 90

Walcott, Derek, 114, 121
Wallerstein, Immanuel, 287, 288, 297
Washington, Booker T., 264
Waterman, Richard, 231
Weinreich, U., 89, 92
White, José, 188
Whitman, Walt, 264
Whitten, Norman E., 298
Whorf, 95
Wilde, José Antonio, 221
Williams, Eric, 106–7
Wolfe, Tom, 264

Zapata Olivella, Delia, 209, 210, 215
Zárate, 196, 203, 209, 210, 214–15, 224